The Orphan
Carpenter

The Orphan Carpenter

ORPHANED AT BIRTH. ADOPTED BY GOD.
A TALE OF HOPE AND A FUTURE.

Kenneth Ian McQuarrie

Carpenter's Son Publishing

The Orphan Carpenter: Orphaned at birth. Adopted by God.
A tale of hope and a future

Published by Carpenter's Son Publishing, Franklin, Tennessee

Published in association with Larry Carpenter of Christian Book Services, LLC
www.christianbookservices.com

All Biblical scriptures quoted are from
New International Version (NIV), by Zondervan.

Cover Illustrations by Brock Nicol

Cover and Interior Design by Suzanne Lawing

Content Edit by Tiarra Tompkins

Edited by Ann Tatlock

DISCLAIMER: The following pages contain stories from my life from my subjective perspective and point of view. My history as a baby together with the people who were in my life during my pre-memory years is pieced together from notes, photos, and journals. Dialogs are representative of conversations that occurred and are not exactly word for word. However, any variations in no way change the essence of these stories and how my life was impacted. Some names of people, places, and companies have been changed, but they still represent actual people or companies. My views do not necessarily represent the opinions of individuals or companies named in this book. The author does not assume and hereby disclaims any liability to any party for any loss, damage, or disruption caused by errors or omissions in this book, whether such errors or omissions result from negligence, accident, or any other cause.

Printed in the United States of America

978-1-954437-54-8

Contents

Chapter 1:

What Just Happened?

About three in the afternoon Jesus cried out in a loud voice,
"Eli, Eli, lema sabachthani?" (which means, "My God, my God,
why have you forsaken me?"). Matthew 27:46

It all happened so fast.

"I'M GOING TO KILL YOU, YOU MOMMY YOU," shrieked nine-year-old Sofia as she lunged toward my wife Celine.

Backing up to get out of the way, Celine slammed into the hotel room vestibule wall as Sofia unleashed a barrage of kicking, scratching, and hitting, all the while wailing at the top of her lungs.

Regaining her composure, Celine slapped at Sofia's legs, hoping to ward off the sudden unexpected attack.

Confusion blanketed the faces of Sofia's eleven-year-old brother, Andrew, and seven-year-old sister, Joanna. They stood by, wanting to help but not knowing what to do.

Jumping to Celine's defense, I approached Sofia from behind, putting my arms around her waist, trying with all my strength to pull her off Celine. But Sofia just yelled louder and louder as she kicked more and more violently.

"YOU MOTHER F%#@ERS, I'M GOING TO KILL YOU," Sofia continued to scream.

Celine got hold of Sofia's legs, trying to keep a firm grasp while trying to sooth her in Tagalog, Sofia's native Filipino dialect.

Celine wanted to calm her while I was trying to hold her back. Instead, it seemed to only infuriate her more. Sofia started violently scratching at Celine's arms, pinching them with such force that she was pulling off chunks of skin.

As Celine's arms became covered in blood, I realized I needed to get her out of harm's way. Reaching around, I grabbed Sofia by the ankles, allowing Celine to pull herself away from the onslaught of injury.

"Mommy, Mommy, we are going to be late, we are going to be very, very late," little Joanna loudly called out as she became more and more concerned.

With me now holding her by the ankles, Sofia leaned over, and I felt a sharp, tingling pain shoot up my arm as her teeth clamped down just above my wrist. She then attempted to pinch off chunks of my skin as she had done to Celine just moments ago, but my leathery hide was strong enough to hold off the assault.

Sofia screamed hysterically, "I AM SATAN'S, YOU MOTHER F%#@ERS, I'M GOING TO KILL YOU. I'M GOING TO KILL YOU JUST LIKE THEY DID ON TV."

Celine started to pray for Sofia, now moaning, muttering, and shaking her head violently. At this, I released my grip on Sofia's legs and gently placed my hand on the top of her head as I began to pray.

Sofia's ear-piercing screams became even louder, if that was even possible. Then, after about a minute of prayer, Sofia suddenly went silent. Finally, realizing no one was holding her, she jumped up and ran into the bedroom, locking the door.

Not a minute later, the bedroom door swung open; Sofia threw the Bibles of all three children plus the dress she had been wearing out of the room.

The Scriptures hit the ground with a resounding thud, followed by the door slamming as Sofia retreated into the bedroom.

"What do we do now?" Celine asked…

• • •

Lord, what just happened? It just doesn't make sense. The children are traumatized. Celine is devastated. I am in complete and utter shock. What will become of Andrew, Sofia, and little Joanna? These were just some of the thoughts whirling around my head as our plane charged down the runway.

Finally, we gained elevation, and Manila faded into the distance. The aircraft banked slightly, turning toward the United States. I would have the next fifteen hours to process what just happened as Celine and I made the long journey back to California.

Lord, where were you this time? Is this how our seven-year-long journey to have children ends? Are we being punished? Are we cursed?

Our attempts at in-vitro fertilization ended in the most disastrous results you could possibly imagine. This followed by a five-year adoption process, supposedly guaranteed but once again ending in spectacularly devastating fashion.

So here we were, homeward bound, no children, and physically and spiritually exhausted from the ordeal that just transpired.

Is this my fault? What could I have done differently?

This adoption seemed so right, and yet I felt like I let down so many people. My head was spinning, and I didn't know how to process any of it. So much prayer went into this adoption over the past five-plus years. I thought I was ready. I really thought I could help these kids.

After all, I myself started life as an orphan.

Lord, did I not learn your many lessons over the years? Some fun lessons, some hard, some painful.

Many times in my life, the odds were heavily stacked against me. Through life and death situations, and terrible things out of my control, somehow, someway, you always showed up. It may have been a sudden change in circumstance, an extraordinarily gifted physician, a chance unexpected phone call, a perfect stranger to help at the last minute, or a friend's timely advice.

Since day one, I have been a fighter. I know you say bad things will happen.

"I have told you these things so that in me you may have peace.
In this world, you will have trouble. But take heart!
I have overcome the world." John 16:33

No matter what life threw at me, didn't I always take it head-on, and with your help, push through? I know you are working in every person's life. You continue to work in my life. Sometimes I don't even recognize it. Whether somebody believes you are working or not, you love them and are working in their lives.

And we know that in all things God works for the good of those who love him, who have been called according to his purpose. Romans 8:28

My crazy life was a testament to this fact. Like an Old Testament Bible character, the stories of my life provide proof that you are always working in the lives of all of us, and I have the scars to prove it.

My unlikely journey has taken me from being cast aside at birth, to growing up with many roadblocks in my life, to experiencing the pinnacle of the North American construction industry.

I was just a little kid in a small city who wanted to be a carpenter. Instead, you used this to propel me on a most incredible journey throughout two countries, complete with a stop in paradise. But I know this is not your goal for my life; this is not my purpose; this is just a side effect, a peripheral blessing of your real intention for my life.

As the plane reached cruising altitude, my eyes became very heavy. The lack of sleep and emotional trauma of the last seven days was catching up as I reclined my seat back and closed my eyes.

Many more detailed thoughts and memories of my life started to flood through my mind like someone had hit the reverse button on the remote control. I grasped for meaning and clarity as faster and faster the memories passed by, taking me back, back to the beginning, the very beginning. Finally, I couldn't fight the exhaustion any longer as I slipped into "la-la land."

• • •

Thoughts flooded my head in the months following our return to California from the Philippines. Those thoughts, experiences, and circumstances led me to this book's writing. My core beliefs had been shaken. To make sense of what just happened, I went back and examined my own life.

As I put my life story into writing, common themes and biblical truths started to reveal themselves, strengthening my faith. As a result, this book contains true stories of my life that are like parables laying testament to the following:

- God loves you and is continually working in your life, whether you realize it or not. Whether you believe it or not.

- God has a purpose for your life. No matter how bad things get, he is working in all things to help you fulfill your purpose.

- God is more concerned about developing your character than your accomplishments.

- God has a plan for your life. They are plans for good and not for evil, to give you hope and a future.

Have you ever wondered where God is? How can this be happening? What did you do to deserve this? Have your circumstances led you to questioning your faith? Does God care? Does he even exist? Life can be hard, and I sure don't have all the answers. I don't think anyone does. What I do have are my life experiences. From orphan to carpenter and beyond, the pages of this book are my life stories. But the book is not about me.

This book is about showing how God is present and active in your life, that he loves you and has a plan and purpose for you. Right now, as you read these words, God is working in your life. So, let's turn the page and take this journey together.

Chapter 2:

In the Beginning

"For I know the plans I have for you," declares the Lord, "plans to prosper you and not to harm you, plans to give you hope and a future."
Jeremiah 29:11

For most people, having a baby is a joyous occasion. Celebrations have been happening since the news first rang out. When I came into this world, there were no baby showers, no celebrations, no father handing out big cigars, or first photo being passed around the office. Grandma, grandpa, aunts, and uncles would not be visiting, pinching my chubby cheeks and saying how cute I was. You see, I was an orphan. Unwanted, cold, hungry, and alone … or was I?

Sault Ste. Marie (Soo Saint Marie) is a small city of about 80,000 people on the St. Mary's River in Ontario, Canada. If you were to look at a North American map, it's where Lake Superior and Lake Michigan almost meet. It was September 6, 1967. The weather forecast was sunny with a daytime temperature of 26 Celsius (79 Fahrenheit), which was on the high side for that time of year. The warm summer winds would soon be giving way to cool autumn breezes and painted leaves. *It was a good day to be born!*

I know very little about my biological mother. Actually, I don't know anything about my biological mother. But, still, I do know a few facts about my birth:

Fact #1: I was born. I am very grateful to my biological mother I was not aborted.

Fact #2: There was no star in the sky, angelic choir, or wise men bringing gifts. Since I wasn't a virgin birth miracle, it's a safe bet that I was a natural baby with a biological father running around somewhere.

Fact #3: I was born at Plumber Memorial Hospital. There were only two hospitals in town. The "General Hospital," which was a Catholic hospital, and the Plumber. I was born in the Plumber, so I must not be Catholic.

Fact #4: I was given up at birth, so I was a Canadian Crown Ward.

Now there is one more thing; I was born with a deformity. I had a rather sizeable tumorous mass on my head's lower left side and a large birthmark on my forehead. The mass was filled with tissue and blood vessels extending to my brain stem. The prognosis at the time was not good. My diagnosis in those early days was I most likely would be (severely) mentally and/or physically disabled.

So, I started life with a bit of a setback: mother gave me up, the doctors didn't give me much of a chance to survive, and I couldn't rely on my looks to get by. I was on my own. The funny thing about being on my own was that I really wasn't. This is the point where the good Lord stepped in and started to work in my life. I'm not talking miraculous signs and wonders or anything like that. From the beginning, Jesus has simply been working in my life, supporting and helping me along my life journey.

OK, and away we go. Day one Sept 6, 1967: I had arrived weighing 8lb 8oz. They say I was a husky little guy. The doctor who delivered me gave me the name of Ian. I was apparently Scottish, and Ian is a Scottish/Gaelic variant of John. It means "God is Gracious." If you ask me, I was off to a good start with a solid name and a good fighting weight. As I mentioned before, there were medical complications. This meant no foster care for me. Instead, I was whisked off to the hospital nursery. I would be setting up residence in the Plumber Memorial Hospital under the name Ian and being observed until I was of age to have surgery. That is, if I survived long enough to receive it. Let's not forget Jesus was in my corner.

You may be asking how I could have possibly known that. Well, I'm going to tell you. I have always had a strong faith. I have never felt totally alone for as long as I can remember. From day one, I was a fighter. Being a fighter is not enough to survive. Babies need love and nurturing to grow and thrive. I was going to need help and lots of it. This is where it all started. It's where the Lord began to send people of all types, cultures, shapes, and sizes into my life to help. The Lord would use perfect strangers to help support, guide, and encourage me in more ways than I could ever list. These people would become the heroes of my life.

First up was Dr. Ann Cole, a pediatrician at Plumber Memorial Hospital. Dr. Cole was my first doctor. I don't know much about Dr. Cole, but I know she was instrumental in getting me approved for foster care. It took her three months, but she did it. You see, before my life could get rocking and rolling, the Lord had to get me out of that dang hospital.

What happened to me during those first three months in the hospital? I really don't know. I imagine I was pretty sick. I will always be grateful to the hospital staff, who must have done a great job looking after me. But on Sunday, December 10, 1967, winter had set in with temperatures now minus 7 Celsius (18 Fahrenheit). The Monkees' "Daydream Believer" was #1 on the Billboard Charts (I always liked that song) and I was getting out of the hospital. I was going to a foster home. Look out, world, here I come!

Ron and Joanna McQuarrie were a young couple just five years into their marriage. They had one four-year-old daughter named Debbie Jo, or DJ as she was often called by her father back then. Ron and Joanna had a rough start to their marriage. I'm not talking about Ron's groomsmen trying to kidnap him on their wedding day or Joanna pulling her groin by hopping a fence as they tried to escape from being followed by their friends on their honeymoon. That's another story for another day (and perhaps another book).

Ron and Joanna first meet at the S.S. Kresge department store in Sault Ste. Marie. Ron's parents, Neil and Minerva McQuarrie, recently moved their family from Southern Ontario to the Sault. Neil had accepted an offer to pastor the Free Methodist Church. Joanna's parents, Andy and Margaret Bjornaa, relocated to the city from Saint Joseph Island, approximately 68 km (42 mi) southeast of the Sault. The move was to help Andy travel less for his work as a carpenter.

One historic day the stars would align at that S.S. Kresge. Ron and Joanna would turn and look upon each other for the very first time. All the noise and distractions of the store magically seemed to silently fade away as the two gazed deeper into each other's eyes.

"I thought he was a twit," proclaimed Joanna as she recalled the story of their first meeting. Ron says he rebounded from that first impression as their relationship grew over the following few years leading up to their marriage on June 23, 1962.

Ron & Joanna Wedding Day—June 23, 1962

Joanna's mother, Margaret, had been diagnosed with cancer. She was a strong yet compassionate woman, the eldest of ten siblings in the fight of her life. This weighed heavily on Joanna's heart as she and Ron started their married life together. They wanted to have a large family of their own. Still, they would rely on faith and prayer as they began to build a life together.

About a year and a half later, the young couple was blessed with a healthy baby girl, Deborah Joanna, aka Debbie Jo. In short order, Debbie developed a close bond with her grandmother Margaret whom she would call "Nanna." Margaret and Andy, now called "Poppa," couldn't be prouder to be grandparents. The joy of a young grand-daughter was a welcome distraction from the reality of Margaret's advancing cancer.

Ron, Joanna, and Debbie took up residence in a basement-level apartment at Andy and Margaret's house. You gotta admit, this was the perfect place for the young family to keep costs down, not to mention the grandparents' free babysitting.

Life couldn't be better. Ron was getting established in his career at the Algoma Steel Mill in the shipping and manifest services de-partment. Joanna enjoyed her job in the Plumber Memorial Hospital pharmacy. What about little Debbie? Well, she was getting to spend lots of time with Nanna. Even Norman Rockwell couldn't paint a bet-ter picture for the young family. A few short months after Debbie Jo's second birthday, Joanna got the news. Yes, you guessed it, baby num-ber two was on the way!

Stephen Andrew McQuarrie was born at 4:00 a.m. on Tuesday, November 15, 1966, weighing 7lb 8oz. Right up to the time of birth, all was good. Joanna and Ron could hardly wait to hold their newborn baby boy. Then suddenly there was a problem and baby Stephen was struggling during the delivery. This was supposed to be the same joy-ful moment they had when welcoming Debbie Jo into the world. There was no way of knowing that the nine months of excitement leading up to their second child's birth would be a countdown to events that would change the trajectory of their lives forever.

The doctors worked frantically as the difficult birth was causing Stephen respiratory distress. Ultimately, only minutes after birth, it became apparent that all was not well. Little baby Stephen was in trouble. He was rushed to the neonatal intensive care unit and placed in an incubator while the doctors worked tirelessly to get little Stephen stabilized.

Ron and Joanna could only watch and pray as their little boy struggled for his life. They didn't get to hold him after he was born, and just to get into the room where he was with the other NICU babies, they had to scrub down like surgeons prepping for the operating room. Even with the precautions they were still only able to touch Stephen through the plastic arms and gloves extending into the incubator.

Nanna and Poppa took shifts watching Debbie and relieving Ron and Joanna at the hospital. Everyone was praying for baby Stephen, but his condition worsened daily. The doctors suspected after about a week that Stephen had a congenital heart defect. The small Plumber Memorial Hospital was not equipped with the tools or the specialists needed to repair his heart and care for him through recovery. Stephen would need to be airlifted to Sick Children's Hospital in Toronto. The timing could not be worse. There was an airline strike, and the hospital could not arrange a flight.

Ron's employer, Algoma Steel, stepped up and offered the company airplane, a definite answer to prayer. But once again, tragedy struck as the Algoma Steel plane developed mechanical trouble. With time running out, Sault Search and Rescue arranged a military aircraft out of Trenton Air Force Base about 160 km (100 miles) east of Toronto (520 miles southwest of the Sault).

In the early hours of Monday, November 25, 1966, the aircraft took off en route to Sault Ste. Marie to get baby Stephen. They would be flying him back to Toronto Sick Children's Hospital, where Dr. Hendrick and his team were preparing for the complex surgery. Ron had his bags packed and headed to the hospital, where Dr. Ann Cole prepped baby Stephen for the ambulance ride to the airport. The plane had just arrived and was fueling for the return trip. Ron got to the hospital but despite all efforts, time had run out. Cradled in Dr. Cole's arms, baby Stephen took his final breath and went to be with Jesus.

The defect they found in Stephen's heart was so rare, Dr. Hendrick would go on to write a paper about it.

This was not how things were supposed to end. Even with their strong faith, prayer, and the support of family and friends, this was devastating for the young couple. Joanna's father, Andy, aka "Poppa," took Stephen's death especially hard. He never had a son and was looking forward to having a grandson to mentor and teach his carpentry trade skills.

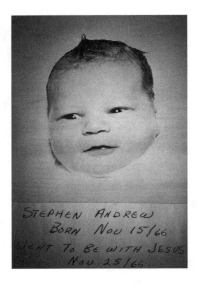

Christmas in the McQuarrie household was just not the same that year. Tragedy leaves us all reaching for answers. So many doubts and questions of faith came up as Ron, Joanna, and Debbie journeyed through and processed their grief and loss.

Why did God take our child?

What could we have done differently?

Where do we go from here?

These were only some of the thoughts swirling around their heads like a northern winter storm. The snowy winter months marched on, and the bitter cold seemed to parallel the bitterness of the tragic loss. The McQuarries leaned on family and faith to get through a winter that felt longer and colder than ever before.

As with every long hard winter, spring finally starts to break through. The hopes and excitement of the fresh spring blooms begin to warm the heart and excite the soul.

One fateful day Joanna was getting a checkup with her family doctor, Dr. Lloyd Sagle. Dr. Sagle told Joanna she was "baby crazy" and suggested she and Ron consider becoming foster parents.

"There are so many children that could use your help, and I think it will be therapeutic after the loss of Stephen," the doctor said.

The couple had the fostering paperwork submitted in no time, followed by the physicals, home studies, and interviews. The whole process took about six months; one year had now passed since baby Stephen went to be with the Lord.

Suddenly, the phone rang on one ordinary, uneventful day toward the end of the first week in December 1967.

"Hello," Joanna answered, just like a thousand times before.

"Mrs. McQuarrie?" asked the voice on the other end of the line.

"Yes, who is calling?" Joanna responded with a hint of curiosity.

"This is the Ontario Children's Aid Society; we have a three-month-old baby boy in need of foster care," replied the social worker in a calm but matter-of-fact tone.

Joanna was beside herself, hardly containing her excitement. "That's wonderful. Yes, we will take him," she excitedly proclaimed.

"Well, that's wonderful, Mrs. McQuarrie, but there are a few things you need to know about this little guy. His name is Ian, and he is a special needs child."

Joanna became silent as she strained to hear over the faint whistle from the steeping tea kettle. The social worker continued, "Ian was born with a tumorous mass on the base of his skull, behind his left ear. He has been a very sick little man. We feel he is stable enough to move from the hospital into a home on his doctor's recommendation. Ian *will not* be eligible for adoption and is being scheduled for surgery at Sick Children's Hospital in Toronto."

It was like a dark cloud was forming over Joanna's head as her heart grew heavy. Suddenly, the weight of grief piled on her shoulders. She had to sit down as the emotional memories of baby Stephen's death came flooding back into her thoughts. The endless days and nights in neonatal, trying to get to Toronto Sick Children's Hospital, having no planes available and ultimately saying goodbye to her little boy.

As Joanna sat there listening to the social worker, the emotion turned to compassion. She could feel her heart beating as if it was outside her chest. Suddenly she felt peace; a calming came over her entire body. It was at that moment she knew, she knew in her heart, "The Lord took my baby and has sent me this one because he needs my help."

Back at the hospital, Dr. Cole prepared me for the social worker, who would take me to my new foster home. I can only imagine what was going through her mind. What was her reaction when she heard I was going to the McQuarries'? Stephen McQuarrie had died in her arms almost one year ago to the day. Was this family ready to take me on? What if I did not survive? She knew I was a fighter, but what would become of me? Only time would tell. The social worker was now at the hospital and it was time to go. It was literally the first day of the rest of my life.

Chapter 3:

The McQuarries

And again, "I will put my trust in him." And again, he says,
"Here am I, and the children God has given me." Hebrews 2:13

Sunday, December 10, 1967, the doorbell rang. Ron and Joanna excitedly rushed to the front entry. They could hardly contain their excitement as they flung open the door. There stood the social worker holding a basket with me snuggly wrapped up inside. In the Bible, Moses was delivered in a basket on the Nile River. I, on the other hand, was dispensed by a social worker driving a Chevy with snow tires.

Joanna quickly scooped me up. Cradling me in her arms, she rocked me back and forth, all the while making funny faces. It was sort of fun but some kind of scary at the same time.

Not much time had passed when suddenly the door flung open. "WHERE'S THE BABY?" the older woman enthusiastically called out.

It was Joanna's mother, "Nanna." She took me from Joanna, and we did some more rocking 'n rolling and funny faces, followed by a little bouncing of me around the room. OK, now it was getting a bit scary; this was more excitement than I'd had my entire life, all three months of it. "OK, Lord, what have you gotten me into? I'm not so sure about this." As always, the good Lord knew what he was doing, I had a tough road ahead of me, and I would need some strong support.

As mentioned earlier, Nanna was the eldest of ten siblings, and there was no question she was the matriarch. For those of you who don't understand the term matriarch, it simply means that she's the boss when it comes to the family. Nanna was a strong, compassionate woman, a straight shooter; you would always know where you stood with Nanna.

Now, Joanna was young and years away from achieving full Nanna status, but when it came to protecting the family, hmmm, well, let's just say, she may not start the fight, but she sure would finish it.

Joanna was a strong woman with a firecracker personality. Still, she was very respectful of her husband Ron, always turning to him for comfort and reassurance. Ron was a kind, patient man, still young and full of energy. He was a pretty good athlete, personable, and enjoyed good conversation and meeting new people. Let's not forget Debbie Jo. She had just recently turned four years old and was enjoying life as the only child. As excited as anyone to have a baby in the household, Debbie watched curiously as the commotion of my grand arrival played out.

Ron and Joanna told Debbie she now had a little foster brother to watch over and protect, an assignment she took to heart.

Ron's parents, Neil and Minerva McQuarrie, just retiring from the ministry, were equally excited. They were supportive of Ron and Joanna as they started their new adventure as foster parents. There was one holdout though; Joanna's father, "Poppa," was guarding his heart and was still not over the loss of baby Stephen.

"It's up to you guys if you want to do this. But I'm not having any part of it," Poppa proclaimed.

Poppa was not in favor of the family taking me in. He was not mean or angry about it or anything like that. Poppa just didn't want to get emotionally invested in a baby that may not be around long one way or another.

After having Ron and Joanna sign some paperwork, the social worker hung around for a bit to make sure I was settled. Then, finally getting into her car, she drove away.

I was going to have to trust in Jesus because my ride had just left.

So, there you have it. I was in my first real home with my new foster family. They even gave me a new name, "Kenneth," after Ron's older brother Ken. In Gaelic, it means "Handsome, Fire Born." Given my deformed head and birthmark, "Handsome" is an interesting description; however, one could argue "Fire Born" was a pretty good fit. So now, my name was Kenneth Ian, translation: "Handsome, Fire Born, God is Gracious."

After three long months, I finally got my first photo for passing around the office. Grandma, grandpa, aunts, and uncles were visiting, pinching my chubby cheeks and saying how cute I was.

P.S. I don't think I came with the red suit; it must have been a loaner

"Kenny is the best baby; he sleeps & eats."
Joanna's Journal, December 1967

Oh, how I long for the days I could impress by merely eating and sleeping. Most newborn babies go home with their parents; every time they cry or fuss, a parent picks them up, feeds them, changes them, or gives them some sort of attention. For us babies who don't have parents from the get-go, we learn pretty quickly you can cry and fuss all you want, but it's hit-and-miss if you get any attention. So, we stop complaining and learn to sleep. We also never pass up a meal; you never know if or when the next one is coming.

Well, that was all behind me; I was getting lots of attention now. I settled right in and made it through my first week in the McQuarrie household. It was Sunday morning, and I was going to church for the first time, the Free Methodist Church. This was a time in my life when sleeping through the pastor's sermon was not only acceptable, but it was also actually encouraged. Not only that, but after church, we went out for lunch. How cool is that? It was right in the middle of the Christmas season, so there were lots of activities and new adventures. My social life was really starting to take off.

As 1967 came to an end, I was in a pretty good place. It was New Year's Eve now, and I was ready to sleep for the night—no staying up 'til midnight for me. I would need my rest; 1968 was going to be a Big Year.

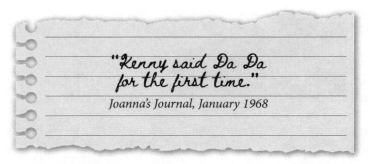

"*Kenny said Da Da for the first time.*"
Joanna's Journal, January 1968

Yeah, I was working it; I needed to stand out in a crowded field. Remember, Ron and Joanna were foster parents, and they were taking other babies, sometimes just for a night, sometimes longer. These kids had parents who couldn't look after them properly or were up for adoption. Sadly, even today, so many children worldwide are in need. It takes an extraordinary couple to take on all us misfits.

On February 1, I was put into a walker for the first time, and I was mobile. Look out, my first set of wheels, and I could make that walker fly. The only problem was I could only go backward, and walkers don't come with rearview mirrors. So, all I can say is, it's a good thing we lived in a basement apartment.

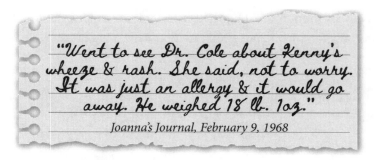

"Went to see Dr. Cole about Kenny's wheeze & rash. She said, not to worry. It was just an allergy & it would go away. He weighed 18 lb. 1oz."
Joanna's Journal, February 9, 1968

Yes, the rash turned out to be caused by a crazy cocktail of mixed cereal and orange juice, an allergy I would outgrow. However, the wheeze was the first recorded incident of something much more, something I will chat about a little later. I was holding my own on the weight, though, being about average for my age.

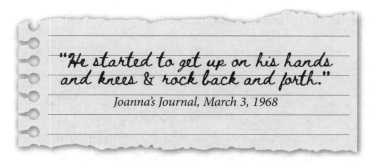

"He started to get up on his hands and knees & rock back and forth."
Joanna's Journal, March 3, 1968

I must have been practicing my football stance, and you never know it may come in handy someday. Also, if I could just get to my feet, I could get outside and explore. I had already spent half my life in a hospital, and I was not getting any younger, you know.

> *"March 15-22, Kenny had company, Donna (Cree Indian) 3 months."*
>
> *Joanna's Journal, March 22, 1968*

Now six months old, I had a little foster sister to look out for. Well, it was only for a week, but good practice being a big brother.

> *"Kenny can sure master the walker. Mom & Dad (Nanna & Poppa) got him a new one as the other was too small & he fell out."*
>
> *Joanna's Journal, March 29, 1968*

I crashed my ride. Fortunately, Nanna and Poppa stepped up and got me a new one with a better seatbelt. Hey, Poppa didn't want much to do with me when I first arrived three months ago, but now he's getting me a new ride. Hmmm, interesting.

> *"Kenny went for his last needle. Dr. Cole made Dr appointment in Toronto, May 14/68, 1:00 pm. Kenny goes back to Dr. Cole on May 1/68. Kenny just screamed when I cleaned his ear on his bad side today. I hope it was just temper, not a bad sign."*
>
> *Joanna's Journal, March 29, 1968*

I was doing well, growing stronger every day. The past three months had been much better than the first three, that's for sure. But it was getting time to deal with the elephant in the room, and I'm not talking about my stuffed elephant I slept with or the elephant lamp on my dresser.

The tumorous mass on the back of my head needed to be dealt with. Within a couple of months, I would be eight months old and have major surgery on the back of my head, brain, and brain stem area. The doctors didn't know what they were dealing with or the potential side effects of the surgery. Remember this was 1968; CT (CAT) scanners would not be around until 1974, and MRIs not until 1977.

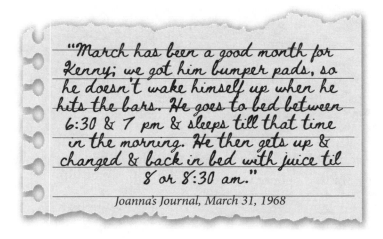

"March has been a good month for Kenny; we got him bumper pads, so he doesn't wake himself up when he hits the bars. He goes to bed between 6:30 & 7 pm & sleeps till that time in the morning. He then gets up & changed & back in bed with juice til 8 or 8:30 am."

Joanna's Journal, March 31, 1968

As you can see from Joanna's Journal entry, I wasn't stressing over my pending surgery. I got my crib bars padded, so I wasn't whacking my head. I got my twelve to fourteen hours' sleep a night, which didn't even include my naps. So, I had mastered the art of putting myself to sleep.

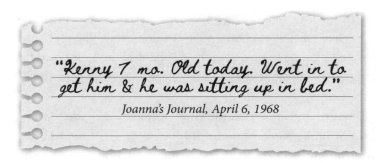

"Kenny 7 mo. Old today. Went in to get him & he was sitting up in bed."

Joanna's Journal, April 6, 1968

OK, I know some overachievers sit as early as four months but wait, maybe this is just the first time Joanna caught me sitting up.

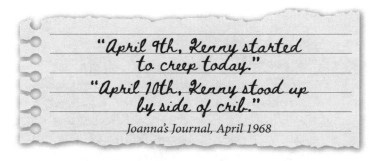

"April 9th, Kenny started to creep today."
"April 10th, Kenny stood up by side of crib."

Joanna's Journal, April 1968

See, in only four days, I went from sitting to standing. I'm a bit of a slow starter, but once I get going, look out!

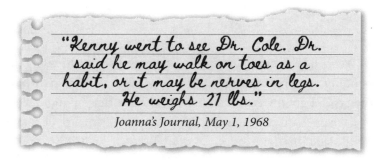

"Kenny went to see Dr. Cole. Dr. said he may walk on toes as a habit, or it may be nerves in legs. He weighs 21 lbs."

Joanna's Journal, May 1, 1968

It was great that I was starting to walk upright. Remember, I was the child they thought would be severely physically and mentally disabled. Still, there was some concern my toe-walking was due to a nerve or muscle disorder like cerebral palsy or muscular dystrophy. Achilles tendon problems could also cause this. However, it was too early to tell; besides, I had to get my head problem fixed first.

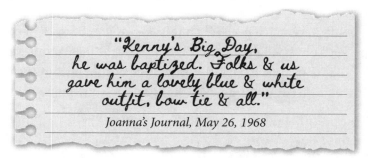

"Kenny's Big Day, he was baptized. Folks & us gave him a lovely blue & white outfit, bow tie & all."

Joanna's Journal, May 26, 1968

OK, as I mentioned, I have always felt confident that the Lord was looking out for me. However, I was only one week away from having surgery on my brain, so I needed to cover all my bases, and baptism seemed like a good idea. Plus, I got a new suit out of it, complete with a bow tie.

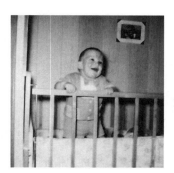

Dressed and ready to be baptized

"May 29 Left Soo for Toronto to have Kenny Checked by Dr. Hendrick."

Joanna's Journal, May 29, 1968

My first plane flight. Thanks to the Ontario government and the Children's Aid Society, I was traveling in style. Someone had given me a book about going on my first plane ride—not the most practical gift, as I couldn't read yet.

I would have much preferred a teething ring or pacifier in case I got nervous on the flight. But hey, it's the thought that counts, right? Wait, hold on to your horses, last-minute change in plans; we ended up driving instead. It was an eight-hour car ride, my longest ride to date.

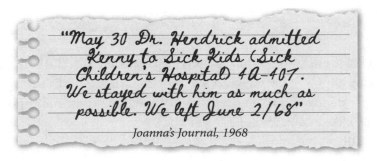

"*May 30 Dr. Hendrick admitted Kenny to Sick Kids (Sick Children's Hospital) 4A-407. We stayed with him as much as possible. We left June 2/68*"
Joanna's Journal, 1968

There I was, on my own again, in a hospital and less than twenty-four hours from major surgery. Ron and Joanna had left, heading back to Sault Ste. Marie without me. Don't get me wrong, it wasn't their fault; they were just my foster parents, after all. The Children's Aid was not financing them to stay in Toronto, plus they needed to get back to their daughter Debbie who was staying with Nanna and Poppa.

Ron and Joanna were quiet during what seemed like an eternity getting back home. Would they see me again? If I survived, would I be the same loveable bundle of joy they had gotten to know over the past five months? OK, total honesty, I don't know about the "loveable bundle of joy" comment, but they were definitely concerned.

There I was, just a few days shy of my nine-month birthday and a lot more aware of my surroundings than the last time I was in the hospital. This time it was a lot more stressful.

I didn't recognize my doctor or all these strange people running around, poking and prodding me. There were so many strange sights, sounds, and odd smells. I missed my crib and my little stuffed elephant.

Then to add insult to injury, I didn't get dinner or my apple juice before bed. So, what's up with that? Something about general anesthesia in the morning. I was getting quite stressed; my airplane book was not doing much good now. I sure could have used that pacifier. I managed to get very little sleep that night. This was not my bed, and I was seriously hungry!

Morning arrived on June 3, my surgery day. Some doctor took a knife and cut me in the leg above my ankle to put in an IV. Ouch, that's going to leave a mark.

I was sure getting a lot of attention from many strange people in masks. They didn't give me my morning juice and still nothing to eat. I mean c'mon, what's wrong with these people? I was tired, hungry, stressed, and hate to admit it, even a bit scared. I was just about to cry.

• • •

Suddenly, I was slowly opening my eyes. Hmmm, I must have dozed off; things were a bit out of focus, and I had a doozy of a headache. I don't think I'm dead, but I'm all alone. I am hooked up to a bunch of machines and can hear some slow beeping sounds.

Usually, when I wake up, Joanna comes into the room, wishes me good morning, and opens the drapes to let the sun in. Sometimes she even whistles or sings me a little song. After that, I get changed and am given some juice, then a little later some breakfast. Most mornings, Christian music is playing considerably loudly on the record player downstairs—The Bill Gaither Trio is a favorite of Joanna's. But today is different, much different, and I feel very sleepy. I think I will just go back to sleep; maybe this is just a bad dream.

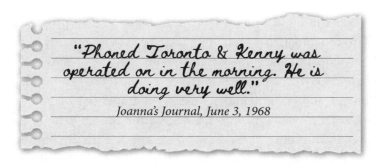

"*Phoned Toronto & Kenny was operated on in the morning. He is doing very well.*"

Joanna's Journal, June 3, 1968

I was doing very well right up until I wasn't. I developed a brain hemorrhage, which is bleeding on the brain. No wonder I had a massive headache. Brain hemorrhage is a type of stroke and very bad. Blood is toxic to the brain and kills brain cells. So, I was rushed back into surgery for a second go-round. My trip to the big city was not entirely turning out as planned as Dr. Hendrick and his team worked tirelessly to get me right in the head. Before you could say, who's your mama? I was back in that room with the beeping machines.

What seemed like only moments was really a few days. I was starting to open my eyes a couple of hours at a time. There was not much to do anyway. But I did enjoy watching the blinking lights on all the monitors I was hooked up to. Finally, they gave me something to eat along with some juice and milk; it was about time.

Here I was, on June 6, my nine-month birthday, although I had no one to celebrate with. My doctors were concerned about possible brain damage before the surgery. I'm sure the added brain hemorrhage did not help my odds. Only time would tell what sort of brain damage I may have incurred. At least I no longer had the tumorous mass. I did, however, have a deformed skull where the tumor used to be.

There was a small hole from the drainage tube and a lesser leftover mass at the base of my skull, but it was between my skull and scalp, so it was harmless. Bordering the surgery site were black stitches. The back of my head now resembled a partly deflated football. On a positive note, I could now wear a baseball cap.

Over the next week or so, I continued my recovery. I didn't give up when I was born, and I was surely not going to let minor brain damage hold me back. Plus, I just knew Jesus was helping out in the background. I had two primary nurses, one for the day and one for the night, then some part-timers on the weekends. Dr. Hendrick stopped by to say hi every few days. Well, it may have been more often, but I slept a lot. Oh yeah, they gave me a few toys to play with, but they didn't have a walker for me to run around in.

I missed my walker, the one that Nanna and Poppa had bought me. I wondered how the McQuarries were doing or if I would ever see them again.

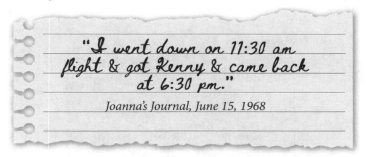

"*I went down on 11:30 am flight & got Kenny & came back at 6:30 pm.*"

Joanna's Journal, June 15, 1968

It was Saturday, June 15, and the day started like any other in the hospital; this was my new normal. After lunch, the nurse dressed me in my street clothes; hey, I must be going for a ride. I would love to get outside. But the journey would have to wait; it was time for my nap. Oh baby, after my rest, I'm going for a ride.

As I started to wake up from my nap, I rolled over and rubbed my eyes. Wait a second, that's not my nurse. As I rub my eyes some more, a familiar face came into view. Hey, it's Joanna! I didn't think I would ever see her again.

It was time to head back to Sault Ste. Marie. I even got a stylish new red jacket for the plane ride. Yes, this time, we're going in style, my very first plane ride.

OK, if you're reading this and you were a passenger on an Air Canada flight from Toronto to Sault Ste. Marie on Saturday, June 15, at 6:30 p.m., I apologize and hope you can find it in your heart to forgive me. After all, I just had brain surgery. Yes, that was me crying at the top of my lungs for the entire flight. The pressurization of the plane was giving me the worst headache ever.

> *"Arrived in Soo tired but happy to have big boy back. We didn't dream he went through so much until we saw him."*
>
> *Joanna's Journal, June 15, 1968*

Ron & Debbie pick Joanna & me up at the airport

> *"Took Kenny to Dr. Cole to have stitches out of leg (They forgot in Toronto)."*
>
> *Joanna's Journal, June 17, 1968*

See, I told you that cut in the leg would leave a mark.

Over the next month, I did well, getting stronger every day. Then, one day, I was out grocery shopping with Joanna when this scary-looking older woman walked up and started staring me down.

Joanna turned to check on me, then she made eye contact with the old lady. At this, the woman lifted her bony finger. Pointing at my head with self-righteousness indignation, she blurted out, "He is ugly; you should cover that boy up."

Joanna looked the woman straight in the eye and fired back, "His scars will heal; what's your excuse?"

From that point on, to build up my self-confidence, every time we went by a mirror, Joanna would hold me up, pointing at my reflection and proclaim, "There's my handsome boy." This practice continued for several months until one day, a woman came up to me and said, "What a cute little man. What's your name?" Standing straight up and with absolute confidence, I replied, "Handsome Boy."

Mission accomplished; my self-confidence was intact. However, I believe that is the last time I was ever referred to as "Handsome Boy."

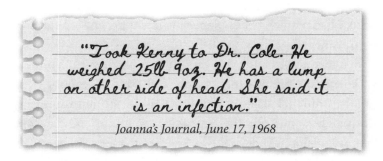

"Took Kenny to Dr. Cole. He weighed 25lb 9oz. He has a lump on other side of head. She said it is an infection."

Joanna's Journal, June 17, 1968

Thank Jesus, this second lump went away on its own; I did not want more surgeries.

The McQuarries continued to take in foster babies. On August 6, a little five-month-old girl named Christine arrived. She had black hair and big eyes. But she didn't stay long. Her father picked her up on August 11, taking her to Sudbury.

I spent most of August working on my walking skills. Still, being unsteady, I would have to hold on to things. Oh yeah, and I continued to walk on my toes, which was causing some concern.

September 6, 1968, rolled around. Woohoo! I was one year old. I made it, beat the odds, not to mention my hair was growing and covering my scars.

I had no signs of brain damage, and my motor skills improved daily. Finally, on September 21, the first day of fall, I started freestyle walking.

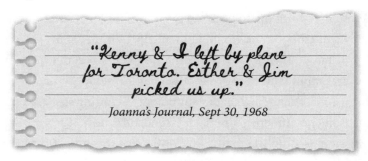

"*Kenny & I left by plane for Toronto. Esther & Jim picked us up.*"

Joanna's Journal, Sept 30, 1968

I was off for my follow-up appointment with Dr. Hendrick in Toronto. I had a much better plane ride this time, and we stayed with Jim and Esther Elliott.

When Joanna was fourteen years old, her parents sent her to Lorne Park College, a Christian high school and Bible college for the Free Methodist Church, located at Port Credit in the Toronto area.

Although Joanna was there for less than a year, she developed a lifelong friendship with a young girl named Esther, who would eventually marry Jim Elliott (not the missionary killed in Ecuador in 1956. This is a different Jim Elliott).

Who could have guessed that the young girl Joanna met as a teenager 690 km (430 miles) from home, now eighteen years later, just happened to be living in Toronto in a perfect position to help us out?

I had my follow-up appointment with Dr. Hendrick on October 1. "Kenny's head is healing up nicely. The surgery was successful, and we don't have to worry about the lump recurring," the doctor told Joanna.

Did you catch that? My head was OK; what an enormous answer to prayer! Of course, I was still an orphan, but at least now I would not be institutionalized due to brain damage. The doctor did mention tonsils and a couple of other things, but who cares? As long as I didn't need any more surgeries, life was good.

One other thing the doctor mentioned was, I should have been wearing a helmet from birth. If I had fallen and hit my head on the tumor, the fluid and blood would have rushed into my brain and most likely killed me.

When Ron heard this, he felt sick to his stomach. Ron's thoughts went to all the times I had taken a tumble, crashed my walker, whacked my head on the crib rails. Not to mention the day before my surgery, he was playing with me, tossing me up in the air.

I guess it proved I was a tough little guy, or more importantly, someone was indeed looking out for me. Joanna and I visited with Jim and Esther for a few days then flew back to the Soo on October 3.

Debbie & me with a foster baby

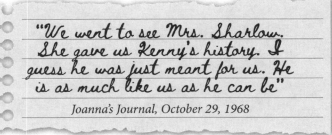

"We went to see Mrs. Sharlow. She gave us Kenny's history. I guess he was just meant for us. He is as much like us as he can be"

Joanna's Journal, October 29, 1968

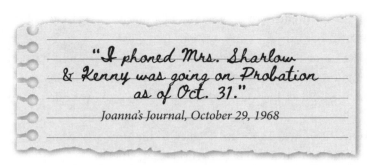

> *"I phoned Mrs. Sharlow*
> *& Kenny was going on Probation*
> *as of Oct. 31."*
>
> *Joanna's Journal, October 29, 1968*

I don't know what Mrs. Sharlow of the Children's Aid Society told Ron and Joanna about me, but it doesn't matter; I was finally cleared for adoption. It was time to stick my past in my behind and move forward.

Hmm, what's all this stuff about probation? The McQuarries had successfully navigated me through a pretty rough first year, and it seems to me they were pretty qualified as parents. Well, one step at a time. Probation or not, I was now eligible for adoption.

Meanwhile, back at the house, the foster babies kept on coming. First, a five-week-old boy named Danny stayed with us for a couple of nights. Then there was an eleven-day-old boy without a name. Ron and Joanna called him Dougie. Finally, after four weeks, Dougie left. Joanna said, "We will miss him as he was starting to get cute." Plus, they liked the name Dougie.

I went to see Dr. Sagle for the first time. Dr. Sagle was the McQuarrie's family doctor. He said I was doing well but would need surgery to remove my tonsils in the new year. Gosh, darn it, another surgery.

> *"Kenny went in hospital for tonsils*
> *and circumcision, he was a pretty*
> *sick boy. He had the flu & cold,*
> *which made it worse. I took sick at*
> *hospital & mom had to take over."*
>
> *Joanna's Journal, April 8, 1969*

Then, to complicate things, Joanna took sick at the hospital, and Nanna had to come to watch over me. When Nanna arrived at the hospital nursery, I was awaiting my surgery. I was very sick and alone, crying in my crib. Nanna arrived on the scene, knowing I was not typically a crier. She then noticed the nurses ignoring me. Well, let's just say those nurses did not know who Nanna was, but they were about to find out. Nanna lit into those young gals and schooled them pretty good.

"You never, ever ignore a crying baby, especially when they are sick," Nanna scolded as she unleashed a verbal lashing those nurses would not soon forget. Never again would I be in a hospital by myself being ignored. I admit this surgery was a lot easier than my previous one, plus I did feel better afterward, which was a good thing, as I was only a few weeks away from a momentous day, a day that would take my life in a whole new direction.

On Friday, May 2, 1969, Ron took off work and Debbie stayed home from school. Joanna was already there looking after me as usual. We all got dressed up in our fancy-pants outfits and drove to the courthouse. When we arrived, this policeman-looking guy brought us into the courtroom.

The courtroom looked like a church with pews facing a platform and a large desk. The policeman guy told us to sit in the front row. After a few minutes, we were told to stand up, then this old guy they called Judge came out wearing a black robe and sat at the desk.

The Judge shuffled some papers, then asked Ron, Joanna, and even Debbie some questions. He then asked me if I wanted Ron and Joanna to be my mommy and daddy. I wasn't sure how to respond, so I just turned and hugged Joanna around the neck.

I guess that was good enough. Next, Ron and Joanna signed some papers, and BAM! I WAS ADOPTED! The coolest part of the whole thing was I got to bang the judge's wooden hammer on his desk.

Or at least, that is how I envisioned it happening. Truth is, on Friday, May 2,1969, Ron and Joanna received a letter in the mail. The letter was signed by a judge declaring I was officially Kenneth

Ian McQuarrie. So, Ron and Joanna were now Mommy and Daddy, Debbie Jo, my sister, and Nanna and Poppa were, well, Nanna and Poppa.

Oh, yeah, May 2 was also Poppa's birthday. Sort of funny how things work out. Poppa was originally against taking me in, and now I officially become his first grandson, right smack on his birthday.

I NOW HAD MY FOREVER FAMILY

My new official sister Debbie and me

I often reflect on the circumstances of my birth and those early months of my life. Baby Stephen McQuarrie died so that I could live. The passing of Stephen was a catalyst that resulted in Ron and Joanna McQuarrie becoming foster parents and, eventually, my parents.

Stephen and I were both born with medical abnormalities; we even had the same doctors. None of this was in our control, but why was I the one that survived? Why did I get a chance? These are questions I've been wrestling with my whole life.

Why am I here, God? What's my purpose? How do I build a purposeful life?

Chapter 4:

Dr. Hendrick

To one there is given through the Spirit a
message of wisdom, to another a message of knowledge
by means of the same Spirit, to another faith by the
same Spirit, to another gifts of healing by that one Spirit.
1 Corinthians 12:8-9

Overnight I went from being my own little man to part of a big family. In the Bible, Jesus had a genealogy, and now I had one too, including a dad, mom, sister, two sets of grandparents, and even a great-grandmother, Nellie Hawdon (Great-Grandpa Willy Hawdon passed away long before I was born). As mentioned prior, Nanna was the eldest of ten siblings, so her brothers and sisters now became my great uncles and aunts. Jesus came from the "Twelve Tribes of Israel"; I was now part of the "Ten Tribes of Hawdon."

Mom had an adopted younger sister, Linda, and a foster sister named Marilyn, which gave me two aunts. Additionally, I had more cousins than you could count—well, definitely more than I could count, given I wasn't yet two years old.

Dad was one of five siblings; his side was a bit smaller. Likewise, I had several cousins on Dad's side of the family too. That said, I was all set with my forever family. I had now moved on from being a foster child to being part of a fostering family. It was official; I was the youngest member in the family business charged with caring for children in need.

Life was changing and it was an exciting time. We had just moved out of Nanna and Poppa's basement apartment to our own house on Primrose Drive in an area of town called "The P. Patch," named for all the streets starting with the letter "P." Here is where I would spend the rest of my childhood.

Our home was a modest two-story, 1,600-square-foot house with a one-vehicle carport on the left side. The carport roof was flat and doubled as an outdoor deck, probably not the best design for a city with ten feet of yearly snowfall.

The house included four bedrooms and one bathroom. (Yes, we all survived with one bathroom.) The main floor was sunken into the ground about three feet. Dad always said the sunken living room kept it cool in the hot summer months, "all ten days of them."

The large grassy backyard was amazing—like nothing I had ever seen before—with a rickety old storage shed and a majestic oak tree complete with acorns and a resident chipmunk we named "Chippy." The Canadian red maple trees would not be outdone by the mighty oak, with leaves turning bright red every fall. Then, we would tap the trees for sap in the spring to make maple syrup.

Primrose Drive bordered the forest, or as we called it, "the bush." So, during the summer months, we would get occasional critters exploring in our backyard. Raccoons, porcupines, an occasional skunk, even a random black bear would wander out of the bush and down the street, looking for an evening snack. But don't worry, Dad told me the bears preferred to eat berries over little kids. This became my new stomping grounds, and for a young Canadian boy, it was about as close to paradise as I could imagine. Oh yeah, I almost forgot. There were many kids of all ages in the neighborhood to play with.

Not too long after moving in, we took in two sisters, Laura, age five, and Tracy, age three. They were so neglected and underweight that poor little Laura had lost her teeth. Tracey, who was a tiny as could be, was suffering a bloated stomach from malnutrition.

One sunny day, Debbie, Laura, Tracy, and I were all playing. Mom told us, "Wait here, it's time for a treat," then disappeared to the kitchen. By the time she returned, Laura and Tracy had gone AWOL. Now, I was only twenty months old at the time, but that was old enough to know if someone mentions the words "stay here" and "treat" in the same sentence, well, there could be a full-on apocalypse outside and I would still be patiently waiting for my treat.

We found the two girls sitting outside on the clothesline stand. Mom asked, "Why did you leave the house?" At this, Laura's eyes began to tear up as she rolled her shoulders and looked down toward the ground; her little voice began to quiver.

"Treats ... are for the real kids, not for us."

Mom, fighting back her own tears, kneeled down. Then she pulled the two girls close with a big hug. "You are in the McQuarrie household now, and in this house, all kids are real kids. Now, let's go get us that treat." Grabbing the two girls by the hand, Mom walked them back into the house. I believe our treat was a little bigger than usual that day.

Over the next few months, Laura and Tracy started to do much better, both physically and emotionally. They gained weight, and Tracy's stomach even went back to normal. Then, at the beginning of September, Laura and Tracy moved to Hamilton, Ontario.

L-R: Me, Debbie, Tracy, Laura

It had been one whole year since my head surgery, and I continued to do well. Yet, I had developed occasional wheezing, nothing major, but the doctors kept an eye on it.

I was a happy little guy, reasonably social, with a good sense of humor. At least that's what Mom always said.

I was beginning to develop quite the advanced vocabulary and communication skills for my age. Mom thought just maybe she had a genius on her hands; however, doctors assured her I most likely was not a genius.

Sometimes babies that have been through traumatic experiences develop communication skills a bit faster than expected. It's more of a survival thing, trying to create attachments with a caregiver. I spent a lot of time in hospitals interacting with various caregivers, so I learned to communicate and socialize.

Shortly after Laura and Tracy left us, I celebrated my second birthday. Now, this was a landmark event for a couple of reasons. Not only was I able to pick the flavor of my cake for the first time, "that would be chocolate, thank you very much." But I had graduated to full-blown toddler, affording me a lot more freedom and privileges, of which I took full advantage.

Doctors and social workers recommended that Mom and Dad not be overprotective, not to hold me back, and to let me set my own limits, within reason, of course. I had survived quite a few physical and emotional challenges in my first couple of years but had proven myself to be an emotionally resilient and mentally astute little guy. Still, the professionals figured it would be imperative that I not be held back or babied. Instead, I needed to be encouraged to find my own path.

Physically, I still tended to walk on my toes. Being an athlete, Dad noticed when I tried to run and got going, I was pretty quick. He decided to put a hold on any treatments or surgeries to relieve the tension in my legs, not wanting to hamper my ability to run.

On September 22, baby Billy arrived, just eleven days old, with a strep (streptococcal) infection. Unfortunately, he also developed a nasty eye infection and rash, to make matters worse. So, on October 7, Billy had to go back to the hospital in isolation for two weeks, after which his mother took him back.

Coincidently, almost the same day Billy went to the hospital, I got sick with an ear infection, battling a fever of 40.5 degrees Celsius (105 Fahrenheit). Mom was quite concerned, saying I would just hold my head and scream in pain. It took me a couple of weeks, but eventually I fought it off and was up and running in no time.

LORD my God, I called to you for help, and you healed me. Psalm 30:2

December 9, 1969, rolled around. Mom and I flew back to Toronto for my final checkup with Dr. Hendrick. Once again, Esther Elliott picked us up at the airport, driving us to Sick Children's Hospital for my appointment. Mom and I sat in the tiny exam room for what seemed like forever until finally, Dr. Hendrick burst through the door with a big smile and a friendly greeting. "How's our little man doing?" he said as he picked me up and set me on the exam table.

After poking and prodding me, the doc opened a folder with an X-ray of my head. He said he was pleased with my progress, and everything looked good. Even the birthmark on my forehead had begun to fade. I was doing just fine, so the appointment focused more on my breathing issues. The wheezing episodes had been getting more frequent, and Dr. Hendrick told Mom it was allergy related. So, I needed a dehumidifier for my room, and my blankets and pillows changed to hypoallergenic. The doctor also gave me two prescriptions, one for every night and another to take when I had an attack. I can still remember the yucky taste of those medicines to this day.

Mom thanked the doctor for all his work and dedication, getting me all fixed up in the head, giving me a chance at a normal healthy life. Dr. Hendrick shook my hand, told me to keep growing strong, and then left the room. That was the last time I would see Dr. Hendrick.

Dr. Edward Bruce Hendrick was not just any surgeon. Many children knew him for his magic tricks and water fights using syringe barrels. Beyond that he was Canada's top pediatric neurosurgeon, heading up Toronto Hospital for Sick Children's neurosurgical unit from 1964 to 1986. Dr. Hendrick trained at Boston Children's Hospital under Dr. Franc D. Ingraham and Dr. Donald Matson, regarded as founders of modern pediatric neurosurgery.

OK, so how does a little orphan baby from Sault Ste. Marie, Ontario, end up getting the number one neurosurgeon in all of Canada? There is no way of knowing how things would have turned out if I had a different surgeon. However, I know with 100 percent certainty that people prayed for me, I got the number one neurosurgeon in Canada, and I fully recovered from brain surgery. Thank you, Jesus.

Now, it was time to get on with my life.

Chapter 5:

The Orphan Carpenter Begins

Your eyes saw my unformed body; all the days ordained for me were written in your book before one of them came to be. Psalm 139:16

Everyone was looking forward to Christmas in 1969, especially Mom and Dad. We were all healthy and were taking a break from foster children for the holidays. The rest and respite were sure welcomed, as the past three years had been quite the emotional whirlwind in the McQuarrie household. As breaks go, this one was short-lived. First, Debbie broke out with red measles on Christmas Eve. You know I couldn't be outdone by Debbie. Simultaneously, I managed to come down with the measles plus scarlet fever in early January. True to McQuarrie form, we pressed onward.

Growing up in a winter wonderland was awesome. First, the snowbanks could get as high as ten feet, which provided hours of fun climbing and sliding down; then, of course, there were snowmobiling and hockey.

Sault Ste. Marie, like most places in Canada, is a big hockey town. More than forty hockey players from the Sault have made it to the NHL, including Hall of Famers Phil Esposito, Tony Esposito, and Ron Francis. We even have a "Junior A" hockey team called "The Soo Greyhounds," which has produced over seventy NHL players, including Hockey Hall of Famers Wayne Gretzky and Paul Coffey. Not bad for a small city of 80,000 people, eh?

Dad's favorite NHL team was the Toronto Maple Leafs. He watched *Hockey Night* in Canada every Saturday night when he got the chance. I enjoyed the cartoon they played between periods called "Peter Puck."

Dad, Debbie, and I would play boot hockey in the driveway for hours, sometimes just us and sometimes with the neighborhood kids. Debbie was good at hockey and liked playing goalie. Me, I was just shy of two and a half. Still, I ran around and took swipes at the ball or puck but could never really get it shot in the direction I was aiming.

Eventually, like clockwork, the warm spring breezes would begin to blow, melting away the high snowbanks and outdoor skating rinks. Soon we would be waking up to the chirping of the red robins returning from their winter vacation in Florida. With the warmer temperatures came longer days and that meant Debbie and I got to spend more time with Nanna and Poppa. Anytime I was around Poppa, he was always building, fixing, sharpening, or cleaning something. Given my natural curiosity, I started following him around everywhere. Just so you understand, Poppa was a carpenter, and you don't just stand there and watch a carpenter.

"If you're going to just stand there, you need to make yourself useful," Poppa said with a slight grin and a gleam in his eye. (That would be from his real eye, not the glass one he got after losing his eyeball in a construction accident.)

Poppa was Norwegian and immigrated to Canada with his family when just a young boy. He had a calm but rugged look in his early sixties now; his skin weathered from over forty years on the construction sites. Standing just shy of six feet tall, Poppa was a very lean 145 pounds. There was not an ounce of body fat on Poppa, and you would also be hard-pressed to find a single grey hair on his head, a side benefit of his Nordic roots. Oh, and he always had a pack of smokes in his front shirt pocket or rolled up tightly in his T-shirt sleeve, a habit he had since he was fourteen years old.

To make myself useful, I would retrieve for Poppa the correct tool from his toolbox, returning it to its proper place when he was finished with it. Sounds easy, right? Well, not so fast. I had to learn the name and function of the tool too. No touching the saws, though! "Saws are too dangerous," Poppa pointed out, at least until I got a little older. Being a quick study, I had mastered my tool-boy job in no time. Poppa also put me on the cleanup crew, picking up bent nails for later straightening and sweeping up.

Poppa would only accept quality work. "If you are going to take the time to do it wrong, why not do it right the first time," he would say as he handed me the broom back to do a better job.

I got paid in chocolate milkshakes, but only if I listened, worked hard, and passed inspection.

Dad, Mom, Me & Debbie

Therefore, in order to keep me from becoming conceited, I was given a thorn in my flesh, a messenger of Satan, to torment me. Three times I pleaded with the Lord to take it away from me. But he said to me, "My grace is sufficient for you, for my power is made perfect in weakness."

Therefore, I will boast all the more gladly about my weaknesses, so that Christ's power may rest on me. 2 Corinthians 12:7-9

As spring ran into summer, my allergies and breathing were growing worse. Finally, one day just like any other, I was playing hard, running around, and having fun. Suddenly, my lungs started to tighten up, and I began to gasp for air. No big panic, though, as I had symptoms like this in the past. All I needed to do was just go inside and rest. Then, after a couple of hours, my breathing will return to normal, right? Well, this time was different. This time my lungs stayed in spasm.

Mom gave me my yucky-tasting medicine, along with some Tylenol. She also put mentholatum ointment on my chest and over my lip. The menthol helped to soothe my lungs and sinuses. That night I was propped up in bed with two pillows. I had to sleep in a partially seated position to breathe.

I was exhausted from the day's activities and soon descended into a deep slumber. Suddenly I awoke, it was so dark and cold. The very air in the room seemed unbreathable. An eerie silence engulfed me, only challenged by the faint sound of the fan on my dehumidifier.

I tried taking a deep breath but was denied. Then, beginning to panic a little, I sat up straight, placing my hands on either side of me; I pushed myself up, trying desperately to inhale air into my lungs, but once again, nothing.

At this point, all I could manage were quick, shallow gasps for air. But no matter how fast I took those breaths, I could not seem to get enough oxygen.

Rolling out of bed, I stumbled the short distance to Mom and Dad's room and tugged on Dad's shirt a couple of times, but he was in a deep sleep. With one last effort, I placed my hands on Dad's shoulders; I pushed him with all my might. That did the trick. As Dad opened his eyes, I forced out what little breath I had, "I can't breathe."

Though she had been sound asleep, Mom jumped up at the sound of my voice and turned on the bedside lamp. Within minutes we were all, including Debbie, on our way to the emergency room of the Plumber Memorial Hospital.

The roads were dark and empty as the dimly lit streetlights guided the way. With no traffic, we were at the hospital in no time. As we pulled up to the ER, Mom jumped out of the car and carried me into the hospital.

Once inside, I was quickly placed on a bed, and the doctor pulled a curtain around us. Then he gave me a needle in the butt. "OUCH!" What's that got to do with my breathing?

A nurse pulled a special oxygen mask over my head with a tiny liquid compartment. I had to breathe through this contraption until all the liquid evaporated. Like filling a balloon at the fairgrounds, my chest expanded as I desperately sucked back as much oxygen as humanly possible. Thankfully, over the next hour or so, my breathing considerably improved. Eventually, just as the morning sun gave rise to a new day, I was allowed to go home. However, I had to lay low for a few days until my lungs fully recovered.

Soon after, I would be diagnosed as a severe asthmatic. My primary triggers were dust, feathers, dogs, cats, cigarette smoke, and cold, damp weather.

"OK, Lord, I have a little problem here. Sault Ste. Marie has plenty of cold, damp weather, and do I need to point out that just about everyone has a dog, a cat, or both."

Oh, and just so you know, back then smoking was everywhere—restaurants, offices, stores, you name it, people smoked there. You know those fast-acting asthma rescue inhalers? Well, they would not be around for another ten years.

If you were gambling in Vegas, you might say the odds were stacked against me. But we were Free Methodists, so we didn't gamble. We just prayed.

Asthma. This would be my thorn in the flesh. I prayed hard for Jesus to heal me, but he never did. Dad taught me a new prayer that we began to pray every night.

"Now I lay me down to sleep. I pray the Lord my soul to keep. If I should die before I wake, I pray the Lord, my soul to take. God bless Mommy, Daddy, and Debbie, in Jesus' name, Amen."

Asthma became my new normal, with regular asthma attacks and many trips to the hospital emergency room. Mom had many a sleepless night monitoring my breathing. Dr. Sagle sent me to a special kids' asthma physician named Dr. John Pierson, who prescribed me even more yucky medicines.

I could live with the medicines and butt needles, but now I could not have any toys in my bedroom. Life was just not fair, ugh! My room had to become a dust-free zone. I had a bed, a dresser, my elephant lamp, and that was it. Mom scrubbed my bedroom down a couple of times a week like it was an operating room, giving me the cleanest bedroom in all of Sault Ste. Marie.

Do nothing out of selfish ambition or vain conceit. Rather, in humility value others above yourselves, not looking to your own interests but each of you to the interests of the others. Philippians 2:3-4

Me babysitting a foster baby

Well, life wasn't all about me as the foster children continued to flow in and out of our home. Many babies and toddlers, including Keith, a two month old with reddish-blond hair, came with a rash and cold. Then there was Kathy, a part First Nations baby with black hair and brown eyes. Mom said she was a doll; we discovered she was allergic to wool and baby oil. Kristine was a three-year-old Black girl. She was a very mixed-up little gal (Mom's words, not mine).

Kristine did well with us, and Mom and Dad wanted to adopt her, but the Children's Aid Society chose a Black West Indian family in Toronto for Kristine.

We took in many more babies and young children, some for a few days and sometimes a few months. Unfortunately, many kids had illnesses or emotional problems, and some had both.

Debbie and I did our part to help to the best of our abilities. Four years older than me, Debbie was much better at holding and feeding the babies. I worked more on the hospitality side of things, sharing my toys and playing with the kids.

When Dad was at work and Debbie at school, I was Mom's right-hand man. If Mom needed something and I knew where it was or how to do it, consider it done. I also helped out in the kitchen; if it required mixing, stirring, or pounding, then I was your guy.

All these foster children were a lot like I once was, needing help and fighting through a tough start to life. So, I found myself in the middle of many other kids, all starving for love and attention.

Mom and Dad always told me how Jesus brought me to them, how they chose me, that I was not an accident, I was a blessing. But I was now almost three years old and sometimes would feel like just one of the many kids. Sometimes, Mom and Dad seemed more interested in all the other children than me.

I've always been a profoundly deep thinker, an old soul, always watching, observing, and analyzing people, even as a little guy. Probably a survival skill from spending so much time in hospitals as a baby.

One evening at bedtime prayers, sensing something was bothering me, Dad asked. "How are you getting along with the other kids?" At first, I didn't say much, but then I let loose.

"Why do the other kids get special treats? When I talk to you and Mom, you don't listen and are busy with the other kids. I was playing in the sandbox with my Tonka trucks, and Johnny took my truck."

I must have rattled off a half-dozen arguments in sixty seconds.

Dad patiently listened to all my evidence, raising his eyebrow and nodding like a wise old judge as I pleaded my case. When I finished, he sat quietly for a moment. Then he took a deep breath.

"I am very, very proud of you for helping your mom, playing with the kids, and sharing your toys," he began as he pulled up my bed covers to tuck me in. "Just like Jesus brought you to your mother and me, he has brought these kids to all of us because they need our help. Sometimes, we have to put the needs of others ahead of ourselves," he continued as he grabbed my stuffed elephant and placed it on the pillow beside me. "Maybe we could pray that Jesus helps find a mommy and daddy for these kids. Would you like to do that?"

It was pretty hard to argue with Dad; he did make some good points, I thought, as I quietly nodded my head and placed my palms together to pray.

"Now I lay me down to sleep. I pray the Lord my soul to keep. I pray Johnny gets a mommy and daddy so they can buy him his own Tonka truck, and he doesn't take mine. In Jesus' name, Amen."

OK, so I was a work in progress. Still, Dad spent a little more time with me the next day, helping me with my baseball swing.

My natural curiosity about life and how things worked continued to develop. I would bug Mom and Dad with hundreds of questions until they provided an acceptable explanation. I'd even debate them if I didn't feel they answered my question correctly. With home maintenance or construction questions, many times the answer would be, "Well, that's a good question for Poppa."

One Saturday, while Dad was outside doing yard work and Mom was in the kitchen, I checked out the front coat closet door, investigating how the doorknob turned and the catch would lock into place.

As I entered the closet to see how it worked from the inside, I noticed a hidden purse sitting on a ledge behind the coats. Hmmm, very interesting, I thought to myself.

I pulled back the top flap of the purse, hoping to find some candy. Mom always had some sort of small candies in her bag. To my disappointment, I didn't find any sweets. I did, however, find something very intriguing. There were all sorts of lipstick containers in the purse.

One by one, I started taking the lipsticks out of the bag, pulling the caps off, and setting them on the ledge.

They were all various shades of red, which just happens to be my favorite color. Suddenly, I got a brilliant idea. I would color the closet walls red. After all, I had been helping Poppa with his projects, so I figured I would do my own renovation project. The first lipstick didn't cover the area very much, but no worries, I had plenty more.

I don't know if you've painted with lipstick before but I'll let you in on a bit of secret: it's very messy. After about ten minutes, I had lipstick all over the wall, my clothes, and even the coats.

It was just about that time the closet door flung open, and I heard the words "KENNETH IAN MCQUARRIE, WHAT ARE YOU DOING!" To which I replied, "Painting the closet, Mom."

Now that is my first memory of really, really getting into trouble.

So, my first solo renovation project didn't turn out so swell. But I did learn a couple of valuable lessons that day:

1. Doing a renovation project, make sure you get approval from the homeowner first.

2. Before starting, clear the workspace of coats, clothing, or furniture you don't want to get messed up.

3. Make sure you put your work clothes on before you begin.

4. Lipstick is tough to get off walls, and paint does not cover it up very well as the paint will not stick to the lipstick. It took Dad and me days to fix the mess.

Third Birthday

Three candles and some wind and I had officially made it to the ripe old age of three. Everyone now paid close attention to my breathing, especially around dust or animals. But thank Jesus, I was not allergic to sawdust.

I now had many doctor visits with Dr. Pierson for my asthma and Dr. Sagle for follow-ups and regular checkups. Dr. Sagle's waiting room had a table with some kids' books and a few toys. One book immediately got my attention. It was a Bible with amazing pictures of all the Bible heroes: Samson, Abraham and Isaac, Joseph and his coat of many colors, Moses parting the Red Sea, and, of course, Jesus and his disciples. This Bible book quickly became my most loved. These were all the stories I had been learning at Sunday school. My favorites were Joseph and Moses.

Joseph had a coat of many colors, making his brothers jealous of him, so they sold him as a slave when he was just a boy. He was taken to a faraway land and had many good and bad adventures. Every time something terrible happened to Joseph, God turned it into something useful. Eventually, Joseph became a great leader, helping his family and forgiving his brothers for being mean to him.

With Moses, to save his life from the Egyptian soldiers, his mother put him in a basket on the Nile River when he was only three months old. He was found and adopted by Pharaoh's daughter. After being raised in Pharaoh's house, Moses escaped to a faraway land. But God was with him and sent him back to Egypt to free his people. Then, Moses became a great leader, leading his people to the promised land. Moses was my favorite because he was once an orphan, just like me. And, just like me, he was three months old when he went to live with his foster family.

Maybe someday, God will send me on adventures to far-off lands like he did Joseph and Moses, I told myself.

As Christmas 1970 approached, the church Sunday school classes started to prepare for the children's Christmas concert, an annual Christmas tradition. I had a Bible scripture to memorize and then recite on cue at the show. Dad practiced me up on my verse every night.

Ultimately, the big day arrived. I was all dressed in my fancy pants, suit, and tie, but I decided right at the last minute that I did not want to participate when my big moment came. I was not shy or scared or anything like that; I just chose not to do it. Everyone was trying to coax and encourage me, but I stood firm—nope, not today.

Finally, after a few moments, Dad walked up behind me, kneeled, and whispered in my ear. Instantly I blurted out my verse with complete confidence and clarity, left the stage, and went back to my seat.

Mom asked Dad, "What did you say to Kenny?"

"I told him if he didn't say his verse, he would be making a trip to the furnace room when we get home."

The furnace room was a utility room at our house with the furnace, washer, dryer, and a freezer Mom used to freeze extra baking items and meats bought on sale. This room is also where we went to get our spankings. In 1970, most parents disciplined their kids with some sort of spanking. Dad did not believe in using any kind of belt or paddle; he would simply make us hold out our hands palms up then slap them a few times with his open palm. It would sting a bit, but that was about it. However, it got the point across.

Mom, however, used a variety of discipline techniques. First, there was the "just wait 'til your father gets home" method or the "you're going to sit on this chair until you are ready to apologize" technique. Last, but not least, was the wooden spoon procedure, or as I secretly called it, "The Persuader."

The Persuader was meant to persuade me to make better choices. Mom could have been a professional drummer the way she could paddle my butt with that wooden spoon.

Regardless of the punishment, it came with a life lesson. Mom and Dad always followed up, so we understood why we were in trouble and how we could learn from it.

So, you may wonder if I was a bad kid. Well, if you ask Mom, Dad, or even Debbie, the response you will get is, "Kenny was very stubborn."

Yeah, but was he a bad stubborn, you may ask?

"He was just plain stubborn."

What about strong-willed?

"Yes, he was that too."

My strong will kept me fighting to survive; I just needed some gentle guidance once in a while. Well, OK, I must admit, sometimes it took more than gentle guidance.

You see, I was very independent and had a mind of my own. I was not giving up on what I believed was fair and proper. But I wasn't mean to other children; I didn't take stuff that wasn't mine, I didn't hit, I played well with other kids, I told the truth (well, at least most of the time), and even though stubborn, I did not throw temper tantrums.

Since we are being totally honest here, full disclosure: on one occasion, I did bite Debbie on the arm, and oh yeah, once I threw a pair of scissors at her. But, both times, Mom used The Persuader with a lesson on why I should never do those things again. You know what? It worked; I never did those things again.

Just ordering me to do something didn't work so well. But if you asked me to do something and explained why, you would have much better luck getting my full participation. As long as I agreed with your argument, of course.

Mom and Dad always gave us plenty of warnings before administering any discipline. But, of course, that warning would come with a consequence of the mischief or misbehavior. Warnings are where my strong will would engage, debating my case and holding my ground. I would make a good argument on a rare occasion, and Mom or Dad would agree, but I would most often take the punishment. Debbie could not understand for the life of her why I would not just give in and take the get-out-of-jail-free card.

One time after losing a punishment debate, I found myself in the furnace room. Dad told me, "Hold out your hands." As he raised his hand for the imminent spanking, I looked him square in the eyes and proclaimed: "You can spank me all you want, but you can't change my mind."

Well, let me just say, I never tried that argument again.

Christmas morning finally arrived, a special family time in the McQuarrie household. Unfortunately, we were not allowed to venture downstairs to the Christmas tree until Mom or Dad gave us the OK. No worries though, we were allowed to open our stockings, which hung on our bedroom door knobs as we did not have a fireplace to hang them on.

As Debbie and I checked out what surprises Santa had left in our stockings, the aroma of roasting turkey started to fill the house and Christmas music softly played in the background.

Mom always liked to get the turkey prepped and in the oven early, before we awoke, so it would be ready when Nanna, Poppa, and Aunt Linda arrived for lunch.

Finally, Dad gave the OK, and we rushed down the stairs to a magical scene of colored lights, ornaments, and gifts around the Christmas tree. The front window drapes were pulled back, revealing the winter wonderland outside as the morning sun glistened through the frost-covered glass. It would make the whole magical scene come alive.

"How did Santa get these gifts in the house? We don't have a fire-place or chimney," I asked.

Being caught a little off guard at my question, Dad responded, "Well, that's a secret."

I quickly ran to the kitchen where Debbie and I had left some cookies and a glass of milk for Santa. Sure enough, all that was left were a few crumbs and about a quarter glass of milk. OK, enough investigation. Somehow Santa got in and out undetected. I was not going to figure the mystery out right now. Besides, it was time for Dad to read the first Christmas Story.

Before opening gifts, Dad would always read about the first Christmas when Jesus was born, reading from Luke Chapter 2 verses

1-21. Then Dad would say a prayer of thanks to Jesus for coming into the world and blessing humankind by paying the price for our sins.

Amen, now it was time for two of my favorite pastimes. Eating Mom's freshly baked cinnamon buns and opening presents. We would open our gifts, one person at a time. It took longer this way, but it was a fun family time seeing each other's reactions as we each took our turns.

Nanna and Poppa arrived, bringing more gifts. Soon, Poppa handed me a very different gift from the others. This one was heavy, and I could feel the box's cold hard surface through the wrapping paper. I thought to myself, is this a briefcase like the one Dad takes to work? Hmmm, I don't need a briefcase yet. With my curiosity at an all-time high, I carefully pulled back the wrapping paper to reveal a plain wooden box. The box had a couple of hinges on one side and a latch on the other.

Pulling back the latch, I slowly started to lift the lid, revealing the contents of the box. Suddenly, Mom gasped so hard she almost sucked all the air out of the room. I on the other hand let out an exuberant yell as I jumped up with excitement; this was the best gift ever! Real tools filled the plain wooden box. Not kids' plastic stuff, but miniature versions of actual tools, with a hammer, three screwdrivers, a small hand saw, a manual drill, and pliers. In addition, a carpenter's pencil, folding wooden measuring tape, and a builder's level completed the tool chest.

I could barely control myself from the rush of adrenaline.

Poppa and I were both down on our knees, examining my new toolset, when Mom finally caught her breath and, standing directly over us, placed her hands on her hips.

"There is NO WAY he can have those tools; it's much too dangerous."

Before I could even respond, Poppa looked up at Mom and fired back, "But he knows how to use them; he will be fine."

"Fine? You do remember the damage he did to the front closet with only a few tubes of lipstick?"

"Yes, but he learns fast, and I have been teaching him how to use all these tools."

Mom picked up the small hammer. "Look at this. Look at it. What if he hits himself with it?"

"Well, if he does, he won't do it a second time," Poppa replied.

Mom and Poppa continued to deliberate about my tools throughout the rest of the day. Dad and I, while curious about the verdict, wisely stayed out of the debate. By the end of the day, Mom and Poppa came to an agreement, or more like a five-point compromise.

I could have the pliers, measuring tape, level, and pencil. I could have the screwdrivers if I didn't run while carrying them. It was OK to have the hammer, but the first time I hammered something that was not meant to be hit, like the coffee table, window, or Debbie, I would be handing it over to Mom. The drill could only be used with adult supervision. And the saw? Well, it just disappeared.

Back then, almost everything needed assembly, and instructions were not always clear. Dad had many talents, none of which included putting stuff together. I couldn't read the instructions yet but had a knack for figuring things out. So, armed with my new tools, I was the official toy assembly boy from that Christmas onward.

That was the official beginning of my construction career. However, I still had many years of training and mentoring ahead of me before I would be ready to head out into the big leagues.

In the Bible, it seems God likes the number three a lot. There are hundreds of references to three in the Scriptures. For example, the Holy Trinity is the Father, Son, and Holy Spirit (Matthew 28:19). Noah had three sons—Shem, Ham, and Japheth (Genesis 6:10). Wiseman brought three gifts to Jesus at his birth—gold, frankincense, and myrrh. (Matthew 2:11). Satan tempted Jesus three times in the desert (Matthew 4:1-11). Three Apostles—Peter, James, and John—were with Jesus in the Garden of Gethsemane (Mark 14:33). Jesus prayed three times before being arrested (Mark 14:35-42). And, of course, Jesus rose from the dead after three days (Acts 10:39-43).

I don't think anyone can fully understand why God uses three so much in Scripture. Still, it almost seems like it's one of his signatures identifying his involvement.

For me, the Lord had given me three mentors, "Mom, Dad, and Poppa." These three would be the most influential people in my life, molding me, or in my case, chiseling me into the person I would need to become. And it was going to take all three.

Dad always possessed a humble strength, and is very patient and gracious with a strong faith and practical wisdom. He always put the family's needs ahead of his own and is the first to admit he's not technically or mechanically inclined. Still, his strengths and talents include loyalty, being a positive encourager, and always treating everyone with dignity, equality, and fairness.

Mom is best described as compassion with an edge, always having a solid faith and a determined will of her own. In addition, she always had a good sense of humor and quick wit. Although growing up in the country and never completing high school, she developed street smarts and a good judge of character. Mom was never afraid to tell it like it is or, as she would say, "call a spade a spade." She had a passion for children and a gift for genuine hospitality. Mom would always be there to help you get back on your feet.

Poppa was the faithful servant carpenter with the technical skills and a heart of service. If it was broken and needed fixing, you didn't even have to ask; Poppa was there to fix it. A logical perfectionist, he was always paying close attention to detail. The only way to do it was the right way; there was no room for shortcuts.

Adults would often ask me, "What do you want to be when you grow up?" Without hesitation, I would fire back, "I'm going to be a carpenter, of course."

But before that could happen, I still had a lot to learn. Life is quite similar to constructing a building. The most important thing is to begin with a good solid foundation.

Chapter 6:

The Foundation

For he was looking forward to the city with foundations,
whose architect and builder is God. Hebrews 11:10

Cold, cold, cold! It was January 1971. The frigid temperatures brought outdoor ice rinks and a new season of boot hockey. This gave us the perfect opportunity to use the new hockey sticks we got for Christmas. Winter in Canada came with lots of snow and ample opportunity to play in it. One of my favorite winter things to do was tobogganing at Finn Hill, a sizeable snow-covered slope across the street from the church. Afterward, Mom welcomed us home with hot chocolate and Sloppy Joes, a welcome treat to warm up the soul from the frigid Canadian winter.

Then there was our annual get-together with Dad's side of the family, at Aunt Ruth and Uncle Charlie's house. They had a couple of acres on the city's outskirts where they lived with their three kids, cousins Henry, Judy, and Michael. Debbie and I always looked forward to getting rides on Uncle Charlie's snowmobiles, a highlight of winter. Well, at least a highlight for me.

Grandpa and Grandma McQuarrie, though retired from pastoring, still attended the Free Methodist Church. Debbie and I would sit with them during Sunday service as Mom and Dad were busy helping out with the program.

Grandma, being very friendly, always talked to me and was interested in my innermost thoughts and opinions. Sometimes though, we would get chatting, and Grandpa would lean over and say, "Shush, the service is starting." You see, Grandpa McQuarrie was a man of few words, at least to me. Most of the time, he would just speak single syllables like sit, stay, go. However, he could be quite talkative occasionally, using more words like sit still, stay here, or go away.

Church service was about to start one Sunday, and I needed to use the bathroom. So Grandpa let me go by myself. Unfortunately, I was too short for the urinal, so I went into the old plywood stall. That's when disaster struck.

After finishing my business, I could not get the darn stall deadbolt open. Rats, it was stuck tighter than a nail in a two-by-four, and so was I.

A few kids tried to get me to crawl under the partition. But this was a terrible idea on so many levels. First, there was not much space, and second, I had on my good Sunday suit. Mom had already warned me about getting my suit all messed up and dirty. Doggone it, I had gotten myself into quite the pickle.

Suddenly I heard Grandpa's voice yell out, "STAND BACK!"

As I moved back, Grandpa slammed his shoulder into the stall door. It surged forward a couple of inches, but the deadbolt gouged itself into the partition frame, desperately trying to hold up against the force of Grandpa's might.

Grandpa recoiled and slammed into the door again. However, this time as if begging for mercy, the door gave way, crashing into the left side of the stall.

Grandpa grabbed me by the arm and walked me over to the sink, lifting me to reach the faucet as I washed my hands. We then— cool, calm, and collected—exited the restroom looking as if nothing had happened. I would probably still be stuck in that stall if not for Grandpa. Unfortunately, the gouge in the stall door frame would remain for the next thirty years until the church finally renovated that bathroom.

From that day on, I figured Grandpa, a retired pastor, reflected Jesus. He was always watching, didn't say much, and was there to rescue me at the last minute.

The smell of spring was in the air, signifying that once again we had survived a long Canadian winter when, one evening at dinner time, Dad told us, "Your mother and I have some exciting news for you guys!"

Well, that got my attention. What could it be? Hmm, I wonder, are we going for ice cream after supper? Maybe we are going camping at Pancake Bay. Even better, could we be renovating the house? I sat up straight, straining to hear, as Mom started to talk with a big smile on her face. "I am pregnant; Kenny is not going to be the youngest much longer."

Whoa, I was NOT expecting that; I was speechless. Mom went on to say it was a real surprise. Well, of course it was! I would be surprised too if I woke up one morning with a baby in my belly. Mom told me I had only nine months to get ready to be a big brother. Nine months? Seriously, that's like forever. But, on a positive note, I would get to help dad make a baby nursery.

Everyone was very excited about Mom being pregnant; it had been five years since she had been pregnant with baby Stephen. Nanna was probably the most excited. The thought of having another grandchild warmed her soul but, at the same time, brought home the reality of her condition. Nanna's cancer was getting worse, and she had to travel to Toronto for treatments. The illness, as well as the procedures, were taking a physical toll on Nanna. As a result, Mom and Dad put a hold on taking in foster children, as Mom focused on her pregnancy and helping Nanna.

Nanna was becoming weak, so Poppa got a wheelchair to help her get around. However, there was one small problem; their house had about six steps at the front and back, making it impossible to enter with a wheelchair. A lesser man would struggle, but not a carpenter.

Poppa had a brilliant idea to build a platform that could move up and down. Then, Nanna and her wheelchair could easily get in and out of the house.

So, Poppa and his trusted sidekick (that would be me) started construction in no time.

Pulling the existing steps back from the house, we built a platform that Poppa rigged up with some homemade hydraulics and electric pullies. During our construction, I caught a pretty good-sized wood sliver in my finger from carrying wood. As my eyes began to well up from the pain, Poppa pulled out his pocketknife and grabbed my hand. Whoa! No, not the knife! I began to whimper, trying to pull back my hand. "Come here. Carpenters don't cry," Poppa asserted as he grabbed my hand and removed the sliver. I then ran into the house where Nanna put a Band-Aid on my finger, gave me a glass of milk, a hug, and a cookie. My finger was now good, and so was I; time to get back to work.

The next big project was the renovation of my sandbox. The sandbox was my happy place, my escape. Most boys my age had an attention span of about ten minutes, and that's on a good day. Not me. You could put me in the sandbox with my Tonka trucks and I was good for hours. I even preferred to be by myself most of the time.

Mom used this to her full advantage. So, if she needed to get something accomplished, she would say, "Why don't you go play in your sandbox." And off I'd go; she never had to ask me a second time. My sandbox was a small patch of sand on the side of the old shed in our backyard. But that was all about to change.

Dad and I built a one-foot-high wood border around the sand patch. Then one day, a dump truck placed a big load of sand in the driveway. So, we spent the next week shoveling and wheelbarrowing that sand back to my sandbox. When all was said and done, I ended up with a massive sandbox twelve feet long by eight feet wide and almost twelve inches deep.

I would spend endless hours constructing roads, sandcastles, and cities in my sandbox. I couldn't tell time yet but had a good sense of it.

So, if Mom said I had thirty minutes, I would plan out my sandcastle complete with moat and get to substantial completion within the given time frame, give or take a few minutes.

One day, Mom called me out of the sandbox. "Get yourself cleaned up; I have some running around to do. You will be spending the afternoon with Poppa at work."

I was so excited; it was a dream of a lifetime. Poppa was the Maintenance Supervisor at the Plumber Hospital. A few years earlier, while Poppa was working as a carpenter on a construction site, he broke his back when three stories of scaffolding he was standing on collapsed. After his recovery, Nanna found out about the hospital's opening and encouraged Poppa to apply.

Mom parked the car behind the hospital. I was all too familiar with the hospital emergency room entrance. Today, I was going through a whole new door. The glass entry door opened with a swooshing sound. We went left to a staircase with cold metal railings leading down to the basement. I leaped off the last step with both feet to see how far I could jump. "Kenny, stop playing. We gotta go," Mom called out as she turned down a long corridor. (Just in case you were wondering, I jumped pretty far!)

Unlike the hospital's main floors, this corridor was empty with no people, no gurneys, no equipment, no nothing. As we walked, the passageway lighting became dim; a ceiling light flickered. The hallway seemed endless as we headed to find Poppa. Farther down the hall, I saw a door partially propped open. Catching a glimpse inside, I noticed all sorts of abandoned equipment and curiosities.

"Can I see in there?" I asked as I tugged on Mom's hand.

"No, come on. Poppa is waiting for you."

I felt a sudden chill as we passed by an unusual-looking door. It had strange letters above it, M-O-R-G-U-E.

"Mom, what's in there?" I asked.

"That room is not for you. Now come on, hurry up."

Finally, we came to an oversized old metal door with a few dents and scratches. As Mom pulled it open, the sweet aroma of sawdust, paint, and grease hit my nostrils simultaneously. I quickly stepped around Mom to get a glimpse. Talk about shock and awe; my eyeballs almost popped out of my head.

There, in front of me, was the most fantastically mind-boggling workshop I ever saw. The room had no ceilings. You could see the exposed structure above; all sorts of pipes and wires ran in every direction. The floor was just bare concrete. This workshop was jam-packed with all sorts of tools, both big and small. Enormous table and radial arm saws sat quietly in the middle of the room. In addition, they had a big bad band saw and lathe. Along the wall stood a humongous drill press, welding equipment, and pipe benders.

Then, there were all sorts of stuff I had no clue what it was, but I can assure you, I was about to find out.

Back in those days, hospitals repaired everything on site. Poppa managed a small staff of tradesmen, including plumbers, electricians, and painters. In honor of my first day in the shop, Poppa made me Junior Maintenance Supervisor. When Poppa went on calls in the hospital, my job was to stay in the workshop and watch the men. In addition, I spent time helping each tradesperson. I learned a lot about mixing paint, cleaning brushes, taking apart electric motors and generators, bending pipes. I still was not allowed to use the power tools but watched from a safe distance. Poppa said I did good. Translation, I listened and did what I was told. Even better was it provided me the opportunity to come back again and work at the hospital with Poppa and his team.

Poppa cut up some wood into blocks so I could practice building my structures when I was not helping the tradesmen. I would stack the blocks higher and higher until they all came crashing down. Poppa instructed me, "Build the base wide and deep. You always need to build a solid foundation first. Without a solid foundation, the part people see won't be able to stay standing strong and tall."

Occasionally I would go with Poppa on rounds to check maintenance requests in various hospital areas. I'll let you in on a little secret:

many doctors had suckers or lollipops, so I usually got a couple when doing the rounds. (But don't tell mom, it will be our little secret.)

One of my favorite things about working with Poppa was the coffee breaks. He would grab me some grape pop and Cheezies from the vending machine. Sometimes, we would even go to the cafeteria and get a chocolate milkshake. Nanna was at the hospital quite often in those days. Sometimes, we visited her room while on a coffee break. She always asked me about what project I was working on and keenly listened as I explained every detail.

As another summer came to an end, Mom continued to get bigger with the baby in her belly. Her belly was getting so big I figured that baby must be pretty near as big as me. Without all the foster kids around, it was just Mom and me most of the time, baking goodies and listening to Christian music on the record player. Every afternoon Mom and I would have our afternoon tea. Well, tea for Mom and juice for me. We would sit at the kitchen table, sipping our drinks and sampling freshly baked goodies, all the while bantering back and forth, talking story, seeing who could outwit each other.

One day Mom laid down on the sofa to watch her soap operas; I headed out to my sandbox. After a while, I heard a faint yelling coming from inside the house. "Kenny, Kenny, help me!"

Dropping my Tonka truck, I ran into the house. Mom had to go pee really bad, but her baby belly was so big that she was stuck on the couch like a turtle on its back. I had to pull Mom's arm with all my might to get her up off that sofa. But mission accomplished, and Mom made it to the bathroom in the nick of time.

After what seemed like an eternity, on Wednesday, December 8, 1971, at 4:23 a.m., my baby brother, Ronald Douglas McQuarrie, more commonly known as Dougie, was born. Dougie tipped the scales at 9 lb. 6 ½ oz. Jeepers, that's a big baby, and they said I was stocky. I think Mom maybe left him in her tummy too long.

Dougie arrived just in time for Christmas, just one month after Mom's sister Aunt Linda gave birth to a baby girl, our cousin Kelly. Nanna was especially thrilled to have two new grandchildren just in time for Christmas. The delight of the new babies helped take her mind off her illness and thoughts of not being around for many more Christmases. This Christmas would be a special one, and we had so much to be thankful for. Nanna was with us, and the Lord blessed our family with two healthy newborn babies.

After Christmas, I continued to help Mom with my new baby brother as best I could. But then, there was talk of me starting school in the fall. What's up with that? Debbie goes to school, so I don't think both of us need to be going. As far as I was concerned, I should just help Poppa and his guys at the hospital.

Do not be deceived: God cannot be mocked.
A man reaps what he sows. Galatians 6:7

One sunny summer day, I took my tricycle across the street to play with some neighborhood kids. My tricycle, inherited from Debbie, was awesome; fire engine red, which happens to be my favorite color. Made of solid tube steel with steel and rubber wheels, none of that plastic stuff.

Around lunchtime, I saw Dad's car coming down the street. Pulling into the driveway, he went inside the house for lunch. I leaped onto my tricycle and headed home to say hi to dad and, of course, get some lunch. Then, parking my trike behind Dad's car, I ran into the house. I am sure you can imagine what happened next.

Dad finished eating, said goodbye, and left for work. Suddenly there was a loud banging, scraping noise. *Oh no, it can't be!* I quickly ran outside where my fears had become a reality. Dad had backed the car over my tricycle, a disaster of epic proportions.

"Why did you park right behind the car?" Dad asked.

Sensing the tone of his speech, I knew it was not a question I'd be wise to answer, so I decided to remain silent.

"This is not good; there could be damage to the undercarriage and the fuel tank," Dad said in his "this is serious" voice.

I wasn't sure what an undercarriage was, but I did understand fuel tank damage. So, I stepped back a few paces just in case the car was going to explode as I had seen on TV. Dad pulled the mangled tricycle out from under the car. It was all twisted and bent out of shape. I took my twisted trike to the backyard as Dad headed off to work. Jeepers, I sure messed that one up. Worst of all, I really liked that tricycle, and now it was destroyed. On a positive note, Dad's car would be OK.

That afternoon, Poppa dropped by and picked up the broken trike. I figured he was taking it to the tricycle graveyard. On the third day after the death of my tricycle, Poppa drove into the driveway. As I ran out to see him, my eyes caught a glimpse of a brand-new red bike. Hold on just a minute here; after further investigation, I discovered it was my old tricycle. Only it was even better than before. My tricycle had been raised from the dead!

Poppa had taken my old, damaged tricycle to the hospital workshop. All the tradesmen worked together to rebuild it. It was still the same tricycle, but now it had been transformed into something new, something even better than before.

"The guys at the hospital heard about your tricycle mishap and wanted to help. They appreciate how you help them when you visit," Dad told me.

Dad explained, "When you are kind and help others, then sometimes when you need help, people will help you. But never be nice to someone just to get something in return. Always remember you reap what you sow."

"Uh, OK. Dad, can I ride my tricycle now?"

It wasn't too long after my tricycle mishap that I heard a strange rumbling noise. As the rumbling got louder, the ground started to shake. I ran outside, and to my delight, a parade of bulldozers, backhoes, and dump trucks was coming down the street. The city was expanding our subdivision. I was ecstatic, like I had died and gone to heaven. A massive construction project at the end of my very own street. How cool is that?

I would spend hours at the end of the road watching the large construction equipment carve out the new streets through the bush. By summer's end, I could tell you exactly how many loads of a backhoe bucket it took to fill a dump truck. Still, I couldn't wait for the new house construction to start.

These would also be my last days visiting Poppa at the hospital workshop. He was preparing to retire. I would be starting kindergarten soon, and there was no way to get out of it; believe me, I tried. Nanna's cancer treatments were no longer working, and there was talk of her coming to live with us.

The fall of 1972 was fast approaching, and I was about to turn five years old. A new chapter in my life was about to begin. This new chapter would overwhelmingly impact me for the rest of my years to come.

Chapter 7:

Like a Bat Out of Hell

"They will fight against you but will not overcome you, for I am with you and will rescue you," declares the Lord. Jeremiah 1:19

Tuesday, September 5, 1972, finally arrived just one day shy of my fifth birthday. It was my first day of school. I was getting older so, much to my disagreement, it was time to start my formal education.

Some kids start preschool when they are four years old, but I was too busy helping Mom look after Dougie and working with Poppa at the hospital. Mom put Dougie in a stroller, and we headed off to school, strolling to the end of Primrose Drive, turning down a back laneway leading to the gravel parking lot of St. Gerard Majella Catholic Church. Making our way around to the front of the church, we crossed Pentagon Boulevard and came to a trailhead. The well-trodden, tree-lined dirt path bordered the bush. It meandered about four hundred yards to the end of Paradise Avenue, which ran along the school property leading to the front of Ben R. McMullin Elementary School.

Now I know all the streets in "The P. Patch" have to start with the letter "P." However, I think having a school street named "Paradise" was a big mistake. I believe "Purgatory Lane" would have been much more appropriate. Mom walked me to my class, hugged me, and tried to kiss me on the cheek, but I ducked out of it. Listen, I was a big boy now and did not want to get labeled as a momma's boy, especially on the first day of school.

"Now listen to your teacher, and I will be picking you up at 11:30 a.m. sharp," Mom said as she left with Dougie. Well, at least school was only half a day for kindergarteners.

I stood back to survey the situation. The floor had square vinyl tiles. I noticed a couple of tiles in the back corner were coming loose. *I think I can fix that,* I thought to myself.

Looking across the room over the small tables and chairs, I could see built-in shelves with toys and stuff. A few kids were already playing at the tables. The walls were plastered with all sorts of things, like the alphabet letters, pictures, and posters. There was an area with hooks to hang our coats and a shelf for our hats and toques (Canadian for knitted hats or caps). We even had our own restrooms separate from the older kids.

Thankfully, I already knew a few kids in my class. First, there was Krista Sepp, and she lived in one of the houses on the street behind me. Our parents had known each other for some time, so we grew up playing together. When we were three years old, Krista said she would marry me, but I was not ready to get married yet.

Susie Wansbrough was also in the class. Susie was adopted just like me and lived behind us on the same street as Krista Sepp.

Johnny Darlow lived a block over from us. I had known Johnny for about a year. I would ride my bike over to Johnny's house, and we would play games in his basement. He had an Evel Knievel action figure complete with a motorcycle that you could wind up and make it jump over stuff, just like the real Evel Knievel.

I settled into class and even made a new friend, Cameron Ross. Cameron lived a couple of blocks from my house; his dad was a church pastor, which I thought was pretty cool.

The teacher read us a story, we did some crafts, had a snack, learned a couple of new songs. As exciting as all that stuff was, my mind started to wander. I wondered what Poppa was doing. Was Mom making it through the morning without my help? I missed my tools, sandbox, and helping Poppa at the hospital.

Suddenly, a bell went off; it was recess time. The teacher opened the door and let us outside. Wow, I didn't see that one coming. Once outdoors, I took a look around for a bit, then decided that was enough school for me. So, back up Paradise Lane I went, down the dirt path, through the church parking lot, and up Primrose Drive to home.

As I entered the house, my unexpected arrival completely surprised Mom.

"Kenneth Ian George McQuarrie, why are you not at school?"

Standing straight up, I puffed out my chest, looked Mom straight in the eye, and declared, "I'm all done with school."

"You certainly are not, young man," Mom fired back as she packed Dougie into a stroller, grabbed me by the arm, and marched me right back to school.

I know what you're thinking, "I'm all done with school" is a pretty weak argument, eh? But in fairness, I was making it up as I went, and that's all that came to mind in the heat of the moment.

Mom also invoked my full name. Unfortunately, my success rate of negotiations after Mom invoked my full name had not been good. This time she even threw in "George." Hmmm, I wonder where that came from? Queen Elizabeth's dad was King George, and of course, there is a monkey called Curious George. Oh well, I'll figure that out later.

Nanna was very sick by the end of September and had come to live with us, moving into Debbie's room at the end of the upstairs hall. Dr. Sagle started making house visits, getting Nanna hooked up to all sorts of oxygen, tubes, and things. Poppa used his connections at the hospital to get her a special bed that went up and down.

Nanna slept most of the time those days. Our house was full of visitors, with all nine of Nanna's brothers and sisters (my great aunts and uncles) and Great-Grandma Hawdon visiting.

Some folks came to visit more often than others. People from the church would bring us meals, so Mom didn't have to worry about cooking.

It was early morning, November 6, 1972, just three days before Debbie's ninth birthday. Dad came into my room and sat on the edge of the bed.

"I need to tell you something about Nanna," he started, then paused a moment to collect his thoughts. Finally, taking a deep breath, he continued. "You know, Nanna has been very, very sick. Last night, Nanna died and went to be with Jesus in heaven."

Dad said a couple more things, but after "last night Nanna died," my five-year-old analytical brain started to spin, losing focus as I tried to make sense of what he had just told me. After a few minutes, Dad was now standing at my bedroom door.

"You take your time and come downstairs when you're ready," he said as he left the room, gently closing the door behind him.

Sitting up in bed, I blankly stared at the closed door for a while as time seemingly stood still. Then, I got out of bed, walked over, and opened the bedroom door.

Standing there in my pajamas, I leaned against the door frame, looking down the hall toward Nanna's bedroom. The upstairs was empty and quiet, except for the dull murmur of adults talking in the kitchen downstairs. As I looked down the long dark hallway, the morning sun was starting to rise, peeking through the cracks of the window drapes in Nanna's bedroom. Beams of sunlight shot across the room, hitting the side of the special bed where I had stood to say goodnight just hours before. Nanna was gone. Nanna was gone and never coming back; she was gone to be with Jesus. My eyes swelled up as I fought back the emotions. A tear broke free, streaking down my cheek, but I fought back the tears, wiping them with my pajama sleeve.

I needed to be strong for Poppa.

"Carpenters don't cry."

As I stood there, my sadness turned to concern, and I silently wondered, *Jesus, are you coming for me next? Am I going to die and go to heaven too?*

These two questions consumed my thoughts for the next few weeks. First, baby Stephen had died and went to be with Jesus, and now Nanna was gone too. Sometimes I had to go to the hospital because of trouble breathing, so would I die soon?

I asked Dad, "Does everyone die?" Much to my dismay, the answer was yes. OK, so not the answer I was looking for. So, I asked Dad many more times, hoping to get a different answer. But nope, the same answer. "Everyone dies."

On about the hundredth time, Dad added, "It's not something you need to worry about for a very long time."

I had to ask, "How long?"

Dad said maybe Jesus would return before then, referring to the Bible where Jesus says he is coming back someday.

Oh, OK, so perhaps Jesus would save me from dying? I guess that made sense, and I never asked that question again.

Nanna was only sixty-one years old when she passed away. Lots of people came to her funeral. I spent most of the evening with my cousin Mark. He was the son of Mom's sister, Aunt Marilyn, and one year older than me.

Everyone was sad but also happy that Nanna was not in pain anymore. She was at peace in heaven with Jesus.

Days after Nanna's funeral, the weather turned frigid cold as fall transitioned to winter. There had been a few early winter snowfalls but nothing permanent yet. The

Margaret Emily (Hawdon) Bjornaa – Nanna Went to live with Jesus on November 6, 1972

daytime sun would melt the snow, but freezing nighttime temperatures would create a thin layer of ice on the puddles.

Since starting school, a few grade-one boys had been picking on me. It was very frustrating, especially given the circumstances with Nanna and all. But, for the most part, they would just make fun of how I dressed or how I walked. Mom always said I walked with purpose. Although, you see, I still had tight calf muscles and Achilles tendons combined with large flat-as-pancakes feet, so my stride was slightly different from other kids. Occasionally, the bullies would push me, trying to knock me over. I did my best just to avoid these kids by running away. Looking at me physically, you would not think so, but I was a surprisingly fast runner.

The school bell rang, signaling lunch and ending the school day for us kindergartners. Most kids walked home for lunch in those days.

We kindergarteners got released a bit earlier than the bigger kids, so we would get a head start on the walk home. On this particular day, I got hung up a bit longer at school. The older kids had already started to walk up the dirt path before I began my trek home. About halfway up the trail, I encountered the group of boys that had been picking on me. As I approached the gang, of course, the main bully started making fun of me. Maybe if I just ignored him, he would go away, I thought, as I kept to the right side of the pathway, looking toward the ground, and just kept walking.

Suddenly and without warning, the bully lunged at me, pushing me off the well-trodden path.

Stumbling, I fell into the tall grass and uneven, muddy terrain. My right knee hit the ground as I reached out to brace my fall with my hand. The cold, wet mud quickly penetrated my pant leg, feeling like frigid prickly needles hitting my skin.

Attempting desperately to get up, I got pushed harder and farther off the path, this time falling to both knees and hands in the icy mud.

I paused for a moment, closed my eyes, took a deep breath, then jumped up, trying to make a run for it.

Getting by my first attacker, my feet hit the solid ground of the path. But as I accelerated, the other boys blocked me off and started pushing me backward, enabling the bully to catch up with me.

Grabbing my jacket, he spun me around, trying to throw me into a large puddle on the other side of the path.

Frantically I tried to pull away, but the other boys jumped me.

My body slammed face down into the puddle with the full force of all the boys on my back, breaking through a thin layer of ice left from the previous night's freeze. The ice shards felt like cold razorblades cutting at my hands and face. The shock of the freezing water caused me to gasp, only to inhale some of the murky, muddy water into my lungs.

I tried pushing myself up with all my might, but my arms collapsed under the weight of the boys as I sank deeper into the muddy depths of the ice-cold puddle.

Desperately I strained to lift my head out of the water for a breath, but to no avail as the bully, now pressing his knees into my shoulder blades, pushed his hands down on the base of my skull, forcing my face gravely deeper into the murky water.

I frantically tried to lift my head one last time but was deprived. Then, finally, the paralyzing cold overcame me, and I gasped for air one last time, yet nothing but mud and water rushed in.

A strange dizziness came over me, and everything started to go black as I felt my consciousness slipping away.

Suddenly at that moment, I felt the weight come off my shoulders. I heard someone yelling, "Kenny, get up, get up!" I pushed up with my arms, gasping hard for air as I choked, coughed, spit, and sputtered the muddy water out of my lungs.

"RUN, KENNY, RUN," yelled my sister Debbie as she pushed the boys off my back.

I took one deep breath and took off like a bat out of hell.

I ran frantically up the old path as fast as my short legs and flat feet could propel me. My lungs started to spasm as asthma started to constrict my breathing, but I didn't dare slow down or look back.

The Catholic church was now coming into view. I kept my eyes focused on the cross as I raced down the trail, across Pentagon Boulevard, and through the church parking lot.

Soon reaching the end of Primrose Drive, Debbie caught up to me. Now freezing and wheezing, I tried taking slow deep breaths to calm my lungs down as Debbie slowly walked me up the street.

Once home, Mom put me into a warm bath to thaw me out. After warming up, my lungs settled down, and my breathing returned to normal. Next, Mom made me some freshly baked chocolate chip cookies, and we watched *The Galloping Gourmet* on TV. The show was about this chef called the "Galloping Gourmet" who traveled the world to find new recipes. It always began with the chef entering the stage and leaping over a chair. Then after showing a video clip of him visiting some far-off land, he would make the new exotic recipe while the studio audience looked on. The show would end with the chef picking someone from the audience to eat the meal he just made.

So, you may be thinking, that's it? A gang of first-grade hood-lums almost drowned you, and you just sat home eating fresh baked cookies and watching *The Galloping Gourmet*! Well, the short answer is, "yes." You see, it was 1972 in a small city in Northern Ontario, Canada. Times were different back then. When something like this happened, there were no police, no lawyers, no psychologists, or even counselors involved. However, that's not to say the situation did not get dealt with.

Dad called the school principal and informed him what had just happened. It turns out the main bully was already a known trouble-maker. *Surprise, surprise.*

When those boys returned to school, they were called to the prin-cipal's office and introduced to the "leather strap." But, of course, if Mom had her way, she would have been the one doing the strapping combined with a few whacks with her persuader. I can't say for sure if the boys actually received the strap or just a demonstration with a warning. But I'm pretty sure some suspensions got handed out that day.

As for me, I stayed home from school for a few days. Then, when it was time to venture back to kindergarten, Dad, Mom, and Debbie had set up a few safeguards. I had to walk with Debbie to and from school for a few months. Mom would also be waiting at the end of the trail each day, making sure I made it down the pathway safely. Mom did have a few choice words for the bully when he passed by her, though.

Then, one day, Mom and the bully's mom had a confrontation. Now that was a big mistake. A mistake on bully's mother's part, that is. All I can say on the topic is after the two-mother show down, that boy never came near me again.

While they were stoning him, Stephen prayed, "Lord Jesus, receive my spirit." Then he fell on his knees and cried out, "Lord, do not hold this sin against them." When he had said this, he fell asleep. Acts 7:59-60

That attack by those bullies was a pivotal point in my young life. My self-confidence was shattered, and for the first time, I felt scared. I sure wished I could take a different path. Sunday school taught me to forgive kids who did mean things to me. The Bible tells a story about Stephen, who forgives people stoning him to death. That's all well and good, but Stephen died and went to live with Jesus. On the other hand, I had to return to school and face my attackers. The possibility of death now became very real to me.

In the Christmas television special *Rudolf, the Red-Nosed Reindeer,* Rudolf, Yukon Cornelius, and Elf Hermey land on the "Island of Misfit Toys," where they find a bunch of toys that are all a little different from regular toys. I felt like a misfit toy. I was just a bit different from the other kids. Maybe I should go live on the Island of Misfit Toys.

Mom and I continued to have our afternoon tea and goodies. We would talk story about all sorts of stuff, and I would fill her in on all the things going on at school. She would ask about the other kids and how I was getting along with them, what the teacher was teaching me, and other stuff like that. Mom always pointed out the humor in all situations. Of course, sarcastic wit was a must if you were hanging with Mom and me at afternoon tea.

But we did have rules! You could be witty but never mean-spirited.

"We don't make fun at other people's expense," Mom would always say.

Mom taught me about bullies and how they are not as bright as they think they are. They bully others because they are insecure and have a low opinion of themselves. Bullies try to control other people, thinking it will make them feel better about themselves, but it doesn't. So, when I started to understand this, I began to see bullies differently. Oh, I was still very aware of the danger. Icy mud water in your face and lungs will do that for you. For me, knowing the bully is the one with the problem somehow made it a little easier to work on that forgiving stuff.

"Do to others as you would have them do to you." Luke 6:31

Mom also made clear I was never to bully another kid. I always needed to remember to treat other kids the way I wanted to be treated. Now, did I ever upset or say something mean to another kid? Well, yes, I was not some holy saint, you know. However, I would mostly feel bad after and usually apologize, being kinder to them after that. Plus, if Mom ever caught me being mean to another kid, well, that would be the end of life as I knew it.

There was some stuff at school that I just did not want to do, like playing a musical instrument or singing. I'm just not musical; I could not remember a tune if my life depended on it. So, with stuff like this, Mom would say, "I don't blame you for not liking it, but just try your best."

Well, I'm happy to report I survived kindergarten, and at the end of it all, we even had graduation, which I have to admit was kind of fun. Except for the fact they made us perform for the parents by singing a couple of songs. Ugh!

About this time, the Children's Aid Society asked Dad and Mom to put together a paper on foster parenting, based on their years of experience. One thing led to another, and within a couple of years, Dad got appointed president of the Ontario Children's Aid Society, and he even did it as a volunteer.

We pretty much had to stop taking in foster children, and Dad would make trips back and forth to Toronto. One summer, we visited a big campground where the Children's Aid ran a summer camp for all the foster kids in the area. It was a crazy number of kids of all ages.

To think, I was once one of those foster children, and now I'm the son of the Children's Aid Society president. It made me realize how lucky I was. Jesus must be looking out for me. I decided, one day, after I get married, my wife and I would adopt at least one child, maybe two or three. But adopting kids for me would be way in the future; first, I had to survive elementary school.

"I am sending you out like sheep among wolves. Therefore, be as shrewd as snakes and as innocent as doves." Matthew 10:16

After being attacked, I developed my bully senses. I figured I could be scared, or I could be shrewd. So, I chose to be shrewd. If I could spot and outsmart a bully early enough, I could avoid any future attacks. I became very cautious and observant, more aware of my surroundings. Always knowing my escape route. Hey, you never know when you may need one.

I would just sit back and watch other people—children and adults. I would notice how they looked, dressed, moved, and interacted with others. Always trying to spot a potential bully, wondering, would this kid be friendly or mean? From time to time, Mom or Dad would tell me to stop staring; it's not polite, you know. However, at afternoon tea, Mom would discuss my observations with me. She was always willing to provide words of wisdom like, "If it walks like a duck and talks like a duck, well it must be a duck," and "Sometimes a little humor goes a long way."

Mom would tell me, "It's good to observe and learn as much as you can, but don't let people know everything you know. It's far better to appear a little dumber than you are than to act smarter than you prove yourself to be." So, I took that to heart and always strived to appear a little dumber than I was.

When I noticed other kids being bullied or teased, it made me mad, but I did not have the confidence to step in, which frustrated me to no end. I wished I could be Spiderman and just zap the mean people with my web-slinger.

I started to make friends with older, bigger kids for added security. Since Debbie was four years older than me, I was able to get to know some of the boys in her class, like Kevin Erickson and Herold Kreps, who lived on our street. Herold's younger brother Ernie was two years older than me, so I would quite often go to and from school with Ernie.

One misty, rainy day, Ernie and I were racing our bikes to school. Ernie was out ahead, but I was determined to catch him. I cranked my handlebars and leaned hard into the turn from the end of our street to the back laneway of the Catholic church parking lot. I could feel the adrenalin as I accelerated through the bend, not noticing the slippery wet rock.

As my bald tires hit that slick rock, suddenly the bike and I were both airborne; the problem was we were flying in different directions.

Everything felt like slow motion until gravity caught up with me, and I came crashing down to earth in a heap of twisted body parts, whacking my left knee on a bunch of rocks and scraping the first couple layers of skin off the palms of both hands.

After deciding I was still indeed alive, I felt a tingling numbness in my knee. Then, my pant leg began to turn a crimson red from the bleeding underneath.

I could barely walk from the impact to my knee as Ernie helped me hobble back home.

Walking in the back door through the kitchen and into the living room, I began calling, "Mom, Mom, MOM!"

Coming down the stairs carrying a laundry basket, Mom took one look at me standing there wet, muddy, and bloody.

"Kenneth Ian George, what did you do to yourself!"

"I crashed my bike racing Ernie to school."

"I told you to be careful on that bike; you never listen to your mother!"

"But I don't know where that rock came from. It wasn't there before."

"Goodness gracious, go sit on the chair in the kitchen. You're bleeding all over the carpet."

Just so that you know, Mom is, in fact, quite compassionate and always nursing people back to health. However, that does not mean she won't call out boneheaded behavior. Especially when it is something she previously warned you about. Looking at my knee, my mom could see I had scraped half the skin right off the bottom part of my left kneecap. The flap of skin was just hanging there. Mom flipped the flap back over and wrapped it tightly with a Tensor bandage.

Poppa came and drove us to the hospital, where Dr. Sagle stitched me back together.

When we got home, Mom made me some chocolate cake to help me heal better. I hobbled around for a few weeks, but in the long run, I survived. Plus, I had another scar to add to my collection.

I settled into the reality of elementary school. The most significant reality was that I had to attend. I didn't stick to one group of friends or clique. I was entirely independent but seemed to get along with most kids. The boys in my class were all fairly athletic for the most part. But I will admit, we could get a bit rough and rowdy at recess playing boot hockey, tag, or keep away with any kind of ball.

For some annoying reason, the teachers would get upset and bent out of shape if we were tackling or body checking while playing. On occasion, they would even take our balls away.

Greg Elsby was sort of the unofficial leader of the boys. He was the tallest and brightest kid in the class, plus he was a good hockey goalie.

We were friends and got along but sometimes would annoy each other. I still had that strong-willed gene, so sometimes, I would have to challenge even an unofficial leader. We often split up into two teams on the playground, and Greg and I always seemed to be on opposite sides.

Playing sports, some folks may say I was competitive. I think intense is a better description. The truth is, I was not very competitive at all. Oh, don't get me wrong. I enjoyed winning just as much as any other kid, especially if I beat Greg Elsby.

But the thing is, I didn't really care that much if I won or lost, especially considering I usually lost. Mom would always say that in sports someone has to finish last, but the important thing is that you do your best, never give up, and continually be a good loser.

The source of my intensity was simply playing by the rules and trying my hardest. I could get quite frustrated when the other kids didn't follow the rules or try their best.

*Swinging for the fences
in Bellevue Park
At bat – me, On deck behind me–
cousin Joey Campbell,
With glove – friend Johnny Tucker*

I wanted to play hockey like many other boys, but my lungs were just not healthy enough. The cold air would trigger my asthma. I often pushed myself to keep up with the other kids in the playground, but then it would take twenty minutes for my breathing to settle back to normal.

While I never used asthma as an excuse, I still had to know my limits. If I didn't it meant a trip to the hospital for me.

I would get hit with a full asthma attack a half dozen times a year. It would generally build in my lungs throughout the day then almost suffocate me at night. It was like the Grim Reaper himself was trying to smother me. After an attack, I would have to stay home from school for a few days lying low for my lungs to recover fully. Of course, I wasn't supposed to move around much while I recovered, so I would watch *The Galloping Gourmet* and help Mom in the kitchen. The more time I spent with Mom, the more she taught me about cooking and baking. Making food is like construction; you have to follow the instructions, and everything needs to be scheduled correctly.

I was no Galloping Gourmet by any means. But, from a young age, I could make a few staples like macaroni and cheese, hot dogs, hamburgers, soup, oatmeal, cookies, chocolate cake, French toast, and pancakes. Of course, that would be homemade pancakes, not the cheap imitation store-bought stuff. We used Nanna's old homemade pancake recipe from her time as a hotel cook back in the 1930s.

How precious to me are your thoughts, God! How vast is the sum of them! Were I to count them, they would outnumber the grains of sand—when I awake, I am still with you. Psalm 139:17-18

Though I was still very young and probably didn't understand the concept, I was learning not to take life for granted. Mom and Dad's attitude was always: every day is a gift from the Lord, so live it as best you can.

My whole family are fighters; if we get knocked down, we just get right back up. One of Mom's most common sayings was, "It's a long way from the heart." (Translation: although it may hurt like a bugger, it's not fatal, so let's have a cookie to make it feel better, then get right back out there). Although it was not discussed, at least with me anyway, Mom and Dad knew that every time I went to sleep at night, there was a chance my breathing would stop, and I would not wake up.

Every night Dad would tuck me in and pray with me. Dad and I would pray for all sorts of things, but I always prayed for two things in my own heart: healing from asthma and for Jesus to watch over and protect me. Some doubting Thomases may say, "Where was Jesus when the bullies almost drowned you? Where was Jesus when you hurt yourself falling off your bike?"

Well, I cannot speak for Jesus; however, Debbie arrived to save me from the bullies seconds before I drowned. If she had not, this would have been an extremely short book. Also, remember, Ernie was there to help me home when I crashed my bike.

For me, I assume Jesus is very busy, and sometimes he has to send other people to help us out, just in the nick of time. I am just saying.

Chapter 8:

The Parable of the Pollywog

That same day Jesus went out of the house and sat by the lake.
Such large crowds gathered around him that he got into a boat and
sat in it, while all the people stood on the shore. Then he told them
many things in parables, saying: "A farmer went out to sow his seed."
Matthew 13:1-3

Around Easter time, *The Ten Commandments* with Charlton Heston as Moses played on TV. I was so excited to watch it since Moses was my favorite Bible hero.

As I mentioned before, both Moses and I went to live with our foster families when we were three months old. There was only one problem. The movie, including commercials, ran for more than four-and-a-half hours, which would take it way past my bedtime. However, as soon as I saw the advertisements, I asked Dad if I could watch it. Eventually, I wore Dad down, and he said yes. I was so excited and couldn't wait to see it.

The week could not go by fast enough, but finally, the weekend arrived. Mom got me some snacks for the movie, my favorite Reese's peanut butter cups.

So, you want to know how I liked it? OK, well, I fell asleep sometime between plague seven and eight. No worries, though; I will try again next year.

As you can imagine, church was a very important part of our lives. We attended the Sault Free Methodist Church every Sunday morning at 753 McNabb Street. It was a small church of about eighty people back in those days. We were always the first to arrive because Dad liked to be early and the last to leave because Dad was very social. Poppa came occasionally, but mostly just on special occasions.

The church met in the basement because there was no money to finish the construction of the main sanctuary upstairs. Dad volunteered as the church treasurer and Sunday school superintendent. Mom helped in the nursery and planned church potlucks and various activities. When I wasn't in my own Sunday school class, I helped Mom in the nursery.

My best friend at church was Johnny Tucker. Johnny and I were the same age, so we were always together at Sunday school. We didn't always pay attention to the teachers and preachers, though. Instead, we would play Tic-tac-toe or Hangman during sermons using the weekly church bulletin for our paper. As long as we were quiet, our parents were usually OK with it.

The church also had a midweek kid's group for ages six to twelve called CYC, which stood for Christian Youth Crusaders. It was a youth group like Boy Scouts but with a mix of boys and girls. You would earn merit badges for Bible scripture memory, helping old people, hiking, and other stuff. Many kids from around the neighborhood would come to CYC, even if their families did not attend Sunday services. There would be crafts, Bible stories, songs, games, and learning about different cultures worldwide.

"Each of you should give what you have decided in
your heart to give, not reluctantly or under compulsion,
for God loves a cheerful giver." 2 Corinthians 9:7

One time the church was doing a mission's focus month. At CYC, the teacher taught us about missionaries in Africa who were helping poor people. We learned about how the African kids had to walk two miles every day just to get fresh water. That was crazy hard to believe; jeepers, I lived right beside Lake Superior, the largest freshwater lake in the world.

Then the teacher said, "I would like each of you to donate one of your toys so we can send it to the kids in Africa."

"I don't have any spare toys," I blurted out without thinking, drawing unwanted attention to myself.

"Kenny, can't you find just one small toy to send a child in Africa?" the teacher responded.

"Nope," I fired back quickly and quietly, shaking my head slightly while staring down at the floor. Well, I hate to say it, but that CYC teacher ratted me out to Mom. When I got home, Mom confronted me. "So, what's this I hear about you not wanting to give a toy to poor kids in Africa?"

"Mom, I don't have many toys."

"I think you have plenty."

"No, I really don't. I have a hockey stick and plastic sled for tobogganing at Fin Hill. Kids in Africa don't have snow and don't play hockey. My tools are not toys. I need my Tonka dump truck and backhoe for my sandbox. I would like to keep my Legos, and I only have five Hot Wheels cars."

"I see," replied Mom. "So, I guess those kids in Africa get nothing." And she turned and walked away, leaving me standing by myself. Over the next few days, I kept thinking of those African kids, having to walk so far to get water. I sure hope the church can find some toys to send them.

Since it was missions month, at nighttime prayers, Dad and I would pray for the African kids.

As the days moved on, I thought more and more about those kids with no toys. Maybe I can look around the house and find something. Dougie was now a toddler, so I conscripted him to help me. Wouldn't you know it, Dougie found one of my old Hot Wheels cars that I thought I had lost. I also found an army paratrooper figurine that used to have a parachute. After finding a few other things, I brought my donation to Mom.

"Here you go, Mom; I have decided to donate these toys to the kids in Africa."

"Good, I'm glad. See, I told you so."

Once school was out for the summer, I had more time to work with Poppa on his projects. I was getting a bit older now, so I was getting to use tools like the electric drill, belt sander, and hand saws. Still no power saws, though. Poppa said, "We want you to go home with the same number of fingers you arrived with."

The new houses were now going up at the end of our street. So, whenever I had the chance, I'd wander down to watch the carpenters and other trades. Well, before you could say Poppas, your grandfather, I was right in there helping the workers. I'd pick up scrap lumber and carry it to a pile near the trash bins. When not picking up scrap lumber, you could find me holding the end of the tape measure as a carpenter laid out the wall framing. And, of course, I was always scrounging for nails that I brought home and saved for my projects.

Meanwhile, Kevin Erickson and his older brother, plus a few of their friends, were building a treehouse in the bush just behind Kevin's house across the street. The boys were about four to six years older than me, so I just sat back and watched.

After spending an afternoon watching them, I thought to myself, *You know what, I think I can do that.*

I explored about twenty yards deeper into the bush and came across a cluster of four trees, all about five to six feet apart. *These trees are perfect for building my treehouse,* I thought. Now I just needed supplies, and I knew just where to get some.

Walking back to the houses under construction, I explained to the project superintendent my treehouse project plans.

"Help yourself to any of the scrap lumber by the trash bin," the man said, pointing over to the pile of scraps I had helped create. I spent the next couple of days hauling scraps of lumber to my tree-house construction site. It was a lot more work than I had expected, but there was no giving up. As Poppa would say, "Once you start a project quitting is not an option."

Finally, I had enough wood to begin building my treehouse. So, grabbing my hammer, a pail of nails, and a hand saw from the back shed, I made my way to my construction site.

I wasn't very tall, so the first thing was to build myself a ladder. Finding some low-lying tree branches, I cut them up and nailed the pieces together for my makeshift ladder. I was now ready to start building.

Grabbing some two-by-fours that were long enough to span between the trees, I hammered three-inch spikes into the end of each board.

Leaning my ladder against the first tree and grabbing the end of one board, I climbed up and, reaching as high as I could, hammered the nailed board into the tree. Then I repeated the process for each board at each tree.

With my perimeter boards now up, I hung off each of them like a monkey to make sure they could hold my weight.

So far, so good. Now comes the hard part, getting lumber up onto the boards to build my floor.

Grabbing a short plank, I placed it under my arm as I climbed the ladder, trying to push it on top of the perimeter boards, but I couldn't quite get it, and the plank fell to the ground. Rats!

Well, if at first you don't succeed, try, try again. And try, I did. Then, after about five more attempts, success, woohoo! I nailed that first plank at each end to secure it, then repeated the process with a couple more planks. I now had myself a small platform in the sky. OK, maybe that's an exaggeration, but it was close to at least six feet off the ground.

After throwing planks, pieces of plywood, and whatever other lumber I had up onto the small platform, it was like the United Nations of wood; every piece was a different color, shape, size, thickness, and length. I then nailed everything together like a giant jigsaw puzzle.

Sitting down in the middle of my new treehouse high off the ground, I felt pretty proud of myself. "This is the most gloriously spectacular treehouse ever. I bet other boys my age can't build a treehouse as good as this one."

> *Pride goes before destruction, a haughty spirit before a fall.*
> *Proverbs 16:18*

Well, break time was over; time to stop admiring my handiwork and get started on my roof.

Pulling my ladder up onto the platform, I leaned it against one of the trees. Now just like I had done for the floor, I prepared another two-by-four and climbed my ladder to nail the first end to the tree. I was now up about ten feet off the ground. Then, leaning around to reach the outside face of the tree trunk, I started to nail my board into place.

• • •

Suddenly, I was sitting on the living room sofa. Mom's Christian praise and worship music was playing. "Hey, what's the deal! How did I get here?" I looked down at my Mickey Mouse watch, and it was 3:45 p.m. Hold on a second. I looked at my watch before climbing the ladder, and it was only a couple of minutes before 3:00 pm. Where did the past forty-five minutes go?

There's an old saying, "To be absent from the body is to be present with the Lord." So, was I absent from my body for forty-five minutes? No, I don't think so; I surely don't remember visiting the Lord. Besides, if I was absent from my body, how did my body get home to the sofa?

Jumping off the couch, I walked into the kitchen where Mom was making homemade pizza for dinner, a weekly Saturday tradition.

"Kenny, do you want to help me make some pizza?" Mom asked as I walked by.

"No, not right now. Mom, how did I get on the sofa?"

"I assume the same way you always do." Mom said, looking back at me like I was Cuckoo-for-Cocoa-Puffs.

"No, Mom, when did I get ON the sofa?"

"About a half-hour ago, you walked in the door and through the kitchen. I asked you if you wanted to make some pizzas, but you didn't say a word. Instead, you just walked right by me and into the living room."

Hmm, what was happening to me? I didn't remember any of that.

I went out front where Dad was doing some yard work.

"Dad, when did I come home?"

"Oh, around a half-hour ago, you walked up the driveway, looking all serious like you were on a mission of some sort."

It's so weird, I thought as I walked across the street, heading back to my treehouse. I passed by Kevin Erickson, so I asked him.

"Kevin, did you see me walk home?"

Kevin said he was working on his treehouse and heard a crash. When he looked over, I was sitting on a pile of lumber on the ground under my treehouse. Kevin said I just sat there for about fifteen minutes, not moving, then suddenly I got up and walked home. It seems pretty clear; I must have taken a ten-foot nosedive off my treehouse. But, crazy, I don't remember anything from the missing forty-five minutes. Adding to the mystery, I didn't have any bruises or even the slightest headache. I can only assume Jesus must have helped me get home safely.

The following week Poppa came by to visit. I was so excited to show him my glorious treehouse. Poppa stood back and took a good long look when we got to the treehouse.

"Well, that's quite the treehouse," he said.

I stood up tall and puffed out my chest at the recognition from Poppa.

Poppa started to walk around the treehouse, pushing and pulling at the boards. After finishing his inspection, he looked down at me.

"Good job. You picked a good location and nice sturdy trees."

Picking up my homemade ladder, Poppa continued. "This is quite resourceful to make yourself a ladder. I can see you put a lot of work into this project. Just a couple things, though. We need to make sure it's sturdy and safe. When you build any house, it needs to be built to the building code. So, tell you what, let's go get some tools, and I will show you what I mean."

After returning with the tools, Poppa started pulling a few boards off. "Here, remove the nails from these," he said.

I started to pull out the nails, and by the time I looked up, Poppa had demolished about 90 percent of my glorious treehouse. "Ahhh, Poppa, that's too much!" I proclaimed in protest.

Poppa looked back at me. "Just grab the measuring tape and the saw; now, let's get to work."

Poppa and I spent the rest of the day completely rebuilding my treehouse.

We finished just as the sun was going down on that warm summer day. After giving the treehouse one last inspection, Poppa looked over at me with a partial grin. "Now, let's go get a chocolate milkshake."

When I stood back and looked at the finished work, I had to admit: The treehouse that I did on my own was OK, but when I let the Master Carpenter help me, the result was something special.

"Poppa?"

"Yes."

"When I grow up, will you help me build a house for my wife and me? That's when I get a wife, of course."

"Well, I hope so, but that's some ways off. You have a lot to learn before then."

"I know I do. But, Poppa, I want to adopt a kid, like I was adopted. Can we build a kid's room in my house?"

"Of course. Now hurry up, it's getting late. I don't want your mother to start worrying."

Poppa gave me a toolbox with my name painted on the side that Christmas. So now I had something to carry all my tools to my tree-house or when helping Poppa.

Me with my new toolbox, Dougie with his tractor, and Debbie just chilling

I spent my childhood growing up with our cousins Bonnie, Sean, Joey, and Dennis Campbell. So, when you add in Debbie, Dougie, and me, we were seven kids in total with eight years' difference from oldest to youngest.

These cousins were the grandchildren of Nanna's sister Dorothy or, as we called her, Auntie Dot. Auntie married Frank Campbell and had three sons, Harold, Dave, and John. John married Greer, and they had four children, Bonnie, Sean, Joey, and Dennis.

John Campbell headed to Toronto to pursue his radio news career and left Greer and the kids in the Sault. Growing up, we did many church and family activities with our four Campbell cousins. Dad and the two moms would pile us seven kids into the station wagon and take us all over the place on our many adventures. Our annual summer trip to Eddy's cottage at Sand Bay on Lake Superior was one such adventure.

Bob Eddy was our one-legged Sunday school teacher. He lost his leg fighting in World War II and had many exciting war stories. Bob and his wife Virene had a family cottage on Sand Bay, on the eastern end of Lake Superior. Sand Bay has an outstanding sandy beach and clear cold water.

It was a sunny Saturday in mid-July. Dad packed the seven kids and two moms into the station wagon. Our suitcases and food supplies were tied on the car roof rack before we set out on our journey north to Sand Bay. With ten of us crammed into a station wagon and no air conditioning, the forty-five-minute drive felt more like three hours.

Finally, pulling off Sand Bay Rd., we turned down a long sandy dirt laneway leading up to the cottage. The car tires made faint snapping and crackling noises as they rolled over the pine needle-covered ground.

The fresh scent of pine and fir penetrated the car as the giant trees stretched high toward the sky, creating a canopy blocking out much of the sun.

"Dad, what's that small shed over there?" I asked as we pulled up beside the cottage.

"I think it's the outhouse," Dad responded.

The cottage exterior was covered with well-weathered reddish-brown plywood siding. And, it turns out, there was indeed no indoor plumbing. Instead, water came from a well. So, the kitchen faucet was a well water pump of sorts, and the little shed outside was indeed an outhouse.

Walking around to the front porch exposed an open view of the sandy beach and scenic Lake Superior. You could hear the waves from the mighty lake lightly crashing on the shoreline, along with the sound of an occasional loon flying over the bay to catch itself a fish for dinner.

Dad stayed the weekend to help us settle in, then headed home for his week's work. So, for the next five days, we were on our own, two moms and seven kids, roughing it in the wilderness cottage. There were two main rules: you can explore but not leave the cottage property under any circumstances and don't dare go over waist-deep in the water.

One of the moms would ring a bell when it was mealtime. After meals, we had to wait thirty minutes before going into the water. Apparently, this was so we didn't cramp up and drown.

If we are only waist-deep in the water, how can we cramp up and drown? I thought. Oh well, sometimes it's just easier to follow the rules.

The lake was lots of fun for seven young kids. There was never a dull moment and so much to explore.

Sean found a couple of bullfrogs that were playing piggyback. Greer said they were mating, and we needed to put them back. Debbie and Bonnie tried skinny dipping at night, but some kids from the cottage down the beach stole their clothes. Greer saw a mouse in the house and set up a barricade, but it turns out the mice were nesting inside the sofa where she was sleeping.

Reject every kind of evil. 1 Thessalonians 5:22

Beside the cottage, a small creek flowed out of the bush and into the lake. Dougie, being the youngest, preferred the stream's calm flowing water over the lake's crashing waves.

Standing on the creek's bank using a small butterfly net, Dougie caught himself a pollywog and a little silver minnow. He placed his new pets in a small water-filled canning jar that Mom let him borrow.

Joey and I spotted a black leech swimming in the lake just below the surface of the shallows. With a coordinated effort, we captured the little black slithery bloodsucker.

Then, with no place to store our catch, we came across Dougie's canning jar with the pollywog and minnow. So, placing our little creature into the jar, we sat back and watched.

At first, the leech swam around with his new friends, each darting around the jar in various directions.

Then catastrophe struck. Suddenly and without warning, the blood-sucking leech attacked the pollywog. Latching on, he began sucking the life out of the little guy as the two sank to the bottom of the jar.

Although I was not totally naïve of the possible outcome of letting a bloodsucker into the jar, the sudden violent attack and Dougie's traumatic response caught me off guard. My first thought was, *Oh crap, Mom is going to kill me.*

Hearing Dougie's cries, Mom caught wind of the commotion. And, as I figured, Mom was beyond angry. Even angrier than when I painted the closet with lipstick or the time I took the wheels off Dougie's plastic riding tractor for my go-cart. Dang, I'm in big trouble now.

"Kenneth Ian George, did I raise you to be mean and cruel to little pollywogs?" Mom angrily shrieked as she poured the leech and pollywog out of the jar.

Mom then hit the leech with table salt, causing the little bloodsucker to release its grip on the pollywog. However, sadly, neither the pollywog nor the leech survived the ordeal. Now, most child experts would recommend a time out of one minute per year old of the child. I was eight years old, but that day I was banished to timeout for about an hour and a half. Mom told me to sit there and think about what I had done.

As I sat there thinking, I thought to myself, *I must admit I'm complicit in the death of the pollywog, but Mom murdered the leech.* However, I decided to keep my thoughts to myself as we only had a few days left at the cottage, and I did not want to spend it banished to my bedroom.

Years later, I would think back about that pollywog. The minnow, pollywog, and leech were all created creatures with a purpose. The minnow and the pollywog were innocent, maybe even naïve. The leech, however, was a predator, a bloodsucker, a killer. If the leech represented evil, I was responsible for allowing evil into the jar. Once the darkness was let in, it attacked, but what did it strike?

The minnow would simply grow into a bigger minnow or fish, but the pollywog would one day transform into a whole new creature, a frog. That dark, evil blood-sucking leech attacked the pollywog, destroying the creature with the most potential. Sometimes bad things out of my control would happen to me, but I needed to be careful not to allow evil into my jar.

From that day forward, I always needed to remember my little "Parable of the Pollywog."

Chapter 9:

What's the Deal, Mrs. Crabby-pants?

Consider it pure joy, my brothers and sisters, whenever you face trials of many kinds. Because you know that the testing of your faith produces perseverance. Let perseverance finish its work so that you may be mature and complete, not lacking anything. James 1:2-4

In Sault Ste. Marie, there is no such thing as endless summers, although some years it would feel like endless winter. The best thing about growing up in a place with four different seasons is that the holiday specials make sense. When *Frosty the Snowman* and *Rudolf the Red-Nosed Reindeer* are on TV, it's winter. Easter Bunny shows up in the spring. Halloween is in the fall when it's cold, damp, and scary.

Mom was always big on holiday traditions, especially those revolving around family and food. She would always prepare us special treats and decorations for the various festivities.

Mom never made it into an over-the-top big production or anything. Instead, she would say, "It's just a little something," or "It's the little things that count."

Those little holiday traditions always gave me something to look forward to, taking my mind of the struggles of life. One of those life struggles for me was school. I had a love-hate relationship with the school. I hated to go and loved it when the school day was finished. Now, in fairness, my school life got off to a rocky start with kindergarten. But I can't say things much improved as that school bell continued to ring.

There was a time the school decided I needed speech therapy because I could not curl the sides of my tongue. They called it "forming a straw." Really? That's craziness. What does curling my tongue have to do with how good I talk? I mean, I wasn't very good at spitting, but I could speak just fine.

Mom agreed with me but asked if I would attend the classes to, in her words, "humor the so-called experts." Plus, she said the speech therapist would give me snacks.

"Well, why didn't you say that in the first place? Then, of course, I'll go."

As far as school learning went, I did all right with subjects that involved studying people and faraway places including geography, history, and social studies. With math and science, well, there were two schools of thought on my skills. The thing about math and science was I could never get the darn tests finished in time. However, on a positive note, I would score 90 percent on the 70 percent part I did manage to complete, which resulted in a C-plus to a B-minus for me in these subjects.

By far, my greatest learning challenges were spelling, grammar, and phonics. I would try my darndest, but the struggle was real. No matter how hard I tried, I barely passed these subjects. Maybe Dr. Hendrick had crossed some wires in my brain when he fixed up my head?

Dad would quiz me on spelling every night before prayer time.

Mom would say, "You need to try hard. If you're not good at spelling and grammar, people are going to think you're not very smart." Which, of course, is a polite way of saying, people will think you're a dummy.

On a positive note, this helped me with Mom's advice about "It's better to be smarter than people think you are."

My absolute worst subject was anything to do with music. Don't get me wrong. I like listening to music. The thing is, I cannot remember a tune or figure out how to play an instrument to produce anything that sounds like music. Of course, at school, they are always trying to get us kids to perform for the adults, like a bunch of trained monkeys. My go-to move was to always deflect with humor, a skill Mom taught me well. However, Mom also fielded many phone calls from music teachers about me being disruptive or not paying attention.

As summer 1976 ended, I turned nine years old, and it was time for Dougie to start kindergarten. Being Dougie's big brother, my job was to walk him to school and watch the playground so the bullies didn't get him.

I was entering grade four, a class I had dreaded for a couple of years, and with good reason!

Grade four was ruled with an iron fist by the infamous Mrs. Crabby-pants. Some people may say she was a disciplinarian; well, I'd say she was just plain mean and scary. But it's like Mom says, "Sometimes you gotta call a spade a spade."

Mrs. Crabby-pants was the oldest teacher in the school. She was a relatively small woman, standing about five foot three, with wiry short curly dark hair transitioning to grey. Her eyes always seemed to be squinting as they pierced through her glasses, causing the wrinkles on her face to be more pronounced than they already were.

She tried to mask the cigarette smell in her clothing with perfume, but she couldn't fool me. Her raspy voice proved to be evidence enough of a chain-smoking life.

Mom already had a few run-ins with the infamous Mrs. Crabby-pants from when Debbie was in her class four years prior. Let's just say Mom was not a fan of Mrs. Crabby-pants, and we shall leave it at that. I was dreading the start of the school year. I already had struggles in school, and I suspected I'd be walking into a situation heavily stacked against me. That's OK though. I prayed every night and knew Jesus had my back. At least, I hoped he did.

Just so you know, Mom and Dad would never let me be disrespectful or sarcastic to adults, and I wasn't. However, I would make non-sarcastic entertaining or witty comments. Well, at least entertaining to me, especially if I felt stressed, pressured, or uneasy in a situation.

It didn't take me long to figure out that Mrs. Crabby-pants did not appreciate my sense of humor, wit, or for that matter, anything about me. So right out of the gate, I drew unwanted attention.

The elementary school teachers seemed to have this thing about children talking when the teacher left the classroom. They would get so mad if they returned to the room to find us kids socializing. Jeepers, that made absolutely no sense to me at all. Like, what was the big deal? You would think children's social interaction would be a good thing, something to be encouraged. What if someday in the distant future, children don't even talk to each other? What if future children only communicate by pressing buttons on their Star Trek communicators or some future device? Oh, well, it wasn't the future; it was only 1976.

One day Mrs. Crabby-pants returned to the room after being gone for about ten minutes to get some supplies. While she was gone, the whole class erupted in mindless social chitchat.

Suddenly Mrs. Crabby-pants appeared at the classroom door. Her wrinkled brow gave way to a burning stare from eyeballs that only seemed contained by the eyeglasses they were piercing through. Then, one by one, all the kids became very quiet as an eerie silence engulfed the classroom. Still, Mrs. Crabby-pants just stood there motionlessly staring. I swear I could see steam coming off the top of her head. Oh boy, this was not going to end well.

Finally, Mrs. Crabby-pants spoke. "That's a half-hour detention for all of you."

Detention? Well, that's just great. I wasn't even talking when she was out of the room. This was not good.

Ever since being attacked by those bullies in kindergarten, I had strict rules to come straight home after school. During detention, I kept watching the clock's minute hand, trying to will it to move quicker. Finally, detention was over and I ran home as fast as possible.

I barely got into the house, and Mom was right there. "Kenneth Ian ... where have you been? You know you are supposed to come straight home after school."

I paused for a moment to collect my thoughts. Then, I had only one choice; I promptly threw Mrs. Crabby-pants under the bus.

It was "Game On." Mom filed a complaint about Mrs. Crabby-pants with the school, stating you can't detain kids without letting the parents know. Mom also added that I was severely asthmatic, and she needed to know where I was for safety reasons.

I think the complaint worked, and our class was never detained again. However, Mrs. Crabby-pants called me a little baby for crying to my mommy about the detention.

I was starting to develop bad headaches and very tight neck muscles. The throbbing pain would begin at the back of my head and neck. The doctors had several theories as to the cause of the headaches. Maybe it was from my asthma medications or stress related. Possibly leftover nerve damage from my surgery.

I also had very tight and overdeveloped neck and shoulder muscles for my age due to years of pushing myself up to breathe when lying in bed. Regardless of the cause, I would sometimes stretch my neck from side to side to relieve the tightness.

One day at school, we were doing a clock-timed multiplication math quiz. My desk was at the back of a row. My neck was sore and tight during the quiz, and I began getting a headache.

Sitting up straight, I turned my head to the right, then left, trying to stretch out my neck, and happened to notice Johnny Darlow was going fast through his quiz.

Suddenly Mrs. Crabby-pants' bony hand clamped onto the back of my neck like a pair of vice grips slamming my face down into the top of my desk. She then pushed down a couple of times, squishing my face against the hard surface. Finally, releasing her grip, she grabbed the back of my seat, pulling me and my desk back about ten feet.

It was then I came to the realization that Mrs. Crabby-pants must be a bully. I guess adults can be bullies too. And what's up with bullies always grabbing the back of my neck and pushing my face into things?

Even with a headache and getting my face mashed into the desk, I still managed to get 70 percent on that quiz.

I did not tell Mom and Dad about the desk faceplant. I didn't want Mrs. Crabby-pants to accuse me of being a crybaby again. I did, however, tell Dad about the math quiz, and he made up some multiplication flashcards. After that, he worked me on those flashcards to increase my multiplication speed every night.

When the next math quiz came around, Mrs. Crabby-pants moved my desk clear to the back of the room. However, this time I scored 85 percent, which for some reason seemed to upset her even more.

Week three, my desk got moved to the very back of the room, turned around in the opposite direction, and Mrs. Crabby-pants stood there and watched me. This time I scored 100 percent. Woohoo! Take that, Mrs. Crabby-pants! Well, I didn't say that, but I sure did think it.

On a cold, damp fall day during recess, we boys got to running around, having fun and playing hard. My lungs began tightening up like they often did in those days. So, once back in the classroom, I was taking rapid short breaths and wheezing.

Mrs. Crabby-pants asked me a question. Being short of breath, I sort of stuttered, trying to talk between my short breaths. Mrs. Crabby-pants took exception to how I spoke and mocked me, making fun of how I was talking and breathing.

Later that day, at afternoon tea with Mom, I sort of mentioned my breathing episode at school and how Mrs. Crabby-pants made fun of me. Well, I'm sure by now you can guess; Mom went ballistic. "That woman has no business teaching children. She needs to be fired," declared Mom.

Dad and Mom had words with the school principal and wanted Mrs. Crabby-pants fired or, at the very least, put on suspension. Well, that did not happen, but Mrs. Crabby-pants did start to ignore me after that, which suited me just fine.

*An angel of the Lord appeared to them, and the glory of the Lord
shone around them, and they were terrified. But the angel said to
them, "Do not be afraid. I bring you good news that will cause great
joy for all the people. Today in the town of David, a Savior has been
born to you; he is the Messiah, the Lord. This will be a sign to you: You
will find a baby wrapped in cloths and lying in a manger."*

*So they hurried off and found Mary and Joseph, and the baby, who
was lying in the manger. Luke 2:9-12, 16*

Christmas was coming and preparing for the annual school
Christmas concert would be starting soon. All grades had to put on a
presentation for the show.

Every year Mrs. Crabby-pants would have her class do a live nativity scene. A few kids would be selected to be put into costumes and
play Mary and Joseph, shepherds, three wise men, and a few angels.
The rest of the kids would be in the choir singing Christmas hymns
like "Away in a Manger," "Hark! The Herold Angels Sing," and "We
Three Kings."

Oh, yeah, and Baby Jesus would be played by a doll.

Mrs. Crabby-pants explained the whole Christmas production
to the class, and I knew there was absolutely no chance I would get
picked to have one of the acting roles. It would be cool to play Joseph
or one of the kings, maybe even a shepherd. Heck, I'd even dress up as
an angel just to avoid being in the choir. But unfortunately, the angel
parts always went to the girls.

Then suddenly, I heard the words, "Does anyone have a parent
with tools who could build us a manger to lay the Baby Jesus in?"

No way, did I hear that right? I shot both hands high in the air,
waving back and forth. Pick me, pick me, please, please pick me. I can
do this. I know I can.

I was so excited I didn't even notice if any other kids had their
hands up. Then suddenly I heard, "Kenny, thanks for volunteering."

What? Did I hear that right? So, Mrs. Crabby-pants actually picked
me? Holy cow, I cannot believe it; she chose me!

Oh darn, now I need to convince Poppa to let me use his table saw.

When I got home from school, I burst into the house. "Mom, Mom, guess what?"

"What happened?" Mom replied, stopping what she was doing.

"I got picked to build a Baby Jesus manger."

"That's wonderful. We'll have to make some fresh chocolate chip cookies to celebrate."

"Thanks, Mom, but first, I need to call Poppa to see if I can use his table saw."

"OK, you know where the phone is."

Calling Poppa, I told him all about my new project, and he agreed to help me. We just needed to find a time I could get to Poppa's workshop.

Unfortunately, all the adults got busy that week, and since I could not drive myself, I didn't get to the workshop. So, Poppa just made something up quick then transported me and the manger to the school to show Mrs. Crabby-pants.

The first version was a bit big. You could have fit a three-year-old Jesus in it. So, we took it back to the workshop and trimmed it down a bit.

Mrs. Crabby-pants was thrilled with the manger. I think it was the first time I saw her smile, at least around me, that is.

After successfully delivering the manger on time and budget, I hoped to get consideration for a costumed role in the live nativity. But nope, I was relegated to the choir. Oh well, it didn't bother me this time. Besides, I had made my contribution, plus we were singing Christmas hymns, and I liked those songs. After Christmas, Mrs. Crabby-pants was a lot nicer toward me. I had this life-size drawing of the cartoon character Popeye that I had colored at CYC, and Mrs. Crabby-pants hung it up on the wall in the classroom.

And get this ... during spring break, Dad and Mom drove our family down to Disney World in Florida, our one big family trip that they had saved up for years to take us on. Anyway, I brought back a record album of "The Country Bear Jamboree," and Mrs. Crabby-pants played it for the whole class. How cool is that?

Mrs. Crabby-pants was a mystery to me. Of all my teachers, she was the only one who focused her class on the true meaning of Christmas, the birth of Jesus Christ. Yet, she was the strictest, meanest teacher I would ever come up against. Mrs. Crabby-pants and I did not get off to a good start, and I don't think I would ever be on her favorite students list. She's definitely not on my favorite teachers list. However, because of Baby Jesus and a wooden manager, everything turned out OK. I had survived grade four. I guess Jesus did have my back after all.

Chapter 10:

Hard to Break

Do not gloat over me, my enemy! Though I have fallen, I will rise.
Though I sit in darkness, the Lord will be my light. Micah 7:8

It was the first day of summer break, and it could not have come fast enough. I had survived the dreaded fourth grade. After finishing my bowl of cereal, it was time to head outside. Primrose Drive had many families with kids of all ages, so it was reasonably easy to find someone to play with each day. Also, with some of the new houses at the end of the road completed, I needed to keep my eye open for potential new friends.

One such friend was David West. His family had moved to the street the previous summer. So, unfortunately, his first year in a new school was in Mrs. Crabby-pants' class. But in the end, we both survived. On a side note, David's dad, David West Sr., and my dad had attended high school together back in the day.

It was still early morning and the sun was just getting up above the trees, starting to warm the air from the chilly northern summer night. I decided to climb the tree in the front yard to survey the street, looking for other kids to play with. This was a multi-trunk maple tree on the right side of the front yard and it was good for climbing. There used to be a low-hanging branch you could pull yourself up with to start your climb. But the limb had cracked, so Dad cut it off, leaving only a stub where the branch used to be. However, that stub was large enough to give me an excellent foothold to get me up and into the tree.

I climbed and climbed until I was more than twice the height of the house. Wow, this was the highest I had ever climbed. For a moment, I just sat there with the warm sun starting to hit my face. It was so peaceful and quiet. Then, a couple of little birds started chirping as I began to reflect on the past year's struggles and contemplate all the fun things I would be doing this summer.

Out of nowhere, a gentle summer breeze began to blow. I held on just a little tighter as the tree branches began to sway. Then, that gentle breeze slowly intensified into a stronger wind. The whole tree was now moving as if trying to shake me out of its branches.

I heard a sudden loud cracking sound as the branch I was standing on gave way without warning. Oh dang!

Everything went into slow motion as, with cat-like reflexes, I grabbed for another branch only to have it snap off in my grasp. Frantically I grasped at branches as I continued in a downward trajectory.

Now, picking up speed, breaking through some branches, and bouncing off others, my body flipped and flopped through that tree like a rag doll in a washing machine.

Nearing the end of my rapid descent, that branch stub that had started my climb caught me just above my right hip. The stub dug in, scraping up the side of my body through my armpit and down the inside of my bicep, tearing my fresh white tee shirt and peeling off the first couple layers of skin as I slammed the ground with a dull thud and a gasp.

The sudden impact knocked every bit of air out of my lungs. Then, taking a moment to catch my breath, I pulled myself together and pushed up out of the divot my body had created in the grass. "Whoa, I just got my butt kicked by a maple tree."

I was bruised all over from head to toe. My once clean white shirt was bloody, torn with grass and mud stains; my hair looked like a bird's nest. I looked more like I had gotten mauled by a bear than fallen out of a tree.

Regaining my composure, I hobbled into the house.

"Mom, Mom, Mom," I called out.

"Goodness gracious, what in the world; what happened?" Mom shockingly exclaimed as she saw me.

"I fell out of the tree."

"What on earth were you doing in that tree? I told you not to climb that tree."

"Actually, you told me, 'If you keep climbing that tree, one day you're going to fall and break your fool neck.'"

Mom just glared back at me, shaking her head in disbelief.

"Get over here. Let's get you cleaned up."

The good news was I didn't break anything except my ego and a few tree branches, of course. However, I was pretty sore for a week or so. The funny thing is, I didn't remember anything when I fell out of my treehouse, but this time I remembered every detail. Well, if there's one thing for sure, I may take a bad fall, but it seems I'm hard to break.

I had proven my body was strong, but now Dr. Sagle wanted to strengthen my lungs. My allergies would trigger asthma attacks, so the doctor wanted to start me on allergy immunization shots. Their theory was if they could strengthen my immunity to the things that triggered my asthma, it would give me a fighting chance.

Mom and I visited the doctor for his initial consultation. After checking my lungs with his stethoscope, Dr. Sagle began by saying, "The first step is to get you allergy tested. Dr. Pierson will be doing the tests."

So, of course, I had to ask, "Why do I need to get tested? I can already tell you what I'm allergic to."

"Well, that's true, but there may be things you're allergic to that you don't even realize. So, we need to inject you with small amounts of various allergens. Small needles will administer these in your back."

"Ah, needles? How many needles?"

"We want to test you for sixty allergens, so that will be sixty needles."

"Sixty needles! No, I'm good. I don't need allergy testing."

Let me just say that sometimes we don't get to make our own decisions in life, and this was one of those times.

To my dread, the big test day finally arrived. Mom and I got to the doctor's office at 9:00 a.m. and were taken into the exam room right away. After meeting with the doctor, Mom then went to the waiting room.

The Torment of Time

I took my shirt off as slowly as humanly possible, trying to delay somehow the torment I was about to face. Then, lying face down on the exam room table, the doctor took a black marker, making sixty small circles on my back in a checkerboard pattern. It sort of tickled, but so far, so good.

Now it was time for the scary part as Dr. Pierson pricked me with sixty individual needles, each containing a different allergen. As I felt the first needle pierce my skin, I held my breath and tightened up all my back muscles. "Just take deep breaths and relax, Kenny," the doctor told me. Easy for him to say; he was not the one getting pricked.

After about eight minutes of sheer torture, the doctor finished and left the room. There I was, stuck there lying face down for thirty minutes in the cold, quiet torture chamber. It was one of the longest thirty minutes of my life.

After all was said and done, Dr. Pierson called Mom into the room to review the test results, and to no surprise, I was highly allergic to animal dander, particularly dogs and cats.

In the next group, I was very allergic to dust, feathers, and cigarette smoke. More moderate allergies included grass and pollens.

On a positive note, I had no food allergies, praise Jesus!

However, I did find out I have a mild intolerance to dairy and corn, to which Mom commented, "No wonder I always have so much trouble getting him to drink milk."

Now just to be clear, this does not mean I cannot have ice cream or chocolate milkshakes. It just means I may get a bit bloated when I have them.

I would now need to go to Dr. Sagle every week for the next three years to get an allergy shot in each arm. Just for the record, this was not fun, but a boy's gotta do what a boy must do to survive.

Dougie was now at the age to help me with my projects. If he weren't playing with the younger kids, he would be assisting me, from building tree houses and forts in the bush to making homemade bow and arrows or slingshots; Dougie was an excellent helper. He even helped me build a go-cart that we rode in the community day parade one year.

Beyond the four-year age gap, we three kids were very different. Debbie was a natural athlete and loved to play and watch all sorts of sports. She also loved animals, especially dogs, and even talked about becoming a veterinarian when she grew up. Of course, having an asthmatic brother sort of put a kink in her chain as far as having a dog, but she never complained about it.

Pushing Dougie in the Community Day Parade

Debbie's patience eventually paid off, though, when we discovered purebred poodles do not shed hair or have the dander of other dogs, so they don't trigger my asthma so much. So, for her grade eight graduation, Dad got Debbie a white miniature French poodle called Julie. We would take in Julie's half-sister Paulette a couple of years later.

Dougie liked science, chemistry, and of course, pollywogs. He had a genuine curiosity about how all that stuff worked. He also had some natural athletic abilities, but athletics was not his focus.

As far as sports went, I continued to struggle. It was not for lack of trying, but I did not have the natural abilities of Debbie or Dougie. When kids would pick teams in the playground, I was always one of the last kids to get picked. Mom would always tell me it doesn't matter whether I was the first one chosen or the last one. The important thing is that when my number gets called, I'm ready to give it my all.

*Listen, my son, to your father's instruction and
do not forsake your mother's teaching. Proverbs 1:8*

Batter Up

That summer, Dad had gotten together with a couple of other fathers to start a boys slow-pitch league. Slow-pitch is like baseball, except you pitch slow underhand and have four outfielders instead of three.

We put together our inaugural team, including my cousins Sean and Joey Campbell and friends Johnny Tucker and David West. We rounded out the rest of the team with other kids from surrounding neighborhoods. I loved playing baseball. However, my baseball skills were much like my other sports skills, which were not very good. I tried hard, could run fast, and throw the ball far, but struggled with agility and coordination.

Grounders seemed to always bounce over my glove. When throwing the ball, it never went where I was aiming. I would swing the bat hard but it seldom made solid contact with the ball.

Dad and Debbie, both athletes, spent hours with me to improve my skills.

My favorite position was shortstop, but my inability to cleanly field a grounder and accurately throw it to the baseman was problematic.

One night at dinner, Dad asked me, "How about we try you in center field the next game." To which I replied, "But, Dad, I'm a shortstop."

Game Time

The big game arrived, and I made my debut in center field. I have to admit, Dad was right. I got to run fast all over the place, chasing and catching all the fly balls. Throwing the ball to the infield, it seldom went to the base I was aiming for, but that's OK; there was always an infielder backing it up. So, other than one throw that went over the backstop and bounced off a car, my wild throws didn't do any damage. When batting, Dad noticed I was always trying to, as he would say, "kill the ball." As a result, I tended to hit off the skinny part of the bat closer to my hands, resulting in many pop flies.

One day, Dad came home and gave me a new bat. It was a bottle bat, a term used for a bat that was the same thickness for the entire length of the bat. So, it had a much larger sweet spot to hit the ball than a regular bat.

Next game, I came up to the plate with my trusty new bat in hand. In came the first pitch and ka-boom; I whacked that ball with all my might.

The ball shot off the bat like it was launched out of a cannon. I stood in amazement, just watching as the ball sailed over the left fielder's head. Then I heard Dad yell, "Run, Kenny, run." I took off like a basset hound chasing a jackrabbit. I could see the outfielders running after the ball as I rounded first base. Then, accelerating around second base, the third-base coach came into view, motioning me toward home plate; I almost ran into him as I rounded third. Hitting the straightaway, I crossed the home plate just a split second ahead of the ball. I had just hit my first home run, thanks to Dad and my new bottle bat.

We scored a lot of runs that game. The only problem was the other team scored more. Well, it's not whether you win or lose, it's how you play the game. Right?

My cousin Joey was our pitcher. I was the backup pitcher when he couldn't make the games. For some reason, I can't throw overhand accurately, but I was pretty accurate tossing underhand, possibly a side benefit of training the eye for distance and levelness as a carpenter. With Dad's coaching and Debbie's help, I earned a place on the slow-pitch team as the center fielder, backup pitcher, and cleanup hitter, learning that perseverance, hard work, and good coaching eventually pay off.

I was now part of my first real team. Look out, world, there was a new athlete in the McQuarrie family.

Fun in the Sun, Summers to Remember

Most summers Dad would take a couple of weeks' vacation and we would load up the station wagon and head off on a new adventure. Although we were not big campers, we may head to Pancake Bay to swim and camp or venture down into Northern Michigan to stay in a hotel with a pool.

Sometimes we would make the eight-hour drive to Toronto and stay with Jim and Esther Elliott. Remember them? They had helped me out when I had my head surgery. Jim and Esther also had three children, Stephen, Laura, and Martha. While in Toronto, we would visit Ontario Place, the Toronto Zoo, and the Science Center or catch a Toronto Blue Jay baseball game.

A regular destination was Ena and Larry's place. We would cross the Sault Ste. Marie bridge to the United States and drive down I-75 about seven hours to their home in Spring Arbor, Michigan.

Ena was the daughter of Nanna's sister Rose. Auntie Rose married Poppa's cousin from Norway, Bernt Gilbertson. They settled on Saint Joseph's Island and started a roadwork construction company and maple syrup production operation.

When the maple sap runs in the early spring, we would visit the "Gilbertson Pancake House" on Saint Joseph's Island. Sometimes Uncle Bernt would drive me around the sugar bush on his snowmobile. Then we would have some pancakes with fresh maple syrup.

If you are in the area around March/April and the sap is running, you can still visit "The Pancake House."

Ena had attended the Free Methodist Spring Arbor College, where she met and married Larry Knowles. Larry, at one point, was a pitching prospect for the Detroit Tigers.

Ena and Larry had two children, our cousins Dawn and Tim, who are a bit older than Debbie, Dougie, and me. Dawn was the flower girl at Mom and Dad's wedding. Tim was adopted when he was young, like me.

The highlight of visiting Ena and Larry was their backyard swimming pool, where I learned to swim. Well, let me rephrase that; it's where I learned not to drown.

I have always been very heavy, very dense, so to speak. Not dense in the head, although there could be an argument for that; I am just big-boned, wide footed, and have always weighed about 30 percent more than anyone would guess. That being said, I am not built to be an Olympic swimmer.

I would practice jumping into the swimming pool deep end and sink until my backside hit the very bottom. Then I'd sit there, holding my breath underwater as long as possible. Once completely out of breath, almost at the point of passing out, I would pull my legs under me and kick up as hard as I could, bursting up out of the water as high as my momentum would take me. I never developed into much of a swimmer. I'm a sinker, not a swimmer, just not that good in the water. My saving grace is the ability to tread water for a long time, a side benefit of big wide feet and strong legs.

One summer activity I didn't get to participate in was staying overnight with Uncle Reg and Aunt Bessie on their Saint Joseph Island dairy farm. Debbie could do it, but I could not stay the night because of my allergies to the animals. Regardless, I always enjoyed visiting Uncle Reg at the farm.

Uncle Reg was the oldest of Nanna's three younger brothers. Of all Nanna's brothers, I was closest to Uncle Reg. He always made a point of talking to me and always answered a question with a question, just like Jesus often did.

Uncle Reg was just a little guy standing only about five foot six, weighing in at 145 pounds soaking wet, with his boots on. He and Aunt Bessie didn't meet and marry until their mid-30s but still managed to have five children. Uncle Reg told me he could relate to me as he also had some medical challenges when he was born. A highlight of visiting Uncle Reg and Aunt Bessie on the dairy farm was the ice cream. They always had lots of ice cream, and Aunt Bessie would fill my bowl with massive amounts.

Back in the Sault, a young couple had started attending the church. Newly married, Dave and Viki Steenburgh and their German Shepard dog, Max, had moved to the Sault from Southern Ontario. Dave specialized in teaching developmentally challenged students.

Dave and Viki hosted a barbeque for some church folks at home one weekend. Early in the evening, a few of us were tossing the baseball in the backyard. Max was having more fun than all of us, running back and forth with his tongue hanging from the side of his mouth, trying to intercept the ball as we threw it. The faster we threw the ball back and forth, the quicker Max would run, eyes gleaming with excitement. I took my eye off the ball for just a split second, something Dad always told me not to do. Then, as the ball whacked the edge of my glove, it instantly dropped to the ground. Quickly, I reached down to grab it before Max could scoop it up.

Max was charging hard for the ball at full gallop when he suddenly noticed me starting to reach down. Trying to slam on the breaks, he desperately dug his claws into the grass to slow his momentum. I felt a sharp pain in my left temple as Max slammed into me like a freight train hitting a brick wall. Trying to stand, I felt nauseous and dizzy, blood now flowing down my face as Dad quickly grabbed me, bringing me into the house.

Mom grabbed a dish towel to apply pressure to the deep gash just above my eye, grabbing the back of my head with one hand while pressing down the cloth on my wound with the other. I tried to pull away. "Stay still," Mom said as Dad went to get the car started.

Putting Mom and me in the back seat, Dad headed for the hospital emergency room, a route he knew pretty well by now.

I was lying down with my head in Mom's lap as she kept applying pressure to the towel over my left temple. The pressure hurt like a son of a gun. Already feeling dizzy and nauseous, I now started getting a headache. I squirmed and tried my hardest to pull free from Mom's "Kung Fu grip." But, as much as I tried to wiggle free, Mom would not let go.

Once at the hospital, the emergency room doctor stitched me up. I had a one-inch gash along the top side of my left eye socket, just along the eyebrow. The doctor told Mom and Dad the injury had nicked my supraorbital artery. That's why I was bleeding so much. It was a good thing Mom applied the pressure or I could have bled to death. It was suspected Max's fang caught me just above the eye in the collision, mere millimeters from causing significant damage to my eye.

Max Steenburgh, Late 1970s
Painting by Debbie McQuarrie

In true McQuarrie fashion, though, it was a long way from the heart, so I would live. That meant back to the barbeque at the Steenburgh's we went.

Once back at the party, I had to stay put on a reclining lawn chair. Max would not leave my side, laying down beside my chair, keeping guard. Max faired a little better than I did and was not injured from the collision. Eventually, Viki took Max into the house because he affected my asthma. All in all, the barbeque was fun for all. Well, maybe not the best for Max and me, but in the end, we both lived to play another day.

The sun set on another memorable summer that started with a nosedive from a maple tree and ended with a potentially catastrophic collision with Max. Some folks would say I had terrible luck, that some dark cloud was following me around trying to strike me down. I say I was very fortunate; someone was looking out for me.

For I may fall hard, I will always rise again, and the Lord will be my strength.

Chapter 11:

Foolish Controversies

But avoid foolish controversies and genealogies and arguments and quarrels about the law, because these are unprofitable and useless.
Titus 3:9

The year 1977 was a big year for hockey in Sault Ste. Marie. The Soo Greyhounds Junior "A" hockey team drafted a young sixteen-year-old phenom named Wayne Gretzky. Gretzky wanted to wear number 9, but another player already took it, so he had to settle for 14. As the season progressed, his coach suggested he wear number 99, a number he would wear the rest of his hockey career, all the way to the NHL Hall of Fame.

Everyone was thrilled about Wayne Gretzky coming to play for the Greyhounds. With all the hockey buzz around town, it made me want to be a hockey player even more. But my asthmatic lungs and the cold, damp air were a bad combination that prevented me from playing league hockey.

In past years, Dad had made a small backyard ice rink for us to play around on. It was great winter fun, but due to all the work and time commitment, Dad decided to stop doing it. So, I asked Dad several times if I could build the rink; that way, it would not be so much work for him.

"OK but understand you will have to shovel it and water it a few times a week," Dad said.

"That's not a problem, I'm ten years old now. I can do that," I assured him.

Every successful construction project begins with proper planning and preparation. My preparation started with building rink boards and hanging lights in November before the snow flew.

NHL rink boards are about forty-two inches high. However, my boards were only ten to twelve inches, just tall enough to bounce a puck off.

It gets dark early in the winter months, so I needed decent lighting for my rink. Dad had a bunch of 150-watt floodlights he got on sale at Canadian Tire. Grabbing about eight of them along with a ladder, I tied my floodlights in the trees around the rink. Then, after stringing together a bunch of extension cords from light to light, I anxiously waited for it to get dark.

After dinner, it was good and dark. Oh boy, time to test my rink lights.

It was a particularly frigid cold night, with temperatures hovering right around freezing. So, I pulled out my big winter gloves, jacket, and boots, venturing outside for my grand lighting ceremony. Pulling my long extension cord over to the electrical outlet inside the carport, it was the moment of truth as I stuck the plug into the outlet. Very quickly I realized something went very wrong.

An enormous fiery flame shot out of the outlet like a fire-breathing dragon woken up from a long slumber. The electric current took hold of my hand, gripping me like I was caught in a vise. As I frantically tried to pull away, a painful numbness engulfed my hand. Then suddenly the electricity shot up my arm, catapulting me backward five feet through the air.

As my butt hit the ground, the sheer force of the jolt caused me to do about three backward summersaults worthy of an Olympic gold medal, followed by all the lights in the house going dark.

"WE'RE HAVING A POWER OUTAGE!" Mom yelled from inside the house.

Oh darn, I was burnt toast in more ways than one; this was not good!

I had blown up the old house electrical fuse box and singed what few hairs I had on my arm. Guess it couldn't handle all my floodlights connected to one outlet, probably combined with some ice buildup on the plug prongs.

"Kenny, you could have been electrocuted. You can't just connect that many floodlights into one outlet," Dad said with shock and awe in his voice.

I guess if there was a silver lining, it was the fact I didn't get in trouble. Dad was more concerned that I almost electrocuted myself than he was about the fuse box. Thank God for quality Canadian-made gloves and boots. Fortunately, Dad had some replacement fuses on hand. But unfortunately for me, he also took away half my floodlights.

I would continue to build our yearly backyard rink for the next eight years. I may not be able to play league hockey, but I could practice my hockey skills in my very own backyard.

Dad eventually had Uncle Jim swap out the old fuse box with a much safer breaker panel. Uncle Jim was an electrician and Aunt Julie's

Dougie and me on the backyard rink

husband. Aunt Julie was Nanna's youngest sister, and get this, only five and a half years older than Mom. Whenever Uncle Jim worked at our house, I was his electrical assistant, meaning I handed him the correct screwdrivers.

Saying Goodbye Too Soon

It was right around Easter 1978 when Grandma McQuarrie got sick, and after only a few weeks, she passed away and went to be with Jesus. She was just in her early 70s, which was on the young side to die even in those days.

Jesus now had two of my grandmas, and I had none. Grandma McQuarrie was always interested in hearing about what I was learning in Sunday school. Dad once told me Grandma was arguably bet-

Grandma and Grandpa McQuarrie

ter at preaching a sermon than Grandpa McQuarrie, even though he was the pastor.

After Grandma's death, Grandpa came out to fewer social events. It was only a few years later that he moved to Algoma Manor Nursing Home in Thessalon, Ontario, about an hour's drive from the Sault. I didn't see Grandpa McQuarrie much after that. He went home to be with the Lord some years later, just shy of his ninetieth birthday.

Do You Believe?

In the summer of 1978, another new friend, Jimmy Brown, moved to one of the new houses at the end of the street. Jimmy would join our slow-pitch ball team and start attending Ben R. McMullin Elementary.

David West, Jimmy Brown, and I would make our daily trek home from school together, having heated debates on topics of the day like who makes the best hockey stick, how fast the "Six Million Dollar Man" can run, or what we wanted to be when we grew up.

One day David asked me, "Have you been saved?"

Hmm, what's he talking about? Let's see, Debbie saved me from being drowned by the bullies in kindergarten. Mom saved me from bleeding to death after the collision with Max. Oh, yeah, the house fuse box and a thick pair of gloves saved me from being electrocuted.

Seeing I had a puzzled look on my face, David rephrased the question. "Have you accepted Jesus as your Lord and Savior?"

Wow, I never had anyone ask me that question before. Of course, Jesus is Lord. Besides, I say my prayers every night. "Now I lay me down to sleep. I pray the Lord my soul to keep. If I should die before I wake, I pray the Lord my soul to take." I also go to church every Sunday, attend CYC, and watch *The Ten Commandments* every year.

Well, I was at the end of my driveway now. "See you tomorrow," I said as I waved to David and Jimmy and walked up the driveway into the house.

Over the coming weeks, I kept thinking about that conversation with David West. Am I saved? Am I going to heaven someday? I am pretty sure I am. After all, I was baptized when I was a baby.

So, I asked Dad, "If people go to church, does that mean they'll make it to heaven?" Dad smiled and responded, "Well, some of them will, but probably not all."

"Well, I was baptized when I was a baby, so does that mean I get into heaven?"

"Your mother and I had you baptized as a baby, showing we were dedicated to raising you in the church and by the teachings of the Bible. So, no, being baptized does not get you into heaven." Dad continued, "The only way to get into heaven is to put your faith in Jesus Christ and accept him as your Lord and Savior."

"OK, so if you believe in God, then you will go to heaven," I responded.

"Not exactly," Dad replied, explaining the Bible says even demons believe in God. Still, demons will not be going to heaven.

You believe that there is one God. Good! Even the demons believe that—and shudder. James 2:19.

Wow, this was a lot for my eleven-year-old brain to take in. Something told me I needed to figure this thing out, as my life depended on it.

The first thing I did was pray to Jesus to ask for some answers. Mom would always say, "Well, did you pray about it?"

I began to pay more attention to the preacher's sermons on Sundays. Not too much attention, though. I still had to focus on beating Johnny Tucker in Tic-tac-toe; he's pretty good, you know. Then, one Sunday, the church bulletin that Johnny and I were using for our weekly Tic-tac-toe game had a scripture verse on it.

For all have sinned and fall short of the glory of God. Romans 3:23

I had heard that scripture before, but it stuck with me this time. If all have sinned, then does that mean I am a sinner? I don't always listen to Mom and Dad, but I think that's normal for a kid, right? I don't hit. I don't swear or steal, and I'm not mean to other kids.

Hmm, but how do I figure out if I'm a sinner?

Then it hit me. The Ten Commandments, of course. That would be the best place to start. I knew right where to look: Exodus 20 in the Old Testament.

1. *"You shall have no other gods before me."* Well, I only worship God, so it looks like I'm OK on this one.

2. *"You shall not make an image in the form of anything in heaven, earth, or water. You shall not bow down to them or worship them."* The Bible also calls these worshiping idols, and I'm OK on this one too. Like I just said, I only worship God.

3. *"You shall not misuse the name of the Lord your God."* I've heard other people use the Lord's name in vain, but I sure don't. I hate when I even hear swear words; it's like hearing fingernails scraping a chalkboard. The very thought makes the hairs on the back of my neck stand up.

4. ***"Remember the Sabbath day by keeping it holy."*** Well, I heard the pastor preach since Jesus rose from the grave, Christians take Sunday as our Sabbath. I go to church every Sunday, so I think I'm good on this one.

5. ***"Honor your father and your mother."*** OK, guilty as charged. I must admit I don't always listen to Mom and Dad. I mostly listen, but not always.

6. ***"You shall not murder."*** This one is obviously a sin. I have not killed anyone, and I wouldn't even think of doing something like that. But wait, I must be honest; I did play a part in the death of the pollywog. I've watched *Perry Mason* on TV, and I think this would be involuntary manslaughter of a pollywog.

7. ***"You shall not commit adultery."*** Not sure what this one is. However, I don't think I'm even old enough to be guilty of it.

8. ***"You shall not steal."*** Well, this is a hard one as it depends on your definition of stealing. I did take some scrap lumber from the houses for my treehouse project. Sometimes the project superintendent was around to give me the OK. Sometimes though, no one was around, and I helped myself.

9. ***"You shall not give false testimony against your neighbor."*** Another hard one. Sometimes I may blame the neighbor kids, even when I don't know if they did it or not.

10. ***"You shall not covet your neighbor's house, wife, servant, ox, donkey, or anything that belongs to your neighbor."*** OK, so none of my neighbors have a donkey or, for that matter, a servant or ox, and I don't want nobody's wife. However, some neighbors have snowmobiles, and I really want a snowmobile, so I guess that's coveting.

Oh man, it looks like I am at least a little guilty on five of the ten commandments, and I haven't even looked at the seven deadly sins of pride, greed, lust, anger, gluttony, envy, and sloth. So, Romans 3:23 is right, and I'm a sinner.

I can't even think of anybody who has not done at least one sin. I know I'm not supposed to judge, but I'm just calling a spade a spade.

A few weeks later, the church bulletin had another verse.

For the wages of sin is death, but the gift of God is eternal life in Christ Jesus our Lord. Romans 6:23

Hey, this is like the verse I see at NFL football games between the goalposts: "For God so loved the world that he gave his one and only Son, that whoever believes in him shall not perish but have eternal life" John 3:16.

In Sunday school, I learned the Bible teaches that I have free will and can make my own decisions. The problem is I choose to sin, which makes me a sinner. It seems to me it would be impossible for anybody not to do at least one sin.

Over the coming months, I paid more attention to the sermons and the scriptures the pastor was preaching.

But God demonstrates his own love for us in this:
While we were still sinners, Christ died for us. Romans 5:8

For God did not send his Son into the world to condemn the world,
but to save the world through him. John 3:17

I was now starting to understand much better. As I began piecing together my Sunday school lessons and the pastor's sermons, I came to some conclusions.

God created the world and all us people to have a relationship with him. He didn't want programmable robots or trained monkeys. God wanted us to be in his image with free will and the ability to do right and wrong. Unfortunately, humankind chose not to follow God and allowed sin into the world, causing a humungous barrier between God and us.

Don't worry, though; God had a plan "B." He sent his Son Jesus Christ to die as a sacrifice to pay the price for our sins. When Jesus died on the cross and rose from the dead on Easter morning, he not only paid the price for all sin past, present, and future, but he also defeated death.

What Jesus did is all well and good but remember my conversation with Dad. Just believing Jesus is the Son of God and died for my sins does not get me into heaven. Satan and the demons also believe this, but it doesn't get them into heaven. Dad told me, "The only way to get into heaven is to put your faith in Jesus Christ and accept him as your Lord and Savior." Going back to the Bible, I came across more scriptures.

Jesus answered, "I am the way and the truth and the life. No one comes to the Father except through me." John 14:6

If you declare with your mouth, "Jesus is Lord," and believe in your heart that God raised him from the dead, you will be saved. For it is with your heart that you believe and are justified, and it is with your mouth that you profess your faith and are saved. Romans 10:9-10

For it is by grace you have been saved, through faith— and this is not from yourselves, it is the gift of God— not by works, so that no one can boast. Ephesians 2:8-9

It's just like Dad told me, to be saved and know that you are going to heaven, all you have to do is admit you're a sinner, accept and declare Jesus Christ as your Lord and Savior, and have faith that through his grace you have been saved. OK, back to David West's question, was I saved? The answer is yes. I realized I was a sinner and had always put my faith in Jesus, declaring him as my Lord and Savior as far back as I can remember. Now I just fully understood it.

That being said, just to be sure, I prayed, "Dear Jesus, I am a sinner, please forgive me of my sins. I accept you as my Lord and Savior.

Please continue to watch over and protect me until it's time for me to go to heaven. Amen."

Life was good over the next couple of years, and I continued my allergy immunization shots. As a result, the asthma attacks were a little less frequent, but I still spent many a night in the hospital emergency room. In addition, the headaches started to become a bit more frequent; the doctor gave me a prescription of Tylenol 3 with codeine to help. Regardless, I didn't let any of this stuff slow me down.

I continued to help Poppa when I got the chance. A few years after Nanna passed away, Poppa got remarried to Violet or Vi for short. She was not a replacement for Nanna, but she helped keep Poppa healthy and was a grandmother to Dougie, who was just a baby when Nanna passed away. Plus, Vi always baked me chocolate cake when I visited or helped Poppa.

During the summer, we went to Aunt Shirley and Uncle Tom's cottage on a small island in Lake Matinenda. They had two daughters, Kim and Lyn, who were younger than Dougie. Our cousin Kathleen came with us that year. Kathleen was a bit older than Debbie and the daughter of Dad's oldest sister, Aunt Marj and Uncle Norm.

The cottage was a fun place that you could only get to by boat, with lots of swimming and fishing. I also got to go snorkeling for the first time. Jeepers, swimming is much easier with fins, mask, and a breathing tube!

Aunt Shirley was Dad's youngest sister. She married Uncle Tom when I was about four years old and moved to Blind River. I was the ring bearer at their wedding—well, sort of. Unfortunately, I had one of my stubborn moments and refused to walk down the aisle. Still, they gave me a toy and a pair of cufflinks for my service with my initials on them. They said I was to save the cufflinks to wear on my future wedding day.

One person considers one day more sacred than another; another considers every day alike. Each of them should be fully convinced in their own mind. Whoever regards one day as special does so to the

Lord. Whoever eats meat does so to the Lord, for they give thanks to God; and whoever abstains does so to the Lord and gives thanks to God. For none of us lives for ourselves alone, and none of us dies for ourselves alone. If we live, we live for the Lord; and if we die, we die for the Lord. So, whether we live or die, we belong to the Lord. For this very reason, Christ died and returned to life so that he might be the Lord of both the dead and the living. Romans 14:5-9

So Many Questions

I was always asking Dad questions about the Bible, so eventually he bought me *Strong's Exhaustive Concordance of the Bible*. This big, thick encyclopedia-type book had all sorts of stuff about the Bible! Including different translations, history, and background of the scriptures. For example, you could look up themes like "love" or "anger," and it would tell you which scriptures have love or anger in them.

During the school year, on our walks to and from school, David West and I continued our discussions on church, religions, and other stuff. David and his family attended a church called "The Gospel Hall." As we discussed things, I discovered David's church did stuff differently from my church, some of which seemed strange to me. For example, all the women had to wear hats, and there was no preacher. Instead, men called elders took turns preaching. Heck, they didn't even have any musical instruments in the church.

But then get this, in my church, we didn't want people to drink alcohol, but in David's church, it was OK to drink alcohol (for the adults, that is).

It was very puzzling to me, all these different rules and regulations. So over time, some of these differences became heated discussions between David and me. I needed to find out which church was right, and which was wrong, and I knew just who to ask.

"Dad, why do women in David's church have to wear hats and women in our church don't."

"Good question," Dad responded. "The Gospel Hall is following the words of the Apostle Paul in First Corinthians chapter 11. Our church's view on this is that Paul was addressing a specific cultural issue at the time. Since we live in a different culture, it is not applicable today."

Another time I asked Dad about the alcohol thing. Dad told me the Bible says you should not be drunk. However, it does not mean you cannot drink alcohol. The Free Methodist Church asks its members not to drink alcohol or smoke as a commitment to membership, not a spiritual law. Dad also reminded me that becoming a church member and following specific rules and regulations does not get you into heaven. After many more questions about different church rules, Dad eventually said, "It's good to discuss these things but don't get too caught up in arguments over various church rules and regulations."

"But Dad, there are so many different churches but only one Jesus and one Bible."

"Yes, that's true. Various churches may put more focus on different parts of the Bible or even have disagreements on secondary issues. But the most important thing is what evangelical churches have in common, that being the Holy Trinity – God the Father, Son, and Holy Spirit, and salvation through faith in Jesus Christ."

Dad also pointed out that the Apostle Paul wrote Titus 3:9, which says, "But avoid foolish controversies and genealogies and arguments and quarrels about the law, because these are unprofitable and useless."

Well, I guess Dad and the Apostle Paul made good points. I decided not to sweat the secondary church differences too much.

The Social Experiment

As I headed into grade seven, the school decided to do some sort of social experiment. They selected seven students out of our seventh-grade class and merged us into the grade eight class. Even though we would be in an eighth-grade class, we would still be only in grade seven. It probably sounds as confusing to you as it did to me at the time.

The seven students consisted of Greg Elsby, Johnny Darlow, me, plus four of the girls. I could understand why the other kids were selected because they were all pretty smart, with good grades and all. I guess I was more the social part of the experiment. As mentioned before, I had my good subjects and my bad. I wasn't what you would call a popular kid, but I wasn't unpopular either. Still, I got along will all the kids while going to the beat of my own drum.

Some adults would say I was a young kid but had an old soul, probably because I was just as comfortable having meaningful conversations with adults as I was with kids. Of course, this was a side benefit of growing up conversing with so many doctors, nurses, and adults. I will say, I had a bit of apprehension when first told I would be in the grade eight classroom, because it put me in the same class as the boys who attacked me when I was in kindergarten.

All had been forgiven, though. Besides, we were seven years older now, so I figured I would probably be OK. There was, however, a new bully in the grade eight class. He was different from any bullies I had dealt with in the past. This bully was more psychological than your garden variety bully. There was just something not right with this kid.

My experiences in kindergarten and the years following had prepared me to deal with the worst of the bullies. I knew Jesus had helped me survive the kindergarten ordeal; I was much wiser now because of it. Even still, I prayed for Jesus to watch over and protect me as I navigated grade seven in the eighth-grade class.

For the most part it worked. I was able to elude the wrath of the new bully. Unfortunately, I think he ended up terrorizing my friends Johnny and Greg much more than me.

Facing Tragedy and Questions of Faith

That same year on Friday, September 28, 1979, our family got the most shocking news of our lives. Dad's older brother Uncle Ken McQuarrie had been killed in a plane crash while on a business trip.

It was so sudden and unexpected that I could not get my twelve-year-old brain around it. We visited Uncle Ken, Aunt Hazel, and cous-

*Cousin Chelley, Uncle Ken, and Me
Circa mid-70s*

in Chelley that past summer in Bellville, Ontario. Now, in only a year and a half, we lost Gramma McQuarrie and Uncle Ken.

Uncle Ken looked like dad but was taller, bulkier, and a couple of years older. He was mechanically inclined and worked in automotive part sales for Chrysler Corporation out of Northern Ontario and Morton's Sales and Service Southern Ontario.

He served as president of both the community fire department and Ladies Softball Association. In addition, he was a board member of the Albury United Church, a member of the Canadian Legion, and a supporter of the Shriners fund for the Sick Children's Hospital.

Uncle Ken was always friendly and easygoing, at least with me. I noticed he really enjoyed his beer. When he would visit, he would always bring his beer as we did not have any alcohol in the house.

Uncle Ken, Aunt Hazel, and cousin Chelley would visit us about every two years or so. Chelley is the same age as I am. I always wondered if it was strange for her to have a dad named Kenneth McQuarrie and a cousin named Kenneth McQuarrie.

Among the people I knew who had died, Uncle Ken was the first who I could not say for sure had gone to heaven to be with Jesus. I simply didn't know whether he believed or not. He was a good man, but had he accepted Jesus as his Lord and Savior? It was a question no one could seem to answer for sure. He grew up in the church but never talked about his faith or where he stood with Jesus, keeping his thoughts to himself. I hope and pray that at some point in his life, maybe as a kid or just before the plane crash, he had accepted Jesus as his Lord and Savior.

The death of Uncle Ken impacted me deeply; it was a turning point in my life. I was starting to question who I am and why was I here.

It wasn't like I wanted to go on a quest to discover my biological parents or anything. It was a lot deeper than that. Through circumstances totally out of their control, Baby Stephen, Nanna, Grandma McQuarrie, and Uncle Ken had died years earlier than they should have.

I could undoubtedly have died many times over in the past twelve years. Head surgery, severe asthma attacks, attempted drowning by bullies, falling out of trees, a collision with Max, electrocution from rink lights, and the list goes on.

"Lord, why am I still here? Are you watching over and protecting me? And if you are, why?"

I wasn't the smartest kid or the dumbest, not the best athlete or the worst. Instead, I was the most extraordinarily ordinary kid from a small northern city in the middle of nowhere. Heck, I don't even really play hockey. These were just some of the thoughts that would drive me forward, seeking to find my place and purpose in life.

After all these years, the church was finally finishing the renovation of the upper floor sanctuary, complete with a new baptismal tank. I was baptized as a baby, but that was my parents' decision. Now it was my decision. I was ready and it was time that I got baptized in the name of God the Father, Son, and Holy Spirit.

Chapter 12:

McQuarrie, Run It Again

So do not fear, for I am with you; do not be dismayed,
for I am your God. I will strengthen you and help you;
I will uphold you with my righteous right hand. Isaiah 41:10

There were a lot of changes happening in my life as I entered grade eight, and I'm not talking about my voice getting deeper or starting to notice girls in a different way.

Aunt Linda had just married Albert "Butch" King. Uncle Albert King was just way too regal a name for our family, so we just affectionately called him "Uncle Butch" or "Butch" for short.

Uncle Butch had a couple of daughters from a previous marriage. His eldest daughter Leeanne lived out west, but his younger daughter Sherry stayed with him. So now Aunt Linda's daughter Kelly had a new younger sister, and we had a new cousin.

Remember that young couple from the church, Dave and Viki Steenburgh? Well, they had started a family with the birth of their baby girl Sarah. Unfortunately, the Steenburgh grandparents lived far away. No worries though, Mom and Dad were there to fill that void.

Little Sarah would come to know Mom as Nanna. After years of looking after, probably, hundreds of babies, Mom had finally achieved full Nanna status.

Dave and Viki would have three more children over the next few years, another girl named Rachael, followed by twin boys Luke and Matthew. You can imagine that Mom's Nanna duties increased, while Debbie, Dougie, and I supplied babysitting support.

I had just completed my three years of allergy immunization shots, and they did help quite a bit. I wasn't as sensitive now to dust, feathers, and cigarette smoke. However, dogs and cats were still the worst culprits for triggering my asthma. Dr. Sagle gave me a drug that was just coming to market called a Ventolin rescue inhaler, and for me, this was the most incredible blessing ever. If my lungs started to tighten up, just one shot of this inhaler, and it was like I had a new pair of lungs. I could now run hard and fast without sending myself spinning into an asthma attack. It was amazing!

I had always run relatively quickly and was starting to develop a lot more strength, and now, with my newfound inhaler, I could actually breathe. Do you know what this means? Look out, sports world, here I come!

There was just one problem, though. I still wasn't blessed with co-ordination and agility. I competed in the 80-yard dash and the triple jump in grade eight track and field. However, I had shorter legs with an unorthodox running style when it came to running. So, although I was quick out of the starting blocks, I often ran out of gas by 100 yards. So, I stuck with the 80-yard race.

My grade eight year was an enjoyable one. It was nice being the older kid at school for a change, which meant no one could bully me. With my trusty inhaler, I took part in all sorts of sporting events. For the first time in my life, I was able to get perfect attendance. I made it a whole year with no sick days, an absolute dream of mine since kindergarten.

Grade 8 Graduation with Dad

High School Here I Come!

David West, Jimmy Brown, Johnny Darlow, Cameron Ross, and I decided to try out for the high school football team, "The Sir James Dunn Eagles."

Because of hockey, high school football is not as big a deal in Canada as in the United States. However, it is still considered a major sport and a chance to prove that I could do a demanding physical sport since I could never play league hockey.

I decided to try out for quarterback simply because I could throw the ball a long way, albeit not very accurately. My biggest challenge was my height; standing only five foot six and three-quarters inches tall, I was a bit short for a quarterback. After the first practice, Head Coach White sent me over to train with the linemen.

Johnny decided he didn't want to play football, and Jimmy, Cameron, and David were all put with the defensive backs. Eventually, David would move onto the offensive line.

I was a solid 160 pounds at fourteen years old, but I didn't envision myself as a lineman. Still, I trained hard and learned to block on offense and rush the quarterback on defense.

At the end of each practice were the dreaded wind sprints. The whole team would line up on the goal line, and when the coach blew the whistle, we sprinted twenty yards, then turned around and did the same thing back. We did ten to fifteen sprints, depending on the coach's mood that day.

I was totally exhausted during one practice and came in dead last on the first wind sprint to cross the 20-yard line.

An assistant coach yelled out, "Hey, Coach White, I think McQuarrie is dogging it." Drawing unwanted attention to me.

At this, I leaned over and, placing my hands on my knees, I took a couple of the deepest breaths my lungs would allow. Then when the whistle blew again, I took off as fast as I could, this time crossing the line ahead of all my teammates.

"See, Coach White, I was right; McQuarrie was dogging it. So, I guess we're going to have to run ten more sprints."

Rats, I can't believe I fell for that. I imagine my teammates were not too pleased either.

The following practice, Coach White moved me to running back. The good news was that the coaches now knew who I was. The bad news, I was about the fourth string on the depth chart. In case you're wondering, first string are the starting players. Second string is the backup player in case the first-string player gets hurt. Third string is the back up to the back up. At fourth string you're lucky to get a helmet that fits, and the coach would probably forfeit the game before ever letting you on the field. I was the proverbial bench warmer.

As football season wore on, I watched and learned, trying hard to improve my football skills. However, playing a contact sport didn't help my tension headaches any. After many a practice, I would stand under a steaming hot shower, letting the water massage the base of my skull and neck to help relieve tension and pain. There was no way a pain in the neck and head would deter me from proving I could play football.

Late in the season, I had moved up the depth chart to second string. Not as much due to my skills but more because of injuries to the other running backs. It was a Wednesday practice before our upcoming Friday game. A job of a second-string player is to run our opposing team plays against our first-string defense. So, I would be standing in for our opponent's running back in this practice.

After running a few plays, the coach called for a "32-Dive." For this play, the right side running back, that would be me, takes the handoff and runs between the right guard and tackle.

We huddled, and the quarterback called the play, "32-Dive on one, break." Getting down into my three-point stance, I nervously waited.

The quarterback started his cadence. "Down, set, hut one."

Lunging up from my stance, I took the handoff from the quarterback and slammed into the backside of the right guard.

"McQuarrie, what was that?" yelled Coach White.

"Ahh, Coach, there was no hole to run through."

"If there is no hole, then you make a hole. Run it again!"

The quarterback started again. "Down, set, hut one."

Taking off this time, I lowered my shoulder, hitting the line hard, squeezing between the guard and tackle. However, now knowing exactly where I was going, the linebacker stepped up and tackled me.

"McQuarrie, get up! What do you think you are doing!" yelled Coach White, now shaking his head and rolling his eyes.

"Running the opposing teams plays against our defense, Coach."

"Is that what you call that! Run it again, and this time I want to see you in the end zone!"

I was now getting exhausted and a little annoyed, not to mention that the entire defense knew precisely where the play was going.

I jogged back to get into position, dropping down onto two knees to catch my breath before getting into my three-point stance.

The cold, wet mud of the field hit my knees like a jolt of electricity as all the memories of that November day in kindergarten came flooding back. Then, all I could think about was those bullies tackling me in that cold icy puddle.

The quarterback started his cadence, seemingly in slow motion, "Down ... set."

I shifted into a three-point stance; I could hear my heart beating as my breathing slowed.

"Hut one."

Exploding from my stance, I snatched the ball from the quarterback's hands, almost taking his arm with me.

Crashing between the guard and tackle, I lowered my right shoulder into the linebacker with force I didn't even know I possessed. Then, keeping my legs driving, I pivoted to the left, breaking out of the linebacker's clutches as my cleats dug hard into the muddy, grassy field.

Gaining traction, I accelerated and busted through the arm tackles of the defensive backs, then scampered the forty yards to the end zone. As I crossed the goal line, I looked up. The sky was blue with white billowy clouds. I could hear a few birds chirping as they flew by. Wow, I've never been here before; it was so peaceful.

"MCQUARRIE! McQuarrie, get back here!" I could hear Coach White yelling from a distance.

I turned and jogged back to the huddle.

"McQuarrie, you're starting at running back this Friday."

What, did Coach White just say I was starting Friday? I was shocked, excited, and scared, all wrapped into one emotion. One thing was for sure, just like Mom always said, "It doesn't matter whether I was the first one chosen or the last one. The important thing is that when my number gets called, I'm ready to give it my all."

Are You Ready for Some Football?

Game day had arrived. It was a home game against the Bawating Braves. Bawating won the coin flip and chose to receive the ball. After the kickoff, the Braves managed to get a couple of first downs. But then our defense stepped up, stopping the Bawating drive, forcing them to punt.

Our punt returner fielded the ball and ran it back to about our 20-yard line.

After taking a shot of my inhaler, I nervously jogged onto the field with our starting offense. The coach sent in the first play; a sweep left. The ball was not coming to me on this play; I would be just a decoy. It was just as well, as I couldn't stop my legs from shaking due to nerves.

Getting that first play out of the way was good, allowing my nervous energy to calm down a bit.

Coach White sent in the next play.

"32-Dive on two," the quarterback called out in the huddle.

It was the same play I ran in practice. But, this time, the only difference was the defense didn't know it was coming.

I dropped into my three-point stance as the quarterback started his cadence. Then, slowing my breathing, everything went silent as I focused on the voice of the quarterback.

"Hut one, hut two."

I blasted out of my stance, taking the quarterback's handoff, as I accelerated between our guard and tackle.

Our linemen opened up a huge hole for me to run through this time. By the time I hit the gap, I was going full speed. The linebacker stepped up for the tackle, but I cut hard to the left, shooting through the defensive backfield untouched. There was now no one between me and the endzone as I raced up the left side of the field, with the defense in hot pursuit.

Straining with every muscle in my body, I raced up the sideline. Finally, after about 60 yards, I started to run out of gas. Doggone it, I had trained for 80-yard sprints, but that was without wearing football equipment.

As the end zone became closer and closer, I slowed down just ever so slightly. But it was just enough for a defender to catch me from behind, wrapping his arms around my shoulders and neck. My momentum kept propelling me forward as I strained to reach the end zone. Suddenly I got hit by a second defender from the side, driving me out of bounds on the 2-yard line. All three of us came crashing down as we slammed into the ground just short of the end zone.

I jumped up quickly to get back to the huddle for the next play. Then, after two steps, I collapsed back down to the turf. Pushing myself up, I tried again, only to crash back down and a second time, my shoulder hitting the grass. What's going on? My right leg was not working. So finally, one of my teammates tells me, "Just take a knee." The referee blew the whistle as I knelt on one knee, and an assistant coach came to help me limp off the field.

My right hamstring was shot; I couldn't even straighten my leg. The assistant coach took me back to the locker room, where he stretched, massaged, and taped my leg. Once back out on the sidelines, I tried to run, but a light jog with a limp was the best I could manage. After all these years of dreaming of a chance like this, I couldn't believe it. This time it wasn't even my lungs that let me down. It was my darn legs. My game was over, and I was off to the hospital to have my leg checked. But, on a positive note, we did win the game.

By the time I got to the hospital, the back of my leg was completely black and blue. It turned out to be a severe hamstring strain, complete with some torn muscle fibers. My football season was over. I was a one-run wonder, the ultimate one-trick pony.

That winter, Coach White got me into the weight room. The goal was to make me bigger, stronger, and faster for the following year's football season. He showed me how to properly lift weights, and the bonus was it also helped with rehabbing my injured hamstring.

Sadly, high school was more than just football. There was still the school part. Sir James Dunn was a school of about 1,200 students, making it one of the largest high schools in the Sault.

Our school had a sizeable technical department with elective courses in drafting, woodworking, building construction, electrical, machine shop, and automotive. I am sure you can tell by now that I signed up for all the technical classes. Despite my excitement over woodworking and building construction, I still had to take the typical academic courses, including English, math, science, geography, and history. However, I was able to avoid music, typing, and French classes. Canada is bilingual, English and French. I already struggled enough with English, so you're not going to find me anywhere near a French class!

Now that I was in high school, I needed a part-time job to make some spending money. Working for chocolate milkshakes is all well and good, but I needed some cash. Dad suggested I talk to Paul Mathewson at church on Sunday. Paul was the owner of Sault Transmission, an automotive transmission repair shop on Pim Street. Paul hired me on as the shop cleaner. I would clean once a week for $50.00. Back in those days, the minimum wage was $3.50 per hour.

I knew from working with Poppa that time was money. The faster I finished, the more money per hour I would make. Once I got a system going, I was able to get the job done in 3.5 hours. That worked out to $14.29 per hour. You and I both know that sounded a lot better than $3.50 per hour!

No Place Like Home for the Holidays

We were all getting a bit older now, but Mom made sure that Christmas and the holiday seasons were still very tradition-filled. Christmas day, we would have a full house with Poppa, Vi, Aunt Linda, Uncle Butch, Kelly, Sherry, and all the Steenburghs. It would be a day of food, fun, and games.

To close out Christmas day late in the evening, we would gather around the dining room table for the second round of turkey and goodies. With lights dimmed, every person would have a lit Christmas candle as Dad would say a prayer of thanks to Jesus for coming into the world so many Christmases ago. Then we had time to share what we were thankful for in the past year.

Once all the touchy-feely stuff was done, Christmas carol sheet music got passed around for a sing-along. OK, personally, the singing part was not high on my list of traditions, but I did sort of participate.

On Uncle Butch's first Christmas with the family, we did a song in which each person got a verse of the "Twelve Days of Christmas." Uncle Butch got the line "Five Golden Rings." He was a good sport but not a good singer. When his turn came, he used his deep baritone voice to hit his lines with the passion of an opera singer. However, the resulting sound was more like that of a wounded water buffalo.

Aunt Linda & Uncle Butch circa 1979-80

From that day on, Uncle Butch became the official "Five Golden Rings" singer at any family or church event.

We would have the same gang over for New Year's Eve, along with our Campbell cousins. Most years Ena, Larry, Dawn, and Dawn's now-husband Vern Hawkins would drive up from Spring Arbor, Michigan, for the New Years' festivities. Dawn and Vern had a couple of babies of their own now, Heath and Brittany. Babies were always welcome in the McQuarrie household.

New Year's Eve would be a time of games and overeating. Of course, the festivities always included a big boot hockey game. It just wouldn't be Canadian without hockey. Not to mention, nothing feels better than beating your American cousins in a good old hockey game.

When spring came around, I joined the Sir James Dunn track and field team. That year I qualified for the Northern Ontario Championships "NOSSA" and the Ontario Championships "OFSSA" in the discus. However, I did get my butt kicked at OFSSA, not even getting by the first round of the competition.

Back to the Gridiron

I managed to make it through my first year of high school, and the following summer, I continued to play on the slow-pitch team.

As summer ended, it was time for a new football season to begin. My offseason weightlifting, along with a bit of a growth spurt, had paid off. I was heading into training camp now 5' 7" tall, 175 lbs, bench-pressing 250 pounds, and running a 4.8-second 40-yard dash. Not NFL caliber by any means, but relatively solid for a fifteen-year-old.

1980s family photo

The week before Labor Day, Mom and Dad needed to drive Debbie to Brock University in St. Catharines, Ontario, to begin her first year at university. Although Debbie loved animals, she decided against becoming a veterinarian. However, Dave Steenburgh was a teacher that specialized in children with developmental disabilities. He introduced Debbie to this field when she was in high school. With the new interest at hand, Debbie would be starting her studies in early childhood education, intending to teach people with developmental disabilities. In addition, she would be playing on the university volleyball team.

I didn't want to go with the family to take Debbie because of football preseason practice. So, Mom and Dad decided they would leave me at home to look after the poodles. Poppa would check in on me to make sure I was doing OK.

I was running low on my inhaler, so Poppa picked me up in his blue 1972 Ford Comet, and we headed to the pharmacy. After picking up the prescription, we hit Burger King at the corner of McNabb St. and Great Northern Road. Then, after we polished off a couple of whoppers and chocolate milkshakes, it was time to head back home.

It was an unusually warm evening, so I tossed my inhaler onto the console under the dash and rolled down the passenger side window. Then, leaning back into my seat for the short ride home, I stuck my right arm out the window over the edge of the door, neglecting to put my seatbelt on.

Poppa continued down McNabb Street. As we approached the Shell Station, he turned his signal on to make the left turn onto Pine Street. The vehicle ahead of us moved into the intersection, anticipating the yellow light coming soon. Poppa also inched forward, keeping tight on the vehicle's rear bumper. With a break in traffic, the first car took off into the turn. Following suit, Poppa hit the gas to get around the corner on the now yellow light. Unexpectedly, some dude stepped into the crosswalk at that exact moment, trying to make his own last-second dash before the lights turned red.

The front car slammed on the breaks to prevent hitting the guy, causing Poppa to hammer on his breaks. I lunged forward from the sudden stop, almost slamming my face on the dash, my right arm still hanging out the window.

Suddenly, I heard the loud sound of a car engine revving. I swung my head around hard to the right, catching a glimpse of the oncoming orangish-red vehicle, now merely inches from my door.

Everything suddenly went into slow motion, and with cat-like reflexes, I pulled my right arm back inside the car as the door began to collapse inward on me.

My shoulder now firmly pressed against the collapsing door, I braced for the impact of my life. All of a sudden, a strange sensation came over me, like I was being pulled back through the air away from the door. The little Ford Comet flew backward through the intersection, slamming into a third vehicle, then everything went silent.

As if I had been holding my breath underwater for an eternity, I gasped for air. Inhaling sharply, I tried desperately to get oxygen back into my lungs. Glancing down, I saw my inhaler still sitting quietly on the console under the dash like nothing happened. Grabbing it, I took a few shots, and within about fifteen seconds, my breathing returned to normal.

At that moment, a police officer reached through the window, grabbed my arm, placed two fingers on my wrist, and checked my pulse. Then, setting my arm back down, the officer said, "Stay here, you're going to be just fine."

Now, two ambulance guys were helping Poppa, who was bleeding from his head and half unconscious (back in those days, the Sault did not have paramedics yet). I saw a second ambulance pull up, and the attendants started helping the man and woman in the car that hit us. After some time, the two ambulances sped off, heading for the Plumber Hospital with Poppa and the two other people. I continued to sit in the car as the police officer had instructed me.

A tow truck came and took the other vehicle away. A second tow truck had arrived and started hooking up to our car. It was strange that the tow truck operator seemed oblivious that I was still sitting inside the vehicle.

After securing the car, the tow guy walked over to the truck, hitting the levers to pull the car into place. At this, I crawled out of the vehicle through the driver's side, cutting my right pinky finger on some shattered glass. Backing away from the car, I moved toward the curb and the crowd that had now gathered.

I then heard my name called out, "Ken." Turning around, I was surprised to see Brian, one of my football teammates. He had been at the Shell station with his father and brother, filling their car with gas as the accident happened. Brian's father told me I should go talk to the police officers as they were preparing to leave the accident scene. The two police officers were parked in Mac's corner store parking lot across the street from the Shell Station.

As I ran across the street, the police car started to pull out of the parking lot and onto Pine Street. I accelerated to catch the car, just barely managing to slam my hand on the trunk as the cruiser pulled away. At this, the brake lights came on.

"Can I help you?" The officer called out as he rolled down the window.

"Yeah, I was the passenger in the blue Comet in the accident."

Looking at me like I was crazy, the officer replied, "There wasn't anybody on the passenger side; that's not even possible."

"Yeah, I know, a good thing I didn't have a seatbelt on so I could get out of the way."

The officer just looked at me in bewilderment. Oops! Maybe I shouldn't have mentioned that part about not wearing a seatbelt. It turns out the orangish-red vehicle ran the yellow light going upwards of 80 km (50 miles) per hour. The Ford Comet didn't even have a passenger side anymore.

I continued, "The other policeman will tell you, the one that took my pulse after the crash."

"Ahh, what other policemen? The only two officers on the scene were my partner here and me."

He referred to the female officer sitting in the passenger side of the police car.

"There was a third officer; he was a bit shorter, maybe 5' 8," and stockier than you. He had the same uniform as you but was wearing his police hat with the badge in front. Just like the one there." I pointed at the cap on the back seat of the police car. "Look, I have a cut on my finger from the crash, and they took my grandfather to the hospital. Can you give me a ride?"

Still not convinced, the officer told me to get into the car. "We'll sort this out at the hospital. Anyway, I need to get statements from everyone involved in the crash."

Once at the hospital, Poppa verified my story. Although the officer took my account down, I don't think his brain believed I could have walked away from that crash.

The hospital let me use the phone to call Aunt Linda and Uncle Butch, and before long, they arrived at the hospital with Poppa's wife, Vi. They also left a message for Mom and Dad at their hotel about the events of the evening.

Poppa had a fractured hip, multiple broken ribs, and needed over twenty stitches in his head. The man and woman that hit us looked like their faces had collided with the windshield. They were all bruised and cut up.

As for me, well, all I needed was a Band-Aid for the cut on my finger.

Mom and Dad cut their trip short and drove home the next day. At the time of the accident, they had been at a restaurant for dinner. During the meal, Debbie mentioned to Dad that she felt something was wrong back home, and he should call me. But, of course, I was not home.

Mom was not happy with the police or the hospital because they never examined me after the accident.

"He could have been in shock or had a concussion or even worse," Mom told Dr. Sagle as he checked me out. I was OK and attended football practice the very next day after the accident.

Poppa's car was a complete write-off. So, Dad and Uncle Butch went to get the personal effects out of the car at the wrecking yard.

Dad said when he saw the vehicle he felt sick to his stomach. "It's a miracle you and Poppa survived," Dad said. As for the mysterious police officer who took my pulse after the crash? Well, no one was ever able to find him; he remains a mystery to this day.

It was the football season opener against the St. Mary's Knights. Naturally, I was nervous, setting out to prove I was more than a one-run wonder.

1970s Ford Comet – Similar to the car in which Poppa and I were in the accident

On our first possession, we drove the ball down the field. Then taking a pitchout from quarterback Mike Joy, I was able to get by the defense and scamper 40-yards for a touchdown. I scored a second time with a 30-yard run later in the second quarter. When the final whistle blew, we were the winners, and I was no longer the one-run wonder.

Ken McQuabbie of the Dunn was a one-man scoring machine in the junior game. He ran for a pair of early touchdowns and added a single with a tackle behind the St. Mary's goal line. Dave Carscadden converted both touchdowns. *Sept. 16/82*

My first newspaper clipping, although they spelled my name wrong

About halfway through the season, we played a Saturday morning game against the Korah Colts, and Mom came to watch me play for the first time. Winning the coin toss, we chose to receive the ball.

I caught the kickoff in full stride at about our 25-yard line. Accelerating up the middle of the field, I then cut hard to the right running up the sideline, getting by all defenders except one, the littlest player on their team.

I figured I was at least twenty pounds heavier and would just steamroll right over the little guy. So, all I would need to do is lower my left shoulder. I could already envision myself crossing the goal line. That was my first mistake. The tiny defender launched himself through the air headfirst at the last possible second. I pulled back my left shoulder to avoid hitting his head, my second mistake.

The defender's helmet hit me full force square in the chest, instantly knocking every bit of air out of my lungs. I hit the ground like a sack of potatoes falling off the back of a flatbed truck.

Pushing up to my hands and knees, I spit out my mouthguard and desperately gasped for air. But no air came, my lungs were not working, I was starting to foam at the mouth. Mom, standing on the sidelines, had watched the entire spectacle unfold. Without hesitation, she started onto the football field. Dad stepped out and grabbed Mom by the arm, "Where do you think you're going?"

"My son is hurt. I'm going to help him."

"You can't do that. A football player can't be having his mom come onto the field to help him. He'd never be able to live that down. Let the coaches help him."

Me and the Steenburgh twins Luke & Matthew, Matthew was obviously cheering for the other team

After a little more persuading, Dad convinced Mom to remain on the sidelines. Then, one of the other fathers leaned over and said to Dad, "Don't worry, sir. If she gets by you, I'll tackle her."

I just had the wind knocked out of me. So, after sitting out the next couple of plays, I finished the game.

Humility First

If anyone thinks they are something when they are not, they deceive themselves. Each one should test their own actions. Then they can take pride in themselves alone, without comparing themselves to someone else, for each one should carry their own load. Galatians 6:3-5

One evening at dinner, Dad told me my cousin Sean Campbell had scored his first touchdown. Sean was playing running back for the rival Bawating Braves that season.

"That's great. How long was the run?" I replied.

"It doesn't matter how long Sean's run was."

"But I wasn't …"

Dad continued, "It's OK to take pride in your achievements, but we should never compare or minimize other people's accomplishments. Instead, you should just be happy for your cousin."

Wow, Dad caught me off guard. After thinking more about it, Dad was right; the only reason for me to ask how many yards Sean ran was to, in my mind, compare it to my touchdowns, and that was wrong. I was happy he scored; even better, that it wasn't against us.

Football season ended, and I made it through without injury, plus I got voted the most valuable player by my teammates. I think any teenage boy would be happy to be voted MVP of their team, and I was no exception. It was only the junior high school football team, but it was what it represented. Despite the joy of having done so well, this had special meaning for me.

Doctors once thought I might not run, and surgery was even discussed to relieve tension in my legs. Asthma had caused limitations preventing me from playing hockey. Throughout the football season, I had to deal with tension headaches. Oh, and let's not forget the season started with a potentially tragic car accident.

I had overcome many physical challenges to be successful on the football field and as a running back, no less. It was the most significant accomplish-

Winning the Football Team MVP

ment of my life to date. It gave me the confidence to keep pushing my boundaries and keep moving forward.

The Lord continued to work in my life, helping me grow stronger, preparing me for what lies ahead. I would learn so many lessons on the football field. In life, I was going to get tackled more often than scoring. Sometimes I would get the wind knocked out of me and sometimes injured. There were always people trying to prevent me from scoring, and on occasion, I would simply fumble the ball. But on my journey, the only person I am competing against is myself.

Whenever I get tackled or knocked down in life, I can always sense Jesus calling out, "McQuarrie, get up! Run it again."

Chapter 13:

Better Get a Trade

If we claim to be without sin, we deceive ourselves and the truth is not in us. If we confess our sins, he is faithful and just and will forgive us our sins and purify us from all unrighteousness. If we claim we have not sinned, we make him out to be a liar and his word is not in us.
1 John 1:8-10

In high school, just like countless other kids, I was just another typical teenager trying to figure out who I was. I was probably way too focused on who I wished I was instead of who I really am. I tended to be somewhat of a loner, not belonging to any particular group. However, I did get along with almost everyone. Of course, I played sports, so I got along with the jocks, but I also took the technical trade courses, which attracted a different group of kids. Still, my analytical mind allowed me to hang with some of the more scholastically gifted guys and gals.

Like in elementary school, I remained not a popular kid, but not an unpopular one either. I was always very focused on what I was doing. Still, I could come across as very emotionless or aloof at times. If I weren't interested in something or someone, I would quietly go about my own business. Occasionally this could come across as a bit stuck up, but people who know me would tell you that's not true.

I never thought I was better than anyone and always treated everyone the same. Plus, if Mom ever sensed I was getting cocky or too full of myself, she'd knock the living cocky right out of me. I have to admit, I didn't do very well with the girls. I couldn't quite figure them out. I only managed two dates with one girl in my entire high school career. One was a group date, so that probably doesn't count. The other time I took her to a movie, *Indiana Jones and the Temple of Doom,* and that was it. It seemed that I just landed in the friend zone with girls, someone they would trust and depend on, but more like a brother. I honestly couldn't tell if they liked me beyond that. So much for the analytical mind, eh?

Winter 1982, one of my long-standing childhood prayers got answered. I was finally getting a snowmobile. I had prayed for one every year since I could remember, but it was just a luxury we could not afford. Yamaha launched the 250 Bravo, and a local dealer had one on sale for just under $1,400. I had saved up $800, and Dougie contributed $100 of his savings. Dad loaned us the remaining $500, which I paid back $25 per month for a year and a half.

My new 1982 Yamaha 250 Bravo

Dad was happy to be able to make one of my childhood dreams come true while at the same time teaching me financial responsibility.

Almost as exciting as getting the snowmobile was David West turning sixteen in January of 1983. David was able to get his driver's license, and we were now mobile.

David's church had a big teen group. Several kids from Bethel Bible Chapel would also attend. Bethel is a similar denomination as The Gospel Hall. The teen group would meet Friday evenings for a Bible study led by one of the church elders. After the study, most of us would head to various kids' homes to hang out, play games, shoot pool, or hit a local pizza parlor.

At these teen group events, I got to know the Pinches brothers, Scott and Rob. Scott Pinches was the same age as Debbie and get this: our mothers shared the same hospital room when they gave birth. So, I guess that almost makes us related.

I continued to help Poppa with his projects during the summer and when time permitted. Uncle Butch also enjoyed woodworking and subscribed to a woodworking magazine. There were plans for building a queen-sized poster bed and dresser in one magazine issue. I decided to try making the bed and asked Poppa if I could use his workshop. Poppa, now in his mid-70s, was happy to help me with my new project.

Poppa didn't have the lathe required to make the four bedposts, so he contracted it out, making a deal with me. He would cover the costs for the posts, but in return, I would work off the price, helping him finish up a few of his projects that summer. That summer, I painted Poppa's house, slurry sealed his asphalt driveway, shingled two garages, and did a few other odd jobs he had contracted.

You see, Poppa was getting older and a bit unsteady. His years of injuries on the construction sites were catching up to him. Truth be told, the family just didn't want him on ladders anymore. Now that didn't stop him from standing partway up the ladder, providing me instruction. As a tradition, working with Poppa would always end up at the Dairy Queen for a chocolate milkshake each day.

The bed was the last project Poppa and I would do together. A couple of years later, Poppa slipped running a board through his jointer/planer. His right hand hit the spinning blades, severing four fingers just above the middle knuckle. After that, he had to stop using power tools.

At school, we students built a small two-bedroom house in the woodshop. It was built over two years then auctioned off.

Mr. McLean was my woodworking and building construction teacher throughout high school. A former tradesman himself, he

Newly refinished Bed and Dresser Poppa and I built almost 40 years ago

knew my desire to become a carpenter and encouraged me in that endeavor. Occasionally Poppa would drop by the school after hours, talk story with Mr. McLean, and check out progress on the house.

As I turned sixteen, I set my sites on getting my driver's license. Unfortunately, we were in the middle of a snowstorm on the day of my test. Gusts of wind upwards of 100 km (60 miles) per hour, wind chill hitting 20-below with occasional whiteout conditions. Luckily, the weather settled down a bit by afternoon, and I could complete and pass my test. I didn't even have to perform all the skills on the test. Guess the instructor figured, if I could control the vehicle in a snowstorm, I would be acceptable as a driver.

After Grandpa McQuarrie left for the nursing home, he gave Dad his old Chevy II Nova. Dad had it fixed up for Debbie to drive in high school.

With Debbie off at college, I now sort of inherited the car. The vehicle had survived a few too many harsh Canadian winters and was on its last legs—or wheels, so to speak. Pop in a cassette tape of your favorite music, and as you accelerate, the music would also speed up.

One day, Rob Pinches and I were out and about in the Chevy when the breaks stopped working. Luckily, I could use the emergency brake to slow down at stoplights for the rest of the evening.

Something as trivial as no breaks was not going to stop a couple of teenage boys from a night out on the town. Just watch where you put your feet, though, as you could see the road going by through the rusted floorboards. It was without a doubt time to get a new car.

Paul Mathewson said he would help me find something I could afford, which wasn't much. So finally, Paul managed to find me a 1976 Dodge Charger for a mere $150. There's only one problem, though: it was up on blocks and didn't run.

But Paul said not to worry, the mechanics at the transmission shop could help me get it running. And with the help of Sault Transmission mechanic Dennis and my high school auto shop training, I was able to get my new ride on the road.

1976 Charger - Before

1976 Charger - After

Dr. Sagle decided to put me on a second round of allergy immunization shots and a drug called Theo-dur (Theophylline). Theo-dur is supposed to keep the inflammation down in the lungs and airways. I kept telling the doctor Theo-dur made my headaches worse, but he assured me headaches were not a known side effect of the drug. To this, I replied, "Maybe the drug manufacturer should give me a call." Mildly amused by my response, Dr. Sagle suggested maybe playing football and weight lifting was causing my head pain. Well, let's just say Dr. Sagle and I agreed to disagree. As a result, I continued playing football and taking the drug. If you look up the drug Theo-dur today, headaches are a listed potential side effect; surprise, surprise, eh!

In the Home Stretch

In my grade12 year, I had a new English teacher, Mr. Aaronson. Our first assignment was to write a 500-word essay. For me, this would be pure torture. I struggled with spelling and grammar throughout my whole life, just barely passing English class each year. Despite my previous essay experience, I'm happy to report that I completed my essay and handed it in on time. Then, a few days later, Mr. Aaronson walked around the classroom, passing out the marked-up papers. He placed my essay face down on my desk as he walked by, continuing through the room.

I slowly flipped over the paper. Jeepers, Mr. Aaronson put more red ink on the page than I had blue. Then my eyes caught the grade in the top right corner, as expected, a D minus. *Wait a second, I didn't see it quite right. It sorta looks like a B minus.*

Mr. Aaronson walked down my aisle, noticing the stunned look on my face.

"Kenny, is there something wrong?" he asked.

"Is that a D or a B?"

"It's a B."

"It looks like you wrote more on my paper than I did. How could I get a B minus?"

Mr. Aaronson chuckled, seemingly amused at my comment. "Well, I would have liked to have given you an A, but your grammar needs some work and your punctuation needs help. But I like your content. You tell a good story."

I was shocked! Finally getting a good grade did motivate me to try harder in class. Later in the year, on a 1,500-word essay assignment, I managed to get a B plus. That would be my highest grade on an English assignment ever. However, I knew my future was in construction, not writing.

It had come to that time of year when I needed to meet with a guidance counselor to figure out my future. Everyone was always saying to get a good job, you're going to need to get a university education. So, I asked the counselor, "Is there a university construction course?"

"Well," the counselor started, "the only thing in construction would be engineering or architecture."

I had taken four years of drafting class and had designed an automotive station and a house. The problem was my designs were very practical and uninspiring, not very architectural.

Before I could respond, the counselor continued. "Architecture and engineering programs are very competitive to get in. You have to be at the top of your class to be accepted by the university, and you need to complete grade 13."

Back in those days, you would graduate high school in grade 12. However, if you wanted to go to university for a degree program, you would need to do an added year of high school (grade 13).

Although my grades in technical classes were excellent, the counselor told me that my academic grades were not the greatest.

"I think we should look at community college for you," the counselor said.

The local Sault College did not have much in the way of construction courses. George Brown in Toronto and Fanshawe College in London, Ontario, had the best construction courses.

Only one problem, and it was a biggie. The Ontario government had tightened up the restrictions on getting student loans and grants. So, unless my parents legally disowned me, I would not be able to get a grant.

I figured asking Mom to disown me to get money for college would not go over too well. So, a grant was out of the question. I didn't qualify for a loan large enough to pay for tuition, books, room, and board for an out-of-town college.

I asked the counselor, "What about the Algoma Steel Technical Scholarship?"

Algoma Steel is the largest employer in the Sault, and they offer scholarships to kids of employees who are pursuing a technical field of study. As a bonus, Algoma Steel will provide you with a job when you graduate college. Responding to my question, the counselor said, "Algoma only gives out a few of those scholarships every year. Since they are the largest employer in the Sault, hundreds of kids apply. With your grades, the chance of you winning that scholarship is doubtful. You may be better off getting a trade."

My last class of the day was building construction with Mr. McLean. After class, I talked to him about my conversation with the guidance counselor.

After looking at the course outlines for George Brown and Fanshaw, he said, "I think this Fanshawe course would be good for you. It doesn't hurt to apply, and if it doesn't work out, you can always start your carpenter apprenticeship."

Mr. McLean pointed out Fanshawe is a co-op internship program, meaning graduation requirements included a four-month and an eight-month internship with a construction company. A paid internship would help me earn added money to pay for college expenses. Plus, it would also give me work experience to use toward my carpentry apprenticeship.

On a side note, Fanshaw College was established in 1967, the very same year I was born. So, was this destiny calling?

I filled in Mom and Dad on my meetings with the guidance counselor and Mr. McLean. Mom said, "We just need to pray about it. You pray about it, and your father and I will pray about it, and we shall see what happens."

Dad did more than pray about it. He filled in the Algoma Steel Scholarship application and submitted it.

A couple of months later, I got notified that I was in consideration for the scholarship. I would need to write a one-page essay on why I should get the award. I would also need to be interviewed by the selection committee.

The pressure was on, and a B was not going to cut it this time. I wrote my essay, focusing on what it would mean to get the scholarship. Since there were no fancy-pants computers back then with spelling and grammar checks, Mom was my spelling and grammar check program.

At the interview, they asked me many questions throughout the forty-five minutes. First, I told a few stories about being adopted, fighting through asthma, and working with Poppa. Next, I mentioned helping Mom with babies and the church nursery.

A couple of weeks later, the phone rang.

Dad answered it. "Just a minute. Kenny, it's for you."

"Hello."

"Is this Kenneth Ian McQuarrie?" the voice asked.

"Yes, that's me."

"This is the Algoma Steel Corporation calling. I am pleased to inform you that you are this year's recipient of one of the Algoma Steel Technical Scholarships."

I was shocked. I was hoping and praying but did not expect to win. Talk about an answer to prayer or more like a miracle.

The scholarship paid for tuition plus $250 per semester for books. Combined with a small government student loan for the first year, plus the money I would have from working the internships, I was good to go to Fanshawe in London, Ontario.

It was now the beginning of May, with only one month left of high school. Once again, I qualified for the NOSSA track and field meet for the discus. This year it would be held in Sudbury, about a 3.5-hour drive from the Sault.

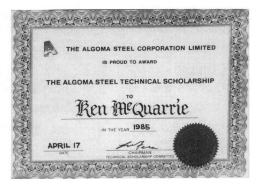

Sir James Dunn was a big track and field school, having won many past city and NOSSA championships. There was always a lot of pressure and school pride on the line to win.

Thursday evening, we arrived at the hotel by school bus, along with many other student-athletes from rival schools.

After grabbing dinner at a restaurant with a few other kids, I made my way back to the hotel, where a few eighteen-year-old students had picked up beer and liquor for the evening—something not allowed but quite common at these events.

I was given a mickey of vodka, a small bottle of thirteen ounces. To put it in perspective, a can of pop is twelve ounces.

I decided to try the vodka, which was my first mistake. It didn't taste terrific; actually, it tasted pretty awful, like watered-down paint thinner. However, it was just a tiny bottle, so I chug-a-lugged it all down at once, and that was mistake number two.

All was good for about twenty minutes, and then the 40-proof alcohol kicked in. It wasn't long, and I couldn't walk straight without falling over.

I was in a room with a couple of other students when I decided to go back to my own room and sleep it off. And that was mistake number three as in three strikes, and you're out or, in my case, completely out of it.

By now, I couldn't quite remember where my room was and kept falling, trying to get there. Finally, one of the other students went and got a couple of the teacher chaperones who helped me to my room, just in time to hurl the entire contents of my stomach into the trash can.

As I crawled into the bed, I felt so sick, like it would be easier just to die. But, once the bed stopped spinning, I passed out for the night.

The following day, I woke up to the worst headache ever, and not the muscle tension kind. My forehead was just throbbing. My mouth was so dry, like I had been sucking sand all night. No amount of water would quench the thirst.

I felt like I should eat something, but just the thought of food made me nauseous. I was still feeling a little dizzy, and to throw the discus, you have to spin around. So, this was not going to be a fun day.

Stepping into the discus circle, I started my spin, but the disk slipped out of my hand, slamming into the back safety net; doggone it!

My successive two tosses weren't much better, landing out of bounds to the right and left.

I had fouled out in the very first round. My competition was over.

Many of our athletes did not do well that day, and I was not the only one feeling the effects of the previous night's festivities.

Sir James Dunn did not fare well at NOSSA that year. Then, after the track meet, we all piled into the bus for the 3.5-hour ride home, arriving back in the Sault late Friday evening.

Monday morning, it was back to school. Only three weeks of classes, then exams and graduation. I was already looking forward to college in the fall.

Tuesday morning, I was in math class when I got the call to report to the principal's office. A rival school had said that Sir James Dunn athletes were drinking at the NOSSA track meet.

The vice principal told me about the complaint. He said he had interviewed students, teachers, and coaches that all verified I was drunk on the evening before the meet. Then he told me, "We are suspending you indefinitely pending further investigation." I was to clean out my locker and leave the school property.

Well, this was not good; talk about fumbling the ball. If I can't finish the next three weeks and write my exams, I will lose the scholarship. I would have to repeat the whole semester just to graduate high school.

I felt sicker to my stomach now than I did after drinking the vodka.

I called home, and Mom answered, but I didn't even get two words out when she fired back, "The school already called. You get yourself home, right now."

Mom was not happy. That was the longest two-mile walk home ever. Talk about the walk of shame.

When I arrived, Mom said, "I don't even want to talk about it. We will discuss this when your father gets home."

Dad arrived home for lunch, and I could tell from his body language he was not happy. I had seen that look before when he backed over my tricycle after I left it behind the car.

Dad didn't yell or anything; he never yelled. He just had a very stern, serious, I-mean-business tone about his voice.

"Sit down. Now, I want you to tell your mother and me exactly what happened at the track meet."

I gave Dad a detailed blow-by-blow description of the events that happened at the track meet. He and Mom quietly listened, not saying a word. Finally, when I was finished, Dad responded,

"If you wanted to try alcohol, I wish you would have just asked me. But instead, you made a very unwise choice that may have some very tough consequences."

"Now you're going to lose your scholarship," Mom blurted out.

Dad continued, "We have a meeting with the vice principal at the school tonight at five p.m. So, I will pick you and your mother up at four-thirty p.m."

After arriving at the school, Dad parked out front, and we entered through the main front glass doors. A few of my teammates just happened to be standing in the hall, looking very somber as we passed by. I imagine they were concerned about what details I would divulge to the school.

The vice principal introduced himself, then led us into a small conference room. Two of the teachers accompanying the track team on the trip were already seated. After a couple more introductions and offers of coffee or water, the meeting started.

The vice principal explained why we were all there and mentioned the complaint from the rival school.

He said, "I have multiple witnesses that verified Ken was drunk and became ill. The only other student drinking that night was a boy having his eighteenth birthday and wanted a beer now that he was of legal age. I can understand that, and we are not going to fault him for it."

That's a bunch of hogwash, I thought to myself. At least a dozen kids were drinking that night, and that's not to mention the ones smoking pot. So why does he think we lost the track meet?

But I kept my thoughts to myself as I figured it would not help the situation.

Then the vice principal pulled out a sheet of paper. It was the parental consent form to allow a student to go on the trip. Showing the document to Dad, he asked, "Mr. McQuarrie, is this your signature?"

Looking at the form, Dad replied, "Yes, it is."

"Well, Mr. McQuarrie, the form states that if a student is caught drinking or doing drugs, they may be expelled and/or banned from participating in future school athletics."

Dad listened quietly as the vice principal continued, "If this was just an in-school incident, we could handle it differently. But since another school reported it, we have no choice but to expel Ken for the rest of the school year and ban him from any future school athletics."

The room went silent; it was a heavy tense silence. Or maybe it was just me as Dad sat there quietly collecting his thoughts. Then, finally, after about ten seconds, Dad began.

"On the consent form, we listed Ken as a severe asthmatic under medical conditions. Also listed are the medications he is on. You stated that he was sick that night. Why was he not taken to the hospital? How do you know the alcohol was not reacting with his medications?"

Dad continued, "It says here that if the student is caught with drugs or alcohol, their parents will be notified at once. It also says the student will be sent home via Greyhound bus at the parent's expense. I find it interesting that my son was allowed to compete at the track meet. That was Friday, and it's now Tuesday. Why am I just finding out about this today?"

The vice principal started to respond, but Dad cut him off.

"I'm not finished. Ken is only seventeen years old, the legal drinking age in Canada is eighteen. I want to know who gave Ken the alcohol because I want to press charges. I will also be filing a complaint with the Board of Education against the school and the teachers involved."

At this, the vice principal jumped in, "Mr. McQuarrie, I'm sure that won't be necessary. Let's talk about it. I'm sure we can come to a resolution."

Dad and the vice principal hashed out the following resolution:

- I would not be expelled but would serve a three-week suspension.
- I would be allowed to come to class to hand in any assignments due or write any tests that would be part of my grades.
- I would be allowed to write all my exams.
- I would get to attend graduation.
- Dad will not take any action against the school, and they will be left to reprimand the teachers involved as they see fit.
- I was banned from future school athletics. However, it didn't matter as I was not returning for grade 13.

So basically, I got the last month of high school off other than coming in to write tests. Well, I couldn't argue with that. Not that I was in any position to argue.

As we left, the vice principal said one last thing. "If Ken knows of any other students who were drinking that night, maybe we could reduce the suspension further."

Seriously, did he just say that? I thought to myself.

Dad quickly replied, "I will leave that up to Ken; it's his decision."

Not a chance, Mr. VP. He must have been smoking something if he thought I would rat out my teammates; no possible good would come of that at this stage.

After we arrived back home, Dad told me, "What you did was very disappointing to your mother and me. It is very unlike you to do something like this. We are so sad that this is how you are ending your high school years.

"So, your punishment is knowing the fact that you let your mother and me down. I hope you learned your lesson. Now let's make better decisions moving forward, OK."

Then he and Mom walked away, leaving me by myself.

Jesus straightened up and asked her, "Woman, where are they?
Has no one condemned you?"

"No one, sir," she said. "Then neither do I condemn you," Jesus declared. "Go now and leave your life of sin." John 8:10-11

Whoa, I felt so bad and embarrassed. Talk about an awful punishment, and it was a punishment that would never go away. I had spent my whole life trying to prove myself, and just like that, I blew my reputation and trust with my parents.

High school was a lot of hard work, and I can't say I enjoyed it, but I managed to survive. When I began high school, I couldn't wait to be done to start working as a carpenter. Instead, now I found myself heading off on a different path, to a strange city for another three-and-a-half years of school, and who knows what.

How did I get to this point?

It started with Coach White challenging me on the football field, unleashing a drive and focus I didn't even know I had.

Mr. McLean, knowing my career goal, offered some timely advice that opened me up to other possibilities.

Finally, Mr. Aaronson encouraged me on my essay writing ability, and it was an essay that helped me win a scholarship.

Could this be Jesus working from afar, using these people to guide me onto a specific life path?

What about all the events that could have drastically changed my course in life? The car accident. A guidance counselor, though well-meaning, pointing me in the wrong direction. The track meet drinking incident that could have destroyed everything.

My earthly father was watching over me and helping me. Submitting the scholarship application, step-

Grade 12 graduation

ping in to help when I screwed up, making sure the punishment was fair and just.

So how much more was my heavenly Father helping me?

At graduation, I won an award, "Most Outstanding Student with a Technical Major." It was a complete surprise. I didn't even know there was such an award.

I thought of sending a copy of my prize to the vice principal and guidance counselor for a moment. But that would be cocky, and Mom would disapprove. Besides, high school was over. Fanshawe College, here I come.

Chapter 14:

On My Own

"The Lord himself goes before you and will be with you; he will never leave you nor forsake you. Do not be afraid; do not be discouraged."
Deuteronomy 31:8

I was all ready for my next adventure, moving to the big city in Southern Ontario. Well, a big city for me. In 1985 London, Ontario, had a population of about 265,000, about three-and-a-half times the size of Sault Ste. Marie.

Unfortunately, my Dodge Charger only got about 20 km (12 miles) to the gallon, and that was driving downhill with the wind behind me. So, I really couldn't afford the gas.

I would be leaving the car behind in the Sault for a bus pass. The plan was to bring the car down once I started my work placement. In the meantime, it was bussing it for me.

Fanshawe College didn't have any student housing. So earlier that summer, Dad, Mom, Dougie, and I made a quick trip down to secure a place for me to stay. We found a studio apartment on Adelaide St. N., just south of Kipps Lane, about a twenty-minute bus ride from the college.

Mrs. Reimer lived in London, Ontario, and helped us find the apartment. Mrs. Reimer was the mother of a family friend, May

Adshead. May attended the Sault Free Methodist Church, and Mom babysat her sons Jason and Brandon for years.

Mom stocked my apartment cupboards and fridge with food. Dad helped me set up a bank account and showed me how to write a check. Then, on Friday morning, bright and early, they headed back to Sault Ste. Marie. I was officially on my own.

Being on my own felt good for about thirty minutes. Then reality set in. *What do I do now?* I was alone. Really alone. I didn't know anybody, didn't have anything to do, or any place to go.

I had a little black-and-white 14" TV but no cable and I only received one channel. Most of the time it was fuzzy anyways. Few people had personal computers and there was no internet back then. Heck, I didn't even have an Atari to play video games.

The first thing I did was call the London Free Methodist Church and introduce myself. Then, talking to the pastor, he mentioned they had just broken ground on constructing a new church building on Commissioners Road, and he would arrange to have someone pick me up for Sunday service.

How cool is that? I thought I would be able to jump right in with this church.

Sunday finally arrived. I was excited to meet some new people and see the church construction site.

Growing up, anytime a college student came to visit our church, they would be welcomed with open arms and invited to people's homes and all sorts of activities. However, I soon found out that this was not normal.

I attended the church service, said hi to the pastor, a couple of people introduced themselves. Then I was driven back to my apartment and dropped off. I wasn't looking for a free lunch, and besides I knew how to cook. I was, though, expecting to be welcomed into the church and maybe invited to a Bible study or something. Instead, I ended up spending another dreary afternoon all by myself with nothing but a tennis match on the TV. Ugh!

It was still a week before classes began. I was there a week early because I had to write an English and math proficiency test as part of my enrollment, but that wasn't until Wednesday. So, Monday morning, I figured I would check out the church construction site.

Unfortunately, it took me two busses and almost an hour and a half to get there. Upon arrival, I introduced myself to the construction superintendent, Dave Johnson.

The church's general contractor was Grace Developments, and they let me help out with the construction. Of course, it was just volunteer work, so I wasn't getting paid, but it gave me something to do until school started.

I wrote my entry exams and, as expected, I did OK on the math test. But the English test? Well, that was another story. The college required me to take an added English course as part of my program. However, on a positive note, most of my classmates also ended up taking it. I guess we construction types just aren't so good at English.

Now in her fourth year at Brock University in St. Catharines, Debbie made the two-hour drive over to take me out for dinner for my eighteenth birthday. It was nice to have big sister visit after a few weeks of virtually no social interaction. After witnessing the torture of a single fuzzy television station, Debbie paid for me to get cable as a birthday gift. Woohoo! And just in time for football season.

Even though nobody was paying much attention to me at the church, I signed up to teach the eight-year-old boys' Sunday school class. I had more experience with preschoolers, but I thought I'd try teaching older kids this time.

One Sunday, Steve Rensberry picked me up for church. What a surprise! I didn't even know he was in town. Steve was about ten years older than me and the son of Pastor Merlyn Rensberry. Pastor Rensberry and his wife Gina pastored the Sault Free Methodist Church back in the '70s. Back in the day, Steve was a teenager when I was just a little kid, so it wasn't like we hung out together or anything.

It turns out Steve and his younger sister Donita were both living in London, Ontario, at the time. Steve had a piano tuning and refinishing business, a trade he learned from his father. Soon, I became one of his trusty piano movers. Of course, we also hit the occasional London Knights Junior A hockey game. Although he was at a different stage in life than I was, Steve became a good friend and supported me during my college years.

Even though I was lonely and on my own, the Lord had provided a familiar face who just coincidently ended up being in London the same years I was there.

There were a few kids around my age at the church, but I never seemed to click with them, always feeling like an outsider. Then, at church, I met a young woman named Angela. We were both the same age and sort of hit it off.

Angela and I started officially dating for about a month or so. The challenge was to see her. She lived with her parents, and it took me an hour and a half commute each way by bus. We would meet at her parent's home and watch Toronto Blue Jay playoff games or movies with her folks. To make creating deeper connections even worse, I had a time limit each visit. I had to leave by 9 p.m. to catch the bus connections back to my apartment.

Once school started kicking in, I decided to focus more on school and my future career than Angela. She was nice and all, but we didn't seem to have much in common, or so I thought.

Have you ever had one of those situations where the more you try to explain yourself, the worse you make it? Well, that's me with matters of the heart. In hindsight, I could have handled the situation with Angela a little better. But unfortunately, I tend to let my logic override my emotions. My college dating life ended before it even really got started.

There were about twenty students in my college class. It was a good group of hardworking guys, many coming from some sort of family construction background. Most students were from the surrounding cities and went home on weekends, so Thursday night was the big night to hit the pubs. I didn't go out with my classmates that first year. Instead, I focused on trying to develop relationships at the church. I was not a drinker and was probably overcorrecting myself from the past high school suspension debacle.

Truth be told, I was still new to being on my own and wanted to make sure I was making good decisions. As a result of my so-called good decisions, I ended up spending most of my time alone. Weekends were the worst. Other than church on Sunday, most weekends I would go from Friday afternoon until Monday morning without seeing or talking to a single soul.

Growing up in the Sault with a big extended family and involvement in the church, there were always people around and something going on. Now, I was on my big life adventure, bored out of my mind and lonely.

I was stuck in a studio apartment with no car. Well, at least thanks to Debbie, I had cable TV. So, I guess I shouldn't complain too much. While attending a nearby conference, Aunt Marion found out I was being overlooked at church. So, she talked to the young pastor and gave him some pastorally advice on pastoring.

Aunt Marion was Nanna's sister and married Pastor John Hyndman or Uncle John. Uncle John and Aunt Marion had pastored Free Methodist Churches for years.

After Aunt Marion's little discussion with the pastor, I occasionally got invited out to lunch by him and his wife on Sundays.

Meanwhile, back in the Sault, Paul Mathewson had done some transmission work on a small Dodge hatchback called an Omni. Sadly, the car owner went AWOL and did not pay Paul, so he took possession of the vehicle. The Omni got about

1986 Picking up my Dodge Omni for my first co-op work term

three times the gas mileage of my Charger. So, I sold my charger and bought the Omni from Paul.

After initially working as a volunteer on the church construction for Grace Developments, they hired me on as a laborer for my summer co-op.

Poppa stocked up my toolbox with all sorts of new hand tools for my work term. That summer, I worked primarily with superintendent Dave Johnson, doing a lot of excavation, backfill, and grading. I also worked on a concrete and formwork crew building footings and foundation walls.

He replied, "You of little faith, why are you so afraid?" Then he got up and rebuked the winds and the waves, and it was completely calm.
Matthew 8:26

One blistering hot, humid summer day, I was working with a small crew pouring foundations for a new church near St. Thomas, Ontario. It was so hot my eyeballs were sweating. As the concrete truck arrived, we saw a summer afternoon thunderstorm brewing in the distance. Those were some pretty ominous-looking clouds, so we kicked it into high gear to beat the rain. There is no stopping a concrete pour once the cement truck arrives. We frantically worked, pouring the concrete as a light drizzle began. The rain was almost a refreshing break from the baking afternoon sun.

A steady wind picked up as the raindrops increased in size and intensity. Flashes of lightning were now making the hair on my arms stand up, followed by booming claps of thunder.

As the winds and rain intensified, so did our resolve. No little storm would deter us from our goal of finishing the pour. Not to be outdone by our resolve, the rain and wind suddenly became enraged.

"Run for cover!" the superintendent yelled.

Dropping our shovels, we made a mad dash for the vehicles.

My little Dodge hatchback was the closest. Five of us burly construction workers shoehorned ourselves into the tiny orange car, slamming the doors behind us.

It was raining so hard you couldn't even see out the windows.

The wind began grabbing at the vehicle like the very hands of God were trying to lift us off the ground, only anchored by the weight of us five bulky men inside.

The car bounced up and down, and side to side, as the winds swirled around us.

After a couple of minutes, the storm gave up and moved on over the horizon, searching for another victim. We finished the concrete pour and ended the day on time and as scheduled.

Once home, I turned on the TV, and a tornado warning flashed across the bottom of the screen. The meteorologist said there were funnel clouds spotted in the area. However, they are still looking for evidence or witnesses of a tornado touching down.

Well, Mr. Meteorologist, I think I found your missing tornado, and it was no match for our concrete pouring crew.

That summer, the church put together a ball team to play in a men's slow-pitch league. We called ourselves the Sky Pilots. It's an old slang term from the 1800s referring to traveling preachers. Slow-pitch is big in Southern Ontario, with many leagues and tournaments. So, I was pretty excited about this. A few of my college classmates also decided to play.

Playing slow-pitch that summer, I developed some closer friendships, but not with the church guys. Instead, I got to know some of my college buddies a little better. Now, I couldn't talk biblical doctrines with my college buddies. Still, we did enjoy common interests of sports, school, and of course, construction.

Once school fired back up in the fall, I relaxed a bit and started hanging out more with my classmates. Oh, I was still that religious, Bible-thumper guy, and sort of intense at times. I was learning to stay true to my faith while at the same time building relationships with folks who may not have that relationship or understanding of Jesus.

My college program covered all aspects of construction. From contracts, engineering, and design to mechanical and electrical systems, surveying, and accounting to round things out. Most of the instructors had previously worked in the industry for large commercial construction companies.

I seemed to have a knack for the "estimating" courses. Something inside me naturally took to quantifying materials, figuring out how much labor was needed, and coming up with a price to build it.

Ever since I was a little guy, I could see a two-dimensional drawing and visualize it already built in 3D. I assume I learned this from Poppa's napkin sketches that he often did with a carpenter's pencil to show me what to do. Not to mention, taking four years of drafting in high school probably helped.

As spring break 1987 rolled around, Mom and Dad wanted to convert a downstairs closet to a second bathroom. It just so happens it was the same closet I tried to paint with lipstick when I was two and a half. It was my big chance to redeem myself. This time I planned and scheduled the project correctly, maintained budget, and of course, had permission from the homeowners: the result, a successful transformation from a closet to a bathroom for Mom and Dad.

As summer began, so did my second co-op internship. This time it would run from May through December for eight months. Once again, I would be working for Grace Developments.

The first month was slow as we were waiting for a couple of projects to get going. Grace Developments had hired a new project manager named John. Since it was slow, John brought me into the office to help with some estimating for the first month. That was all well and good, but I couldn't wait for some projects to start so I could get my tool belt back on.

Finally, a project needed some help. It was a Wesleyan Methodist Church in Markham, Ontario. The problem was it was east of Toronto and a two-hour-plus drive from my apartment, which was too far to commute every day.

Was I going to have to quit my job? That would put me into a whole other can of worms; I needed a certain amount of work hours to graduate.

Talking with Mom, she said, "Well, have you prayed about it?"

"No," I replied.

"Well, you pray about it, and your father and I will pray about it, and we shall see what happens."

Do not be anxious about anything, but in every situation, by prayer and petition, with thanksgiving, present your requests to God.
Philippians 4:6

Well, my prayers were quickly answered, sort of. The project superintendent really needed help that first week, so he offered to have me crash on his sofa for a few days.

Since I was in the Toronto area, I decided to call Jim and Esther Elliott to say hi. The last time I saw them was when they visited Sault Ste. Marie, about three years prior. Jim told me he and Esther had just moved into a brand spanking new house in Pickering, Ontario, a small community west of Toronto.

Jim invited me to drop by for dinner after work the next day. It turns out Jim and Esther's new place was only about a twenty-five-minute drive from the construction site.

After dinner that evening, Jim and Esther offered to let me stay with them for a couple of months until the church construction was completed. I would pay them a token amount for groceries, and Esther would even make me bag lunches every day.

It's sort of crazy. Ever since I was a baby, the Lord always somehow arranged to have Jim and Esther in the perfect location to help me. Fortunately, this time the location was close to the construction site.

The real miracle and answer to prayer were I never even mentioned to them I needed a place to stay; they just offered.

The church project was running behind schedule, so Grace Developments fired the superintendent, and project manager John came out to run the project. John was a decent guy but could get pretty fired up on the construction site. I guess he was under a lot of stress to complete the project on time.

The London church did not continue the slow-pitch team in the summer of 1987. Nevertheless, a few of my classmates including Scott Lupa, Murray McPhail, Frank Romano and I formed a new team. A car detailing company sponsored us, so our team's name changed from Sky Pilots to Zimmies Fine Shine.

I would make the two-hour commute from the Toronto construction site to the ball field on game nights. Then get up at 4:00 a.m. the following day to drive back to work. On weekends we played in a few tournaments at Softball City.

Early July rolled around, and my work at the Wesleyan Methodist Church ended. Grace Developments wanted to send me to another project even farther east of Toronto. But it was just too far away, especially with no living allowance or place to stay.

Fortunately, Dave Johnson, the superintendent I had worked for the previous summer, had a couple of his own projects on the go in the London area. So, Dave was able to give me about six weeks of work.

As usual, all good things come to an end. By Friday, August 7, I found myself out of work and attended a meeting at Fanshawe College with a co-op placement officer.

The officer reviewed my performance evaluation paperwork given by my employers. Unfortunately, with Grace Developments, John gave me a somewhat discouraging evaluation.

I was pretty surprised. I know I was not the fastest worker, but I thought I worked steadily and hard. Not to mention they had offered me another project. But unfortunately, I had to turn it down.

However, there was one interesting statement. It was under the question: Is there anything else you would like to comment about the student? John wrote he is good at estimating. Well, that's sort of random, but OK, at least he said one positive thing.

The placement officer told me it's not uncommon when you quit an employer for them not to give you the best evaluation. He said, just take what you can, learn from the comments, and move on. Besides, Dave Johnson gave you a complimentary assessment.

I spent the rest of the week dropping by construction sites handing out resumes. I needed to find another placement through December.

Friday, August 14, I drove three and a half hours to Ena and Larry's in Spring Arbor, Michigan, to attend the Spark Plug 400 NASCAR race at the Michigan International Speedway.

Paul Mathewson, Dave Steenburgh, and a couple of others from the Sault were driving down to attend. Once again, Bill Elliott was victorious, driving his Coors Ford Thunderbird.

After the race, I hung around Spring Arbor to let traffic die down before my long drive back to London, Ontario.

As I pulled out of Ena and Larry's driveway, the clock on my dash read 7:45 p.m. So, I figured that if traffic cooperates, I should get to my apartment by 11:30 p.m.

Turning onto Spring Arbor Rd. I followed the signs to I-94. Once on the interstate, I settled into my long drive to the Canadian Border.

At about 8:35 p.m., as the sun was beginning to set, massive thunderstorm clouds started to form directly in front of me. The lightning bolts were giving off a spectacular show against the setting sun.

It was like I was on a collision course with the storm as I raced down I-94. Soon the rain began; soft at first, then picking up intensity. Finally, the downpour got so hard I could barely see the road. So, I decided to pull to the shoulder and wait out the storm.

There were flashes of lightning instantaneously followed by ear-shattering claps of thunder as the torrential rain ran up and down the hood of my car.

Bringing the vehicle to a stop, I placed it in park, turning on my four-way flashers. I checked my time, and it was 8:43 p.m. I had been driving for an hour. Just as quickly as the storm kicked up, it passed. I put my signal on and started to accelerate as I pulled back onto the freeway; it was now 8:45 p.m. Just as I was getting to my cruising speed, the air was filled with a tremendous explosion. Without warning, the fiery ball of bright orange flame and black smoke shot hundreds of feet into the air, lighting up the entire skyline just up ahead.

What the heck! Was that a bomb?

That was my first thought as I sped down the freeway toward the location of the explosion.

Nah, it must have been a building or a warehouse explosion.

As I approached the explosion site, I drove into a thick bank of fog and smoke, and I could hardly see where I was going. The road became very rough and bumpy as I slowed down to a crawl, hoping not to hit another car, concrete freeway barrier, or worse.

Man, this stretch of road is rough, I thought. They must be working on repaving this section of the highway.

Looking out the window, I could see tufts of shrubs and what I assumed were pieces of the building on fire. There was this putrid odor in the air, filtering through my vents along with the smoke. I took a shot of my inhaler to help me breathe. As I drove out of the smoke bank, I could now hear the sound of a helicopter overhead and barely see its flashing red light.

Clearing the explosion site, I sped up to 75 miles (112 km) per hour, trying to make up for the lost time. I finally arrived home at about 11:30 p.m. It had been a long day. So, I went straight to bed and crashed for the night.

The following morning my alarm set to a radio station went off.

"Last night just past 8:45 p.m., Northwest Airlines Flight 255 crashed shortly after takeoff from Detroit Airport, killing 154 people on board. The sole survivor was a four-year-old girl."

I quickly sat up in utter shock.

What? Did I hear that right? Am I still sleeping? I must be dreaming, some sort of nightmare!

It was no nightmare. I had seen a plane crash.

Emotions of seeing a disaster like that are hard to describe, from the sheer horror of realizing what I had seen to the thankfulness of a rainstorm that had slowed me down. I had unknowingly driven right through the middle of the debris field only minutes after the crash. The fact that I did not hit anything is a miracle in itself.

What about all those people that died that day? Why did it happen, Lord? Why didn't you prevent it? So many people's lives were affected, family and friends in shock.

A little girl lost her parents and brother. An event like this cannot be unseen. It's seared into my memory and will never be erased. The totality of the events that weekend made my worries about not having a job seem almost selfish. My prayers were once again soon answered when I received a phone call from one of my classmates, Murray McPhail.

Murray had been working as a superintendent for David K. Hill and Company, a small local general contractor. Dave Hill was a graduate of Fanshawe College, now in his mid to late '30s.

Dave's company was doing well, and he hired me on. I helped out on the construction sites working with the carpenters. I did a little of everything, including demolition, concrete work, mixing masonry grout, framing, installing doors, cabinetry, and drywall.

Dave Hill even made use of my drafting training. He would send me out to visit potential residential clients. I would discuss with them and document the scope of work they wanted.

Then I would take measurements and draw up floor plans for presentation and pricing.

On Sunday, December 6, 1987, I talked with Mom on the phone. She said I might be getting a call from Uncle Reg, as he and Aunt Bessie were down in London for her eye surgery. London, Ontario, is a major medical center, and sometimes people from the smaller cities are sent there for procedures.

Mom told me Uncle Ed and Aunt Merle had also made the trip with them. Uncle Ed was Nanna and Uncle Reg's youngest brother.

I had planned to drop by the hospital for a visit on Monday but didn't finish work until 9:00 p.m., so it was way too late to head to the hospital. I wanted to get over and visit Aunt Bessie, but it was a bad week. We were going to be burning the midnight oil, trying to keep a project on schedule. I just didn't know how I would be able to break free for a visit.

Tuesday, December 8, afternoon rain clouds started to move in, and by 3:00 p.m., it was raining cats and dogs. Due to the rain, we had to close down the construction site early that day.

Taking advantage of the rain delay, I figured I would head home, clean up, and visit Aunt Bessie in the hospital.

When I got to my apartment, Mom had left a message on my answering machine.

"Your aunt is in a secure recovery area, so you will need Uncle Reg to get you signed in at the hospital."

Arriving at the hospital, I walked to the front desk.

"Can you tell me where Bessie Hawdon's room is?" I asked.

The receptionist checked her screen. "Mrs. Hawdon is in a secure recovery area. Can I see your ID?"

"Where is that?" I asked as I pulled out my ID and prepared to explain who I was. But, at that very moment, the reception phone rang.

The woman picking up the phone quickly engaged in a rather heated exchange with the person on the other end. After about fifteen seconds, she pointed me toward the recovery care directional sign on the wall as she continued her phone conversation.

Well, that's pretty lax security, I thought as I placed my unchecked ID back in my pocket and headed to recovery.

As I approached the closed doors, I wondered how I would get Uncle Reg's attention to let me in. Of course, there were no cell phones back in those days, but at that very moment, the door swung open.

Someone inside must have come too close to the auto opener because nobody came out the door. I walked in and right past an unattended nurse's station. After wandering around for a while, I finally found Aunt Bessie.

She was propped up in her hospital bed, with white gauze wrapping around the side of her head, covering one eye. I noticed her glasses sitting on the bedside table.

"Hi there, do you know who I am?" I asked, now standing at the foot of her bed, wondering if she could see me at all.

"Well, of course, I'm not totally blind." Aunt Bessie responded with a smile. "Your uncles and Aunt Merle just left to go get some dinner."

Aunt Bessie asked me many questions about how I was doing with my schooling and what Debbie and Dougie were up to these days. She told me Poppa was very proud of me and always kept Uncle Reg updated on my work.

"I hope Reg gets back soon so he can see you," she said just as her dinner was delivered.

I quickly noticed the small scoop of ice cream sitting on her dinner tray. I couldn't help but comment, "Well, that's a pretty tiny scoop of ice cream, sure not like the bowls you used to give me."

Aunt Bessie laughed, then suddenly started gasping and taking rapid breaths as she tried to speak. I thought she was hyperventilating as her one uncovered eyelid started to flicker rapidly.

A nurse rushed over, pulling the cubical curtain around the bed. She told me I needed to leave now. A second nurse walked me out the door and said, "Wait here."

After about ten minutes, the one nurse came back and told me, "You're not going to be able to go back in tonight."

I waited around for about fifteen minutes to see if, by chance, I could catch Uncle Reg. But no luck, so I headed home for the evening. I figured maybe tomorrow I'll take an extended lunch break and visit again.

It hit me as I left the hospital; nobody ever asked who I was.

I stopped and got some dinner on my way home, then picked up some groceries. Entering my apartment, I saw the flashing red light on my answering machine. Then hitting the play button, I headed to the kitchen to unpack the groceries.

"It's your mother here. I just wanted to let you know your Aunt Bessie passed away this evening, just in case you planned to go to the hospital. So, give us a call when you get this."

What? It can't be. Did I hear that right? I ran over and hit replay on the answering machine. Then I hit it a third time. Something is not right; this makes no sense. Aunt Bessie is only sixty-eight years old, and I was just talking to her at the hospital.

I quickly called Mom.

Mom said she didn't have all the details, but it must have been a blood clot or stroke. Mom suspected the reason I was not allowed back into the room was that Aunt Bessie was already gone.

I originally planned to work until December 23, then go home for the week at Christmas. I would then be back at school Monday, January 4, to complete my final eight months of classes.

However, given the circumstances, I felt I needed to drive to the Sault for Aunt Bessie's funeral.

I discussed this with Dave Hill, and he agreed I should quit work a couple of weeks ahead of schedule and make the trip back to the Sault. Auntie Dot walked over to me at the funeral, grabbed me by the forearm, and looked me right in the eyes.

"One of your Aunt Bessie's prayers was that she would not be alone when she died."

Auntie Dot then smiled, patted me on the arm, and walked away. The Lord had often sent people into my life that provided an answer to my prayers. This time he used me to answer one of Aunt Bessie's prayers. This time it wasn't about me; it was about the Lord's faithfulness to Aunt Bessie, right to the day and time she took her last breath. I look forward to the day I see her again in heaven. I'm sure she will be waiting with a big bowl of ice cream.

With only a couple of months left before finishing college, I couldn't wait to be done with school. Actually, I wanted to be done with school on that first day of kindergarten back in 1972, but Mom made me go back. Now here I am sixteen years later, finally almost finished.

I planned to start my carpentry apprenticeship at David K. Hill and Company and get credit for all those hours logged on the construction sites over the past few years.

That was my plan, but the Lord was preparing a different plan for me. Another change in direction setting my feet on yet another new path.

One day our estimating instructor Mr. Tindale asked if I could hang back after class. It turns out he had been talking to a large commercial general contractor in Toronto. It was one of the largest general contractors in all of Canada, and they were interested in interviewing me for an estimating position in their Toronto Office.

"Thanks, Mr. Tindale, but I'm planning on doing a carpenter apprenticeship, plus I'm not a big city guy."

"That's good, but I think you have good instincts for estimating. It doesn't hurt to just go to the interview."

Well, I didn't want to live in Toronto, nor get stuck in an office, but I couldn't get the talk with Mr. Tindale out of my head.

I called Poppa to talk it over. He told me working the tools is fun, but it gets much more challenging when you get into your fifties and sixties; the aches and pains start catching up to you.

Poppa said he enjoyed the less physical managerial office work that he did at Plumber Hospital toward the end of his career.

Fanshawe College Class of 1988 Construction Engineering Technology Management

Advice in hand, I decided to go for the interview, and wouldn't you know it; they offered me the job. I would be starting work as an estimator the day after Labor Day, Tuesday, September 6, 1988, which also happened to be my twenty-first birthday.

I liked London, Ontario, but I was moving on to the Big City of Toronto now. I had grown up a lot over my three and a half years in college—having learned how to live on my own, support myself, and what it meant to be lonely. I attended the London Free Methodist Church for three years, and not once was I invited to anyone's home except, of course, to Angela's parents' place a few times. All in all, it was OK and I believe it worked out that way for a reason. I needed to experience what it was like to be alone. It made me appreciate the people the Lord sent into my life all the more. I discovered that I could have friendships with people who may not share the same beliefs. I learned to set boundaries that enabled me to keep my core values and faith in Jesus Christ without compromise.

This chapter of my life was ending; a different chapter was about to begin. I was on a new path, a collision course with the construction Big Leagues.

Chapter 15:

The Big Leagues

"Suppose one of you wants to build a tower. Won't you first sit down and estimate the cost to see if you have enough money to complete it? For if you lay the foundation and are not able to finish it, everyone who sees it will ridicule you, saying, 'This person began to build and wasn't able to finish.'" Luke 14:28-30

Wouldn't you know it, the week before leaving for Toronto, my Dodge Omni died. It lasted just long enough to get me through college, then gave up the ghost. On my way out of town, I bought my first truck, a red 1988 Chevrolet S10.

Jim & Esther

My biggest challenge in moving to Toronto was finding somewhere to live. The affordable rental availability was less than 1 percent at the time. In addition, I had the added difficulty of allergies and asthma, eliminating places with dogs, cats, smokers, or too much dust.

Once again, Jim and Esther came to the rescue. They knew a fella named Paul Severn, who just happened to be looking for someone to rent a room in his house on Gooderham Drive in Scarborough, Ontario.

Paul was a fellow Christian and a high school teacher in his mid-forties who had never married. He was also a big football and hockey fan. The NFL season had just started, so we got along great.

I found out that my high school friends, Scott and Rob Pinches, had recently moved to Toronto, which was great news as I did not know anybody in Toronto other than Jim and Esther, of course.

Mom got me set up with a new wardrobe for the office. It was time for ditching my steel-toed boots, blue jeans, and T-shirts for dress pants, button-down shirts, and ties.

On September 6, 1988, I arrived for my first day of work, dressed up all fancy like I was going to church. Stepping off the elevator, I entered a large front reception area with floors made of polished granite. The walls were covered with photos and murals of landmark construction projects, including office towers, hospitals, and sports arenas.

An impressive life-size company logo was on the wall behind the long marble reception desk. I felt like that first episode of *The Beverly Hillbillies* when they arrived in the big city for the first time. After getting all signed in with the Human Resources Department, I was taken back to my very own personal office. It was a ten by twelve-foot space with a large eight-foot-tall solid wood entry door. An aluminum plaque with my name clung to the door at about eye level.

In the office on the left was a desk and one of those office chairs on wheels. To the right was a long plan table, where I could lay out my blueprints for estimates.

A box of business cards, a notepad, and a hard hat were sitting on top of the desk, all with the company logo and "Ken I. McQuarrie" printed on them.

I sat down and spun around on the chair a few times. Have you ever found yourself in a place you feel you just don't belong? Well, that was me. I thought, *Jeepers, this is way too fancy for a guy like me. I don't deserve this.*

My first assignment was to complete a concrete structure estimate for a forty-seven story, five-star luxury condominium complete with a multi-level underground parking garage.

My job was to do all the quantities for the concrete and formwork. Then, I would summarize on a Lotus 1-2-3 spreadsheet for pricing once finished. It was going to be the first attempt for the department to do an estimate on a computer. Dang, I guess I should have taken a typing course in high school.

A senior estimator met with me, and after showing me an example, explained how I should quantify and summarize things for pricing. Once I finished, he would review my work and price it with me. I had three weeks to complete the task. Finally, the senior estimator said, "Come see me if you have any questions," then he left my office. This particular senior estimator was being groomed to take over as chief estimator. A chief estimator is a senior manager that runs the entire estimating department. I guess that would make him "Little Chief" for now.

A forty-seven-story concrete estimate was a pretty tall order for my first assignment, and to be honest, quite overwhelming. Sure, I had done some small estimates in the past, but this was an enormous project. I sat there a while, just staring at the stack of blueprints. There must have been a thousand sheets. Then I heard Poppa's voice in my head, "If you don't get started, you will never finish." Armed with a scale rule, a box of pencil crayons, and some highlighters, I dug into my task at hand.

You estimate a project like you build it, starting with the foundations, and ending with the roof slab, in this case, some forty-seven stories up in the sky. The project must have had thirty different types and sizes of foundations, not to mention hundreds of structural details to understand and quantify.

The ground floor structural slab was a nightmare of beams and slab thickenings. Being my first time tackling anything like this, I had hundreds of questions.

Every time I went to ask Little Chief a question, he seemed annoyed, and at times quite snappy in his responses. He was not much help at all. I was just wanting to make sure I was doing it correctly. Whatever happened to the saying, "There is no such thing as a dumb question"? Luckily an older senior estimator helped me out a lot.

I was putting in crazy long hours trying to meet my deadline. Getting to the office by 7:30 a.m., I rarely left before 9:00 p.m. I even worked on weekends. A senior vice president happened to drop by the office two weekends in a row. He asked me, "Kenny, why are you working weekends?"

After showing him what I was working on, he said. "I'll let you in on a little secret; you will get more done if you take at least one day a week off. Working seven days a week, you are going to burn yourself out." I guess he was right; even God created the world in six days, then took a day off.

It was late on Friday night, my three weeks were up, and I wasn't done with my estimate. I had failed and was probably going to get fired. That night Mom called to see how I was doing on my deadline.

I told Mom that I would not be able to finish. At this, Mom responded, "But you still have two days left."

"Yeah, but there is no way I will get finished. It's a forty-seven-story tower, and I just finished the ground floor. The underground parking took me forever."

"Did you pray about it?"

"Mom, it's too late; praying is not going to help now."

"I see; well, you need to listen to your mother. I will hang up the phone, and you're going to pray about it. Your father and I will also pray about it, and we shall see what happens. Now I want you to go to the office over the weekend and work your butt off. I didn't raise you to be a quitter."

Reluctantly I listened to Mom. I had a surprisingly good sleep Friday night, considering all the stress I was under. I hit the office bright and early Saturday morning. Then by Sunday at 6:00 p.m., I turned off the lights in my office and stepped onto the elevator.

I was finished. Not finished as in I would lose my job. But, finished as in I had completed my estimate.

Prayer had worked! That whole weekend, my mind was clear and focused. Once I quantified the tower's second floor, the next forty-four floors were similar, or as we call it in construction, "typical."

After three weeks, I knew the drawings and details inside out, so I was able to quantify and record quantities fast and furious like the building was on fire.

Some doubters may say, well, you were almost finished and just didn't know it. My response to that is, I was tired and burnt out after three long weeks. So, prayers went up, and Jesus came down, giving me energy and clarity of mind, filling my brain with ideas of systems and shortcuts to help me complete my task.

Monday morning, Little Chief seemed surprised that I had finished. There was no "Excellent job" or "Attaboy." He simply reviewed and priced my work. His only actual comment was that I went into too much detail, but that's better than not enough detail, right?

Oh well, I finished, so I had survived to estimate another day.

Socially I was trying to adjust to the big city. Most Saturday nights, I would hang out with Scott Pinches. He worked in guitar sales at Steve's Music Store on Queen Street, downtown Toronto. It was a popular place in the Toronto music scene; many professional musicians, both famous and aspiring, would frequent Steve's Music. Scott is a guitar player himself and was trying to get a Christian rock band started. So, he and I hung out with many musicians in those days.

Rob Pinches was engaged to be married to Cathy and living up in Barrie, Ontario, about an hour's drive from Toronto. I wouldn't see Rob as often, but we still found time to get together and discuss relevant life matters. Like who between us could throw a baseball the hardest and farthest. Oh, yeah, and why he and his brother were such big Pittsburgh Steelers fans. Like, come on, Steelers fans are the most obnoxious fans in the entire NFL.

Regardless, Scott and Rob are like brothers to me, and it was fantastic having them down in Toronto those years.

I got my next assignment back at the office, bidding on an 850,000 square foot office complex complete with a four-level, 750,000 square foot above-grade parking garage shaped like an enormous pork chop.

My task was to prepare the estimate for the pork chop garage. In addition, I would be working with our in-house structural engineer to design and price out the formwork systems for the concrete monstrosity.

Once again, Little Chief was the lead estimator on the entire project pursuit. As with the previous bid, he was of little help when I asked questions. I know he was under a lot of pressure, but I was surprised he was not more helpful. After all, we were on the same team, and I was trying to help him.

Starting my quantity takeoff, I noticed the garage's curved concrete perimeter walls consisted of about seven similar radiuses that repeated themselves. So, this meant we could prefabricate seven different sets of forms, one set for each radius. That way, each form type could be reused multiple times, saving lots of time and money for construction.

Taking my garage floor plan, I color-coded the walls a different color for each different radius. Then, working with our engineer, he designed unique curved forms for each color-coded section.

The forming crew could now use each section of formwork fifteen to twenty times as the parking garage gets built. My color-coded blueprint was the key to the whole plan.

After weeks of preparing the estimate for bid, it was time to review with the company owner and executive vice president.

Little Chief did not want me in the estimate review meeting. However, he wanted me to stick around in my office to be available for questions if needed. So, I set up the conference room with all the plans and specifications for the big meeting, including my color-coded garage wall layout.

About an hour into the review meeting, Little Chief comes to my office and says, "I need that color-coded drawing you did for the parking garage formwork."

"I put it in the conference room earlier with all the other drawings."

"No, you didn't; you better find that drawing." Then Little Chief retreated back to the meeting.

Frantically I started to look around the estimating department for that drawing. I could have sworn I had put it in the conference room.

A few minutes later, Little Chief returned. "Well, where is it?"

"I'm sorry I can't find it."

"You better find it, or tomorrow you may not have a job!"

Desperately, I tore the office apart, looking for that drawing, but to no avail. I had no idea what could have happened.

A third time, Little Chief returned. "Well?" he said as he shrugged his arms.

"I looked everywhere. It's gone!" I said with panic in my voice.

At this, Little Chief just angrily grunted, now all red in the face, looking at me with eyes like daggers as he turned and went back to the meeting.

The estimate review ended at about 7:00 p.m.; everyone left without telling me. I was still sitting in my office when the structural engineer passed by, surprised to see me sitting there.

"The meeting is over, Ken; you should head home."

"Gee, thanks; how did it go?"

"It went well. Oh, just so you know, I walked by the conference room; Little Chief was cleaning up after the meeting. When he pulled back the stack of plans, your color-coded garage plan was at the bottom of the pile. Then when Little Chief saw it, he crumpled it up and tossed it into the trash can."

I couldn't believe what I was hearing; the drawing was in the meeting all along. From that moment on, I knew I could not trust Little Chief. I was dealing with yet another type of bully.

Whoever is patient has great understanding, but one who is quick-tempered displays folly. Proverbs 14:29

As you can probably guess, I did not get fired the next day for not finding the garage plan. Little Chief did ignore me all day, though.

My first thought was to walk into Little Chief's office and thump him, but I have never hit anyone, and I was not about to start. Instead, I wished I could get Little Chief onto a football field, and then I could show him what it feels like to get tackled, tackled hard, very hard.

Finally, bid closing day arrived, construction's version of game day. So, thumping Little Chief would have to wait. Our estimate was complete; it was approved by upper management. All that remained was to receive the subcontractor quotes, finish our price, and submit our bid by 2:00 p.m. sharp. If you are one second late, you're disqualified with a lump sum bid.

We would be receiving over the telephone more than 350 quotations from various subcontractors and suppliers competing for the project. So, our mission was to develop the best combination of about seventy trades to build the job with the complete scope of work for the lowest possible price.

Sounds easy, right? Well, we had only six hours to complete the task, and the subcontractors kept changing their pricing throughout the day, vying to be the low bidder. It was a fast-paced day of wheeling and dealing, and that clock kept ticking.

About twelve of us were in one large conference room or "The War Room," as we called it. Each person was armed with a telephone and a blank pad of phone quotation sheets and was assigned a few trade sections to analyze. I was assigned the excavation and backfill, plus the concrete placing and finishing. My first order of business was to call all the subcontractors in Toronto relating to my designated trade sections. It was an exhaustive list of over one hundred companies. I made my calls and discovered twelve excavation companies and eight concrete placing companies bidding. I had scoped out my subcontractors, and all that was left was for the numbers to come in.

With only about an hour and a half to the deadline, the companies began calling in their pricing. Not just my subcontractors but also the subs of the other folks in the war room.

It was sheer pandemonium. Phones were ringing, everyone trying to talk over each other, wheeling and dealing back and forth. Some pricing even came in over this new device called a fax machine.

We gave our lowest price combinations to Little Chief, who was compiling all the low bids as the clock seemed to be picking up speed. The numbers kept changing as time was running out. Finally, with only two minutes to go, Little Chief relayed our final bid price over the phone to the bid runner, who was using a 1988 mobile brick phone for the first time.

The runner nervously wrote our price onto the bid form, placed it in a sealed envelope, and sprinted to hand it to the owner's representative with now only seconds to go before the 2:00 p.m. deadline. We did it; our bid was submitted. The tension in the room snapped back like a rubber band as we all went brain dead after the stressful countdown to closing.

I had just taken part in my first hard bid closing. It was an exhilarating but mentally exhausting experience. Shortly after, we heard the news. We won the bid! Woohoo! After so much effort put into a big project like that, it felt like we had won the lottery. The whole office paused to celebrate. However, the celebration was a short one because it was on to my next project the next day.

This time it was a big hotel. I still wasn't sure what to do about Little Chief and the missing parking garage plan. I suppose a holier man than me would pray about it and instantly forgive. However, I was not that man. I did pray about it but was not quite ready to forgive. I figured I was still in the danger zone, so forgiveness would have to wait.

As the year progressed, I took on more responsibility for each project. Eventually, it got to the point that I was the lead estimator on the smaller projects and the concrete structure guy on the larger ones. It was a tremendous amount of work, and the long hours continued. I rarely left the office before 7:00 p.m. and worked at least one day most weekends.

Now, one may think I was making a lot of money working those long hours. Well, one would be wrong. I was a salaried employee now, meaning I got a salary based on a forty-hour work week, nothing more, nothing less. It sure was different from when I was on the construction sites getting paid for every hour worked. So many days, I wondered if it was even worth it.

Little Chief was a bit friendlier after winning the big bid, but he still had moody moments. Plus, I didn't trust him. Thankfully, more and more, I was working under the big chief estimator, given I was taking on more responsibility.

Throughout the year, I quietly observed and carefully listened to all the goings-on around me. But unfortunately, this big-league construction stuff seemed to be quite cutthroat. I silently saw a few things that I disagreed with from an ethical perspective. They say it's the "grey area." However, I had always been pretty black and white. I guess I can thank Mom and Dad for that. With us McQuarries, what you see is what you get; it's as simple as that. Maybe I was getting a bit paranoid after what had transpired with Little Chief, but I just had this sense; perhaps this is not the place for me. So, I continued to pray that the Lord would protect me, and if need be, open another door for me to go through.

Meanwhile, back in Sault Ste. Marie, love was in the air. David West asked Lori Niemi to marry him, and fortunately for David, she said yes. David had hung back in the Sault for grade 13, the year I left for college. That same year he started dating Lori. With college behind them and their whole life ahead, it was time for a wedding. David asked me to be one of his groomsmen. The date had been set for July 29, 1989.

I had a little challenge getting time off to attend the wedding festivities. I had already used up my vacation days for college graduation and some time to go home at Christmas. Although at Christmas, I did bring work home with me.

I asked the chief estimator if I could advance one day's vacation from my next year's allotment to drive up Friday for the wedding rehearsal. I figured it wouldn't be a problem given all the extra time I had worked.

To my surprise, the chief estimator said no. He would not let me take any more vacation until I accrued more days into my second year.

I pointed out that I worked most weekends over the past year and took work home over Christmas. But unfortunately, his answer was still no.

That really sucked. I mean, on numerous occasions, I had run personal errands for the chief. For example, I picked up fresh lobster for his dinner parties, used my truck to deliver new French doors to his home. Not to mention all the beer runs I did for the estimating team on nights before bid closings. And I don't even drink!

This response did not sit well with me, but I didn't argue. Instead, I took a deep breath and prayed about it. "Lord, I don't think these are the kind of people I want to be working for. I need direction on where I should go from here. P.S. I also need to find a way to get to David's wedding."

It was now one month before the wedding, and we were bidding on yet another large project. This time everyone was excited as we would be competing against PCL Construction. So, I had to ask, what's the big deal, and who is PCL?

"You don't know who PCL is?" asked a senior project manager. Well, the short answer was no. I'm from a small northern city; I don't know about any large general contractors.

It turns out PCL Construction was the largest general contractor in all of Canada and one of the top 10 largest contractors in North America. The company was started by Ernie Poole back in 1906 under Poole Construction Ltd.

Ernie Poole's two sons sold the company to senior employees in 1977. Then on March 1, 1979, the company changed its name to PCL Construction Ltd. So now I knew who PCL was. Not only that, but we beat them out on the bid that day. This got me to thinking, maybe PCL could use some help. I pulled out the yellow pages about mid-week and looked up PCL Construction. They had an office in Etobicoke, off Highway 427.

I called the phone number, and the receptionist answered. "PCL Construction, how may I direct your call?"

"I'd like to speak to the person in charge of estimating, please."

"Just a minute while I transfer the call."

I waited nervously, and after about a minute, a voice answered. "Hello, this is Ted."

"Hi, Ted, my name is Ken, and I am a junior estimator about a year out of college. We just beat you guys on that bid last week. However, I'm not very happy here and was wondering if you could use any estimating help?"

It turns out I was talking with Ted Cook, PCL's vice president of development. Ted was in charge of the business development and estimating for PCL's Toronto District office. Ted wanted to meet with me, so I dropped by PCL's office after work the next day. The interview went well, and Ted called to offer me a job the next day. I got offered a 10 percent higher salary than I was currently making. Oh, and get

David, Lori, the ring bearer, and me. I'm the one on the right. Sorry about the lousy smile; the sun was in my eyes.

this, with three weeks annual vacation instead of the standard two. Talk about an answer to prayer. Have you heard the saying, "Go big or go home"? Well, I was going big, all the way to the top of the Canadian construction industry. But I was also going home, to David and Lori's wedding, that is.

I gave my two-week notice to my current employer, with a last day of work Wednesday, July 26, just in time to drive up for Dave and Lori's wedding rehearsal Friday.

Jesus had opened up a new door, and the timing was perfect, with even one day to spare.

Get rid of all bitterness, rage and anger, brawling and slander, along with every form of malice. Be kind and compassionate to one another, forgiving each other, just as in Christ God forgave you.
Ephesians 4:31-32

I still had to forgive Little Chief for his actions. I was working on it, but I can't say I was quite there yet. But then, my previous employer called about a month after I started working at PCL. That big office complex and porkchop garage was now under construction. Before leaving for PCL, I had priced a sizeable structural change order for the project manager. Now the owner was disputing the cost. So, the project manager asked if I could attend a meeting to review my pricing. The manager said he would pay me a consulting fee. After thinking about it, I told him I would help him free of charge; professional courtesy, so to speak. So maybe I was farther along on forgiving Little Chief and that company after all.

It had been a whole year now since I graduated from college. I missed working on the tools and the sounds and smells of the construction site, but I was on a new path now. I didn't know it at the time, but this path was going to take me on adventures beyond my wildest dreams.

Chapter 16:

Fireside Chat

"Forget the former things; do not dwell on the past. See, I am doing a new thing! Now it springs up; do you not perceive it? I am making a way in the wilderness and streams in the wasteland." Isaiah 43:18-19

My first month at PCL was reasonably light-duty, at least lighter than I had experienced in the previous year. PCL had a proprietary computer estimating program. It ran on a Disk Operating System or "DOS" platform, as referred to back then. With work being slow, I practiced my computer skills while learning the estimating program.

Chief estimator Steve Jackson was much more approachable and supportive than the guys at my previous employer. Unfortunately, that support was short-lived. A couple of months after I started work, Steve took a medical leave of absence.

Ted Cook began to use me for his business development proposals. I would do the quantity takeoff for his high-level concept budgets. Of course, the quickest way to a potential client's heart is to give them something for free. In this case, it was a free budget estimate on their project.

A large office complex came in for us to bid. All the senior estimators were preoccupied with other projects, so Ted gave this one to me. It was my first big chance to be the lead estimator on a significant project. Light duty time was over; it was time to get to work.

I sprang into action, getting my request for bid letters out to all the subcontractors, followed by pulling together all the contract and financial information. Our finance and administration department needed to review this stuff, ensuring there were no contractual deal-breakers.

As I read through the technical specifications, I set up my trade sections in the PCL estimating program.

I was now ready to start my concrete structure estimate. As usual, I would work with in-house engineering and purchasing departments on form systems, cranes, and hoists. After about three weeks and a lot of late nights, I had all my structural and architectural quantities completed and, in my estimate, ready for pricing.

Chief Estimator Steve was still on leave, so I asked Ted who I should get to help me price the estimate.

"Talk to Chris Morris," Ted said.

Chris was a senior estimator and had been working on a GMP for the massive Bay Adelaide Center project, a large office complex on Bay St. and Adelaide St. W. in downtown Toronto.

GMP is short for a guaranteed maximum price, a contract type where the general contractor guarantees the overall cost and schedule before the design is even complete.

With a GMP contract, if the final price comes in lower than the stated contract amount, the owner and general contractor split the savings. Sounds pretty good, eh?

Well, hold your horses. The general contractor takes 100 percent of the loss if the price goes over the GMP. Thus, the term guaranteed maximum price.

Meeting with Chris, he looked over my estimate and asked a few questions. Then he said, "Looks like you have a pretty good understanding of things. How about you take the first pass at pricing everything, then I'll review it."

"OK, I'll give it a go," I responded, always up for a challenge.

Chris gave me a binder full of PCL historical concrete and form-work productivities, as well as some crane and hoist production charts. He also gave me a copy of an estimate he had priced of similar size and magnitude. The following week, I would study the historical information and price up my estimate. After I finished pricing, Chris reviewed, making a few adjustments. I was now ready to review the project with our vice president and district manager, Al Troppmann.

Al was in his early forties and, just a year prior, had been appointed Toronto district manager. Like me, Al had come from a smaller northern city and spent time estimating at the beginning of his career. Al was about the same height as me, standing about five foot seven, give or take an inch. The main difference being I was built like a football running back in those days, and Al was, well…not. He was a big football fan, so we had a few things in common.

Al told me to walk him through the drawings. Of course, there wasn't any actual walking involved; he just meant for me to show him the plans and tell him about the project.

After our little stroll through the drawings, Al started to flip through the pages of my estimate, asking questions as he went.

"What trades are bidding curtainwall?"

"How many ceramic tile bidders do you have looking at the project?"

I think these were just some softball questions to get me warmed up. After the warm-ups, Al dug into the concrete and formwork estimate.

Now the hardball questions began as Al interrogated me on each item in my detailed concrete estimate.

"Why did you use that unit productivity?"

"What projects did we achieve that unit?"

"How did you arrive at that material price?"

"How many formwork reuses are you anticipating?"

I had to explain my thought process and provide my backup info for each fastball question Al threw at me. I have to admit Al could throw some heat.

Sometimes, I didn't have a good response, but I nervously debated my case as best I could.

But Al, with a half-grin on his face, seemed to enjoy watching me squirm as I tried to explain myself.

"You are not convincing me," Al would say, followed by "double it" or "bump that unit up twenty percent."

After about an hour and a half of interrogation and debate, my brain was reduced to a mental marshmallow. Al, seemingly to take mercy on me, finally said, "Good job. Make the changes we talked about, and print me a revised copy of the estimate."

Whew, I survived my first Al Troppmann review. I had learned a lot from meeting with Al. Now that I knew all his go-to questions, I would be more prepared next time. Next up, I was sent to Ottawa to budget an office building on Sparks Street. PCL had the Ottawa World Exchange Plaza under construction and wanted to establish a new district office there.

The company booked me into the Four Seasons hotel on Albert Street as it was within walking distance to the office. Talk about a hillbilly moment; I had never been inside such a fancy pants hotel like this. Also, it had a doorman who wanted to carry my suitcase. "Nope, I can carry my own bag, thank you very much."

The hotel room was bigger than an apartment. I checked the room service menu, but the prices were insane. So, I walked to a nearby submarine sandwich shop for a much more economical meal. Even though PCL was footing the bill, I didn't want to take advantage of the company.

PCL eventually sent a young up-and-coming manager named Paul Douglas to be the Ottawa district manager. I met Paul when he visited the Toronto office shortly after arriving from Edmonton.

Then the news came that our chief estimator Steve Jackson would not be returning. So, Chris Morris became the new chief estimator.

Based on my performance leading that previous estimate, Chris let me be the lead estimator on all my projects from that point on. Being a lead estimator was a lot of pressure and responsibility, but I was up for the task. I would log in plenty of long hours to make up for my lack of experience, studying cost forecasts and historical data. Of course, when I got the chance, I still visited the construction sites, always asking the superintendents and tradespeople loads of questions to incorporate into my estimates.

I struggled to find the right church to attend that first couple of years in Toronto. You may think a church is a church; what's the big deal? The deal is that many churches preach Jesus Christ's gospel but have different styles of going about it. I like good old theological preaching and biblical history, stuff that would challenge me and make me think. But not so theological that the preacher uses big words like presuppositions, ecumenical, and immutability. Remember, I didn't do so well in English class. Being in my early twenties, I was also looking for a church with an active twenty-something group.

Eventually, I settled into Kingsview Free Methodist Church in Etobicoke. They had a sizable 20s group and a bunch of guys that would rent ice time in the winter to play hockey. So, armed with my trusty inhaler, I was finally playing real hockey with skates, pads, and a helmet.

Like most major North American cities, traffic in Toronto is very congested and slow most of the time. It took me upwards of an hour each way to make the daily 30 km (20 mile) commute.

Not to mention, the hot, humid Toronto summers were brutal. Sitting in traffic for hours in my non-airconditioned truck was not fun. So, I traded in my truck for an airconditioned Pontiac Sunbird.

I also ended up moving from Paul Severn's house in Scarborough to a high-rise rental in Mississauga called "The Mansion." It was a nice building. However, my 590 square-foot, one-bedroom unit was hardly worthy of the name "The Mansion." It was, however, only about a fifteen-minute drive from PCL and the church.

Debbie had graduated from Brock University with her bachelor's degree in early childhood education. In Grimsby, Ontario, she took a job teaching severely mentally disabled kids and adults. Grimsby was about an hour's drive from Toronto—if you don't get caught in a traffic jam, that is. Occasionally I would visit Debbie on the weekends and help her with minor home maintenance or renovation projects. We would also take an annual bus tour to see a Buffalo Bills NFL football game. Debbie is a big Bills fan.

Back at the office on a winter evening, I worked late on an estimate for a new sediment tank at the Ashbridge's Bay sewage treatment facility. I struggled to figure out a specific detail on the large football field-sized tank's structural concrete. I needed to ask our formwork engineer how this item should be quantified and built.

I walked around the office, and it was empty except for one other person, PCL president of Eastern Canada, Ross Grieve.

Ross was just packing up his briefcase and putting on his overcoat. It was about 6:30 p.m., and he was rushing to get out to an evening appointment. Catching me out of the corner of his eye, Ross turned. "Kenny, what are you doing still here?"

"I'm trying to figure out this tank detail, but no one's around."

Ross looked at his watch, then said, "I've only got a minute, but let's take a look."

He ended up spending about ten minutes with me, looking at the detail and making a couple of suggestions, then checked his watch.

"Sorry, I need to get going. But I think you're on the right track."

Jeepers, at my previous employer, Little Chief seemed annoyed when I asked questions. However, here the Eastern president took the time to help me out; maybe that's how PCL became the largest contractor in Canada.

Although not as frequent, I still couldn't shake those darn muscle tension headaches. Thankfully, they never flared up when I was cranking on a deadline. Instead, the headache would usually arrive a day or two after the submission, which seemed bizarre.

Why would I get a headache once the pressure was off? If there was a positive, the head pain helped me develop high pain tolerance. My high pain tolerance was challenged by four impacted wisdom teeth that had decided to grow sideways. I was going to need surgery to remove all four teeth.

Mom flew down from the Sault for my surgery. Poppa, who was now eighty years old, decided to come as well. Even Debbie took the day off work and drove over. I thought that was a lot of help for a relatively simple procedure, or so I thought.

As I entered the dental surgeon's procedure room, my eyes were drawn to the flickering fluorescent light recessed in the water-stained ceiling panels. All the equipment in the room seemed ancient. Even the old dental chair had seen better days, with duct tape covering up a tear in the leather.

Wow, this old place is in bad need of a good renovation, looking more like something out of a cheesy horror movie than a modern-day dental procedure room.

A nurse put an IV in my arm. The anesthesiologist placed a mask over my face and had me count backward from ten.

"Ten, nine, eight, seven…" and the next thing I remember was waking up feeling cold, lying on a small bench in a tiny room, actually more like a closet. I didn't even have a pillow or a blanket.

They brought Mom in from the waiting room to get me. As you can imagine, Mom was not impressed with the facility, but she held her tongue as her focus was getting me up and out of that place.

Mom drove me back to The Mansion, still disoriented from the drugs coursing through my veins. I began to feel terribly nauseous on the drive, rolling down the window to get fresh air.

Entering the apartment, I sat down in my big armchair, taking a moment to catch my breath. Mom grabbed a trash can from the bathroom and set it beside me, just in case. And it was a good thing she did. No sooner did she put it there, and I lost my breakfast. I don't think I had ever been that sick, not even at the high school track meet drinking incident.

Minutes later, I developed my worst headache ever. I had experienced some pretty bad headaches in my day, but none as intense as this. After a sleepless night, the throbbing of my brain continued. The following day, Mom contacted the dental surgeon's office, and he issued me a prescription for Vicodin. While Mom and I were out getting my prescription, Poppa took a nasty fall. He had slipped while taking a shower and whacked his ribs on the side of the bathtub. So, Poppa and I sure made good use of the Vicodin that week. Thank you, Jesus, for good drugs.

Mom had been looking forward to a week's vacation in Southern Ontario. She hadn't anticipated her two rugged construction guys being taken out of commission by a maniacal dental surgeon and an unforgiving bathtub. Instead of sightseeing, Mom spent her week nursing us back to health.

By the end of the week, I was feeling much better. Poppa was still in pain but managing. Mom headed over to Grimsby to stay the night at Debbie's while Poppa and I held down the fort at The Mansion. Saturday, I decided to take Poppa on a tour of Toronto construction projects. First, we drove by a couple of high rises on which I had done estimates.

The first project had a concrete structure up about thirty stories, and the exterior glass was chasing close behind. Another was just a big five-story deep hole in the ground, where the underground parking would soon start to take shape.

We spent most of the afternoon talking about construction, reminiscing about the past twenty years, and looking at the big projects. I had come a long way from Sault Ste. Marie and that first treehouse project that Poppa helped me rebuild when I was just seven years old.

Poppa had always supported, encouraged, and believed in me. Now he was getting to see firsthand how far his influence in my life had taken me. After a special day of touring with Poppa, we headed back to the apartment. But not before stopping at Dairy Queen for a couple of chocolate milkshakes.

The following day Mom and Poppa headed back to the Sault. Oh, and it turns out Poppa had broken ribs from his fall in the tub. So, he was still pretty tough at eighty years old.

It wasn't long before I was working on my next estimate, another large office building. This project was large enough that it would need to be reviewed by PCL's chief executive officer Bob Tarr. Bob would be in town, so he wanted to review it with me in person. Yikes, talk about feeling the pressure.

Before the big CEO review, I would first need to review with Al Troppmann. No problem, this time, I prepared my estimate, considering all the things Al had previously questioned me on.

Walking into the meeting, I had much more confidence than last time. Well, it only took about two minutes for Al to shatter that confidence as he asked a whole bunch of different questions, ugh!

After Al finished going through my estimate, he took the time to "prepare me" for the CEO review.

I was to keep quiet and say as little as possible. If Bob Tarr asked a question, Al would take the lead on answering. If Al needed my help to answer, he would say, "Ken, can you explain that?"

Now, like every good quarterback, Al put in an audible. If Bob addressed me directly on a question, I was to wait a couple of seconds, allowing Al to jump in if needed. After my pregame briefing with Al, I was ready for my first CEO estimate review. I had the meeting room all prepared, drawings and specifications were on the table, and copies of my estimate printed and ready to go.

Eventually, Bob and Al entered the room where I was nervously waiting. Al introduced me to Bob, who smiled but looked pretty serious like he had a lot on his mind. I guess I would have a lot on my mind if I were CEO of the largest general contractor in Canada.

Bob first asked Al a few questions about the project owner, financing, and contract terms. Then, turning toward me, he asked about the subcontractors we had bidding. We reviewed the concrete structure pricing and discussed our staffing for the project.

Bob's demeanor was matter-of-fact, and his questions were very particular and to the point, as were Al's and my responses. There was no joking or goofing around involved. It was all business. The review finally ended. The stress of the situation seemed to overshadow the fact that everything went smoothly.

Later in the day, Bob Tarr walked down the hallway and stepped into my office. He asked me a bit about myself and was easier to talk to than in the earlier meeting. He even joked around a little. As Bob left my office, he said, "Nice job today. Keep up the good work."

Sadly, that was the first, and the last time I would review an estimate with Bob Tarr, as he became very ill and passed away in 1991.

Joe Thompson became the new CEO. Joe had joined PCL back in 1967, the same year I was born. However, a change in CEO didn't affect me much as I still had a lot to learn.

You Need To Listen To Your Mother!

One time I had an extremely short deadline for a budget on an enormous project that engulfed a couple of Toronto city blocks. There was no way I was going to make my deadline.

About three in the afternoon, I found myself on the phone with Mom. She asked, "How are you doing?"

"Well, I have this large project budget to do, but there is no way I'm going to get it done in time."

"Did you pray about it?"

"No, Mom, I have not. This estimate is different from last time; I was a rookie back then and didn't know what I didn't know. This time I know for certain I do not have enough time."

"I see. Well, you need to listen to your mother. So, I am going to hang up and pray about it, and you are going to pray about it, and we shall see what happens."

I sort of slammed the telephone receiver down in frustration. Then, looking up at the office ceiling, I blurted out, "Lord, I need help."

It couldn't have even been fifteen seconds later when Ted Cook entered my office. "Ken, the developer has to make a sudden trip to Europe. You now have four more weeks to get that budget completed."

OK, Lord, I got the message. Next time I will pray to you before I call Mom.

Twice a year, PCL assembles the entire staff for updates on the overall status of the district office and company. These are called fireside chats and occur at mid-year and year-end. They review things like financials, new work, new opportunities, and other significant company news.

I received the memo for the mid-year fireside chat. It was to be 4:00 p.m. to 5:30 p.m. on Wednesday.

Rats, that's the same day I had a date to take a woman to a Blue Jays baseball game. I really didn't want to cancel this date. I didn't get many dating opportunities, you know. Actually, it would be my first date since my first year in college.

Mom and Dad always said they were praying I would meet a lovely young lady who would love me for who I am. Not sure what the "for who I am" part meant, but I welcomed the prayer.

I figured out a game plan. First, I could show up for the PCL event and sit in the back row. Then, if I snuck out at, say, 4:45 p.m., I would have just enough time to get through rush hour traffic, meet my date, and get to the game on time.

I arrived at the fireside chat at 4:00 p.m. sharp. The first half-hour was just snacks, drinks, and socializing. So, I went to the bar to get my Diet Coke. That's when this older guy started talking to me.

After about a minute, I realized who I was speaking with. It was PCL's chairman of the board and former CEO Bob Stollery. Bob was a legend in the Canadian construction industry and had orchestrated PCL's employee buyout of the Poole family and later rise to the number one general contractor in Canada.

Bob and I chatted for a while. He was very interested in how I started in the construction business and my childhood recollections with Poppa.

As the presentations began, I took my seat in the back corner, watching the clock so I could sneak away at 4:45 p.m.

Wouldn't you know it. Bob Stollery walked over and sat in the empty seat right beside me.

Oh darn, how am I going to sneak away now?

Panic was starting to creep in. Unfortunately, there were no cell phones to warn my date that I would be late. Luckily, at precisely 4:48 p.m., Bob got up to use the restroom. Whew, seizing my window of opportunity, I bolted out of the room and made it to my date on time. Looking back, considering how my date went, I would have been far better off spending the evening talking with the construction legend. But I was twenty-three years old, so I didn't always make the wisest decisions.

Speaking of decisions, on a whim, I answered a talent search company ad saying they were looking for potential actors. Since I was a kid, I have always been a big movie fan, especially *The Ten Commandments*. So, I signed up and went to the screen test.

Of course, they said I had potential and wanted me to pay $250 for some acting workshops.

So, I know what you're thinking: that's what they tell everybody; all they want is your money. And you know, you are probably right, but I figured it would help me in my construction career with interviews and presentations.

After completing the workshops, they took a casting photo of me and mailed it to casting agencies in Toronto.

After about six months, I received a call from an agency that wanted to sign me. However, they were more of an extra agency versus an actor agency. Nevertheless, the agency booked me on several Canadian movie and television shoots.

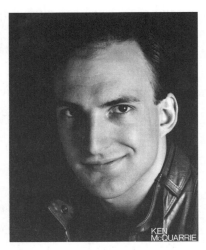

1990 Casting Photo

One weekend I was on the set for a television courtroom scene. The director was David Cronenberg, who had directed Steven King's 1983 movie *The Dead Zone* starring Christopher Walken and 1986's *The Fly* starring Jeff Goldblum.

I was part of the audience in the courtroom for this particular scene. While setting up the shot, David Cronenberg suddenly stopped and whispered to his assistant as he pointed in my direction.

Is he looking at me? I think he is. Am I being discovered by a Hollywood director?

"You there in the red tie," called out the assistant.

Hey, I'm wearing a red tie. The director is talking about me.

"You need to move to the other side of the room; your tie is drawing focus away from the actor."

OK, so I wasn't going to be moving to California just yet, but a Hollywood director did notice me. I enrolled in more acting classes from the money I made from doing extra work. It paid off in the fall of 1991 when I landed my first role. It was the play *Harvey*.

Theater Etobicoke, a local community theater group, was performing the play. *Harvey* is a 1944 comedy-drama play about a man who claims his best friend is a six-foot three-and-a-half-inch invisible rabbit. It was also a 1950 movie starring Jimmy Stewart.

I would be playing the part of Marvin Wilson, the orderly at the sanatorium (insane asylum).

The news got back to PCL, particularly district manager Al Troppmann, that I was acting in a play. Al got a good chuckle out of the thought of me as an actor and bought a ticket to come to see me perform.

The theater held about 350 people; I could hear Al laughing in the audience during the performance.

The next day Al didn't say much about the play. He did indicate he enjoyed it, though. Every time Al walked past me in the hall, he would laugh, shake his head, and keep walking.

PCL was now into our annual charity drive to raise money for the United Way. There were two weeks of fundraising events planned for the staff. Everything would culminate at our big year-end fireside chat.

One of the activities back then was the personal-assistant-for-a-day auction. First, individuals would volunteer to be assistants. Then, the remaining two hundred employees bid on them, with the individual assistants going to the highest bidder. All the funds raised would go to the United Way.

The successful bidder could have their assistant do simple tasks like getting them lunch, cleaning up their office, polishing their shoes, etc.

I was asked to be one of the personal assistants. On auction day, Al Troppmann outbid everyone for me. He made his first bid at $250, and nobody tried to outbid him.

Oh man, what in the world is Al going to make me do? Well, the days marched on, and Al gave me no tasks. Instead, he would just chuckle to himself every time he passed by in the hall.

It was now the fireside chat, and Al still had not used me for any tasks. I know he was busy; maybe he forgot.

At the very end of the meeting, Al announced the total funds raised for United Way. Then he mentioned the personal-assistant auction, saying that his assistant Ken has an extraordinary skill. "He's an actor, and he is going to perform for us right now," Al told the staff.

The room went quiet as everyone turned and just stared at me. Oh boy, what do I do now? Fortunately, I had been working on a comedic audition monologue. So, I gave everyone a quick synopsis of the scene.

"I will be playing the part of a typewriter repair technician who is very awkward around the ladies. In this scene, my character is trying to compliment a woman by comparing her to a typewriter.

"Al, you will be playing the part of the woman." I pulled a chair over and had Al sit there as I performed my five-minute monologue.

When I finished, everyone applauded. I don't know if the applause was for my performance or that everyone could now get to the food and refreshments. Al did get a good laugh out of it, and I fulfilled my duties. Plus, we had raised lots of money for the United Way.

After my fireside chat performance, some of my coworkers started calling me "Rock Quarry" or "Rock" for short. A take on when Rock Hudson guest-starred on *The Flintstones.*

All in all, I ended up doing three plays with Theater Etobicoke, then landed my first professional gig with an evening dinner theater that would pay a whopping $50 per performance.

The early nineties were uncertain times. In April 1990, Canada officially entered into a nasty recession. By August 1990, the lead-up to the Gulf War began with Operation Desert Shield. The actual war, Operation Desert Storm, began on January 17, 1991. The Canadian Ontario construction industry was in free fall. PCL had projects under construction that came to a halt as owners and developers tried to keep their businesses afloat.

PCL Office morale fell to an all-time low as monthly layoffs continued throughout 1991.

"Peace I leave with you; my peace I give you.
I do not give to you as the world gives. Do not let your
hearts be troubled and do not be afraid." John 14:27

It was a stressful time for the estimating department. The pressure was on to get work, but the number of projects out there was getting scarce. When we did find an opportunity to chase, the competition was bidding the job below cost. Al Troppmann kept lowering our fees, but some contractor was always more aggressive no matter how low our bid was. I was concerned I would soon be out of a job but continued to work longer hours as PCL tried to pick up more work and stop the layoffs.

Many of the staff told me you have nothing to worry about. In a recession, we need estimators to get projects. Plus, at only twenty-four years old, you still don't make much money. You have been doing the job of a senior estimator, minus the big salary.

I took a break and went home to Sault Ste. Marie for Christmas. It was a good Christmas time with family. Debbie and Dougie also traveled back for the holidays. Dougie had just finished his first semester studying biochemistry at McMaster University in Hamilton, Ontario.

With Poppa now into his eighties, we didn't know how many more Christmases he would be around. So, it made the holidays just a little more special. I just had this sense that my world was about to change throughout the holiday season. PCL was moving to a new office space. It had been under construction for about six months, and we would be moving in that coming March. I just felt I would not be moving into that office.

Those were crazy thoughts; after all, my coworkers were right. I was doing the job of much more senior estimators and for half the price. I got along well with Vice President Al Troppmann; I think he even liked me as an up-and-coming estimator. Well, maybe that's an overreach, but I was almost sure he didn't dislike me. If I were going to get laid off, it would have happened months ago.

On February 27, 1992, I had just returned from lunch. My inter-company phone line rang. It was Al Troppmann. "Can you come to my office, please?"

The hallway seemed a lot longer than usual that day as I slowly walked to Al's office.

Al asked me to take a seat and proceeded to tell me what I knew was already coming. I was being laid off.

Over the past year and a half, the Toronto office had gone from over two hundred salaried employees to less than eighty. We had hundreds of millions of dollars of work just stopped or canceled. If there was any consolation, it was the fact I was one of the last employees to be laid off. But that's like getting a participation ribbon at a slow-pitch tournament.

Some people said the unemployment in the Ontario construction industry was as high as 40 percent in those days. Not a good time to be out of work, for sure. On a positive note, Al gave me one-month severance pay, plus I got paid out from three weeks of unused vacation days.

Al seemed a bit choked up about letting me go, and I could have sworn I even saw a tear forming in his eye, but it may have just been allergies. However, he did write me a reference letter and allowed his executive assistant to type up my resume.

I packed up my office into a box, walked around, and said goodbye to all my coworkers. Then I made one last call from my office.

"Hello," Mom answered.

"I just got laid off."

"Oh my. OK, I'll let your father know. I guess we have something to pray about."

Chapter 17:

Go West, Young Man

*Trust in the Lord with all your heart and lean not
on your own understanding; in all your ways submit to him,
and he will make your paths straight. Proverbs 3:5-6*

As the weekend arrived, my mind was spinning. It was like I went from starting running back for the Superbowl champs to getting cut by the team. What could I have done differently? Could I have worked harder? Should I have worked longer hours?

After all, I was one of the last people to leave the office most nights, not to mention all the weekends I worked. I studied all PCL's historical information, learned from their superintendents and engineers. What did it get me? One month's severance pay, a handshake, good luck, goodbye, and good riddance.

Dad suggested I move back to the Sault to work for Algoma Steel. Part of my college scholarship included the promise to provide me with a job at the steel mill when I graduated.

I thought about trying full-time acting for about five minutes, but them was crazy thoughts. Stay focused, Kenneth, I told myself.

I tried to pray to the Lord for direction, but I was stressed; my mind couldn't focus.

Monday, I made many phone calls to my connections in the construction industry, putting the word on the street I was looking for work. Meanwhile, Dad contacted Algoma Steel to see what they had available in their facilities and maintenance department.

By the end of the week, I had three irons in the fire. Two midsize Toronto construction companies were interested in me, and Algoma Steel had a potential position.

A new company called Granville Constructors had been building a high-rise apartment complex just down the street. It certainly couldn't hurt, so I decided I might as well drop them off a resume.

Entering the front lobby, I walked up to the receptionist. "Can you give this resume to your chief estimator?"

As I headed for the exit, the receptionist called after me, "Albert, our chief estimator, can see you right now."

I was not expecting that. I was on my way to the gym wearing a T-shirt and sweatpants, not the best interview attire.

Albert Chow was a tall, athletic-looking guy in his mid-thirties. He had an engineering degree and had worked previously as a project manager before taking the chief estimator position. The interview went well, and Granville Constructors made me an offer.

Granville Constructors was a newer start-up company that began in Edmonton, Alberta. Owner and president Bill Smith and vice president Juri Rupra had coincidentally worked for PCL early in their careers. So, amid 40 percent construction unemployment, with a lot of prayers and the strength of PCL on my resume, I had four job opportunities within a week, including two midsize Toronto construction companies, Algoma Steel, and Granville Constructors.

I prayed hard for direction. "Thanks, Lord, but you do realize it would be a lot easier if you had just provided me one opportunity."

After more prayer, I felt I should take the job with Granville Constructors. However, this went against all logic and common sense as it was a newer company and the lowest-paying offer.

Dad was very pleased I had once again landed on my feet. And Mom? Well, Mom was a little more apprehensive about my choice.

"The economy is terrible. Aren't you taking a big gamble with a new company over three established companies?" Mom said in her concerned voice.

"I know, Mom, but I prayed about it, and I feel this is the right decision."

"OK, then I guess we shall see."

I was no longer in the big leagues, but that was OK; I had a job. Besides, I was just a small-town guy and not really a big-league type of player. So, within weeks, PCL seemed like a distant memory.

After two months with Granville Constructors, I was given a small civic building to bid in Vancouver, BC. The company wanted to test the West Coast market. That meant flying out to British Columbia the weekend before the bid closing day. It was already dark as I landed in Vancouver at about 9:30 p.m. Flagging down a taxi, I made the thirty-minute commute to a downtown hotel.

The morning finally arrived. I flung open my hotel room drapes, revealing the most breathtaking view I could ever imagine.

Majestic snow-capped mountains surrounded the city, cascading down to touch the clear blue ocean waters of Burrard Inlet and the Strait of Georgia. Across the Strait stood the mountainous Vancouver Island, shielding the mainland coast from the mighty Pacific Ocean. It was like I was standing in a fairy tale. I had no idea scenery like this even existed. Sure, I had seen mountains in books and movies, but pictures don't do justice to literally being there.

Scott and Rob Pinches' parents, Chuck and Mona, attended Capenwray Bible School on Thetis Island. Thetis was a small island off the coast of Vancouver.

Monday was Victoria Day, a Canadian holiday commemorating Queen Victoria's birthday. So, I took a two-seater float plane over to Thetis Island to visit Chuck and Mona.

The scene from the plane was even more spectacular than from the hotel. The morning sun glistened off the mountains that went on forever. Schools of porpoises chased the shadow of the small plane in the water below as we approached the island.

It was fun spending the day with familiar faces from Sault Ste. Marie in such a scenic and far-off place.

The bid closing went well that Thursday, but we ended up in second place. So, I flew back to Toronto Friday and enjoyed a relaxing weekend after a long, busy week in Vancouver.

Monday morning, I was back in the Toronto office. Vice president Juri told me they wanted to open a full-time office in Vancouver and would like me to move there permanently.

Whoa, was not expecting that. Vancouver is nice and all, but it's a couple thousand miles away from my hometown.

"Let me know your decision by tomorrow. We want you there in a week," Juri said.

I called home. "Mom, Granville Constructors wants me to move to Vancouver."

"Vancouver? That's so far away. When do they want you to move?"

"Next week."

"NEXT WEEK! Just a minute, I need to sit down."

Mom continued. "How stable is this company? What if they go out of business and you are stuck in Vancouver? What about your asthma, your doctors?"

"Mom, the Vancouver construction market is in better shape than Toronto right now, and I can find new doctors in Vancouver. Besides, my asthma has stabilized. I could breathe just fine when I was there last week."

"OK then, I will fill your father in when he gets home from work. We will call you later tonight."

Dad called me back that evening and, quoting the famous phrase from the 1800s, told me, "Well, they always say: Go West, Young Man."

Dad thought it would be an opportunity of a lifetime. But, on the other hand, Mom was happy for me but just a little apprehensive about how far away I would be from family.

"Just be sure you pray about it," Mom said as they hung up the phone.

Within a week, I was on a one-way flight to Vancouver. Because another contractor was already using the name Granville in Vancouver, we changed the company name to "Granwest Constructors."

We leased a small office space in Richmond, BC, and hired a part-time administrative assistant. I would man the office, prepare the estimates, and Juri Rupra would fly out from Toronto on bid days to help close the bids.

Just as I was settling into my new surroundings, Juri called me. "Ken, we have an opportunity to bid on a renovation and addition to the University of Alberta Cross Cancer Hospital in Edmonton, Alberta. Unfortunately, our estimator in Edmonton is busy on another bid, so I would like you to prepare the bid."

Wayne Gretzky became famous for winning Stanley Cups for the Edmonton Oilers in the 80s. So now I was going to get to visit. Not visit Wayne Gretzky, of course, as he was currently playing for the Los Angeles Kings. But visit the West Edmonton Mall hockey arena where he played in the Stanley Cups. There was one more thing: I would be bidding against PCL on this one. PCL's head office is in Edmonton.

But wait, it gets even better. Remember PCL legend and chairman Bob Stollery, who I met at my first PCL fireside chat? Bob was very active in philanthropic support of the University of Alberta and the Cross Cancer Hospital, or so I was told.

So, this was set up to be my David and Goliath moment. Small town boy working for a small company going head-to-head with the "Giant" PCL Construction on their home turf.

This story had a twist, though. This time, the Giant had taught the boy how to fight.

Those years of long hours and late nights spent studying PCL historical data and productivities were now about to pay off. The file cabinet of my brain was filled with PCL knowledge. I even knew how they priced overhead and profit, their bonding and insurance rates, and how they would staff the job.

As I readied my estimate for bid day, I prayed, "Lord, be with me on bid day; I pray everything goes well, and please help me not to screw this bid up."

It was a fast-paced, dynamic bid closing. The subtrade prices kept changing right up to the last minute when I relayed our cost over the phone to the bid runner. Then, we anxiously awaited the results. Finally, after ten minutes, the phone rang. It was our bid runner calling back with the results.

"WE WON! We were the low bidder!"

I fell back in my chair. I couldn't believe it. It was the most satisfying victory in my professional career to date. Just four months after being laid off by PCL, I had come back and beat them on their home field. Thank you, Jesus!

Cross Cancer Hospital wanted to meet with us for a project kickoff meeting about a month later. I would be flying from Vancouver back to Edmonton, where Granville Constructors president Bill Smith and I would attend the meeting.

Getting on the plane in Vancouver, I walked down the aisle, looking for my seat. Suddenly I heard, "Kenny, what are you doing way out here in Vancouver?"

I turned, and to my surprise, it was PCL Eastern Canada president Ross Grieve. Ross had moved to Edmonton head office the previous year to take on new responsibilities. He was flying back to Edmonton from a meeting in Vancouver.

I told Ross how, after being laid off, I hired on with Granville Constructors, who moved me to Vancouver, and I just outbid PCL for the Cross Cancer Hospital project.

I think I kinda caught Ross off guard with that last part about beating PCL. He was very gracious, though, and wished me well with my new company.

Having to leave Toronto so quickly, I could not be in that dinner theater play. But I decided to look for a new acting agency in Vancouver. After contacting several agencies, I finally found one that would meet with me.

The agent I met with was not very nice, to say the very least. He did not like that I would only work weekends and evenings. He said I needed to decide if I wanted to be an actor or not.

Well, I went with the "or not" option. I needed to focus on my day job, the one that paid the bills. Truth be told, that day job was becoming insanely busy.

With PCL, I mainly worked on large, more prominent, privately funded projects with private sector owners and developers. The projects were primarily negotiated guaranteed maximum price (GMP) type work and some lump sum bid work sprinkled in for good measure.

I usually would have about four to six weeks to prepare my estimates or budgets with the complete resources of PCL, including a sizeable estimating and purchasing department plus an on-staff structural engineer. In addition, I'd have superintendents and project managers to help figure out schedules and constructability concerns.

It was also easier to get subcontractor bids as all the trades in Canada wanted to work for PCL.

I had none of that support with Granwest in Vancouver. We were a minor start-up operation, and Juri wanted me bidding two to three projects per month. Time was ticking, and we needed to win work to pay for the overhead cost of starting up an office.

The projects were smaller than the mega-jobs I worked on at PCL and included many elementary and high school projects plus a few university buildings. These jobs were all public lump sum bids with a lot of tough competition. I was up against all sorts of challenges, including I was still young in my career and still didn't know what I didn't know. Not to mention, the subcontractors didn't know Granwest or me, so it was hard to get them to give me bids.

If that wasn't enough, there was no chief estimator to mentor me or additional estimators to back me up. Without a purchasing department to get me pricing on materials, I had to do this by myself. Plus, there was no snazzy computer estimating program, so I was back to doing estimates the old-fashioned way, by hand.

On top of all the work challenges, I was utterly alone. I did not know anyone. My family was over 3,200 km (2,000 miles) away. So, as I celebrated my twenty-fifth birthday alone, I was under a tremendous amount of pressure and responsibility.

"Lord, I hope you know what you're doing because I sure don't."

I began attending the Surrey Free Methodist Church, a small church of maybe one hundred people. They did have a small college and careers group, but they were primarily college-age kids in a different life stage than I was. The rest of the church mainly was married folks of various ages.

Pastor George Fleming was very welcoming and invited me out to dinner several times. That was a nice change from the churches in southern Ontario. Still, at the end of the day, I spent most of my time by myself, working long hours at the office or home alone.

Most weekends in Toronto, I had something to do. I'd be hanging with Scott and Rob Pinches, catching a movie, or watching a football game with Paul Severn. There were also get-togethers with Jim and Esther Elliott and their family. And don't forget playing hockey with the guys from the church.

Of course, in those days, my family was only a car ride away, albeit a long car ride.

Although very lonely, I was in a beautiful place. I know the Lord had me here for a reason. I was thankful to have a job as the country was just starting to pull out of the recession. I needed to pray for a good attitude and continue to push forward.

In downtown Vancouver is Stanley Park. The park is over 1,000 acres surrounded by the waters of Vancouver Harbour and English Bay. It has a 10 km (6 mile) walking/biking trail around the park's perimeter along the oceanside.

When I would start to feel too stressed or overwhelmed, I would head to Stanley Park for a long walk. The fresh ocean air and incredible scenery would have a calming effect. It could even melt away a headache.

My days were spent with a telephone attached to my ear calling subcontractors, getting to know them, convincing them to bid to me. Next, I used the fax machine, sending out thousands of bid invites for the projects. Then I would work on my estimates in the evenings and weekends.

I was constantly juggling two or three project pursuits at a time, making hundreds of phone calls, and sending thousands of faxes, creating an illusion that we were a sizeable operation moving into the Vancouver market in a big way.

When the occasional contractor would drop by the office, they were shocked to find just me.

One such contractor was Edgar Heyde of Fraser Valley Industries, a large architectural millwork and cabinetry shop. Edgar was about twenty years my senior and originally from Argentina. He was German and had been in Canada for many years. Edgar is also a devout Christian who speaks fluent German, Spanish, and English.

Edgar gave me preferred pricing on the millwork bids. He also filled me in on who's who in the Vancouver construction industry, providing me with business insights that helped me immensely. With his guidance, I soon developed relationships with several other vital subcontractors, which helped me get more competitive on my bids. Finally, I landed an elementary school in Richmond, BC, and a new building for Emily Car College of Art & Design.

With the two new projects, Juri Rupra hired an area manager, project manager, full-time administrative assistant, and of course, a few superintendents to run the work.

It was nice to have a few more people in the office. Granwest was starting to put our mark on British Columbia.

I started taking Chinese Kung Fu lessons to help relieve the stress of the fast-paced days and get myself in shape. Unfortunately, my weight had been creeping up with all the long work hours and fast-food lunches. Back in college, I studied a bit of Korean Taekwondo. I ended up stopping after losing a fight by knockout in a Detroit tournament. In that particular tournament, you could kick to the head, but punching to the head was illegal. So, I went to punch my opponent in his chest protector when at the last second, he ducked. The problem was he ducked his jaw right in front of my fist, and the force of the blow rendered him almost totally unconscious. Thus, I was disqualified by knockout.

Scott Pinches and his wife, Heather, visited his parents on Thetis Island. Scott had married Heather the year before I left Toronto. I served as a groomsman and master of ceremonies at their wedding.

L-R: Heather & Scott Pinches, Mona & Chuck Pinches, Rob Pinches, Me

I flew over to the Island to visit Scott and Heather for the weekend. Then, Sunday morning, we all went to church at a small chapel. After singing a couple of songs, the pastor came out and addressed the twenty or so people in the congregation.

"We have a special guest speaker today who was sailing around the islands and decided to join us this morning. His name is Graham Kerr."

Graham Kerr, that name sounds so familiar; where have I heard that before?

"You may know him better as the Galloping Gourmet," the pastor announced.

No way, that's crazy. It had been almost twenty years to the day since I was attacked on the way home from kindergarten. That day Mom and I sat in the living room eating chocolate chip cookies and watching *The Galloping Gourmet* on TV.

Graham Kerr told us his story of how a series of almost tragic events, health issues, and prayers of a staff member led him and his wife to accept Jesus Christ as their Lord and Savior. Graham talked about how that decision had impacted their lives over the past twenty years. It was a memory I will never forget. Wow, talk about a blast from the past.

After a relaxing weekend in the islands, it was back to work. I sorta thought once we started picking up work, the number of projects we were chasing would slow down. Well, I was sorta wrong. If anything, the company wanted me to increase the number of projects I was pursuing.

It was just not humanly possible to bid on more projects per month. Like, when was I supposed to sleep?

Without putting the proper time and analysis into the bids, mistakes or underestimation would happen. I felt I was being set up for failure. It was just a matter of time. I needed to figure out how to get faster and more efficient producing estimates.

I would first do quantity takeoffs on all trade scopes to produce an accurate estimate. On the surface, this isn't rocket science. For example, if you're going to get new carpet or tile in your house, you'd measure how much carpet or tile you will need. Sounds easy, right?

Well, not so fast. Remember, on a commercial construction project, there are upwards of seventy trades that need quantifying. Not to mention the thousands of pages of specifications to read through.

Still, many details or scopes of work could fall through the cracks. Not literally fall in cracks, but these scopes may not be picked up by any trades. So, I had to allow for these items in my estimates. These could include custom design items or special caulking, flashings, etc.

Then don't forget I would also have to figure out our costs to manage the project and do a detailed concrete and formwork estimate because we may do that scope of work ourselves.

Once I had all the trades quantified, I put the quantities into my estimate and applied what we call a plug price to the scope of work. A plug is a price based on past experience and historical information. Finally, all the pricing gets totaled up to arrive at an estimated cost for the total project. Subcontractors make up 80 percent of a project cost. So, when the subtrade bids come in, I replace my plug pricing with the actual trade pricing. The result is our final bid amount to construct the project.

As you can see, for one person alone to produce three or more of these estimates a month was a bit of a challenge. Thus, I began taking shortcuts, only quantifying areas of work that may be complicated or confusing to the subtrades. I had to understand these complications to analyze subcontractor pricing on bid days.

For the remaining trade scopes, I would plug my estimate based on high-level rough areas, ratios, and percent of the total cost with some prayer and gut instinct thrown in for good measure. It was definitely trial by fire. However, continuing to follow Mom's advice of praying first and never giving up, my instincts for focusing in on the most significant risk and cost items improved over time.

Finally, in 1993, Juri hired a second estimator; he was an older guy in his fifties. This only meant instead of bidding on two to three projects at a time, we were expected to bid four to six. Ugh! While I was fighting to keep my career alive, my brother Dougie was just finishing his second year of biochemistry at McMaster University.

Dougie worked with Debbie in Southern Ontario during the previous two summers, helping with her disabled clients. Unfortunately, this work only paid a minimum wage, less than $4.00 per hour Canadian.

I was able to get Dougie a summer job with a concrete forming company in Vancouver for $12.00 per hour. Due to his hard work, he eventually got himself a raise to $14.00 per hour.

Dougie arrived out west in May. We had a fun summer, working hard during the weeks and exploring all over British Columbia on the weekends. We hiked Whistler Mountain, went sailing through the islands, played on a co-ed church softball team, and attended a Christian singles retreat on Thetis Island. We even saw an Aerosmith concert.

It was a lot of fun that summer. Dougie was no longer that little kid brother that I left behind when I went to college. He was taller than me now. The summer eventually ended, Dougie went back to Ontario, and once again, I was on my own.

I will instruct you and teach you in the way you should go;
I will counsel you with my loving eye on you. Psalm 32:8

Things continued to be busy at work. The projects we had under construction all had their own challenges. Not the least of which was some of our superintendents struggling to manage the work.

Granwest did not want to pay the higher salaries the more experienced industry superintendents would demand. That meant we ended up with lower-level field management. They were good tradesmen and foremen, some with potential to be excellent superintendents, but none the caliber of superintendents I was used to at the big-league companies.

I couldn't worry too much about field management. Instead, I needed to focus on my estimating challenges. With PCL, I always had lots of support on bid closing days, with as many as twelve or more staff helping analyze and scope out subcontractor bids. But, at Granwest, we only had three or four people helping on bid days.

Without the senior staff's input reviewing the estimates and helping scope out the subcontractors, a lot of work coverage and legal challenges fell between those proverbial cracks.

As a result, we ended up with a few problem subtrades on our projects. They either did not have the financial means to complete the job or missed scopes of work in their bid.

I proved the philosophy: you don't know what you don't know. Unfortunately, I had not been in the industry long enough to develop all the knowledge, instincts, and political savvy to avoid the problems down the road. I was kind of like the rookie NFL quarterback—he may have many physical skills, but until he learns the instincts for reading the defense, he tends to get his butt kicked.

The trial by fire continued and I was learning fast! At the same time I was trying to understand what the purpose of all this was. I loved construction, but I felt like a hamster on a treadmill. The faster I ran to get off, the quicker the treadmill would spin. Work became all-consuming; no matter how hard I tried, it never seemed good enough, so I kept trying harder.

I prayed, "Lord, what's up with my life? Is there a purpose in all this? I'm under constant pressure and stress working so hard all the time with no end in sight. Here in British Columbia, I have no life, no close friendships, no family. Where is that nice Christian lady my parents are always praying for me to meet? Is she hiding?

"Lord, I know you say to trust you and lean not on my own understanding, but a little direction would help right about now, amen."

I found out that those two midsize companies in Toronto interested in hiring me did not survive the recession. Both ended up going out of business. Even the hometown company Algoma Steel struggled financially through the '90s. So, the Lord had steered me right with Granville/Granwest, helping me thread the needle on my career, so to speak. I could not see it at the time, but the Lord was preparing me, training me for something much bigger. By the grace of God and with family backing me up, I had already overcome many challenges in my life.

Now I needed to learn to survive on my own by putting my trust solely in the Lord alone and not leaning on my own understanding. The rest of my life would depend on it.

Chapter 18:

Poppa

*"He will wipe every tear from their eyes. There will be
no more death or mourning or crying or pain, for the old
order of things has passed away." Revelation 21:4*

Soon after Dougie headed back to university for his fall semester, I received a call from Mom. Poppa was not doing well, and the doctor said the family should come home as he did not have much time left. Talk about a gut punch. I knew this day was coming, but this was very unexpected.

Poppa was now eighty-three years old. He went in for routine hernia surgery, and they ran into complications. His old body, beat up from years of injuries on the construction sites, was just not strong enough to pull through the operation. Even with all my deadlines looming, I wasted no time booking my flight home to see Poppa one last time. I didn't even ask the company for permission; I just went. I wouldn't even be in construction if it were not for Poppa, so if I got fired over this, so be it.

Poppa was in the intensive care unit, and only one or two family members could be in the room at a time. We all waited in a private waiting room and took turns sitting and visiting with Poppa. When it was my turn sitting with Poppa, we would reminisce about past construction tales. He also liked to talk about politics and how current events affected the construction industry.

I had brought a roll of blueprints for a new elementary school project I was bidding. So, Poppa and I flipped through the drawings. He was particularly interested in the wood timber framing details over the large atrium on this project. By now, he could barely see or speak but wanted to make sure I had enough labor figured in my estimate for the tricky timber framing. It would be his last teaching moment.

Poppa seemed to stabilize somewhat as the week progressed, although maybe it was more wishful thinking than actual truth. Regardless, after a little over a week, I needed to return to Vancouver. I said my goodbye and offered Poppa a prayer, knowing this was the last time I would see him this side of heaven.

It seemed lengthier than the usual flight back to the west coast that next day. Even though a week behind on my deadlines, I was not feeling the stress of returning to the office. My thoughts were with Poppa and all the good memories of a life lived.

A couple of weeks later, on Tuesday, October 5, 1993, my office phone rang. It was Mom. "Your Poppa is gone."

The finality of that call is not something you're ever prepared for. My mind went blank; I was done for the day. Something that kept bothering me was not knowing for sure if Poppa had accepted Jesus as his Lord and Savior.

I knew Poppa believed in God. He even donated to the church and would come to service on special occasions. But he just didn't talk about it, at least not with me. When I arrived in the Sault for the funeral, Dad told me the pastor had spoken with Poppa during those final weeks. Dad confirmed that the pastor had prayed with Poppa, and he had accepted Jesus as his Lord and Savior.

Friday evening, October 8th, the at-rest viewing was at the Barton & Kiteley Funeral Home. The funeral service would be the following day at 1:00 p.m.

The immediate family arrived for a private viewing and to pay our respects to Poppa an hour before guests arrived.

I approached the casket where Poppa lay peacefully wearing a suit with his hands crossed over his waist. I thought I would be much more emotional as I stood there looking down at Poppa, but I felt calm, at peace, almost emotionless.

After standing there for about five minutes, I reached down and put my hand on his shoulder to silently pray a quick blessing for him.

As I touched Poppa's shoulder, a jolt of emotion shot up my arm, and my eyes started to well up. Instantaneously a flood of memories hit me like a gust of wind.

"If you're going to just stand there, you need to make yourself useful."

"Saws are too dangerous; we want you to go home with the same number of fingers you arrived with."

"If you are going to take the time to do it wrong, why not do it right the first time."

"He knows how to use them; he will be fine."

"Yes, but he learns fast, and I have been teaching him how to use all these tools."

"We need to make sure it's sturdy and safe. When you build any house, it needs to be built to the building code. Tell you what, let's go get some tools, and I will show you what I mean."

"Come here; carpenters, don't cry."

"Now, let's go get a chocolate milkshake."

Overcome with emotion, I pulled back my hand and walked into the adjacent room. *Come on, Kenneth, pull yourself together, man,* I thought as I sat down on a chair to gather my composure.

Mom, noticing me struggling, walked over and sat down beside me. Placing her right arm around me, she started to rub my shoulder. At this, I completely lost it; I was a blubbering, sniffling mess. So much for "Carpenters don't cry."

Thirty minutes and two boxes of tissue later, I finally calmed down my emotions a bit. I was still overcome to the point I could not speak. However, I did pull myself together enough to stand and shake guests' hands as they offered their condolences.

The next day we had a simple, straightforward funeral service. The pastor gave a short message, followed by the hymn "In the Sweet By and By."

After the hymn, there were a couple of scripture readings.

The Lord is my shepherd, I lack nothing. He makes me lie down in green pastures, he leads me beside quiet waters, he refreshes my soul. He guides me along the right paths for his name's sake. Even though I walk through the darkest valley, I will fear no evil, for you are with me; your rod and your staff, they comfort me. You prepare a table before me in the presence of my enemies. You anoint my head with oil; my cup overflows. Surely your goodness and love will follow me all the days of my life, and I will dwell in the house of the Lord forever. Psalm 23

"Do not let your hearts be troubled. You believe in God; believe also in me. My Father's house has many rooms; if that were not so, would I have told you that I am going there to prepare a place for you? And if I go and prepare a place for you, I will come back and take you to be with me that you also may be where I am. You know the way to the place where I am going." Thomas said to him, "Lord, we don't know where you are going, so how can we know the way?" Jesus answered, "I am the way and the truth and the life. No one comes to the Father except through me." John 14:1-6

The service ended with the singing of the hymn "Glorious Freedom."

After the service, we made the fifty-minute drive to St. Joseph's Island for the interment at Holy Trinity Cemetery. The pastor read a few more scriptures and recited a committal reading. Then, Poppa's casket was lowered into the grave, right beside where Nanna had been laid to rest twenty-one years before.

It was a cold overcast day; a bone-chilling light rain began to fall just as the ceremony finished. A reminder that winter was coming.

Andrew John Bjornaa
- Poppa
Went to be with Jesus and
Nanna on October 5, 1993

The small crowd retreated to the little Anglican Chapel for refreshments and goodies. I hung back and stood still, quietly watching the two men backfill Poppa's grave. I began to shiver as the rain and wind picked up. But I continued to stand guard, ensuring the two guys did a quality job. Poppa would have expected nothing less.

"If you are going to take the time to do it wrong, why not do it right the first time."

Poppa's death was a real turning point in my life, and as I flew back to Vancouver, many thoughts ran in and out of my head. Not the least of which was, where do I go from here?

Initially, Poppa was against the family taking me in, but he became my greatest supporter once I arrived. Did he spoil me? Well, yes, of course, he did. When updating family and friends about my progress, he would simply refer to me as "The Boy," as if there were no other boys around.

I have heard and read many stories about adopted people. Some knew they were adopted, and some found out later in life. In most cases, those people would go through a season in life wanting to know who their biological parents were.

I think it's natural to want to know who you are, where you come from, what's your actual family history. For some folks, I suppose it's just a natural curiosity or wanting insight on genetic health history. Others are looking to fill a void; they lack a sense of belonging or have felt an emptiness that they cannot quite figure out. I had been very blessed. Not only did the good Lord place me into a loving family, but he provided me with something special to fulfill that sense of belonging.

Deep down, I was quite different from the McQuarries. One might say I was very much my own little man growing up. Poppa helped to fill the void that Mom and Dad could not reach. He understood me at a different level. Poppa helped nurture my analytical mind and steer my drive and determination. No matter how frustrated I would get, he was always there to support, encourage, and back me up.

Though one may be overpowered, two can defend themselves.
A cord of three strands is not quickly broken. Ecclesiastes 4:12

The Lord had provided me Mom, Dad, and Poppa, my very own cord of three strands to start my life. Now that cord had been broken, I was being untethered.

As I landed in Vancouver, I felt loneliness even more so than before. I needed to push forward, moving on without Poppa's support. It was time for me to become my own man.

I was at the point in my life's journey where I truly started to focus on seeking God's purpose for me. I'm still here, and baby Stephen is not. There must be a reason and come hell or high water, I'm going to figure it out.

When Juri Rupra flew out for the next bid closing, I decided to talk to him about my concerns with how the projects were being bid and run. I explained how we should bid less work and put more resources into getting the bids right, sharing how PCL approached estimating and bidding.

I also talked about the skill level of our field management, how we needed to employ higher-level supervision. Finally, I explained to Juri that we might build fewer projects if we did all this, but we would be more profitable at the end of the day.

Juri just sat there and patiently listened to everything I said. Then he slowly leaned back in his chair and said with a smile, "If you are so good and knowledgeable, then why did PCL let you go in the first place?"

Well, so much for becoming my own man. Juri's words hit me like a knife to the chest. But he was right; if I'm so good, why did PCL lay me off?

Project manager John gave me a less than stellar evaluation back in college. Not to mention, I've made mistakes on estimates. Poppa always believed in me, but maybe that's all just an illusion. Poppa's gone now; did his praise give me a false sense of my abilities?

For by the grace given me I say to every one of you: Do not think of yourself more highly than you ought, but rather think of yourself with sober judgment, in accordance with the faith God has distributed to each of you. Romans 12:3

As the year ended, my self-confidence was at an all-time low. I flew back to the Sault for two weeks at Christmas, our first family Christmas without Poppa. It was a nice break from a hectic year. I was looking forward to 1994 and what the Lord had in store for me. It was a new beginning.

Chapter 19:

Methodical Ways

Humble yourselves, therefore, under God's mighty hand,
that he may lift you up in due time. 1 Peter 5:6

As the new year began, nothing much had changed. I continued to crank out the estimates faster than I could think, with no end in sight. Making a mistake is just an opportunity to learn, and I was sure getting a lot of learning opportunities. I figured it this way, similar to exercising: the harder I worked at it, the smarter, faster, and stronger I would become. But, of course, the downside was I did not have much of a life outside of work. I was making inroads within the Vancouver construction industry, getting to know more people all the time. At a Construction Association event, I even ran into PCL Vancouver's chief estimator Dave Housser. We would cross paths now and then over the next few years. PCL didn't chase after the smaller elementary and high school projects often, so I hadn't competed with them yet in British Columbia.

Direction toward purpose was all I was praying for. And I was praying hard. Instead of answers, I got crickets. I was not getting any signs or guidance. Not that I was expecting God to speak to me in a burning bush like he did Moses or anything like that. But any sign of the path I should go would be welcomed. I did have a curious conversation one day with a mechanical contractor. He said, "If I were a young guy like you, I would move to the United States." His reason being, the United States population is almost ten times larger than Canada, which equates to ten times the opportunity.

He also believed you could make a lot more money in the USA with technical ability than in Canada. I laughed. Making more money in the USA is crazy talk; why would I leave Canada? I mean, the US is a nice place to visit, and they do have cheaper gas. But I love Canada and particularly British Columbia. Not to mention, I have asthma, and I have heard nightmares about the Unites States medical insurance.

Anyway, I did not give the conversation about moving to the United States a second thought. Mom and Dad were flying out to Vancouver for a vacation. They had not ventured out of Ontario or Michigan except for our family trip to Disney World in Florida when I was eight years old. As Mom put it, this was going to be a trip of a lifetime. Just like me, Mom and Dad were amazed at the breathtaking scenery of beautiful British Columbia. We explored everywhere, from the glaciers at Whistler Ski Resort to sailing the Strait of Georgia.

A highlight for Mom was our trip to Butchart Gardens near Victoria, Vancouver Island. This historic fifty-five-acre garden started in the early 1900s when Jennie Butchart converted her husband's former limestone quarry into spectacular gardens.

We attended an authentic "Victorian High Tea" at Butchart Gardens. Mom's dream had been to take part in an authentic Victorian Tea since she was a little girl. The tea was also reminiscent of the afternoon tea and goodies that Mom and I shared growing up. Alas, all good things must come to an end, and it was time for Mom and Dad to head back to Ontario. So, after putting them on the plane home, it was back to work for me.

I was at a business lunch with Edgar Heyde of Fraser Valley Industries. He told me about how he and a couple of partners had set up a development company building houses. But unfortunately, they could not keep the business going during the recession.

I told Edgar about Poppa and how we had talked about building a house someday, but now that would never happen. However, I still wanted to construct a house, if for no other reason than as a tribute to Poppa.

Edgar said, "Well, why don't we work together to try and get a house built. We can start with one, then see where we can take it from there."

I liked Edgar's idea. Maybe this is the direction the Lord is taking me, getting me back to my carpenter roots, becoming a home builder. After months of planning our exciting new business venture, we had everything we needed except the land and money, of course.

Since I didn't make much money and definitely didn't have any cash for a mortgage down payment and Edgar was still cleaning up financial obligations from his previous business, we hit a wall. As hard as we tried, the banks were just unwilling to play ball with us. Unfortunately, our house-building dreams soon faded away.

Dougie again came out for his summer break, picking up where he left off the previous year with the formwork company. We had discussed a bit about Dougie moving to British Columbia after he finished school. But those plans were also fading. The summer Dougie had worked with Debbie in Southern Ontario, he met a young intern named Grace Zimmerman. Dougie and Grace had continued to keep in touch, and romance was in the air. They talked on the phone almost daily as Dougie finished what would be his last summer working in Vancouver.

Debbie also came to visit that summer. One highlight was Debbie, Dougie, and I watching game seven of the 1994 Stanley Cup Finals between the hometown Vancouver Canucks and the New York Rangers. The game was being played in New York, so we went to a local sports bar to cheer on the Canucks with other local fans. I selected the bar, finding one that didn't allow smoking. It turns out the game was on at 3:00 p.m. West Coast time, and the bar was not allowed to serve alcohol until 6:00 p.m. Debbie joked, "Kenny, you are the only person on the planet that could find a sports bar that does not serve alcohol for a major sporting event."

I just smiled as I sipped my Diet Coke. Oh yeah, the Canucks lost the game by one goal.

After a fun spring and summer showing family around British Columbia, I was back to being on my own, heading into the fall season.

Spiritually, I had gotten to the point in my life where I needed to personalize my faith. I had just turned twenty-seven years old and needed to separate what I had simply been taught from what my true convictions were. I wasn't questioning my salvation or anything like that. I just wanted to understand things at a deeper level. Maybe it would give me insight as to where my life was heading. Since I grew up attending the Free Methodist Church, I figured that would be as good as any place to start my investigation.

I paid attention in Sunday school as a kid, so I already knew the Free Methodist Church was a protestant evangelical church that had separated from the central Methodist Church back in 1860. The word "Free" was added because the founders had several freedom principles:

1. Freedom from slavery. Methodists have always been against any form of slavery.

2. Free pews. It's hard to imagine but renting or purchasing pews back then was common practice. By ending this practice, it provided full access to the poor.

3. Freedom of worship in the Holy Spirit versus strict formality and protocols. Jesus always healed, taught, or prayed in different ways or locations. So, it's essential to allow people to express worship through the Holy Spirit, not a bunch of man-made rules and rituals.

4. Freedom from oaths and secret societies. Loyalty is to Jesus Christ alone. It's OK to join a membership but avoid oaths and secret societies.

5. Freedom from church authority abuses. If church leaders start claiming authority over you that is not scriptural, run and don't look back.

6. Freedom to experience transformation by sanctification through the Holy Spirit versus just sin-management. Gotta let the Holy Spirit work in a person's life to cleanse sins as we grow in our faith and focus on Jesus.

The Methodist Church was founded by a guy named John Wesley back in the 1700s. I figured I should learn more about this John Wesley guy to see what he believed. It turns out he was an Anglican Priest under The Church of England. John and his brother Charles started a "Holy Club" at the University of Oxford. The Holy Club focused on living a holy life and outreach to the sick, poor, and prison inmates. The other college students nicknamed the Holy Club "Methodists" because of their methodical ways. I can relate, as my brain is pretty methodical also. In 1738, John Wesley experienced an evangelical conversion. He suddenly felt a warming of the heart and complete faith and trust in Jesus Christ. From that day on, he became a fearless evangelist and theologian.

John Wesley traveled over 250,000 miles on horseback, preaching over 40,000 sermons and giving away tens of thousands of dollars. OK, so that's all fine and dandy; now I knew more about John Wesley and the Free Methodist Church history, but what was their core belief? I knew they were Protestants, but what does that mean? For this, I had to go back in time a bit further, all the way to the early 1500s and the Protestant Reformation.

The Reformation was the start of Protestantism and the split of Protestants from the Catholic Church. The leaders in Western Christianity felt the Roman Catholic Church was claiming authority and controls that had no foundation in the Bible. The reformers felt the church had drifted away from some of the original teachings of Christianity. The Reformation wanted to refocus Christianity back to the original message of Jesus and the early church.

Martin Luther is credited as being the prominent leader in the Reformation, but there were numerous others. Five points emerged from the Reformation, summarizing the core beliefs of Protestant Christianity called Solas.

1. **Sola Scriptura** – "Scripture Alone." The Holy Bible is the only authoritative scripture.
2. **Sola Fide** – "Faith Alone." We are saved through faith alone in Jesus Christ.
3. **Sola Gratia** – "Grace Alone." The grace of God alone saves us.
4. **Solus Christus** – "Christ Alone." Jesus Christ alone is our Lord, Savior, and King.
5. **Soli Deo Gloria** – "To the glory of God alone." We live for the glory of God alone.

All Scripture is God-breathed and is useful for teaching, rebuking, correcting, and training in righteousness. 2 Timothy 3:16

For it is by grace you have been saved, through faith— and this is not from yourselves, it is the gift of God— not by works so that no one can boast. Ephesians 2:8-9

"Jesus is 'the stone you builders rejected, which has become the cornerstone.' Salvation is found in no one else, for there is no other name under heaven given to mankind by which we must be saved." Acts 4:11-12

So whether you eat or drink or whatever you do, do it all for the glory of God. 1 Corinthians 10:31

After more reading and studying, I felt I understood my core beliefs and faith better. It didn't matter as much which denomination I attended, be it Catholic, Anglican, Lutheran, Baptist, Methodist, or nondenominational.

The important thing was that the denomination or individual church preached to the entire Bible as God's authoritative Word without any additions or deletions. You can't just cherry-pick out parts and pieces of Scripture, like building a car and leaving out the parts you don't think you need. The car seems to work, but in the long run, it will break down.

The church needs to acknowledge that salvation comes through faith in Jesus Christ. After all, Jesus is the one who paid the price for our sins. No matter how many rules, regulations, and good deeds I do, I'm still a sinner and won't be able to earn my way into heaven.

"Therefore go and make disciples of all nations, baptizing
them in the name of the Father and of the Son and of the Holy Spirit."
Matthew 28:19

Let's also not forget about the Godhead: God the Father, God the Son (Jesus), and God the Holy Spirit. He's one God existing in three forms, just like water can be ice, liquid, or steam, but it's still all good old H2O. Like Dad said when I was a kid, pointing me toward the Apostle Paul's words in Titus 3:9, "But avoid foolish controversies and genealogies and arguments and quarrels about the law, because these are unprofitable and useless."

I had come to the realization it's not about rules or religion. It's about a relationship with a loving God through Jesus Christ by the power and conviction of the Holy Spirit. I developed a firm belief that if I held to the Five Solas of the Protestant Reformation and, for good measure, the Free Methodist Church's six freedom principles, I would stay on track no matter what the world throws at me.

Each of you should use whatever gift you have received to serve others,
as faithful stewards of God's grace in its various forms. 1 Peter 4:10

As I continued studying and personalizing my faith, I felt I needed to get more involved with the church. Since I had left home, I looked for the church to provide me with something. But now, it was time for me to start helping the church serve and support others. Most churches are set up with elders and deacons. Elders look after more of the spiritual oversight of the church. The deacons report to the elders but do more of the church's physical business, like building maintenance, helping serve the church's people, etc.

The Free Methodist Churches have trustees instead of deacons and an official board or board of directors instead of elders, but they serve the same functions. I became a trustee, serving as the assistant treasurer and helping manage church maintenance on the building committee. I also began my first home Bible study group that met weekly at my place.

Along with my day job, these added responsibilities kept me quite busy. I may not have known the Lord's direction for my life yet, but at least I was getting involved in serving in the church. I began to pray about my career situation. I was feeling burned out. The housing thing with Edgar didn't work out. So, was there another career I should be trying? Should I start some sort of business?

As Mom taught me, I did pray about it, and we shall see what happens.

Chapter 20:

Back to the Big Leagues

He replied, "Because you have so little faith. Truly I tell you,
if you have faith as small as a mustard seed, you can say to this
mountain, 'Move from here to there,' and it will move.
Nothing will be impossible for you." Matthew 17:20

In early 1995, one of our project managers, Bob Walters, walked into my office. Bob had worked for PCL in Edmonton back in the day but had left to pursue a business venture. He had been working for us for about a year, preferring the milder Vancouver climate over the harsh Edmonton winters.

Bob placed a newspaper ad on my desk. Dominion Construction was looking to hire a senior estimator.

"Who's Dominion Construction?" I asked.

Bob told me Dominion Construction was an old western Canada construction and design firm owned by the Bentall family. It was a big-league construction company and competitor of PCL in western Canada. Dominion worked more on negotiated and private development work, so I had not run up against them in the lump sum bid school market. They even had a full-service design department, including architects and engineers on staff.

I said to Bob, "But I'm not a senior estimator." To which Bob responded, "I think you're underestimating yourself. You've learned a lot in your trial by fire over these past three years. But you've gone as far as you can with Granwest. It's time you return to the big leagues."

I had nothing against Granville/Granwest Constructors. After all, they had given me a job when I needed it most and moved me to Vancouver. However, Bob was right; after three years, I needed something more, both professionally and personally.

So, I interviewed with Dominion Construction within a week, and guess what? I got the senior estimator job! Not only that, but they were going to pay me 60 percent more than I was making at Granwest.

Woohoo! I was back in the big leagues. How's that for an answer to prayer.

I really enjoyed working for Dominion Construction. It was still busy work, but nowhere near the hours I was putting in at Granwest. I even had time to lift weights at a downtown YMCA gym during my lunch hours.

Dominion's chief estimator, Norbert Bonkowski, was in his mid-forties. He was an old tradesman who had transitioned to the office years ago, making him a perfect mentor for me.

Dominion Construction did a lot of design-build work. First, the design department would do the design and engineering. Then the building department would construct the building. Thus, the term "design-build."

Dominion was where I first heard the expression "pre-construction." You see, estimating is figuring out how much a building will cost to construct, considering labor, material, subcontractors, schedule, staffing, site logistics, etc. Pre-construction is everything that comes before construction, including design, permitting, figuring out the schedule and logistics, awarding contracts and of course, estimating.

I had simply performed budgets for clients or lump sum bids in the past. Now I would be working hand in hand with our in-house designers, providing cost input to the design as it was developed.

Soon, I began to learn about what truly drove the cost of a project and how to avoid overruns by studying the early selection of structural systems, aligning it with building function, schedule, and price. I learned how ratios of exterior wall area compared to the floor area could significantly drive the cost of a project up or down.

Not only was I learning, but I liked my coworkers. In addition, senior management was supportive and made me feel valued as an employee, which helped rebuild my confidence. David Bentall was in his early forties and had recently taken over as president and CEO of The Dominion Company from his father. He was a devout Christian and also a champion water skier.

One weekend David was looking for volunteers to help with building a facility for a Baptist retreat center on Keats Island just northwest of Vancouver. That was right up my alley, so I volunteered. David had just bought himself a new ski boat, so one other employee and I met David down at Stanley Park, and we all headed to the island in his new ski boat. It was a lot of fun that day, racing across the Strait of Georgia and swinging a hammer again to frame up the new building.

Doug and Grace Wedding
July 1, 1995

A highlight of that particular summer was my brother Dougie and Grace's wedding. I was honored to be Dougie's best man, as well as master of ceremonies.

I had now served in four weddings, being a ring bearer, groomsman twice, the best man once, and master of ceremonies twice. So, I now had experience playing all the positions except the groom.

Dougie and Grace would eventually buy a house and settle down in Beamsville, Ontario.

It was late November, and I was preparing dinner when the phone

Wedding Day
L-R: Dad, Debbie,
Dougie, Mom, Me

rang. It was Uncle Reg. The last time I saw Uncle Reg was at Poppa's funeral two years prior. Uncle Reg was now eighty-two years old.

"I'm coming out to visit you. I want to see the Pacific Ocean before I die," said Uncle Reg.

"No problem. I can take you to Stanley Park."

"Nope, I want to look out and see nothing but open ocean. I've been to the Atlantic but still need to see the Pacific."

"OK then, when are you coming?"

"Friday night, I land at 9:30 p.m."

"Oh, that soon, eh, OK, I shall pick you up at the airport at 9:30 p.m. Friday."

Friday came, and I picked up Uncle Reg. As we drove to my apartment, I said, "It's quite a long trip to the open ocean on the west side of Vancouver Island. It's going to take over six hours each way. Maybe we should spend Saturday night at a hotel in Tofino?"

"Nope," Uncle Reg responded, "my return flight is early Sunday morning. I don't want you to miss church."

"OK then, I guess we have a big day ahead of us."

Uncle Reg had a heart condition, and the next day on the way to the ferry, he had to take a nitroglycerin pill for chest pain. I suggested I take him to the hospital to get checked, but he wanted nothing to do with that.

"If the Lord takes me on the way to the Pacific, then so be it, at least we tried," declared Uncle Reg.

All I was thinking was, *Oh Lord, I was the last person to see Aunt Bessie alive. Please don't let Uncle Reg die on my watch too.*

Numerous times on the way, it looked like Uncle Reg was not breathing. I'd call out, "You still with me?" and after a few seconds, he'd call back, "Still here."

Arriving at the Tsawwassen terminal, we embarked on a two-hour ferry ride to Nanaimo, British Columbia. Although it was a chilly, overcast day, we stood out on the upper ferry deck, watching a school of porpoises swimming out ahead as if to lead the way. Uncle Reg greeted everyone on board the ship as we strolled the ferry's decks.

Once we landed in Nanaimo, we took Highway 4 across the mountainous island to the beaches of Tofino. Interestingly, the sunset was at 4:30 p.m. that time of year, so we couldn't dillydally.

The low-lying clouds were very dark; a light but steady rain was now falling. Not uncommon for that time of year. So, I felt terrible that the heavy cloud cover would hide the sunset.

After a long journey and a couple more nitroglycerin pills, we arrived at Cox Bay Beach, Tofino, around 3:00 p.m.

As we pulled up and parked, almost as if on cue, the rain stopped, and the clouds cleared, revealing a bright orange-yellow sun, making its way toward the horizon.

Taking off our shoes and socks, we rolled up our pant legs and walked out into the shallow surf of the mighty North Pacific. The water was so frigid cold, I could barely feel my feet. But it didn't seem to faze Uncle Reg as he looked out over the vast Pacific Ocean. I filled up a Coke bottle with some sand and water as a souvenir for him to take back to St Joseph Island.

Suddenly Uncle Reg said, "We need to get heading back."

"But there is over a half-hour before the final sunset. We can watch it, then get some dinner before heading back across the mountains. We will still have plenty of time to catch the last ferry."

"Nope, I'm good. I just sense the Lord telling me we need to get going."

"OK, well, I can't argue with that."

So, we piled back into the car and began our return journey, and it was a good thing.

A thick marine layer rolled in about a half-hour into the three-hour drive to the ferry terminal. The fog was so thick I could barely see the car's front hood, and the twisty, windy road through the mountain pass suddenly became very treacherous. One wrong move, and we could disappear over a cliff.

I edged the car along at about five miles per hour, just praying I did not hit oncoming traffic or worse on the narrow two-lane road.

Eventually, we made it back to Nanaimo, but not in time for our ferry launch. No worries though, we could catch the last ferry of the day at 10:45 p.m. So, we finally got back to the apartment about 2 a.m. Sunday.

I asked Uncle Reg again, "Sure, you don't want to change your early morning flight? You're going to be very tired."

"Nope, I've been tired before, and I'll be tired again," he replied in a matter-of-fact tone.

Uncle Reg wanted to give me some money for being his chauffeur. But I didn't want to accept it; nevertheless, he insisted.

So, I told him. "OK, but here's the deal. I'm going to use this money to get some Christmas decorations. That way, every year when I take out the decorations, I will remember our adventurous journey."

To this day, I still have some of the decorations, including a porcelain nativity set that I put out on display every Christmas season.

Early Sunday morning, I drove Uncle Reg to the airport and dropped him off. Then, with his parting words, he said, "Next year, if I'm healthy enough, I'm coming back, and we're going to go on the Alaskan Cruise."

That was the last time I saw Uncle Reg. He was just getting too old to travel. However, he did live for eight more years. Then on January 6, 2004, he passed away just a couple of months past his ninetieth birthday. I'm sure as soon as he got to heaven, he told Aunt Bessie and Poppa all about our adventurous journey to the mighty Pacific Ocean.

Uncle Reg and Aunt Bessie

As 1995 rolled into 1996, work was going well, and I continued to enjoy working for Dominion Construction. We were now starting to use computers and the internet. We also had this new technology called email, although not many people were using it just yet.

During late summer 1996, I bought my first home. It was a two-bedroom, two-bath condominium apartment in a brand spanking new building called "The Observatory" at the Gateway Skytrain station in Surrey, BC. I would take the Skytrain to work at the Bentall Center in downtown Vancouver.

One of the projects I was working on through design and pre-construction was the new Coquitlam City Hall. Although Dominion Construction had the contract to manage the project, we had to competitively bid on the concrete structure due to city requirements. I would be competing against none other than PCL Construction Vancouver for the concrete structure bid. So, one could say I was pretty stoked to go head-to-head with my old company once again.

As the bid date drew closer, chief estimator Norbert and I worked to strategize and price our structure. Although I knew all PCL's historical averages for concrete and formwork, Norbert, being an old tradesman, wanted me to take a different approach to this estimate. "Historical averages are a good guide, but if you stick to averages, you will underprice the difficult work and overprice the easy stuff," explained Norbert. "You have experience building formwork yourself. So don't look at the historical average to build twenty column foundations. Instead, think about what it would take if you put your tool belt back on and build one foundation."

Taking Norbert's advice, I thought about it. How long would it take if I was given the task of building one foundation? How many helpers would I need? Where is the material coming from, and how do I get it to the location?

Once I figured out everything to build one, I was then able to multiply by twenty to get the total cost and labor hours to complete all the column foundations. I also factored in the learning curve. Meaning once I built one, I would get faster as I made the remaining nineteen. I followed Norbert's method, pricing all the other structure components, including the walls, columns, and slabs. As a result, I was less than the average on some items and more than average on others.

I finished up my bid and submitted it to the City of Coquitlam, and I'm happy to report once again I kicked PCL's butt and won the bid. Not that anybody was keeping score, but I was now 2-0 in head-to-head competition against PCL.

Working with Norbert taught me to use my experiences growing up and working on the construction sites and apply them to my estimates, helping me develop a whole other level of instincts for estimating. I was now combining my field experience with historical cost data and subcontractor input to determine costs and schedules. Working with our design teams, I learned more about building codes and design challenges, figuring out how a project design would affect pricing and schedule.

Work was busy but manageable. I had settled into a good place career-wise when I started getting these phone calls from a recruiter wanting me to interview for a large general contractor out of Utah looking to expand into Hawaii and California. The recruiter said there was much more opportunity for me in the United States. "Thanks, but I've heard that before. Not interested," I told him.

Things were finally firing on all eight cylinders in my life. I enjoyed my job with Dominion Construction. I was active in the church serving God. I lived in a beautiful part of the world and had just moved into my new condo. Life was good!

The year 1997 was just around the corner, and I would be turning thirty years old. Wow, it felt like I had just graduated high school yesterday, and suddenly I was going to be thirty. The past ten years had been a whirlwind. I was still lonely living on my own, so I decided to get a dog. I found a local breeder of miniature poodles with a litter of puppies.

You may be thinking a miniature poodle is not the dog you would picture for a single guy who used to play football, trains Kung Fu and lifts weights. Remember, though, my asthma. So, I had to have a hypoallergenic dog, and my allergies did the best with miniature poodles.

I selected the smallest dog of the litter, a little black-haired female. She was the littlest in stature but had the biggest personality of all the puppies. I named her Gabriel after the angel Gabriel in the Bible. People would say, but Gabriel is a boy's name, and the puppy is a girl. My response, this little dog will be my guardian angel to watch over and protect my home while I am at work, and angels are neither male nor female.

Gabriel and I went everywhere together. She was very friendly and never growled or snapped at anyone. Gabriel felt it was her job to greet and entertain anyone she came into contact with.

She was also scary smart. One day I was putting loose change into paper rolls to take to the bank. I had everything spread out on the floor, and Gabriel was helping me, well, sort of. She kept trying to steal the rolls of coins stacked on the floor, but I kept telling her, "No."

Suddenly Gabriel grabbed one of the empty coin wrappers and ran into the master bedroom. I ran after her in hot pursuit. She ran back between my legs into the living room, where the rolls of coins were sitting. Then, barely breaking stride, she grabbed one of the full coin rolls and ducked through her dog door onto the balcony. She then turned and looked at me through the glass sliding door, wagging her tail.

Yes, I just got outsmarted by a miniature poodle puppy.

As the months rolled on, my health took a sudden turn for the worse. Sadly, my lungs began to fail me, and soon even my rescue inhaler was not helping.

Mom suggested I must be reacting to the dog. "It can't be," I said. With dogs, first my sinuses get stuffed up, and then my lungs get affected. This time my sinuses were fine; it was just my lungs were deteriorating fast. The doctor sent me for testing, and I failed my lung test miserably. Two-thirds of the capacity of my lungs was gone. I could only manage short, shallow breaths. The doctor said if we don't get your lungs working, you'll end up on a ventilator.

Maybe I'm not going to make it to my thirtieth birthday, I quietly thought to myself. I had cheated death a few times, so perhaps it was now catching up with me.

The doctor said I should send Gabriel to live with my family, and he was going to put me on steroids, trying to save my lungs. That week I put Gabriel on a plane to Debbie's in Southern Ontario. Eventually, Gabriel would go to live with Mom and Dad. The condo seemed empty without my little buddy Gabriel.

Once again, I was all alone.

It took a long six months; slowly but surely, my lungs gained capacity, eventually returning to full strength. The doctor told me although poodles are hypoallergenic, I would still be allergic to the dog's saliva and urine. Being a puppy, Gabriel used doggie pee pads inside the home when I was away at work. The odor from the urine was toxic to me and overwhelmed my lungs. The doctor told me if I wanted to make it to old age, I better stay away from dogs and cats.

Gabriel puppy photo

Gabriel all grown up. P.S. She didn't like the ribbons in her hair, but agreed to wear them for the photo

The Surrey Free Methodist Church had a new pastor for a little over a year now. Dave Barbour and his wife, Jacki, were an energetic couple in their mid-thirties with three young kids. They both happened to be ordained ministers.

Dave had attended a training from Pastor Rick Warren of Saddleback Church in California called "The Purpose Driven Church." There was a lot of excitement in the small Surrey Free Methodist Church as we set out to grow the church using Pastor Rick Warren's guidelines. Our goal was to proclaim the good news of Jesus Christ to our North Surrey neighborhood. We had set the operating budget for our upcoming year. The budget would be presented to the church membership for approval on Sunday. Pastor Dave worked for a meager salary as the church just couldn't afford to pay much. Unfortunately, we wouldn't be able to increase the pastor's salary this year.

As the day approached to present the budget, my heart was troubled; I couldn't sleep. Was it fair that we expected Pastor Dave to work full time but not provide a livable salary? He needs to be able to support his family. Not to mention, Jackie was also an ordained pastor and worked for free.

Being the assistant treasurer and a construction estimator, I kept reviewing the budget while praying for direction. "Lord, why am I in such turmoil about this? What should I do?"

Dave and Jacki were working on faith that the Lord had them at the Surrey Church for a purpose, even though they could better support their family elsewhere.

After much prayer, I had a firm conviction that if, as a church, we wanted to grow, then we needed to also step out in faith.

At Sunday's meeting, I stated my conviction to the church membership. I quoted scripture from Matthew 14:22-32 about the Apostle Peter stepping out of the boat in faith and sinking when he started doubting Jesus. I also quoted Matthew 17:20: He replied, "Because you have so little faith. Truly I tell you, if you have faith as small as a mustard seed, you can say to this mountain, 'Move from here to there,' and it will move. Nothing will be impossible for you."

I then challenged the membership to step out in faith and increase the pastor's salary. If they do that, I will also personally take a leap of faith.

Then pulling out a check from my pocket, I held it up for everyone to see.

"I have written a check for the increased amount. It's signed and post-dated to one year from today. If, at the end of one year, the church cannot cover the increased salary amount, then you can cash this check."

The membership accepted my faith challenge to raise Pastor Dave's salary. *Wow*, I thought. *Did the Lord just use me? Is this the start of my calling, my purpose?* Is the Surrey Free Methodist Church going to be like Rick Warren's church, reaching thousands for Christ? Maybe this was my Moses burning bush moment. Only time will tell.

Well, time will always tell, and it did not take very long. At the next board of directors meeting, the church leadership discussed my challenge of faith. They discussed that I was not currently tithing to the church and questioned if I would honor the check.

After more deliberating, the church board voted to reverse the decision to give the pastor his raise.

No one from the board of directors even talked to me about it; they just made the reversal. I wasn't angry or anything like that; I was just disappointed.

A person's tithing is strictly confidential and should never be revealed, let alone discussed at a board meeting.

If they had just asked me, they would have found out someone needed help with their mortgage payment, and for a couple of months, I had used my money to help that person. So, unfortunately, I couldn't afford to give the church money in those months because of this.

Tithing is a voluntary charitable donation, and there is no law saying you need to provide the same amount every month. So, I planned to make up the difference from my yearly work bonus.

Oh well, there was nothing more I could do. I felt convicted by the Lord to challenge the church in faith, and that's what I did. So, my job was done, but that was not the end of it.

As the month passed, a series of unfortunate events started to happen to those board members. I was being told this information by a third party, so I cannot precisely confirm what events happened. However, I was told they were things like a sudden cold or flu virus, car trouble, vandalism.

The events were not life-threatening or anything like that, but enough to convict those board members to reverse their reversal. So, I'm pleased to say Pastor Dave did get his raise after all.

At the end of the year, the church ended up underspending its budget, so everything worked out just fine. The church ended up with more money and a little more faith than initially planned. Oh yeah, and my check was returned uncashed.

Meanwhile, my hometown Sault Ste. Marie church was contemplating a $150,000 addition and renovation of the existing building. An architectural draftsman drew up some sketches of the intended work. Dad asked me if I could look at the project and provide my opinion on how much it would cost.

I prayed about it and prepared a reasonably detailed estimate from the conceptual sketches. My assessment totaled closer to the mid $300,000 range. Of course, I told Dad, I had to make a lot of assumptions, and I don't know the current Sault Ste. Marie's construction market, but around $350,000 would be a more reasonable budget to target for the work.

Dad presented my budget estimate to the church building committee. Well, the cost of $350,000 did not go over very well. Some committee members doubted my budget and questioned many of the costs. Dad, getting a bit annoyed at the responses, said, "Kenny gets paid to do this professionally. So, I don't think we should disregard it." Ah, but disregard it they did. After all, what does Kenny know about construction in Sault Ste. Marie?

Months later, the pastor talked with a pastor from another church that had just completed a similar size renovation.

"Hey, what did that building addition cost you guys?" he asked the pastor of the other church.

"We ended up spending well over $300,000 on it."

Well, my hometown church eventually raised its construction budget. So, I guess, once again, I was just the messenger to the church. But it seems Jesus was the one sending the message.

Over the years, I developed a friendship with Vince Furlong. He was in his mid-fifties and specialized in stone and masonry contracting. Vince had provided me with subtrade pricing both in Toronto and Vancouver.

When Vince found out I was turning thirty, he invited me to his timeshare in Cabo San Lucas, Mexico. It turns out Vince, along with his wife, brother-in-law, and sister-in-law from England, we're all going down to Cabo in September. The timeshare was paid for, so my only expenses would be airfare, food, and entertainment.

I thought a trip to Cabo would be an excellent way to celebrate my thirtieth birthday. Not to mention, it had been a somewhat challenging year with my lung condition and all. So, I could use a vacation.

The year began great. Life was good, and work was going well; I was active in the church and settling into my new condo with my dog. But I should have known better. Over the past nine months, a storm was brewing. It started with my lungs getting bad and having to send my dog away. This was followed by not one but two churches disregarding me. Oh yeah, I haven't even mentioned yet that David Bentall and his siblings decided to sell Dominion Construction. Hence, my enjoyable job situation may be heading for an upheaval.

Since purchasing my condo, the value had dropped by over 10 percent, and to top it all off, I had overextended myself financially on buying the condo and some bad investments.

So yes, a tropical getaway sounded good right about now.

The first few days in Cabo were very relaxing, although very hot. Then, toward the end of the first week, we got the news a tropical storm was heading our way. Isn't that just perfect; a real storm was brewing.

The storm gained intensity, and we now had category four hurricane Nora bearing down on Cabo San Lucas with sustained 215 km/h (130 mph) winds.

I didn't sign up for a category four hurricane, so I called the airline to see about getting an early flight back to Canada, but no luck; all flights were booked.

Rats, there was no choice but to ride out the storm in Cabo.

Fortunately, Nora tracked west of Cabo San Lucas, but we did get a few days of high winds, heavy rains, and 6-meter (20-foot) waves. The massive waves carved up the beach pretty good. There was a six to eight-foot cliff of sand about halfway up the beach line from the water. The sizeable crashing storm waves had carved back the beach into the depths of the ocean.

After the storm passed, the sun came out, and I decided to go for a long walk on the beach. As with the aftermath of many a storm, it was peaceful and calm; I walked and prayed as the ocean waves rolled up and hit my ankles.

"Lord, where do I go from here? What do you want from me? I'm thirty years old now. I didn't even think I would live this long. I still have not found my purpose in life. I'd like to get married and start a family of my own, but so far that's not happening. If I have no real purpose, then maybe you should just take me home to heaven."

I was getting tired, walking in the sand under the hot sun, beads of sweat rolling off my bald head and down my face. Exhausted and looking down at the ground in front of me, I slowly trudged along.

Suddenly I heard a loud roaring sound. Turning my head to the right, I saw a wall of water coming straight at me. It was a rogue wave coming off the back of Hurricane Nora.

Oh crap! My heart rate took off running, not even waiting for my brain to catch up with the magnitude of danger bearing down on me. I turned to run from the tidal wave, only to be trapped at the bottom of the sand cliff. Frantically I tried to scamper up the sandbank as the colossal wave slammed down on me. The initial weight of water felt like being tackled by an elephant. I held my breath as, face first, my entire body was squashed into the sand under the swirling water.

Swiftly the water reversed course, grabbing at me like hundreds of tiny hands trying to pull me out to sea. I desperately grasped at the sand, trying to escape the clutches of the retreating wave. After about fifteen seconds, I once again felt the hot sun hitting my back. My swim trunks were now down to my knees.

Getting up, I regained my composure, pulling up my shorts; I walked on the road the rest of the way to the resort. Now, I don't want to over-spiritualize this event, but I will say this: if you're ever questioning God about why you are here, don't do it with your back to the ocean. I am just saying.

The Cabo trip was a fun time, and I did a lot of praying and soul-searching over those two weeks.

While in Cabo, I also grew a goatee and, upon returning, shaved off my already thinning hair for the first time. Several people said it was a good look for me. Nobody had ever commented on my looks before, so a shaved head and goatee became my new signature look.

Mom was not thrilled about my new look.

"Your scars from your surgery will show," Mom said.

"My scars have healed, Mom. Besides they're on the back of my head. I don't even see them."

A lot more than my hairstyle or lack thereof was changing. I decided to move on from the Surrey Free Methodist Church officially. Now thirty years old, I felt the Lord was just leading me in a different direction. I desired to get married and have a family of my own, including adopting

My new signature look

at least one child. Unfortunately, that wasn't happening at my current church, so I needed to go somewhere to meet more people in my age group and stage of life.

Things at Dominion Construction had started going in the wrong direction. At least wrong for me. A new vice president was put in charge, making all sorts of changes. First, the design and engineering department was split off from the construction company. Then a lot of staff were laid off. Chief Norbert and I were the only ones left in the estimating department.

Soon after, the new vice president talked about not needing an estimating department. He figured the project managers could do their own estimating. Then, if that wasn't bad enough, he wanted me to start bidding on a couple of schools per month. No need to do as detailed an estimate, the vice president said.

That was it for me. I had been there, done that, and did not want to go back to that kind of estimating. In February 1998, I picked up the phone and called PCL's Vancouver chief estimator Dave Housser.

After telling Dave what was going on at Dominion Construction, he said, "Can you drop by our office? We have a new vice president and district manager named Bob Martz that I'd like you to meet."

I met with Dave and Bob before work the following day, and they had a job offer already prepared for me. And just like that, I was back at PCL. My only regret was leaving Norbert at Dominion Construction after learning so much from him over the past three years. He was like my Mr. Miyagi, the karate expert in *The Karate Kid.* He taught me to rely on instincts and take my estimating and pre-construction abilities to a whole different level.

I tried to convince Norbert to come to PCL, but he said he was too old and set in his ways to make a change.

Nineteen ninety-seven ended up being a very strange year. I guess it turned out to be a transitional year for me; it started with lots of promise and ended with a big storm. All of that was behind me now. It was February 1998, and after six years away, I was returning to PCL.

I had learned a lot in those past six years, both professionally and spiritually. But I was still grasping for a purpose and direction in life. I started attending a new church called Panorama. With a new church and a new start at PCL, maybe 1998 will be the year I find my purpose.

Chapter 21:

Mr. Herzog

For we are God's handiwork, created in Christ Jesus to do good works, which God prepared in advance for us to do. Ephesians 2:10

Change is always the constant, and more than a few things had certainly changed in the six years I had been away from PCL. Chairman of the Board Bob Stollery had wholly retired. Joe Thompson moved from being CEO to chairman. Eastern Canada President Ross Grieve, who had helped me with my estimate years earlier, was the new CEO. Toronto Vice President (and my biggest acting fan) Al Troppmann, was still around but had been promoted and moved to the United States. He served as PCL executive vice president, overseeing Denver, Seattle, Minneapolis, and Orlando. VP of Business Development Ted Cook, who had initially hired me back in 1989, was now the Seattle office vice president and district manager, reporting to Al Troppmann. Other than a reshuffling of the executives, things at PCL were pretty much the same. Within a couple of days, I was back working on an estimate, and it was like I had never left.

PCL had really upped their game with new technology while I was gone. They had converted the old PCL estimating system from a DOS-based system to Windows. In addition, email was being widely used throughout the company. I began attending Panorama Church in Surrey, British Columbia. They met in a high school theater and had contemporary praise and worship music, which was a big deal back then.

You see, Protestant churches were in the middle of this cultural shift with style and music. Younger folks wanted to be less formal, preferring modern contemporary praise and worship over the traditional hymns. The older generation still wanted their pastor in a suit and tie, behind a pulpit, with good old hymns and a pipe organ. The funny thing is, the Bible does not dictate the style of praise and worship, only that we "should" praise and worship. I joined a home Bible study group to get to know some folks in the church. I also volunteered to help with Sunday services, being assigned as an assistant Sunday school teacher for the four and five year olds. I may not look like your typical kindergarten teacher, but it was a good fit for me. After all, I had a lot of practice helping Mom out with the kids at church back in the day.

One of the single guys in my Bible study group suggested checking out the 30-something singles ministry at the large Willingdon Church in Burnaby. That night I met a young single mom in her late 20s named Susan. She was from Argentina and didn't get out much, having a two-year-old boy named William and no car. I thought, hey, my friend Edgar is from Argentina, and he was now dating Marta, also from Argentina. So, I figured I should introduce Susan to them.

My cousin, Sherry, was now living in British Columbia and had a child's car seat that her son Christopher had outgrown. So, I borrowed

Edgar, Marta, and Me

the car seat, and in doing so, was able to help Susan and William to various church events and get-togethers, including taking them to meet Edgar and Marta.

That summer, singles from the Panorama Church started playing volleyball at Crescent Beach on Sunday afternoons and invited me to join them. A couple of the guys thought I should meet Lisa, a single mom in her mid-20s who attended the church. They figured I was well established in my career, and Lisa and I would be a good match. Not to mention with my car seat, I could offer to bring Lisa and her two-year-old daughter Victoria out to volleyball on Sundays. Lisa, Victoria, and I started spending more time together throughout the summer months. Getting along well with Lisa's parents, I had long theological discussions with her dad, while little Victoria and I spent hours putting puzzles together.

Our families even got together for Thanksgiving when my parents visited in the fall of that year. With all the time Lisa and I spent together, we only officially dated for about five minutes. Although we were probably a pretty good match on paper, the problem was we just didn't see eye to eye on a lot of things, which may have been because Lisa is an inch taller than me.

Regardless, our relationship was not meant to be and never got out of the gravitational pull of the friend zone.

We have much to say about this, but it is hard to make it clear to you because you no longer try to understand. In fact, though by this time you ought to be teachers, you need someone to teach you the elementary truths of God's word all over again. You need milk, not solid food! Anyone who lives on milk, being still an infant, is not acquainted with the teaching about righteousness. But solid food is for the mature, who by constant use have trained themselves to distinguish good from evil. Hebrews 5:11-14

As the year passed, I started to have some misgivings about the church I was attending. Of course, the people were friendly and all, plus I was having more social outings than ever before. Still, there was just something missing, a feeling I couldn't quite put my finger on. I began to notice all the sermons were very—how should I say—"feel good." Of course, it's great to have encouraging sermons about love and all. But sometimes, our world is not all that loving, and for us to grow in faith, it's essential to learn how to deal with some things.

I wanted to have some meat and potatoes in the teachings and not all this baby milk stuff.

I learned basic kicks and punches at the lower belts when training in martial arts. Then I graduated to putting combinations of moves together, which became more challenging. As I progressed to the higher belts, my body developed muscle memory. It almost automatically started reacting without my brain getting in the way.

Eventually, self-defense became second nature. I was now quite different from when I first began. I had been transformed and could defend myself, at least as well as any other blue belt in the class.

Growing in faith is similar to martial arts. Initially, you're praising and worshiping, learning to understand how much God loves you. But then you start discovering more about the nature of God and who he really is and how much he truly sacrificed for you.

Eventually, through the power of the Holy Spirit, your faith and knowledge grow and strengthen to the point it's just part of who you are. Now you are better prepared to take on life's challenges with a strong faith and trust in God. I just didn't feel the church was challenging people to grow in their faith and knowledge of who Jesus really was. I also noticed at non-church social events, a lot of alcohol was being served and not very responsibly consumed.

Talking with some church leaders, they said the church was trying to be "seeker-sensitive."

"Seeker what? What the heck is seeker-sensitive?"

Apparently, the thought was, many people stopped attending church in general because it was too rigid, maybe even legalistic. The old fire-and-brimstone preaching didn't attract people to the loving-kindness of Jesus, that's for sure. Panorama Church tried to be more open and contemporary, reaching the current culture. Thus, being more sensitive to those seeking Christ.

I agreed with them in principle, but I said there needs to be more spiritual growth. People will not grow in their faith if it's just all good music and feel-good sermons. What you end up with is a big social club.

Social clubs are fun, but when life hits you hard, you need to have strong faith to get you through the tough times.

Just like with martial arts, it's fun learning the kicks and punches, but if you don't move on to the more advanced stuff, when you get into a real fight, you're going to get your butt kicked.

The church leaders did clarify they wanted that deep-rooted spiritual growth to come through the home Bible study groups. Sunday service was intended to be a celebration of praise and worship. It seems I was just an old soul, being quite conservative in those days. Actually, I'm still quite conservative. It's just, back then, I was still learning how to be conservative while at the same time not too judgmental or legalistic.

I had a strong faith in Jesus Christ and a fair amount of biblical knowledge. But I still needed more work on my heart, balancing core convictions, and that loving your neighbor stuff.

That being said, I was struggling with the presence of alcohol at social events and the seeker-sensitive Sunday services. I decided Panorama Church was maybe not the best fit for me. At least not at this point in my life. I had gotten to know Lisa and little Victoria, but I wasn't developing the deep-seated friendships I knew I would need in life beyond that. I spent the next couple of months looking for a new church to attend. In January 1999, I checked out Peace Portal Alliance Church in White Rock.

Pastor Ross Hastings was the senior pastor, and he had not one but two doctorates. One in theology and the other in organometallic chemistry. His sermons were definitely not seeker sensitive. Well, maybe I should put that another way. It's not like the sermons were insensitive to newer believers. It was just that his sermons were more meat and potatoes than baby milk. It was like choking down a thick juicy steak and baked potato with a small glass of milk.

I liked theological sermons. But I have to admit, occasionally, I had to research some of the words Pastor Ross used to understand what he just said. However, beyond being very smart, Pastor Ross was very genuine, and I always found him quite approachable.

So, I joined a home Bible study group that had about ten or eleven people, including Pastor Phil Vanderveen and his wife, Karen. Pastor Phil was only a few years out of college and served as the church's praise and worship music pastor. He also had a good sense of humor, so we got along great.

I settled into attending Peace Portal Alliance Church. One Sunday, I was helping take down chairs after service when I met a couple of guys, Phil Rozander and Ben Sykes. Phil and Ben, both about five or six years younger than me, were heading to meet a couple of friends for lunch at Iguanas, a restaurant along White Rock Beach. So, they invited me to come along.

At lunch that day, I met Scott Yewchuk for the first time. He was a high school French, English, and physical education teacher in his early 30s at the time. He had also done a stint as a missionary in Africa.

I was getting to know people in the church quickly. The singles group put on a spring weekend retreat at a retreat center across the border into Washington State. That weekend and in the weeks following, I met all sorts of new friends.

Shortly after the retreat, Shannon McIlwain, Christine Brotherston, and I decided to start a home Bible study group. We began with a study on prayer, led by Shannon's father, who was a pastor. Our group had eight to ten regular attendees and met weekly at my condo.

It was a fun summer with quite a few weekend activities plus weekly volleyball games in the park. About twenty-five of us even went on a big church camping trip in August.

Scott Yewchuk and I hit it off. Scott's a good athlete and even played on the university volleyball team back in the day. He also has a good knowledge of Scripture and strong faith.

Being close to the same age and stage in life, Scott and I had a lot in common. Not the least of which was the innate ability to get stuck in the friend's zone with any ladies we fancied.

So, my social life had greatly improved, but my financial situation was not getting any better. I had cashed in some registered retirement investment funds to cover some debt. The problem was that Revenue Canada was coming hard after paying the tax penalty on the early fund's withdrawal.

To complicate things, my employer, PCL, which is employee-owned, offered me company stock to purchase. I had to come up with a twenty percent down payment to buy the stock. It was an excellent long-term investment, but I had to advance the down payment off my credit card to get the ball rolling.

So, with that, I had tipped the scales on my finances. I was now using my Visa card to make minimum payments on my Mastercard and vice versa.

To say I was stressed about my financial situation was an understatement. To make matters worse, I had no one to blame but myself. It was pretty embarrassing for someone who makes their living as a numbers guy to be so upside down on personal finances.

So embarrassing, in fact, that I didn't even feel I should pray about it. Why should I expect God to bail me out? It was my bad to be in this situation. I needed to get myself out of it.

I did get some financial relief when PCL sent me to Calgary, Alberta, to bid on a university project for six weeks in late August. The timing couldn't have been more perfect, as PCL would be paying all my expenses, including food, travel, and accommodations.

Sunday afternoon, I boarded the plane in Vancouver, taking my aisle seat on the right, just ahead of the wing. I settled in for the eighty-minute flight as the plane raced down the runway.

As we gained altitude, suddenly, there was a bang, bump, and kerthump. It was like the sound and feeling you get when you drive your car too fast over a speed bump in the parking lot.

My brain's first thought was we hit an expansion joint in the runway. But wait a minute; that can't be it; we're already airborne.

As the plane continued to gain altitude, two panicked-looking flight attendants suddenly ran by toward the aircraft's rear. "Oh dang! This can't be good."

Then the loudspeaker came on. "This is your captain speaking. Some of you may be noticing smoke coming out of the right jet engine. My sensors are not showing anything wrong, but we will be returning to the Vancouver airport to be cautious. Flight attendants, secure yourself for landing."

Suddenly and without warning, the pilot banked the plane to the left like a gulf war fighter pilot in a dog fight. I hung onto the armrest for dear life and tightened my safety belt to keep from falling out of my chair.

The guy in the seat next to me slammed up against my shoulder from the force of the pilot's maneuver. Then, banking out of the turn, the front of the aircraft dipped straight down as we accelerated toward the ground.

My heart was now beating faster than my brain could process; my stomach felt like it was trying to climb out of my throat.

Looking out the side window, I could see the ground getting rapidly closer as the plane began to shake and vibrate. I clenched my butt cheeks, teeth, and armrest as I prepared for imminent impact.

With seemingly seconds to go before the crash, the pilot pulled up the aircraft's nose. The landing gear slammed the runway as the breaks came on, and the engines reversed. We skidded from side to side like we had just hit a banana peel. Fire trucks were now running beside us as the plane came to a screeching halt.

The pilot shut off the aircraft, and we just sat there for about fifteen minutes before slowly being rolled back to the gate.

Once off the plane and back in the waiting area, we were informed they were getting us a different aircraft. So finally, after about a three-hour wait, we were back in the air on our way to Calgary.

As the plane reached cruising altitude, the pilot addressed the passengers. "I apologize for today's delays. I wanted to talk to you in the airport waiting area, but too many other people were around.

"As we were taking off, we hit a flock of large birds. The impact on the right engine broke off some of the jet fan blades and sucked them into the engine turbine, causing the engine to catch on fire. Then the automatic fire suppression system put out the fire and shut down the engine. We could have made it to Calgary on one engine, but I thought it best to return to Vancouver."

Somehow, I don't think that was the whole story. Finally, however, we landed in Calgary. I was tired but still alive, so all was good. I figure any flight you walk away from is a good one, right?

Humble yourselves, therefore, under God's mighty hand,
that he may lift you up in due time. Cast all your anxiety
on him because he cares for you. 1 Peter 5:6-7

Work on the Calgary bid was going well but as the second week of September began, I ran out of money and time on my finances.

It was Wednesday evening, and in just two days, I had credit card and mortgage payments due. Unfortunately, I simply did not have the funds to make the minimum payments this time.

As hard as I tried, I simply couldn't do it on my own. So, I had no choice but to pray about it and wait. Talk about a Hail Mary.

The next day, late afternoon, I received a call from the Vancouver office. It was Chief Estimator Dave Housser.

"Sorry, Ken, I didn't notify you sooner, but you're getting a salary increase of 4.5 percent. The raise is proactive from September first, so the funds will be deposited into your account this Friday, which is tomorrow."

"No way, really?" I was ecstatic; the extra income was just enough to clear my payments. Thank you, Jesus!

Never again would I be so prideful as to not pray for help, even if it was my fault that I needed help in the first place.

We placed second on the Calgary bid, so it was back to Vancouver where Pastor Phil told me he was planning on doing the theatrical musical *The Christmas Post* this coming Christmas season.

The play is based on a couple of Norman Rockwell magazine covers set in 1947, Indiana. Alice Garfield, a second-grade schoolteacher, takes a part-time salesclerk job at Herzog's Department Store over the Christmas season. Her husband was killed in World War II, and she needed to make extra money to buy her daughter a Christmas gift.

I told Pastor Phil I don't sing but have some experience with acting and theater. So, I would be willing to help out behind the scenes. Taylore Fox was a retired Broadway actress, music teacher, and producer that attended the church. She volunteered to be the director. I would be Taylore's right-hand man/assistant director.

We picked a couple of excerpts from the script for each role during the auditions. Then, as people auditioned, I would read the opposing character.

The main antagonist or villain, so to speak, was Mr. Elliott Herzog Jr. He was in his mid- to late-30s and the managing owner of Herzog's Department Store.

Mr. Herzog Jr. was very insecure and overcompensated by being a scrooge and very demanding on his staff. He always wanted to be in the Navy, so he wore a Navy Admirals uniform and used naval references like "on board" and "shipshape" while running around blowing his Navy boatswain whistle.

When I read some of Mr. Herzog's lines, they just seemed mean-spirited to me. The play was supposed to be a comedy-drama. So, I figured the only way to make this guy funny was to play him so over the top that no one would take him seriously, like a cartoon character.

After the auditions, Taylore Fox told me she liked what I was doing with the Herzog character and asked if I would take on the part.

"It would be a fun character, but I can't sing."

"Let's go to the piano, and I'll run you up the scales," replied Taylore.

After about two minutes, Taylore said, "You're right; you can't sing. That's too bad. I really liked you for that part."

The next day, Taylore told me. "Mr. Herzog only has one solo, so we are going to change that a bit. We will have Mr. Herzog leave the stage, and his staff does the song as a comical mockery of him."

And with that, I became Mr. Herzog Jr. in *The Christmas Post*.

Scott Yewchuk, who can sing quite well, took the male lead part of Maxwell Seldon, Herzog's store manager. It was two months of hard work and rehearsals getting the play ready for the two-weekend run, including a dinner theater night. But everything came together and the show was a success.

There were always many business-related social events during the Christmas season, including the Vancouver Construction Association Christmas party, with over sixteen hundred construction professionals attending.

So, I was at the Association party, minding my own business, drinking a Diet Coke when this guy started talking to me like he knew me. I was thinking, *Who is this guy? Do I know him? Maybe he is one of the hundreds of subcontractors I have met in the past?*

At that moment, he says, "And you were my son's favorite character."

It took me a second to clue in. "Oh, you've seen the play. I'm glad you enjoyed it."

Over three thousand people came to see the play that Christmas season, hearing about Jesus and the true meaning of Christmas. It was a humbling experience, and I thank God for being used to reach people for Jesus that way.

For we are God's handiwork, created in Christ Jesus to do good works, which God prepared in advance for us to do. Ephesians 2:10

Hmm, it makes me wonder. Playing Mr. Herzog in *The Christmas Post* in 1999 was the last time I acted, and it's been over twenty years since. Was the actor training I did in the early nineties simply the Lord preparing me in advance to play Mr. Herzog in that one play?

Christmas 1999 Playing Mr. Herzog Jr.

Regardless, the Lord used my training at that moment in time to help proclaim the good news of Jesus Christ that Christmas season.

After the holidays, the new millennium began. It was hard to believe it was the year 2000, and I was thirty-two years old. Finally, after eight years in British Columbia, I felt settled, found a good church, and developed some good friendships with people my age and in the same stage of life.

Not only that, but my health also was good, and work at PCL was going well. I was optimistic that I would soon meet that one special lady to spend the rest of my life with and raise a family.

PCL District Manager Bob Martz came and talked to me just into the new year. The company needed estimating help in our Seattle office. Bob said he would like me to stay in Vancouver, but there was more opportunity for me in the United States. Hmmm, where have I heard that before?

"I think in the United States you could be a chief estimator in three to five years, but here in Vancouver, it's going to be a long time before the chief position becomes available," Bob said.

Chief estimator! Wow, I couldn't comprehend ever getting to the chief estimator level at a big company like PCL. Jeepers, I often felt overwhelmed, just trying to get my estimates done, let alone being the boss. I thanked Bob for the vote of confidence but told him I wanted to stay in British Columbia. After all, life was good, and there are more valuable things in life than climbing the corporate ladder. Plus, as I've said in the past, the United States is a nice place to visit, but I think Canada is a better place to live.

The Seattle thing kept popping up over the next couple of months, and I kept batting it down. Ted Cook, who had initially hired me back in Toronto, was running the Seattle district.

Ted said, "Why don't you drive down for a day to check out the office and the area? Maybe you could just help us out for a few months to see if you like it."

Bob Martz was not in favor of loaning me out to Seattle for a few months as he needed to plan for the coming year's workload. So, it was decided I would drive down, check out the Seattle office on Thursday, which was actually located in Bellevue, Washington. Then I would have to decide by Monday morning if I was moving or not.

Early Thursday morning, I made the two-hour drive to our Seattle office. After meeting with Chief Estimator Grant Morehead and a few others, I drove around and toured the area.

After eight long years, I had finally built a life for myself in beautiful British Columbia. *What am I even doing down here?* I thought as I drove back to Vancouver. I was at a real crossroads. In three days, I would have to make a decision that would completely change the trajectory of my life.

As I made the drive back home, I prayed. "Lord, is this what you want for me?

"I've spent eight hard years in British Columbia building a life for myself. I'm finally in a good place, with a church, friends, and a job. Am I just supposed to walk away from all that into the unknown?

"I'm tired; all I want to do is settle down and start a family. I'm done always chasing tomorrow. I want to start living for today."

I got home just in time for Thursday night's Bible study group. Scott Yewchuk came to the group that night, knowing the big decision

I had ahead of me. I shared with the group what was happening, and everyone took turns praying for me.

That night, I could not sleep. As I tossed and turned, I prayed to the Lord for guidance and made my case to him why I should stay in British Columbia. You may be thinking, what's the big deal? If you want to go, then go. If you're going to stay, then stay. Exactly, I agree, and that's the conclusion I came to as I fell asleep about 5:00 a.m.

I had decided to stay in British Columbia, and no one was going to convince me otherwise.

One short hour later, my alarm went off; it was 6:00 a.m. and time to get up for work. Not only was I exhausted from my sleepless night, but now I had a strong feeling I was supposed to move to Seattle. I thought this was insanity, as my mind started bouncing back and forth like my brain and spirit were having a boxing match.

Mid-morning, I got a call at work. It was Scott Yewchuk; he said, "I was praying for you last night, and I have a strong feeling I am supposed to say, you need to move to Seattle."

Hey, Lord, that's not fair; now you're ganging up on me. Throughout the past few years, I had subcontractors, recruiters, coworkers, and now friends saying I should move to the United States. OK, I got it; I can take a hint. Without any further ado, I agreed to move to Seattle.

I knew moving and starting over again would have challenges. But I've always had faith in God. In my heart, I trusted he would be looking out for me, even in a different country.

"OK, Lord, now that I'm going, what about my condo? It's now worth twenty percent less than when I bought it."

I contacted a property manager, and he told me it might take months to find a renter. *Well, that's just great, I thought. More financial hardship.* But when God wants you to move, God wants you to move. Surprisingly (or unsurprisingly), I had a renter within twenty-four hours of placing the ad. Wow, even the property manager was shocked.

OK, so I'll give the Lord credit on the renter thing, but my car was a different story. It had some costly mechanical issues. Transferring it to the USA could prove problematic without getting it fixed. Not to mention, the cost to fix it exceeded what I could get from a sale. So, I didn't know what to do other than add the car issue to my prayer list.

A few days before leaving town, I ran over a nail in the road. Just perfect. *Lord, you do realize I'm moving in a few days, I don't have time to deal with this.* When I took the car to get the tire fixed, I mentioned to the mechanic about moving to the United States in a couple of days.

When I returned to pick up my car, the mechanic said, "With you going to the USA and all, would you be willing to sell me your car? My daughter will be heading to college this year, and I was looking for a vehicle for her."

"Sure, but it needs some repairs."

"Yeah, I know. I checked it out. Those repairs would cost you a lot of money because of all the labor hours involved. However, I can make those repairs myself at a minimal cost."

So, thanks to prayer and a small nail in the road, I sold my car at a reasonable price.

A few days later, I tossed a couple of suitcases into a rental car. The moving truck had just finished packing up my condo and began its journey to Seattle. It would be a week before my belongings would arrive at my apartment. I don't know why it would take a week, something about clearing customs.

I crossed over the Peace Arch Border Crossing with my immigration paperwork. After four hours at United States Immigration, I received my L1A Visa.

OK, Lord, I sure hope you know what you're doing because I sure don't.

Look out, America, here I come!

Chapter 22:

Coming to America

But our citizenship is in heaven. And we eagerly await a
Savior from there, the Lord Jesus Christ. Philippians 3:20-21

That first couple of weeks were pretty hectic. I rented an apartment in Redmond, Washington, about a twenty-minute drive from the PCL office. Since my furniture was still visiting with customs, I stayed in Bellevue's Doubletree Hotel during my first week. There is so much to do when you move to a new country. First off, I had to get my United States social security number, similar to a Canadian social insurance number. You need this number to work in the country legally.

Once I had secured my new social security number, it was time to get my driver's license. The state made me do both a written and driving exam. Unfortunately, there were no free credits for having a Canadian driver's license. Another priority was to find a family practice doctor. Finally, I found a doctor's office taking new patients. First, they asked for my health insurance information, which I had from PCL's insurance benefits program. Then the doctor's assistant asked me for my social security number.

"Uh, my social security number?" I questioned. "That's my tax identification, so unless your initials are IRS, I won't be giving you that number, eh."

"Well, sir, that's how we identify you."

"That's insane. In Canada, the only folks we give our social insurance number to are our employer and Revenue Canada."

"Well, I guess you'll be driving back to Canada for your medical treatment then." And with that, she hung up on me.

Interesting. Well, that didn't go very well; maybe it was my Canadian accent.

I mentioned the encounter to one of my coworkers. He told me that most medical professionals require you to provide your social security number for identification purposes in the United States. That's insane, or so I thought. However, I figured I had only been in the country for two days and would probably not be changing the American system just yet.

I eventually found a good doctor and set up an appointment.

"Doctor, I need prescriptions for an asthma inhaler and some Tylenol 3 with codeine for my headaches."

"Tylenol 3 with codeine?" responded the doctor. "Codeine is a narcotic and addictive."

"I'm not addicted. I've been taking it for headaches since I was twelve years old."

"That's exactly my point," the doctor exclaimed.

The doctor gave me a prescription for the muscle relaxant Soma (Carisoprodol). In addition, he recommended I use simple over-the-counter Advil for headaches. Truth be told, the Soma and Advil killed the headaches much better than Tylenol 3. But the Soma did make me a bit light-headed at times.

That week, I received my first American paycheck. At first glance, I thought there must be some mistake. The amount of money was way higher than I had anticipated.

PCL had given me a 10 percent raise for coming to the United States. However, the tax deductions were substantially less than I was used to seeing. My taxes were lower mostly because Washington State does not charge state income tax, and British Columbia charges provincial income taxes.

The result was my net pay after deductions was 35 percent higher than in Canada. Now here's the real kicker. Of course, I was getting paid in US dollars, and at the time, one US dollar was worth about a buck fifty Canadian. It was like I had won the lottery. All the debt I was struggling with was in Canada and Canadian dollars. So, overnight my financial situation completely changed for the good.

It had been about seven months since I sent up that Hail Mary prayer on my financial problems. Was this move to the USA all part of God answering that prayer? Or did he just use my bad financial decisions as a way to move me toward my destiny? Well, that's hard to say, maybe it was both, and perhaps it was neither. You will have to ask God about that one. All I can say for sure is that I was in the United States now and a lot better off financially.

With my newfound cash flow, I leased a 3-series BMW. I needed a car and had always heard about BMW's excellent engineering, how they hugged the road and maneuvered so well. I had wanted to drive one for years, and this was my chance. It was my gift to me for coming to America.

There were a lot of subtle cultural differences I was running into living in the United States. Not the least of which was the terminologies. Now, I have spoken English my whole life, but suddenly, it seems people did not know what the heck I was talking about.

While at a restaurant, I asked the waiter, "Where is your bathroom?" The waiter's response was, "You mean restroom?"

"Is there a toilet in your restroom because I need to go pee. I don't need a nap."

The waiter did not seem to appreciate my witty response.

Another time I asked, "What kind of pop do you have?"

"You mean soda?" the waiter responded.

"Ugh, yes, can I have a Diet Coke, please?"

Back at the office, the language barrier was even worse:

• "Do we have an elastic to wrap around this set of blueprints?"

"You mean a rubber band?"

- "Do we need a six-foot or eight-foot hoarding around the perimeter of the site?"

"You mean site fence?"

- "How many meters of dirt can you dig out of the hole in a day?"

"I don't understand meters of dirt."

"Oh, sorry. How many cubic yards of dirt can you dig?"

- "Is that a two or three-inch Q-Deck?"

"What the heck is Q-Deck?"

"Oh, sorry, metal deck."

- "When is the tender due?"

"You mean bid?"

Don't get me wrong, I understood people not knowing some of the foreign terms like Q-Deck. Still, it was kind of annoying when I used common words like bathroom or pop, and they would say, "You mean." It felt like I was not using the politically correct term for something and was getting corrected or scolded all the time. I did not realize that moving to the United States meant learning a new form of English. I needed to learn to speak American, eh.

Canadian English	American English
Elastic	Rubber Band
Pop	Soda
Freezies	Freeze pops
KD (Kraft Dinner)	Mac and Cheese
Parkade	Parking Garage
Hydro Bill	Utility or Electric Bill
Tobogganing	Sledding
Timbit (from Tim Hortons)	Doughnut Hole
Tap	Faucet
Tender	Bid
Serviette	Napkin
Pencil Crayons	Colored Pencils
Homo Milk	Homogenized Milk

Housecoat	Bathrobe or Dressing Gown
Toque	Knit Hat, or Stocking Cap
Stag	Bachelor Party
Keener	Brown Noser
Knapsack	Backpack
Eavestroughs	Rain Gutters
Garburator	Garbage Disposal
Chocolate Bar	Candy Bar
Klick	Kilometer
Chesterfield	Sofa
Kerfuffle	Scuffle
Pogie	Welfare
Molson Muscle	Beer Belly
Thongs = footwear for the beach	Thongs = G-string underwear
Give'r!	Go for it
Soaker	When you step in a puddle and the water penetrates your shoes
Grade One, Grade Two, etc.	First Grade, Second Grade, etc.

Beyond the language barrier, there were a few other differences I noticed. Like in Canada, we had used bank cards to pay for stuff since the mid-1990s. You could use your bank card at almost all fast-food restaurants, gas pumps, and grocery stores. I didn't even need to carry cash around anymore.

In the year 2000, going cashless in Washington State was risky, as many places still did not accept bank cards. People would even pay for groceries with a personal check, which was unheard of in Canada. Now, there was no shortage of Americans telling me how great the United States of America was. Unfortunately, I guess those were the ones that had never visited Canada.

It didn't take a psychologist to tell me I was struggling with a bit of culture shock. I wasn't a hundred percent sold on the whole *moving to the USA* thing.

Probably compounding the issue was Canada being less than a two-hour car ride away. So once or twice a month, I would drive up for the weekend and crash on the floor of Scott Yewchuk's place. Occasionally friends from British Columbia would drive down to Redmond for a visit. I told the Lord. "OK, so here's the deal. I'm here, but I don't think I can deal with this long-term. So, after five years, I plan on moving back to Canada."

Now that we had that settled, I needed to find a church to attend while living in the United States.

I began attending Westminster Chapel, a non-denominational church in Bellevue, Washington. Westminster had a reasonably large singles ministry, with a weekly Bible study and other social events.

So, once again, I started to meet new people. However, with the combination of work, quick trips to Canada, and dealing with my cultural adjustments, I wasn't putting in the effort I probably should have to make friends.

I didn't continue training in martial arts in the United States, so I was getting a bit soft around the middle and started hitting the gym pretty hard.

Not having much of a social life, the gym workouts helped fill my spare time, reduce my spare tire, and relieve stress from work.

I found myself gravitating toward non-Americans, other immigrants like me. I seemed to have a certain kinship with people from different countries going through some similar adjustments as I was. Although my culture shock was probably much less, since I had only moved from Canada.

That being said, I developed a whole new respect for people who take that leap of faith and immigrate to a new country.

At Westminster Chapel, I met Justin Auld, an Australian working on contract for Microsoft. I also met John Lee, from Hong Kong, working for Microsoft. We added Matt Prout, our token American, and started our own little United Nations Bible study group.

In the fall, I began dating a Latvian woman who had immigrated to the United States with her family from the Soviet Union at the end of the cold war. She wanted to go on the three-hour Argosy Christmas Ship boat tour. I picked us up a couple of tickets when she asked if I could also buy a ticket for a friend of hers, shattering my plans for a romantic Christmas excursion on the waters of Puget Sound. Well, the two ladies ended up bailing on me, so I had three tickets and no date. No problem, Justin Auld and John Lee stepped up and went on the Christmas boat tour with me. It wasn't quite as romantic with the guys, but we did get a free photo with Santa.

Hanging with Santa L-R: Me, Santa,
Justin Auld, John Lee

Things at work were going well. I had put together a successful bid for a forty-seven-story Class A office building at the corner of Fourth and Madison in downtown Seattle. It was a lump sum proposal for the structure of the building. We would also be providing preconstruction services and negotiating a guaranteed maximum price for the projects remaining scope of work.

It was nice to get that first big win under my belt, being new to the office—and to the country, for that matter. But I was coming up on one year since leaving Canada and was unsettled. So, as 2001 got going, I made a couple of changes.

I heard about a multicultural church meeting at Kirkland High School. A former Westminster Chapel youth pastor pastored it, so I decided to check it out. That first Sunday, I arrived at Antioch Bible Church. I quickly ducked into the restroom just before service was about to start.

I was standing at the urinal doing my thing and minding my own business. This tall, heavyset guy was doing the same in the urinal beside me. Finally, as we both stepped toward the sinks to wash our hands, the big guy asked me, "How are you doing?"

"Doing good, this is my first time attending. Have you attended here long?"

"Been going here since the church began."

"Is preaching any good?"

"I think so. Enjoy the service."

"Thanks, man."

After the few lively opening songs, Pastor Ken Hutcherson stepped out onto the platform. Oh, no. The pastor was the tall, heavyset guy from the urinal! Yes, that's right, I had asked the lead pastor in the restroom if "his" preaching was any good.

Pastor Hutcherson, known as "Hutch," was a former NFL linebacker who played for the Dallas Cowboys, Green Bay Packers, San Diego Chargers, and the Seattle Seahawks. Pastor Hutch had a larger-than-life personality and gave very energic, biblically sound sermons. It was exactly what I was looking for. I decided to start attending Antioch Bible Church regularly. In no time, I started developing good friendships with Ray Bittner, Tim Hayward, Dennis and Deirdre Sims, plus a few others.

Ray also worked for Microsoft, but he's not your garden variety computer geek. Ray is quite the outdoorsman and would often organize hiking and camping trips for the group and always invite me. Ray and I even attended a conference on J.R.R. Tolkien's *The Lord of The Rings*. These friends were all natural-born Americans, so maybe I was getting through my immigrant culture shock stage. Plus, these guys didn't correct me when I spoke Canadian. I don't know if they always understood what I was saying, but at least they smiled and nodded.

Wednesday morning, February 28, 2001, I was reviewing an estimate with Ted Cook when I heard a faint rumbling sound. Then, the rumbling intensified; I thought a large truck was going down the street. Within seconds the conference room table began to vibrate while the office floor started moving up, down, and side to side at the same time. Then the building's structural steel connections made popping sounds as they desperately tried to hold themselves together.

"We're having an earthquake!" yelled someone from the hallway.

I began feeling nauseous from the movement of the building. Is this the end? Did the Lord bring me to the United States only to die in the rubble of a collapsed building?

About forty-five seconds later, the 6.8 magnitude earthquake subsided. Our three-story office building was still standing, although my nausea remained.

Fortunately, there were no deaths directly related to the earthquake, but quite a few injuries throughout the city. Many older buildings were damaged, especially in the First Hill and Pioneer Square areas of Seattle. In addition, several bridges and buildings were closed temporarily for inspection and repairs after the quake.

As for me, I felt like a magnet for natural disasters. I had now survived a tornado in Southern Ontario, a category four hurricane in Mexico, and a 6.8 magnitude earthquake in Washington State. It seemed as though these natural disasters were chasing me wherever I went. I was still alive, so I guess Jesus must still be looking out for me.

June of 2001, I decided to take a two-week trip to The Gold Coast and Cairns, Australia. Besides taking time off for friends' weddings and visiting family, I had never taken a real vacation.

Growing up in the North, I had never been to a fully tropical location like Cairns. It was a long way to travel alone and lonely at times, but it was a nice break to slow life down and do some soul searching. The past couple of years had been a whirlwind, and I needed to get myself refocused on God and seeking my purpose in life.

I took all sorts of tours in Australia, including snorkeling on the Great Barrier Reef and visiting Cape Tribulation, where Captain Cook grounded his ship the Endeavour in 1770. It was surreal walking the isolated stretch of a tropical beach where, 230 years prior, Captain Cook and his men set up camp to repair their boat.

I went to an Australian zoo to see all the unique animals we don't have in North America, even getting my picture taken with a koala. When I arrived for my photoshoot, the young female koala was sleeping and not too happy when the trainer woke her up.

Handing me the koala, the trainer said, "Our little girl is in a bad mood."

I cupped my hands about waist level and was given the cute little animal. The small koala grabbed my love handles around my waist, pinching rather forcefully with her rear claws as she looked at me with angry eyes.

"Ouch!" I grimaced as the koala's claws sunk deeper into my skin.

As I held the little gal, I spoke to her, "How are you? Having a bad day, are we?"

Me and my new friend in Australia

She did not appreciate my witty banter and grabbed my chest with her front claws squeezing as hard as she could, all the while staring me down.

"Ouch!" I cried out.

At this, the photographer says, "Look here." So, my new little friend and I turned in unison, looking at the photographer just in time for the flash of the camera.

I had claw marks on my chest and waist for about a week but ended up with a good photo.

My vacation was concluding, and I was much more relaxed than when I had first arrived. It had been some good quiet time seeking God's will for my life, and I was ready to head back to the United States and fulfill my destiny.

Do not turn to mediums or seek out spiritists, for you will be defiled by them. I am the Lord your God. Leviticus 19:31

One of my last excursions before making my way back to the United States was a scenic train ride to Kuranda's mountain village. It was a remote village 20 miles (30 km) northwest of Cairns.

This place was almost 9,000 miles (14,500 km) from my home-town of Sault Ste. Marie, Ontario, Canada. I don't know if the Lord was leading me there for a reason, but I was a long way from home regardless. I strolled through the village shops, observing all the new and strange sights and sounds. Then, finally, I passed by a table where a hippie-looking guy sat. He was a tall, gaunt-looking man with his long, partially grey hair tied back in a single ponytail. The man's bright yellow and orange tie-dye T-shirt stood out in the crowded village, drawing your eyes to him.

Behind the hippie man was a big sign proclaiming, "Psychic, 25 years' experience." He sat looking down in a trance-like state and wav-ing his hands over several tarot cards on the table. A young couple was seated, intently watching and listening to every word and breath of the self-proclaimed psychic.

I had an uneasy feeling as I passed by, staring at the hippie psychic, but he did not break his trance or even look up at me. Fading back into the crowd about fifty feet and to the left of the table, I took one last look back at the psychic. I remembered a sermon in which the pastor said only God could know our thoughts. Evil spirits can only hear us; they cannot read our minds.

Looking back toward the psychic, I whispered softly, "Can you see me? Do you know that I am here?"

At that moment, the psychic quickly lifted his head, looked straight at me as the crowd between him and me seemed to separate for a split second. He blinked twice, and his brow wrinkled as if angry as our eyes locked on each other.

Then, I stared back into his eyes. Who are you? At this, he quickly turned away and went back into his trance.

I think maybe the Lord was trying to show me something in that remote place so far from home. But one thing is for sure: the experience was hair-standing-up-on-the-back-of-your-neck freaky. Multiple verses in the Bible give warnings about mediums and psychics. So, I decided to stay away from that side of the village for the rest of the day.

My Aussie friend Justin picked me up at the Seattle airport Friday evening. We grabbed some dinner as I filled him in on my adventures in his native homeland. Justin did mention I seemed way more relaxed than before the trip.

Shortly after returning from my vacation, I moved out of my apartment in Redmond. Aaron, a guy from the church, was renting a room in his Kirkland townhouse. I decided to save some money and rented the room, placing most of my stuff into storage. I was planning on looking for a place to buy within the following year.

The church singles ministry pastor offered a multi-week course titled "Identity in Christ Workshop," or something like that. Given my cultural adjustment struggles with moving to the USA, I quickly signed up for the course.

One exercise we did was break our life down into specific time periods. For example, my periods were birth through age five, elementary school, high school, college, Toronto years, and Vancouver years.

We then took a piece of paper for each life period, drawing a line down the sheet's middle.

On the left side of the sheet, I was to list all the positive things I remember from that period of life. While on the right side, I listed all the negative stuff. I then repeated the exercise for each period in my life.

The purpose of the exercise was three-fold. First, it was to identify negative experiences which turned out to be positive later in life. An example would be that I was orphaned as a baby, but that led to being adopted by stable, loving parents, showing how the Lord can redeem something terrible in my life for good.

Secondly, the exercise was to expose recurring themes in my life. If a lousy situation keeps repeating itself or manifesting differently over the years, then just maybe the Lord is trying to strengthen me to break through a stronghold in my life.

For me, a stronghold was getting stressed about deadlines. The more I worried, the shorter and more difficult each deadline seemed to become. It wasn't until I always remembered to pray and trust God about the deadlines that they became more manageable, thus breaking the stronghold that deadline stress had on me.

The third part of the exercise was to connect the dots, so to speak, and see if the Lord was training me for a specific task or leading me in a particular direction. The day came to share my exercise results with the pastor and the group. I read through the positives and negatives of each period in my life.

When I finished, the pastor said, "So what's the common theme in your life? I think it's pretty obvious."

"Obvious to you, maybe, but I have no idea."

"You're an overcomer."

"A what?" I replied.

The pastor explained. "No matter what setback happens to you, be it physical, financial, emotional, or spiritual, you've always overcome it and moved forward. I think it's pretty obvious that the Lord is working in your life to mold and strengthen you."

"That's great, but to what end?" I asked.

"Well, that's for you to figure out. First, you should pray about it."

Another part of the exercise was to take a spiritual gifts evaluation. The Scriptures tell us that God gives people different spiritual gifts. A number of these gifts are identified in 1 Corinthians 12 and include wisdom, knowledge, faith, healing, prophecy, discernment of spirits, speaking in tongues. Other gifts include evangelism, giving, mercy, hospitality, etc.

After taking the evaluation, my top three gifts were hospitality, faith, and works or helping others. One could argue I also had a bit of discernment of spirits given my experience with the psychic in

Australia. The last part of the course was to take a personality temperament test that aligns your temperament with people in the Bible. It turns out, my temperament and personality are similar to Moses. Wow, I didn't see that one coming. But I guess that's maybe why he is my favorite person in the Bible.

At first, I questioned the accuracy of the test. Moses led over a million people out of Egypt. I'm not that guy. As for me, I prefer to do my thing in the background quietly. I'm not too fond of all the drama involved with leading a large group of people.

The pastor laughed and said, "Your statement just proved the test is more accurate than you think. Remember the burning bush? Moses tried to debate with God about going to free the Hebrews."

The pastor then asked me, "Do you ever feel God is leading you in a direction, and you find yourself coming up with all sorts of excuses why you should not go?"

I immediately thought of not wanting to move to the United States. I even told God I was planning on moving back to Canada in five years. So, guess I'm guilty as charged.

The pastor explained. "This exercise matches your personality and temperament with someone in the Bible to show you what God did with somebody just like you. We tend to limit ourselves based on our weaknesses, but with God, all things are possible."

At the end of the workshop, the pastor talked about how we become citizens of heaven when we accept Christ as our Lord and Savior. Whether we live a long or a short life, we are just passing through this world. In short, it's OK to have a certain amount of pride in the country we live in, but our identity should be that of citizens of Heaven.

The Identity in Christ Workshop helped me to put things into perspective. Struggling with my Canadian pride, I was comparing the United States to Canada, but to what end. If my true citizenship is in Heaven, then I should be trying to impact the world for Heaven.

The workshop was a turning point in my life as I pressed forward to find my way in the world.

Me and Scott Yewchuk   *Lila and Scott Yewchuk*

Meanwhile, back in Canada, love was in the air once again as Scott Yewchuk married Lila. Scott's two brothers were his best man and groomsman. I was the backup groomsman and the chauffeur to drive the newlyweds to the airport after the wedding.

Work continued to be busy as PCL had me chasing lots of new projects. That year I was lead estimator on PCL's successful design-build bid for the Everett Events Center in Everett, Washington. This project included an 8,250-seat hockey arena and a separate practice ice rink. The building also consisted of a 50,000-square-foot convention facility.

Even with the earthquake, it was turning out to be a pretty good year. I enjoyed Antioch Church, was making new friends, had a trip to Australia, won the Everett Event Center bid, and refocused my attitude as a citizen of Heaven. Just when things start going well, life throws you a curveball. On September 11, 2001, terrorists hijacked four planes. Then, they executed the deadliest terrorist attacks in history against the United States, with almost 3,000 fatalities.

For our struggle is not against flesh and blood,
but against the rulers, against the authorities,
against the powers of this dark world and against the
spiritual forces of evil in the heavenly realms. Ephesians 6:12

I cannot even begin to imagine the horror this 9/11 attack was to the people and families directly affected. The thought that a group of individuals could be so deceived as to perpetrate such evil is beyond comprehension.

As the country and the world grappled with the fallout from the terrorist attacks, work in the greater Seattle area continued. PCL had started the process for my United States Permanent Resident Card, more commonly known as a "Green Card."

In mid-November, our office received a call from Armand Cote in Hawaii. Back in the mid-90s, PCL built the Hawaiian Convention Center, and Armand was the owner's representative for the City of Honolulu. Armand was now representing a developer who wanted to build an assisted living senior facility in Honolulu called Kahala Nui. The Hawaii general contractor doing the preconstruction was struggling with the budget. So, Armand wanted PCL to propose on the project. It would be a bid-off between the current general contractor and PCL. Proposals would be due just before the Christmas break.

When I heard about the Hawaii opportunity, I got this strange feeling I was going to Hawaii.

Hawaii was probably just wishful thinking, as I wasn't even going to be working on the Kahala Nui estimate. I was currently working on a bid for a large new Seattle high school, which was due simultaneously. Gerard Lim Kong would be the lead estimator on the Kahala Nui project, and Dennis Smith would head up the proposal.

Dennis was a PCL senior construction manager who had been in charge of the Hawaiian Convention Center's design and construction back in the day. It was Dennis's relationship with Armand Cote that had led to this opportunity.

A few days before Thanksgiving, Dennis Smith walked into my office. "Well, Ken, how would you like a trip to Honolulu?" I was ecstatic. I guess my wishful thinking was not just wishful thinking after all.

A key to winning the project was for PCL to self-perform the concrete and formwork. Since I had many years of concrete structure experience, I would put the self-perform concrete pricing together. So, we canceled the Seattle high school bid and dug into the Kahala Nui project.

Kahala Nui was a 637,000-square-foot luxury senior living complex with 383 living units in six concrete midrise buildings. The project also included a 406-stall, two-story underground parking garage with two full-size soccer fields built on top. In addition, part of the project was a new 72,600-square-foot parish and school building for the Star of the Sea Catholic Church.

Dennis, Gerard, and I flew to Honolulu for a few days to meet with Armand Cote and visit the job site. We would also be meeting with Glen Kaneshige, president of Nordic Construction.

Nordic was a small local Hawaii general contractor that we had joint ventured with on the convention center. We would be bidding on the Kahala Nui project under the joint venture company "Nordic PCL, a Hawaiian Joint Venture."

Before Christmas, we submitted our proposal to Armand Cote. Then I flew home to Sault Ste. Marie to spend Christmas with my family. All Christmas, I just had a feeling I was going to be moving to Hawaii. Those thoughts were absolutely ridiculous. First of all, we didn't even know yet if we would be getting the project. Secondly, even if we did get the project, Gerard would be the lead estimator and handle any preconstruction estimates from Seattle.

PCL would be sending a construction manager to Honolulu to attend weekly design and owner meetings. Not to mention, PCL did not want to set up a permanent office in Hawaii.

It took some time, but we got the call toward the end of January 2002. PCL was being awarded the Kahala Nui Project. It was a big team win and a great way to start the new year. About a week later, Ted

Cook asked me if I would be willing to go to Honolulu for the next four to six months.

Say what! Did I hear that right?

It turns out the Kahala Nui project was about 5 percent over budget. The owner wanted PCL full-time in Hawaii to help get the project back on track. Unfortunately, the assigned PCL construction manager Jeff Westphal was on a large project in Minneapolis, so he was not available. Gerard Lim Kong was also not available. In addition, Dennis Smith was retiring back to Canada that year, so he wouldn't be going. Since this was more of an estimating and budgeting assignment, combined with the fact I was the single guy, PCL decided I should be the one sent to Honolulu.

Before I flew off to Hawaii, Al Troppmann visited the Seattle office. Al was now president of PCL Construction Services for our United States operation.

Al walked up to me with a worried look on his face. "I hear we are sending you to Hawaii because no one else is available. But, you know, there is a lot at stake with this project; it's a risky one for us."

"Yeah, I know, it's going to be a lot of work to get back on track."

"When I heard they were sending you, my first thought was to sell all my company stock while I still had a chance," Al replied with a bit of a gleam in his eye and a smirk on his face.

Translation: This is a big opportunity for you, kid, but I think you're ready for the challenge.

Or maybe he meant: Don't screw it up.

Regardless, Al had given me his vote of confidence, I think.

With that and two suitcases, I boarded a plane to Honolulu.

Look out, Paradise, here I come.

Chapter 23:

The Cost of Paradise

"Have I not commanded you? Be strong and courageous.
Do not be afraid; do not be discouraged, for the Lord your
God will be with you wherever you go." Joshua 1:9

Dennis Smith and I arrived in Honolulu from Seattle mid-after-noon and headed to the Ala Moana Hotel. Jeff Westphal flew in from Minneapolis a couple of hours later. After having some dinner, we retreated to our hotel rooms. We were all exhausted from the long plane rides and time zone changes.

It was February, and there was a two-hour time difference between Seattle and Honolulu, making me wide awake bright and early. So, before breakfast, I decided to head down to the open-air hotel fitness center for a light jog on the treadmill. I needed to clear the cobwebs in my head from the long flight and jet lag.

The early morning temperature was a comfortable 65 Fahrenheit (18 Celsius). There was a calm northern trade wind barely gusting enough to cut through the tropical humidity. Soft Hawaiian music was playing on the overhead speakers. As I jogged, looking out over the pool deck and Ala Moana Park, the sun began to rise, revealing the swaying palm trees. I could hear tranquil ocean waves hitting the beach in the distance. It was going to be a great day in Paradise.

After a quick breakfast, Dennis, Jeff, and I headed to downtown Honolulu for a project kickoff meeting. We decided I would attend the weekly OAC (owner, architect, contractor) meetings. In addition, the developer would be flying in once a month for an extended OAC meeting. Dennis Smith and/or Jeff Westphal would fly in from the mainland when the developer was in town.

Eventually, as Jeff finished up his Minneapolis project and became more available, he would completely take over for Dennis, who would retire.

Armand handed me a list of potential changes to save money and get the project back on budget. These items were called value engineering options. I started to flip through the list, page after page. Gee whiz, there must have been over 200 items! Some ideas were small and simple, but many were quite complicated, which translated into a lot of work to figure out.

"When do you need pricing by?" I asked.

Armand responded, "Can we get them all priced within the next two weeks? The design is progressing, and we need to make decisions on these changes ASAP."

"OK, if that's what you need," I responded. At the same time, I was thinking in the back of my head, *How on earth will I get this monumental task completed in two weeks?*

To put things into perspective, two weeks is ten working days. So, I would need to do at least twenty mini estimates a day to make my deadline.

After the meeting, we drove to the office of our joint venture partner, Nordic, in Waipahu on Ka Uka Boulevard, right beside Costco. I would be working out of the Nordic office for the preconstruction duration.

After having lunch with Nordic's president Glen Kaneshige and chief estimator Rob Spangler, it was time to get to work. I had so much to get done in the next two weeks, not to mention I still had to find a furnished rental apartment on a month-to-month lease.

First things first, I needed to get the value engineering information sent to the subtrades for pricing as time was ticking. Email systems were in use, but they were still pretty rudimentary; you couldn't email large attachments or files. Combined with the conundrum, most Hawaii subtrades were not using email yet.

I prepared a fax document of value engineering and sent it to the two or three low bidders in each trade division.

I also called all the subtrades, but nobody seemed to be available to talk to me, so I left many messages, asking them to give me a call back.

It was getting late in the afternoon. Dennis, Jeff, and I packed up and headed to meet Armand Cote for dinner.

Since I was in the process of getting my green card, I had all my identification and legal documents in my briefcase, as I couldn't risk leaving them in the hotel. Documents included my birth certificate, United States work visa, passport, social security card, checkbook, and new Palm Pilot.

Palm Pilots were these nifty new devices in which you could store all your contacts and phone numbers, and they even had a built-in calendar for your appointments.

Dennis, Jeff, and I tossed our briefcases into the rental car's trunk and drove off to meet Armand at the Kahala Nui sales center in Kaimuki. We found a parking spot right in front of the building on Waialae Ave.

Armand invited us into the sales center to take a quick look at the Kahala Nui scale model and marketing brochures.

We stepped inside the building for about ten minutes, during which time Dennis grabbed some of the sales brochures. As we exited the building, he hit the trunk release to place the leaflets in the back.

"We've been robbed!" Dennis yelled.

It took a second for the magnitude of the situation to hit me. But when my brain caught up to my eyes staring at an empty trunk, reality hit me hard with a full-on gut punch.

I suddenly felt dizzy and sick to my stomach. "My briefcase, it's gone!"

We had all left our cases in the trunk, and some dirty rat had stolen them when we were in the sales center.

"Oh, no! My wallet!" I called out as I quickly reached for my back pocket.

I couldn't believe it. I had taken my wallet out during the day. As we left the office, I had stuffed it in the front pocket of my briefcase. Rats!

For those of you keeping score, I was on an island in the South Pacific just five months post-9/11. I had just lost every piece of identification I had, including my passport, work visa, driver's license, banking information, credit cards, and health insurance cards.

My Palm Pilot was also gone with all my phone numbers, account numbers, and even my home address. Not to mention I still had to find a place to live and complete over 200 mini estimates in the next two weeks.

As I stood there in the middle of Waialae Ave., I felt utterly naked. I had just been stripped of my entire identity. Heck, even my BMW and possessions were sitting in a storage facility back on the mainland.

I was in the middle of the South Pacific, with only the clothes on my back and whatever I had stuffed into a couple of suitcases.

When I die and go to heaven, I can't take anything with me, but it will be Paradise. Apparently, though, in this world, when you go to "Paradise," they take everything from you.

I guess that's the cost of Paradise.

I was up all night, flipping through the phone book and making calls from my hotel room. By the time I got my credit cards canceled, the crooks had already purchased over $2,500 worth of electronics and a large meat-lovers pizza with anchovies.

The bank would rush me a new credit card, but it would take forty-eight hours to get there, so Dennis and Jeff gave me the cash in their wallets, totaling about $65. After dropping the guys off at the airport, I headed to Nordic Construction's office.

My brain was now numb from jet lag, no sleep for over twenty-four hours, and the sheer panic of having all my identification and financial information stolen. In addition, the pressure to meet my work deadlines and get the Kahala Nui project back on budget was squeezing me like I was caught in a vise.

After pounding back about three coffees to wake me up, I called my bank back on the mainland. The bank manager was accommodating and recommended steps to protect my identity and start the long process of getting my identification replaced.

The first thing was to close my bank account and open a new one. Next, I called the three major United States credit bureaus, Equifax, Experian, and TransUnion, and placed a fraud alert.

I called Mom and Dad to fill them in on what happened. Being my parents, they were able to go to Sault Ste. Marie City Hall and get me a new birth certificate. Dad would also mail me a Canadian passport application with my birth certificate.

I needed to get back to Seattle for my driver's license, social security card, and work visa. But there was no time for such a trip. I had deadlines. Ted Cook and Al Troppmann had put their trust in me, and come hell or high water, I was not going to let them down.

Remember also, Mom didn't raise me to be a quitter.

I called PCL's immigration attorney who was working on my green card. Luckily, he had photocopies of my passport and driver's license that he could fax me. Of course, he then billed me for the phone conversation and the photocopies.

Gotta love those attorneys, always there to help—for a fee, of course.

It was now mid-afternoon, and I needed to get back to work on the task at hand, namely the value engineering. But, wouldn't you know it, as the day ended, not a single subcontractor had responded to my faxes or phone calls. This was not good, as time was ticking.

Rob Spangler told me that trades are not likely to call you back in Hawaii if they don't know who you are, especially if you're perceived as a mainlander haole (pronounced: how-lee). Haole means you are not from Hawaii and are most notably a white person.

Well, that's just great. I hadn't even been there for three days, and the locals had robbed me and wouldn't return my calls. Welcome to Paradise, eh!

I worked late that night but was exhausted, both physically and mentally. On my way back to the hotel, I stopped by a midweek service for New Hope Christian Fellowship singles ministry.

New Hope was a large church founded by Pastor Wayne Cordeiro. A couple hundred twenty- and thirty-something singles were at the service that night. Pastor Mike Lwin was the speaker.

I had talked to Pastor Mike on the phone before leaving the mainland, and he had invited me to check out the service when I got to town. That night at the service, the people were friendly, and the praise and worship music was lively, but I was not in a praise and worship mindset. Instead, I was feeling beat down and worn out. My mind was spinning on my current situation and how I would survive the next few weeks. I felt alone and abandoned, both physically and spiritually. My head just wasn't in it; I walked out of the service halfway through and headed back to my hotel.

Lying down on the bed, I tried to pray, but my mind was spiraling. I couldn't keep focus. How was I going to make my deadline? Is someone else using my identification? Is my credit rating going to be ruined, or something worse?

Rats, I still needed to find a furnished rental apartment. I hadn't even had a chance to start looking that day. Not being able to clear my mind to pray, I simply said, "Lord, have you sent me to the middle of the South Pacific to abandon me and let me fail? Am I being punished? I could use a little help here."

With that final thought, I fell into a deep sleep from pure exhaustion.

In all this you greatly rejoice, though now for a little while you may
have had to suffer grief in all kinds of trials. 1 Peter 1:6

In the morning, Hawaiian hotel music was once again playing. I had managed a decent night's sleep. I felt much better physically, but I was still an emotionally stressed mess. However, there was one thing that had changed. I remembered it was almost exactly ten years ago I was sent from Toronto to Vancouver, totally alone and inexperienced, to break into a new market for Granwest Constructors. I then worked for the Design-Build Company Dominion Construction, learning how to design projects to budget.

It was like the Lord reminded me, "I've already helped you. I put you in a similar situation before, and that training and experience prepared you to meet this greater challenge today."

I hit the office that morning with renewed energy, determination, and optimism.

Now don't get me wrong, I was still stressed, but with a new attitude. "I can do this; the Lord is with me."

My first ever cell phone had arrived. PCL sent a Nextel Flip Phone; it was the latest technology and included a two-way radio function as a walkie-talkie.

The phone also had this new function called text messaging, but nobody used that function. It was a real pain typing messages using a telephone keypad, as each number button represented three letters.

I started calling all the subtrades again. This time I left a different message. "Hey, this is Ken from PCL. I'm working with Nordic Construction here in Waipahu. I know this Kahala Nui project has been kicking around for a few years with budget problems. But I've got some ideas, and I need your help. I think if we work together, we can turn this into a real project."

The trades slowly returned my calls to my surprise and excitement, providing the pricing I needed. In addition, many subtrades dropped by the office to meet me and help me settle into island life. I was even invited to attend the NFL Pro Bowl game at Aloha Stadium, a dream of mine since I first took the field for the Sir James Dunn Eagles high school football team so many years ago. So just maybe this was Paradise after all.

It was a tremendous amount of work, but I made my deadline the following week. At the OAC meeting, a number of the value engineering items were accepted and incorporated into the project. But it was not enough to get the job on budget, plus we got hit with a few other unforeseen scope items.

Kahala Nui was getting hit with all sorts of unexpected design creep, as we call it, so PCL needed to come up with savings to counter these added costs. We also had to do detailed constructability reviews as the drawings developed, including revising schedules and construction logistics plans.

This project would prove to be a real tiger by the tail, and I needed to settle in for the long haul. Part of that settling in was getting a place to stay. So, I contacted a Realtor that dealt with short-term rentals that got me into a private furnished apartment at the Waikiki Banyan Hotel on Ohua Avenue.

My accommodations may sound luxurious, but it was far from it. The building was built in the 1970s and still had the original decor and furniture. However, the unit was clean and included a fridge, stove, two twin beds, and a queen-sized pull-out sofa bed.

The night before the next week's OAC meeting, I fell into a deep sleep. I started to have a weird dream, sort of like a nightmare, but I was not scared.

This shadowy figure was stabbing a knife into my lower left side. As the sharp pain intensified, I tried to spin around to see who it was, but I could not bring the shadow man into focus. I grimaced in pain and suddenly woke up.

Looking at the clock, it was 2:00 a.m. I was in a cold sweat, and my lower left side was very sore. I must have pulled a muscle, I thought.

Rolling over, I fell back asleep. At 3:00 a.m., I woke up again, and this time the pain was more intense. I took a painkiller and decided to take a warm shower to see if it would help, but it did not.

It was now pushing 4:00 a.m. and the pain was too intense to sleep. So, I decided to get dressed and head to the office. I was wide awake now, so thought I might as well get some work done before my 9:00 a.m. meeting in downtown Honolulu.

As I walked through the hotel lobby, I suddenly doubled over in pain. A security guard asked me if I was OK.

"I'm fine. I think I pulled a muscle."

"You sure? I think you should go to the hospital, Brah."

"You're probably right. I'll hit the hospital on the way to the office."

Suddenly the pain became so intense I had to clench my teeth and hold my breath for fifteen seconds at a time. The security guard called 911 and an ambulance was on the way.

Now Honolulu is known for its bad roads with plenty of potholes. I could almost swear that the ambulance driver was trying to hit every pothole on the way to the hospital.

Every bump intensified the pain in my side, but I was strapped to a gurney and couldn't move. I just clenched my teeth with every jolt as the emergency medical technician (EMT) kept telling me to breathe.

As we pulled into the hospital, the driver asked me how the ride was.

"Painful. Good job on hitting the potholes; I think you got 'em all."

"Sorry, Brah, a bit of a rough ride."

"No problem. Thanks for getting me here alive."

I have a lot of experience sitting in hospital emergency rooms waiting hours to see a doctor. I'll tell you what, though, you get some serious attention when you arrive by ambulance. I must have had six people working on me as they wheeled me off that ambulance.

After all that, it turned out to be a kidney stone. One of the happiest moments in my life was when they put that IV in my arm and hit me with the intravenous pain killer.

Whew, I could breathe again. After a few hours, armed with some serious painkillers, the hospital released me. I took a cab back to my apartment, got my car, and headed off to work as I had no time to be sick.

A couple of days later, I gave birth to a 2.5mm kidney stone.

I had now been in Paradise for a whole month and had experienced being robbed and a kidney stone.

I would go on to have my rental car broken into three more times in the following few months. They didn't get much, though, just a pair of Christian CDs and a cheap pair of sunglasses. Oh, yeah, and a gym bag with a wet towel and shorts left in the trunk after a workout.

The kidney stone's timing was strange, as I had never had a kidney stone before that day. Funny thing is, I've never had kidney stones since.

After a month, I was caught up in work enough to fly back to the mainland for a few days to get my new identification and work visa. The problem was it had only been seven months since the 9/11 terrorist attacks. You couldn't just walk onto a plane without proper identification.

I needed to visit the consulate to get proof of identification to travel. Canada does not have a consulate in Hawaii, but the Australian Consulate in Honolulu handles Canadian services.

Well, I had visited Australia, so at least I spoke the language.

I told the Consul-Generals staff about my story of the past few weeks and my current dilemma. I also shared a couple of accounts of my trip to Australia, just to break the ice, eh.

They said, "We will make you a proof of ID and put you on a plane back to Canada."

"Canada? I can't go back to Canada."

Without my visa, I wouldn't get back into the United States. I needed to get back to Seattle, Washington. So, after a little more convincing and a few more stories, they made me a proof of ID and arranged to get me on a plane to Seattle.

The next day, armed with my proof of ID, I was on a flight to the mainland. As we hit cruising altitude, the flight attendants started serving refreshments. Then, all of a sudden, the fasten seatbelt sign popped on, and the captain made an abrupt announcement. "Flight attendants, take your seats. Everyone, please stay seated and fasten your seatbelts."

The attendants scrambled quickly and buckled in, leaving the food cart in the aisle just up in front of me.

Unexpectedly and without warning, the plane dropped. Then the food and drinks on top of the food cart hit the ceiling, somehow managing not to conk anyone on the head as they fell to the floor. Next, the food cart tipped over with a loud crash; soda cans began to roll down the aisle.

It felt like the bottom just fell out of the plane, and we dropped a hundred feet or more, like being on the Demon Drop ride at Cedar Point amusement park in Ohio.

The aircraft, catching an updraft, floated up quickly in the opposite direction, now being tossed around like a paper glider in a windstorm.

The captain came back on the speaker. "Sorry about that, folks, we are into some significant turbulence. The storm is too high to get above and too wide to get around. Please stay seated with seatbelts on; it's going to be a rough ride for the next thousand miles."

Say what? A thousand miles? You can't be serious!

It was like I was living some low-budget horror movie, where the evil force was trying to keep me from leaving the island; it was the worst plane flight ever.

I remembered that God told the prophet Jonah to preach in Nineveh in the Old Testament. But Jonah disobeyed and got on a ship in the opposite direction. A violent storm overtook the vessel. Jonah told the crew to throw him overboard; it was his fault for being disobedient to God. When the crew tossed Jonah into the sea, the storm subsided.

"Lord, did I miss something? I don't recall getting a message from you, and I really don't want to tell the captain to toss me out of the plane."

We eventually landed safely in Seattle, and I could get everything taken care of. Then, a few short days later, I was back in Honolulu.

In May, I attended a weekend retreat on Maui for the New Hope thirty-something singles group now called "Mosaix." It was a fun weekend of good food, fun, and fellowship. I got to know several new

Can you spot me?

people that weekend, including Jeff Pagay and his girlfriend, Donna. Jeff, a local artist, had a quick wit and a good sense of humor, so we got along from the get-go.

Jeff and Donna invited me to attend their Bible study group that met weekly at Mocha Java coffee shop in Ward Village, Honolulu. It was a small group, including Jason Uesato, Richard Chun, and a couple of non-regular part-time players. We would simply pick a Bible chapter, read it, then discuss any thoughts and questions for the study. It was a nice, quiet, and relaxing midweek break from my hectic day job.

Jeff and Donna were also part of the Mosaix leadership team. I tagged along to help out where I could, and I did have some experience working on a church leadership team. It was nice having something to focus on other than work.

New Hope Church promoted daily reading through the entire Bible in a year, journaling, and praying. Go figure promoting Bible reading to Christians. Surprisingly, though, many professing Christians have not even read the Bible other than a few scriptures here and there. I was guilty as charged. I had read and studied much of the Bible over the years, but I could not say I had read the entire book.

I decided to take Pastor Wayne up on his challenge to read the Bible as a whole over the next twelve months.

I picked myself up a copy of *Halley's Bible Handbook*. Halley's is a Bible reading guide filled with historical and cultural information. The handbook doesn't interpret the Bible, but it gives historical background and cultural significance, helping me understand the context of the original scriptures. Over the next twelve months, I followed the New Hope one-year Bible reading and journaling plan.

In July, Scott and Lila Yewcuk visited Honolulu from Vancouver. Just in time for their first wedding anniversary. Exploring the island with some old friends from Canada made for a fun week. We even headed to the Big Island to view the lava flows from the Kilauea volcano. It was quite a sight for a bunch of Canucks.

The weeks turned into months, and before I knew it, Christmastime had arrived. Now retired from forty years at Algoma Steel, Dad and Mom flew from Sault Ste. Marie to Honolulu for a two-week Hawaiian Christmas Holiday.

Hawaii was a trip of a lifetime for Mom and Dad. It was almost like God was giving them an all-expenses-paid trip to Hawaii as a bonus for all their years of helping orphan children. We tried to attend the Christmas Eve service at New Hope Christian Fellowship. However, after standing in line under the baking sun for an hour and a half, we were denied entry into the jam-packed auditorium, as it had reached capacity.

The usher at the entrance said we could attend the second service in two hours. To which I responded politely, "No, thanks. Unless Jesus himself is going to be preaching, there is no way we are going to wait another two hours."

It was on to plan "B." First, we hit a Starbucks for a coffee and snack, watched the sunset, then headed to Honolulu City Hall to view the impressive Christmas lights displays. After waking up and getting the turkey in the oven Christmas morning, Dad read the Christmas story from Luke Chapter 2, verses 1-21. Then we got our coffee and cinnamon buns that Mom had cooked up the day before. It was just like Christmas mornings so many years ago, minus all the snow, of course. It was a special Christmas that year, exploring the Hawaiian Islands with Mom and Dad. We went to a Hawaiian Luau, visited the giant sea turtles on the beach in Haleiwa, spent a day at the Hawaiian Cultural Center, and explored all the shops and hotels in Waikiki. In addition, we visited Bellows and Kailua Beaches for a quick swim and long walks along the ocean sand.

One day we took a catamaran boat ride to see whales and porpoises. The whales were a no-show and almost everyone on the boat got seasick. Mom, Dad and I had good old Canadian Gravol (similar to Dramamine) for motion sickness, so we didn't get sick.

After each day's adventure, we would relax in the hot tub, watching the sun set on another day in Paradise.

Once we finished exploring the entire island of Oahu, it was off to the garden island of Kauai, taking the boat ride up the Wailua River to the Fern Grotto. We even saw the abandoned Coco Palms Hotel, where Elvis Presley had filmed part of his movie *Blue Hawaii.*

After visiting Kauai's Waimea Canyon, it was off to Hilo and Volcanos National Park on the Big Island.

We stayed at the Volcano House Hotel and had a couple of exciting days exploring the Kilauea lava flows. Then, driving down Chain of Craters Road, Mom filled her purse with some lava rock to take back to Sault Ste. Marie.

"Hey Mom, you know there is supposed to be a curse that bad things will happen if you take lava rock off the island."

According to ancient superstition, Pele, the Hawaiian goddess of volcanoes, will curse anyone who removes lava rocks from the islands.

Mom laughed. "Kenneth, we're Christians; we don't have to worry about any ancient superstitions," she said as she stuffed a couple more pieces of lava into her purse.

The next day we arrived at the Hilo airport for our flight back to Honolulu. After arriving at our gate Mom and I sat down on a bench while Dad walked over to the glass, looking out over the runways.

A half-hour before flight time, dark clouds started to form, followed by thunder and lightning. Finally, an announcement came over the loudspeakers saying the flight would be delayed forty-five minutes due to weather.

"Wow, that storm came out of nowhere," Dad said, looking back at Mom and me.

I looked over at Mom, making eye contact. I then looked down at her lava-filled purse sitting beside her. Mom pulled the bag closer to her side, then gave me the look; there was no way that lava rock was not going with her.

It took over an hour, but finally, the weather cleared, and we loaded onto the plane. After we all buckled in, the plane raced down the runway.

Unexpectedly, the aircraft reversed its engines and slammed on the breaks just short of the runway's end. Mom was still clutching her lava rock-filled purse as the pilot announced that we had mechanical problems and needed to get another plane.

Mom and I didn't say a word as we exited the plane. A couple of passengers were complaining about the bad luck of the delays. Dad was quick to point out to the two guys, "Would you prefer instead to be crashed in the middle of the Pacific Ocean?"

Dad was right; this was not bad luck or a curse. On the contrary, it was a blessing that we were still safe. Not to mention the airline gave us free meal coupons while we waited for the new plane.

Three hours later, and after grabbing a bite to eat with our free coupons, we were finally in the air on our way back to Honolulu.

After landing safely, we drove back to the apartment. Dad, however, was not doing well. He was feeling very nauseous. It wasn't long before he was hugging the porcelain with the worst food poisoning he had ever had.

*Mom and Dad Aloha from
Hawaii*

After emptying the contents of his stomach multiple times, Dad crashed on the bed. As for Mom and me, we felt fine, so the two of us went down to the pool deck for one last hot tub and sunset before Mom and Dad flew back to the Sault the next day.

To this day, those lava rocks reside at Primrose Drive in Sault Ste. Marie, Ontario, Canada. As for Mom and me, we still don't fear ancient curses. And as for Dad, he recovered.

I guess you could say as far as the curse of Pele goes, Dad took one for the team on Mom's Hawaiian adventure.

It was now early 2003, and I was in the home stretch on the Kahala Nui preconstruction. The project finally got its funding; demolition, excavation, and site utility work were already underway.

I worked around the clock, preparing the final pricing on the 95 percent construction documents, with all the subtrades, and ensuring that the hundreds of accepted value engineering items had been incorporated into the plans.

It was Saturday afternoon, and I had a headache from the long work hours. So, I decided to drive to Kailua Beach for a long walk along the ocean. Similar to Stanley Park in Vancouver, Kailua Beach was my go-to place to take a break and relieve work stress. Before my beach walk, I pulled into a Kailua drug store to get some painkillers for the headache.

I pulled out of the parking lot onto Hahani St. As I approached Kailua Rd., the stoplight turned red, and the vehicle in front of me stopped. As I came to a stop, I reached to grab the bottle of Advil I had just bought.

WHAM! My head snapped back, hitting the headrest. CRASH! I flung forward like a life-size bobblehead doll as my car slammed into the vehicle in front of me.

OK, now I had a real doozy of a headache as I opened the car door. Stepping out of the vehicle, my legs feeling a bit wobbly under me.

A pickup truck had slammed into me from behind. Unfortunately, my poor little rental car got the worst of it, being smashed into the vehicle in front of me. The middle part of the rental was now sitting about twelve inches higher than the car's front and rear bumpers. Fortunately, no one appeared injured. But unfortunately, it seems I got the worst of the collision with a sore shoulder, neck, and now throbbing headache. After exchanging insurance information with the other drivers, I slowly drove my mangled car back to the rental facility and exchanged it for another one.

Getting back to the apartment, I had a Diet Coke, some pizza, and about four Tylenol 2, the good stuff with codeine that Mom had smuggled into the country for me.

Praise Jesus for moms and good Canadian drugs.

The following week, Dennis Smith and Jeff Westphal came to town to finalize our pricing and contract for construction. Unfortunately, there was a bit of a tense moment when the project's cost unexpectedly jumped up two million dollars at the eleventh hour.

There were about twenty-four hours when I thought, *Well, that's the end of my career.* After a year of preconstruction, the project is dead. The value engineering didn't work; how could my pricing be that far off?

Dennis was good at the political stuff and calmed the developer down, buying us a couple of days to correct the issue.

Jeff took the incoming heat from the PCL brass and vouched for the work I had done, reassuring corporate that the project was not dead. However, he also told executives how they sent me to Hawaii on my own with very little support or resources.

I appreciated Jeff coming to my defense, but now we needed to solve the problem, or soon both Jeff and I may be out of a job.

It didn't take long to find the problem. The specifications issued with the final set of drawings had some added mechanical operating controls that were not supposed to be in the project and a few other things. The specification writers must have incorrectly copied these from another project. There were hundreds of specifications pages, and the error was in just a couple of lines. It was the proverbial needle in a haystack. We corrected the specifications, and the pricing came back in line.

Disaster averted. The preconstruction was a success, and the developer signed the final contract.

I had completed my official preconstruction duties and was praying PCL would start up an office in Honolulu. However, the word came down from corporate that we would not be opening an office, so I would be heading back to Seattle. I stayed in Hawaii an extra month to help Jeff Westphal and Craig Warner get the subcontracts awarded.

Craig was a PCL senior project manager from Seattle sent out to work on the Kahala Nui construction. Craig had also been the project manager on that Everett Events Center that we had won back in 2001. So Kahala Nui would be the second of my projects on which Craig would be the project manager.

Jeff, Donna, and a few Mosaix leadership team took me out for dinner on my last night in Honolulu. I would miss the friends I made these past months in Hawaii. On the flight back to Seattle, I had a chance to reflect on my time in Paradise. For me, it was indeed an adventure of a lifetime, beyond my wildest dreams, if Poppa could only see me now.

The Lord had taken me from a kid building tree houses in the bush on Primrose Drive to managing the preconstruction of a large project in Honolulu, Hawaii. It had been a year of personal and professional growth. Professionally, I had proven I could take on a large, complicated, over-budget project and successfully manage it through preconstruction.

On the personal growth side, I was sent to an island in the South Pacific for fourteen months. Then I was stripped of all my possessions except two suitcases, robbed four times, lost all my identification, gave birth to a kidney stone, endured the plane flight from hell, and walked away from my second major car accident.

The Lord God was there every step of the way, and with his help, I had overcome everything the island threw at me. Even with all that adversity, I grew spiritually, studying and reading the entire Bible. At Jeff and Donna's weekly Bible study, being able to discuss, challenge, and dig into biblical truth with a small group of friends was very encouraging.

As I flew back to the mainland, I was a very different man than when I arrived in Honolulu those many months ago. It was like I had graduated somehow, just like Moses. God took him from Egypt far into the desert for forty years. During that time, the Lord changed Moses, humbled him, and prepared him for his most incredible mission of leading the Hebrews out of Egypt.

OK, I know, fourteen months in Honolulu is nothing like forty years in the desert. Regardless, I was a different person now. I had grown a lot on that island in the South Pacific. Now the Lord was bringing me back to the mainland. I must be heading back to fulfill my purpose.

The purpose the Lord had for my life.

Chapter 24:

The Detour

Do everything without grumbling or arguing, so that you may become blameless and pure, "children of God without fault in a warped and crooked generation." Then you will shine among them like stars in the sky. Philippians 2:14-15

Being back on the mainland felt like a culture shock. I was back in the Seattle district office. Justin Auld had helped me secure an apartment on Mercer Island a couple of weeks before I left Hawaii. Ted Cook had retired, and Ed Olsgard was now the Seattle vice president and district manager. Ed was an older senior construction manager when I first left for Hawaii. I always found Ed to be very approachable and easy to talk to. He was like a father figure or wise old uncle with a good sense of humor and one of only a few people to still called me Kenny.

It wasn't long before I was back on the horse and off to a good start landing my first win. It was the Seattle Public Library Ballard Branch. The project was an award-winning design and included a 10,000-square-foot underground garage, 15,000-square-foot library, and a 3,100-square-foot customer service office. The unique thing about this project at the time was the heavy wood timber construction, landscaped roof, or "green roof," as we call it, and the photovoltaic solar glass panels. It also had a two-story, five-mirror periscope that allowed you to look out over the roof garden from the lower floor.

I resumed attending Antioch Church. While I was in Hawaii, one of my friends, Ray Bittner, had switched from Antioch to attending my old church, Westminster Chapel, where he started dating Lorna. I already knew Lorna and her friend Maria from my days at Westminster Chapel. While hanging out with Ray, Lorna, and me, plus a few others, Maria would meet our friend Tim Hayward from Antioch Church.

Complicated, I know, but I do have a point to this story. At least I think I do.

Ray would eventually marry Lorna, and Tim would marry Maria. I cannot take full credit for the two marriages. Still, I could vouch for Ray and Tim's character with Lorna and Maria, so I will take one-half of one credit for helping these two couples find each other.

The real credit goes to Jesus and how the Lord brings people into our lives, maybe just for a season, to help gently guide us in the direction we should go. In this case, I was blessed to be part of the group of friends helping these two Christian couples find each other.

Busy was the name of the game for spring and summer of 2003. Ray continued to plan weekend hikes and a couple of camping trips

L to R: Tim & Maria Hayward, Deirdre Sims, Lorna & Ray Bittner

for the group. It was also nice to once again be able to drive up to Vancouver, British Columbia, and visit Scott and Lila Yewchuk as well as Edgar and Marta Heyde.

My summer adventures in the mighty Northwest were about to be cut short when Ed Olsgard called me into his office.

"Kenny, Al Troppmann just called, and he wanted me to ask if you're willing to move to Orlando, Florida. However, just so you know, I want to keep you here in Seattle, but Al is asking, so I have to give you the option."

"Orlando! Is Al asking? Or am I being voluntold?"

"Al said to ask you. But so that you know, I'm not giving up on Hawaii and think there may be future opportunities there."

I told Ed I wanted to stay in Seattle and would love to do another project in Hawaii. Ed said he would let Al know, and I went back to my office. That's interesting; I believe this is the first time I have ever said no to Al. I wonder how he is going to take it?

A minute later, my office phone began to ring. It was Ed calling. "Al is now asking if you would be willing to go to Orlando for six months, just to try it. He also wants you to help with a bid on a large project in New Orleans."

I knew it. Al was not accepting no for an answer. I figured I better not push my luck and agreed to head to Florida for six months.

Within the week, my BMW was back in storage, my two suitcases packed, and I was on a plane to Orlando, Florida.

A lot was happening in our Orlando office. A former special projects manager, Deron Brown, had just been promoted to Orlando district manager, and the current chief estimator would be retiring in about a year.

They had promised the chief position to a young senior estimator named Eric Orquiola. I believe Eric had actually left PCL, but they enticed him back with the chief estimator opportunity. Deron Brown had a lot of significant work to chase in the upcoming year and wanted to shore up his estimating and preconstruction resources. The first opportunity was a lump sum bid for a massive addition to the New

Orleans Convention Center. Al Troppmann had pulled together a senior team from across a few districts to bid the convention center.

It was a considerable two-and-a-half-month effort to pull together our bid for the massive project. First, I did our self-performance estimates for grading and earthwork, concrete foundations, and structures. Then I also oversaw the landscaping, site work, and deep foundation pricing.

Many of us split our time between New Orleans and Orlando, but unfortunately, we placed second on the bid and did not get the project. However, I did continue to help Eric Orquiola and our Orlando office with budgets on other projects.

I enjoyed working in Orlando, although it sure got hot and humid in the afternoons. Man, it was so hot it made my eyeballs sweat. Every afternoon there would be a thunder and lightning storm from the build-up of humidity.

Deron Brown eventually arranged to have my BWM shipped down to Florida. I appreciated that, plus it saved money on a rental car.

One weekend, I went to church with Eric Orquiola and his wife, Cathy. Cathy had worked for PCL early in her career but was currently a project manager for another contractor. After church, the Orquiolas treated me to dinner at a fancy pants restaurant.

Eric continued to sell me on Orlando's positives, trying to convince me to make the big move. Still, he also understood I wished to return to Hawaii someday.

I did manage to break away for the week of my birthday to the Caribbean. Ben Sykes, a friend from Peace Portal Church in British Columbia, was working as a scuba diving instructor on the island of Saint Thomas. It was a fun week, learning to scuba dive and explore the Caribbean. I even made a new friend.

It was getting to big-decision time as we moved into the fall season, and I needed to figure out if I would move to Orlando or not.

There were a couple of advantages to Orlando. First, house prices were almost half the cost of the greater Seattle area, plus you got a lot more house for your money. Second, Florida was much closer to

Making a new friend in the Caribbean

my family in Ontario, Canada, and, for that matter, my cousins in Michigan.

My time in Orlando was relatively uneventful for a change. There were no automobile accidents, no calls to 911 with mysterious pain, no plane incidences, and I didn't get robbed.

Well, except for being delayed in Puerto Rico on my way to the Caribbean due to the connecting flight having mechanical issues. Then there was this cockroach the size of a small bird landing on my head while I was reading Scripture before bedtime. Oh, yeah, then there was this time I went for a long afternoon jog and got caught in a lightning storm. So, I had to sprint a mile and a half to my apartment with lightning strikes happening all around me.

But other than all that, it was a quiet, uneventful few months.

On the downside, I missed Hawaii and did not want to lose out on an opportunity to return to the islands.

As the weeks went by, I decided to make a deal with God. If Deron Brown makes me an offer to move to Orlando, I will accept it. But, if he doesn't say anything, I will return to Seattle and, hopefully, Hawaii. I heard from another employee that Deron wanted to make me an offer, but only if I told him I wanted to move to Orlando. He wanted me to want to move and not just agree to move because I felt pressured to do so. At the end of the day, I never asked for an offer, and Deron never made me an offer.

My last weekend in Orlando, I went to Disney World. It was a real walk down memory lane from our big family trip twenty-eight years before. So much had happened in my life since I was eight years old, but somehow, it also felt like my life was just beginning.

On Friday, November 21, 2003, I boarded the plane back to Seattle. The next week was the USA Thanksgiving holiday. I spent Thanksgiving day with Ray Bittner and Lorna. Lorna's family put on this big dinner with all sorts of relatives and friends. It was a fun, relaxing day, and a nice break before returning to work in Seattle the following Monday.

Back in my office Monday morning, I got a phone call from Darin Chestnut. Darin had been a construction manager and oversaw business development for PCL in Seattle before I went to Hawaii.

Darin and I had worked together on several pursuits, including the Fourth and Madison office tower and the Everett Event Center.

When I was in Hawaii, Darin had transferred to PCL's Southern California operation and had just been appointed area manager for a new PCL San Diego office.

Darin called to ask me if I would move to San Diego to head up the estimating department. His goal was to build up enough work volume in San Diego to become a full district office. Once a district office, Darin would become district manager and me the chief estimator.

I thanked Darin for the offer and the vote of confidence but told him I hoped to get back to Hawaii.

At this, Darin said, "But we are not going to be establishing a Hawaii office."

"Yea, I know, but regardless, I think I will wait and see."

A couple of days later, Ed Olsgard called me into his office. "Well, Kenny, I have good news. Marriott Vacation Club wants us to bid on constructing a 209-unit, 14-story timeshare at KoOlina on the island of Oahu."

Ed went on to say that the Hawaii construction market was heating up, and he wanted to move me to Oahu to start bidding more work with the hopes of setting up a satellite office in Honolulu.

I was beside myself with excitement. Finally, on January 1, 2004, I was on a one-way flight back to Honolulu, Hawaii, hopefully for good this time.

OK, Lord, what was up with the eight-month detour to Florida? I mean, why could I have not just stayed in Hawaii? It would have made way more sense. Orlando and New Orleans were interesting and all, but we did not even win the convention center bid. Ironically, the opportunity to take me back to Hawaii was due to Deron Brown developing business development relationships with the Marriott Vacation Club executives in Orlando.

Did Deron Brown want me to work for him full-time in Orlando? Hmm, he never did make me an offer. Oh well, I guess it doesn't matter now. I went and helped out without grumbling or complaining, so I hope that's good for something. The plane landed in Honolulu, and soft Hawaiian music played in the airport. Finally, I had made it back to Paradise.

Thank you, Jesus.

Chapter 25:

Kapolei

He heals the brokenhearted and binds up their wounds. Psalm 147:3

Back in Paradise, I rented a townhouse in Waipahu on Lumiauau St. It was a tiny two-bedroom ground-floor unit close to the Nordic office. We would be continuing our joint venture with Nordic, and for the time being, I would be sort of working out of their office.

Glen Kaneshige had his team set me up a small office in a temporary trailer on the backside of the parking lot. When I say small, I mean tiny. My office was ten feet long by four feet wide, just enough space for a plan table, chair, fax machine, and water dispenser.

Rob Spangler assigned a couple of his estimators to help me with the Marriott bid. In addition, Doug Sprute, a senior estimator from our Seattle office, would put together the concrete structure estimate. The help was welcomed and allowed me to focus on getting good sub-trade bid coverage and figuring out things like site logistics and schedule with our Senior Superintendent Terry McCombs. The Marriott Timeshare was Phase Two and Three of a multi-phased project. Our main competition would be the general contractor that had just completed the construction of Phase One.

Terry and I met with every subcontractor that had previously worked on the Phase One project, tracking them down using the "Coconut Wireless."

The greater Honolulu area has about one million people, but it's still like a small-town community. Everyone knows everyone's business and is more than willing to talk story or talk stink as the case may be about others. Thus, the "Coconut Wireless."

Meeting with the subtrades, Terry and I interrogated everyone about what went well, what went wrong, and how to improve from phase one. By the end of the week, we had extracted plenty of helpful information to make our bid more competitive.

One late afternoon, I walked out of my tiny trailer office, and a homeless man was wandering the parking lot. I could see in the distance a couple of women wanted to get to their cars, but the peculiar man was between them and their vehicles. The police had escorted the man off the property earlier in the day, but he had since returned. I walked toward the stranger. His face was leathery and red from sun exposure, further accentuated by his matted red hair and beard. A torn dirt-stained white T-shirt hung off his shoulders like an old rag. He had an old bed sheet wrapped around his waist and between his legs like a diaper.

This guy was in bad shape, hobbled over and walking with a substantial limp. My nostrils caught a whiff of his pungent body odor as I approached. All the while, he kept to my right, keeping one step ahead of me.

"Sir, I think the police officer told you to leave the property."

He turned his head slightly toward me, exposing his uniquely blue eyes, a mirrored remnant into the person he once was. Yet as he looked back at me, his eyes glazed over in a fog, and his pupils became large.

"I know you; you're the bastard," he said in a guttural raspy voice.

The man's statement caught me off guard for a split second. A bastard is an illegitimate child, a child born out of wedlock. I've already mentioned I don't know the circumstances that brought me into this world. Still, odds are my biological parents were not married, thus truly making me a bastard.

"I'm sorry you feel that way, sir," I responded.

He then proceeded with a barrage of profanity that was just short of impressive. I mean, he spewed out every swear and curse word I had ever heard, and a few I hadn't.

At this point, I was at a loss for words, so I simply said, "I'm sorry, sir, can I pray for you?"

Suddenly, the man stood straight, running off the property and down the street like an Olympic sprinter. How bizarre, I thought as the diapered man ran down the road. That's not something you see every day. Add that to the list of strange and yet unrepeated moments of my life. I never saw that man again.

Bid day finally arrived on the Marriott project, and after all the hard work, we placed second. However, all was not lost. Marriott had said they would be open to proposed value engineering options to save money. So based on the value engineering options I provided, Marriott awarded the project to PCL.

Gotta love it when a plan comes together. Thank you, Jesus.

Craig Warner got promoted to construction manager and would manage the Marriott job, making this the third job in a row of mine that Craig would work, including the Everett Events Center and Kahala Nui. Superintendent Terry McCombs moved from Seattle to Kapolei to be the superintendent.

I continued with Jeff and Donna's Bible study group at Mocha Java. The group had expanded while I was in Orlando. New regulars included Nancy Dela Cruz, Linette Maier, Kevin Higa, Joanne Nagamine, Lara Myers, Brent West, Anthony Akamine, Edmond Au, Geri Galanto, Patrick Rorie, Selina Chen, and this new guy from Minnesota, Brent Martinson.

With so many attending now, we would split up into two groups. Jeff and Donna would lead one, and I would lead the other as we discussed various Bible chapters. I jumped back in, serving on the New

Hope Mosaix ministry team. It was a lot of work helping plan the weekly Friday meetings.

In addition, Jeff, Donna, and I prepared some social activities for the Mosaix group. During these activities, I met and developed a good friendship with Dave Brodie, a YWAM (Youth With a Mission) missionary specializing in the teaching of apologetics.

Apologetics is a branch of theology devoted to defending the Christian faith's beliefs and practices based on scientific, historical, philosophical, ethical, religious, and cultural evidence.

Dave was on hiatus from his regular mission work in India. So, he started attending the Mosaix group, even teaching at one of our Friday night group meetings.

After securing the Marriott project, it was time to look for a house.

After months of looking for a house in my price range with zero luck, I was getting exceedingly frustrated. What would Mom have to say about that? Well, you guessed it, "You need to pray about it, and we shall see what we shall see."

I prayed. "Dear Lord, I really would like to find the right house. If you help me, I will be sure to dedicate it to you and use it for ministry. It will be your house; I will just be the caretaker. In Jesus' name. Amen."

Later that same week, I received a call from my Realtor. "I want to show you Kapolei Knolls. I have a friend who bought in the Knolls. Unfortunately, there are no houses available, but I can keep an eye out over the next few months if anything opens up."

"Sure, let's check it out," I replied.

Kapolei Knolls was a housing development only a few years old at the time, on Oahu's Leeward Coast in Kapolei. We drove around the neighborhood, then turned down Paaoloulu Way.

"My friend lives at the end of this cul-de-sac. Maybe you can see what one of these houses looks like inside," the Realtor said.

After giving me a tour of their home, the friend mentioned a neighbor just a few doors down would soon be listing their house for sale.

It was now dark outside, but my anticipation grew as we made the short walk down the moonlight street; a calm trade wind rustled the trees' palm branches along the road. We knocked on the neighbor's entry, and sure enough, they were retiring to Arizona, so the house would be going up for sale.

That night in Kapolei, I negotiated a deal for the home, and my prayer was answered.

My Realtor handed over the house's closing to her Realtor partner Joleen Young Dias. Joleen's husband, Tony Dias, was a mortgage broker. Tony was able to secure me the financing. Then on Friday, June 4, 2004, I took possession of my house in Kapolei Knolls on the Island of Oahu, Hawaii.

That first weekend in my new house, I prayed once more. "Thank you, Lord, for providing me with this home; now show me how you want to use it for ministry."

Pastor Mike Lwin had graduated from leading the singles ministry at New Hope and started a satellite church called "New Hope Leeward," meeting at the Leeward Community College.

I told Pastor Mike about getting the house in Kapolei Knolls and asked him about doing a home dedication or blessing.

"I'd be glad to," Mike said. Then he asked if I would be willing to host the New Hope Leeward singles Bible study for a few weeks. The group met Thursdays at Pastor Mike's home, but he would be busy for the next month or so. Well, it sure looked like the Lord was wasting no time showing me how to use my house for ministry. So, the following week, I hosted the Bible study group.

That next month came and went, but the New Hope Leeward singles group stayed. We continued to meet at my home in Kapolei Knolls for the next three years.

We had three marriages from people getting to know each other in the group, including Konane & Celeste Maluo, Galen & Anne Yee, and Ryan & Kyleanne Braman. Other core group members included Michael Fors, Monica Faux, Derek Shimizu, Kent Anderson, Tate

Goodman, Shelly Kagawa, Angie Andoe, Noelani Noe Ah Sam, Edge Yeun, Brianna Singson, and Evangeline Logan.

Back at work, PCL assigned Wayne Melnyk as the new Hawaii area manager, and it was time to set up a new PCL office and get me out of the trailer at Nordic's parking lot.

Wayne was a long-time PCL'er. He worked his way up from carpenter foreman in Toronto to a superintendent to a general superintendent and most recently operations manager of PCL's Los Angeles district. In the mid-90s, Wayne had been the general superintendent on the Honolulu Convention Center, so he was familiar with the Hawaii construction industry and knew how to use the coconut wireless.

We rented office space at Alii Place on the corner of Alakea St. and S. Hotel St. in downtown Honolulu. Wayne hired Debbie Asato as office manager. Debbie wore many hats covering the roles of an executive assistant, estimating coordinator, marketing manager, and event planner. In addition, Stephan Loubser, an estimator from the Seattle office, volunteered to move to Hawaii to help me with estimating. He was a former quantity surveyor from South Africa and became my right-hand man in Honolulu.

To say the construction market started to boom is an understatement; it was more like an explosion. Every time Wayne picked up the phone, a client wanted a budget, bid, or proposal. It was a good problem to have but tremendously stressful at the same time.

We just didn't have the staff to keep up with the volume of work. Everyone in our office was working around the clock to secure new projects. The stress levels were high, but the work was fun and rewarding.

A Hawaiian office was a high-profile venture within the conservative collective of PCL; thus, we were getting a lot of attention from our corporate executives. Some of this attention was coming from PCL's chief operation officer responsible for USA operations, Peter Beaupre, who was Al Troppmann's direct boss. I hadn't met Peter yet in all my years at PCL, but I was about to. Originally from Canada, Peter took over the US operations in 1997. He would now make frequent trips to Honolulu and pay very close attention to all the new work Wayne and I were chasing.

We would also get visits from other PCL corporate executives and the board of directors.

At one point, PCL's chairman of the board and former CEO Joe Thompson even asked me to hire his granddaughter into my estimating department. She wanted to live in Hawaii for a while, and he figured the estimating department was a good place for her to start.

PCL's director of preconstruction Steve Vrable came to Honolulu from Denver to help me out. Steve and I worked well together as he further mentored me in progressing a project through design and preconstruction.

Marriott was happy with our work on the KoOlina Phase Two/Three project, and in 2005 awarded us KoOlina Phase Four/Five. They also awarded PCL the preconstruction and construction for The Ritz Carlton Club & Residences at Kapalua Bay, Maui.

The Ritz Carlton Club was the largest project of my career to date. It was a luxury resort on 19.7 acres with six residential buildings, a spa, parking garage, restaurants, and pools. The project would cost over $380 million to build back in the mid-2000s. PCL general superintendent Bryan Troell flew out from California to build the massive project.

The Ritz Carlton project would tie up most of my estimating and preconstruction resources, so I hired Tim Schoder, a senior estimator who worked in the islands for several years, plus another solid young estimator who had just moved to Honolulu from the mainland.

Amidst all the busyness, on March 3, 2005, I received my permanent residency card or "green card." Ironically this came almost precisely five years after I had told the Lord I planned to return to Canada in five years.

"So, Lord, OK, I will be happy to stay in Hawaii and forgo the move back to Canada thing. In Jesus' name. Amen."

It was a busy time of my life, but if there wasn't some organized church event or I wasn't working, I spent most of my evenings and weekend time alone. For most of my adult life, I had lived alone. I knew lots of people from all over the place, but knowing people is not friendship. I had a couple of close friends in every province or state I lived in, but they had their own lives. So, I could go weeks at a time alone, especially on the weekends.

I was in my mid-30s now and had not met that special woman to marry and start a life together. That didn't stop me from dreaming and praying about starting a family and building a house. Mom and Dad continued to pray that I would meet a special lady that was just right for me and me for her.

"A new command I give you: Love one another. As I have loved you, so
you must love one another. By this, everyone will know that
you are my disciples, if you love one another." John 13:34-35

I had two choices: sitting home alone and feeling sorry for myself or doing something about it. I figured if I felt lonely, other singles were probably feeling the same way. I had been blessed with a house, and I needed to maximize this blessing to bless others. I needed to spread more aloha.

I started hosting regular parties, nothing formal, just opening up my home so people could come to hang out, eat good food, play games, or watch a movie. I also cooked a turkey at Thanksgiving and gave an open invitation to friends that may not have a place to go.

Although I had some challenges in life, I was blessed with loving, supportive parents and family. But, as I opened up my home to so many people, I soon realized my positive upbringing was an exception and not the norm. I've always had sympathy for the emotional pain and struggles people coming through my home may be dealing with or living through.

My challenge was, I'm a contractor, not a counselor. So, I had difficulty relaying the fact that I cared as much as I did. I always lived my life with the philosophy of fighting, surviving, forgiving, forgetting, and not necessarily in that order.

When a person opens up to you about a challenge or emotional struggle, they need a friend like a warm, comforting lotion, gentle, and soothing to the skin. I'm more like fine-grit sandpaper; I'll take off the bumps but may leave a few scratches in the process.

It's like Mom always said, "You gotta call a spade a spade."

I've always held my emotions very deep inside; they may come bubbling up if I'm giving a wedding or funeral speech, but that's about it. I'm just not good with the touchy-feely drama stuff. Even though I was not good at showing my emotions or stress and would often deflect with humor, I became very discerning over the years in Hawaii.

Watching and observing how people dressed, walked, and interacted with others gave me a window into who they really were instead of who they pretended to be. I was learning to have patience and love others as Christ commands us without trying to fix them. You see, I knew how to repair any problem with a house; I just wasn't so good at refurbishing the people living in the house.

Jeff Pagay, Brent Martinson, and I started mountain biking. Soon we became like the Three Amigos or maybe the Three Stooges. Brent and I had a lot in common. He grew up in North Dakota just south of the Canadian border, played college football in Minnesota, and moved to Minneapolis after college. Minnesota is only about a ten-hour drive from Saul Ste. Marie, Ontario.

Although growing up in Hawaii and being half Filipino, Jeff's mother was from Minnesota, so he had visited several times and has Minnesotan DNA in his blood. Come to think of it, my missionary friend Dave Brodie was also from Minnesota. So, it seems folks from Minnesota and North Dakota are pretty similar to Canadians; they must be distant cousins or something like that.

Jeff and Donna had become like family to me. Jeff and I both have a quirky sense of humor, always seeing the funny side of life's challenges. Brent and I would attend college football's Aloha Bowl at Aloha Stadium every Christmas Eve. We would also host a college national championship watch party at my place in January.

However, the championship party was usually just Brent and me. Sometimes Monica Faux from the Thursday night study group and her husband Tony would join us. Monica and Tony were missionaries eager to get back to the mission field.

With my return to Hawaii, I ended up making a vehicle change. My island lifestyle and Honolulu's potholed roads didn't suit the BMW. Plus, it was hard stuffing a muddy mountain bike in the back of a BMW. So, I returned to my roots, ditching the car for a black GMC Canyon pickup truck.

Biking Kaena Point with Brent Martinson (center) and Jeff Pagay (right)

Back at the office, the construction business continued to boom. From past experience and a lot of prayers, I was getting a feel for putting budgets together, sometimes in mere hours off simple sketches or descriptions of projects.

However, many of my budgets were initially 20 percent higher than our local competitors. Wayne Melnyk would challenge me on my pricing. But I'd present my data and explain the costs, considering current market conditions and future cost inflation as many projects would take up to three years to design and build.

"I keep challenging Ken's numbers until he starts fighting back," Wayne would joke.

He wanted to make sure I wasn't padding things to the point we lost the job but at the same time was respecting my instincts.

I decided not to use "Well, I just prayed about it" to justify my numbers, although that was the truth. My gut told me Al Troppmann, Peter Beaupre, or Ross Grieve would not be willing to base PCL's Hawaii success on a literal wing and a prayer. So, I always provided as much backup data as I could.

We lost a couple of large projects early on due to my pricing being higher than our competitors' pricing. However, Wayne Melnyk backed me up with PCL corporate and stood by my numbers. As for me, I continued to pray.

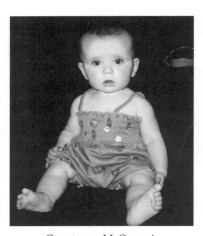

Courteney McQuarrie

Months after losing some work, Wayne received a call from a couple of developers.

"Tell Ken his numbers were right; we should have used PCL for this project."

Suddenly, PCL had a lot of credibility on costing with local developers opening up the flood gates for more work.

A highlight of 2005 was the birth of my niece Courteney to my brother Doug and sister-in-law Grace. Courteney was a real blessing to the family, making Mom and Dad official grandparents for the first time.

Love was in the Hawaiian Air, and after years of dating, Jeff and Donna were engaged to be married. Jeff asked me to be one of his groomsmen.

Shortly after the wedding, I started dating a great gal I had met over a year prior through mutual friends. She was from Hawaii and

*Jeff and Donna Pagay's wedding.
I'm the guy in the middle*

a few years younger than I was. Things just clicked, and the relationship moved quickly. In less than three months, we were engaged with a September wedding date set.

I know, that's fast, but we had known each other casually for about a year. Besides, my good friends Scott Pinches and Scott Yewchuk met their wives and married within six months. So, my fiancée and I just figured if stuff came up, we would pray about it and everything would work itself out.

One Thursday evening, shortly before Easter, I prayed.

"Lord, everything seems right with this marriage. Thank you for blessing me after all these years with a special lady to spend the rest of my life with. For the first time in my life, I don't feel alone. But, God, if this marriage is not your will for either of us for some reason, please end it quickly. In Jesus' name, Amen."

Three days later, the engagement was over, the relationship finished, and I was absolutely devastated. OK, Lord, thanks for the quick answer to prayer, but seriously?

It was like a dark cloud moved in and parked itself squarely over my house. I put all Bible studies, house parties, and activities on hold.

This hurt like I had never experienced before; the emotional pain gave way to actual chest pains. I felt like going to the Big Island and hurling myself into the volcano. Not that I would do that; of course, I was not suicidal. It was just that this pain was something a chocolate chip cookie could not fix.

"He is ugly; you should cover that boy up," the old woman told my mom many years ago.

I now felt ugly and just wanted to hide under the covers and never show my face again. What sort of a hopeless wretch was I? Unfortunately, I had to pull myself together sooner than later. I had a lot of people depending on me at work.

Wayne Melnyk was off on his yearly cruise with his family, leaving me in charge of the office. We were finalizing the GMP pricing on the Marriott KoOlina Phase Four/Five project. Wayne had confidence I had things well under control while he was away, and I couldn't let him down. Truth be told, I did have things under control right up until my engagement crumbled. And that solid mainland estimator? Well, he up and resigned on me just before the GMP due date. So, still reeling from the sting of my engagement breaking up, I was forced to step in and finish the estimate myself to meet the deadline.

The Sunday following Easter, I attended the New Hope campus, where Pastor Wayne Cordeiro preached.

Pastor Wayne had a side note to single people during his sermon that day.

"If you break up in a dating relationship, don't go chasing after it. Instead, pray about it, and if God is in favor, he will find a way to bring it back around for a second chance. If God doesn't bring a second chance, then move on."

Whoa! There were probably six hundred people in the auditorium that day. But it sure felt like God was sending me a direct message through Pastor Wayne.

God never brought a second chance around with my former fiancée, so I started down the long road of moving on. With most of my setbacks in life, I had bounced back pretty quickly, but it was different this time. This time my big heart was shattered into tiny pieces. I found no comfort in prayer, feeling like a hideous creature destined to be alone. I saw this psychologist on television talking about relationships. He said if you are single in your thirties and struggling to find a relationship that leads to marriage, you need to look at the common denominator – "YOU."

Ouch! That hurt, but he was right. I needed to be honest with myself; maybe I was not ready for marriage. I wanted to find answers, so I began reading all the popular Christian books on relationships about what women want. I read about love languages and love banks, about women's brains being like spaghetti and men's like waffles, and a few other relationship books. I soon became a self-proclaimed black belt in relationship theory. The problem was I lacked practical experience.

On April 22, 2006, my missionary friend Dave Brodie was back in the mission field and married Mariluz, a YWAM missionary from Chile. I was so happy that Dave had found Mariluz.

I figured if the Lord could help orchestrate Dave from Minnesota meeting Mariluz from Chile on an India mission field, then there is still hope for me. Right?

On the heels of Dave Brodie's wedding, Brent Martinson began dating Maggie Li. She had started attending the Mocha Java Bible study group a few months prior. Now Maggie always went to bed early. So, Saturday nights after he dropped Maggie off at her home, Brent and I would hit the latest action movie at the Dole Cannery theaters.

My love life may have been in the tank, but my professional career was booming. PCL Honolulu now had close to $600 million of projects under construction, and we were negotiating on a billion dollars of preconstruction. With the booming success, PCL decided to change the Honolulu office from Seattle's satellite office to a fully independent district office. Shortly after becoming the Honolulu district, Wayne Melnyk got promoted to vice president and district manager, Craig Warner to operations manager, and me to chief estimator.

With my promotion, they gave me this new device called a Blackberry. I could use it as a phone for texting and even getting my email messages. Becoming a district office and getting promoted was undoubtedly a highlight of 2006. But it all seemed hollow somehow. It sure didn't feel like it was my purpose in life.

My whole goal in life was to be a carpenter building cabinets in Sault Ste. Marie, get married, have children, adopt a child or two and build my family a house. How did I get here, thirty-nine years old, a chief estimator for a multi-billion-dollar construction company in Honolulu?

Now don't get me wrong, I enjoyed having a successful career and all the fringe benefits that come with that. My job had taken me to places beyond my dreams. But I was missing something, a greater purpose, a reason for being.

I had contemplated going to seminary and possibly full-time ministry. However, I didn't feel a calling to full-time ministry; maybe it was just me grasping to make sense of my life. Early that September, I took a walk around Diamond Head with a lady friend. Diamond Head is an ancient volcanic cone just southeast of Waikiki.

We walked along the sidewalk of an isolated stretch of Diamond Head Road. Suddenly, my friend moved around from my left side to my right, saying, "That guy's crazy; he scares me."

Glancing to my left across the street under a tree, I saw what appeared to be a homeless man having a heated conversation with the wind.

As I made eye contact with the man, he jumped up and started walking toward us. My friend was right; this guy was some sort of scary with long matted hair and a beard that had not seen a barber's scissors in many years. His clothes consisted of an old burlap sack with holes for his head and arms. Around his waist was a piece of rope tied in a knot. The weathered man was dirty and shoeless, spewing all sorts of profanity as he walked toward us. My friend grabbed my right arm, squeezing tight as he approached.

I gazed directly into the oncoming man's eyes as I whispered under my breath, "Stop, in the name of Jesus."

The moment I uttered those words, the strange man abruptly turned around and went back under the tree to my shock and amazement. Then, sitting down, he wrapped his arms around his knees and started rocking back and forth, making murmuring sounds.

It was my second strange experience with a homeless man, but I never saw that man again either.

November 18, 2006, Mom's 70th Birthday

Later that fall, Mom and Dad made a return trip to Hawaii to celebrate Mom's seventieth birthday on November 18, 2006. We stayed local on Oahu and avoided any ancient island curses this time around. We finished every day watching the sun set and taking a swim at the KoOlina Lagoons. Mom even cooked a Thanksgiving feast for a number of my friends.

Having a house in Hawaii, several friends visited from the mainland. My brother Doug, sister-in-law Grace, and niece Courteney came for two weeks when Courteney was two and a half. My sister Debbie kept talking about visiting, but life kept getting in the way.

The economic boom of the 2000s continued. So, in 2007, I hired John Gallagher, an estimator from San Clemente, California. John

Grace, Courteney, Doug, and me at Pearl Harbor

343

was a watersport guy and had moved his wife and young family to experience the aloha and surf warmer waters. I now managed an estimating staff of eight estimators, with the overall district office pushing close to one hundred people.

Who of you by worrying can add a single hour to your life?
Since you cannot do this very little thing, why do you worry
about the rest? Luke 12:25-26

We landed the preconstruction on a massive resort project in Wailea, Maui. The construction budget for the hotel/condominium was a very ambitious $280 million. I ran a quick napkin sketch budget and told Wayne, "I think their numbers are way off. This project will be like $380 to $400 million to build."

"It can't be," Wayne responded.

"Yes, it can. This job will be similar in square footage but way more complicated than our Ritz Carlton, Kapula Bay project."

"If we tell the client that, they won't believe it, we'll lose the job, or the project will get canceled. Besides, they don't have a design yet and are not asking for a budget. So, let's wait and see what they come up with for concept design, then we can do a detailed budget."

Upon receiving the Wailea design development plans, Steve Vrabel did a detailed budget estimate with subcontractor input, totaling around $360 million.

Wayne, Steve, and I consulted with Al Troppmann, and the consensus was subtrades were inflating their pricing due to the booming economy. Therefore, it was decided we should propose a $320 million design to target budget. The big caveat to hitting the $320 million was the developer letting PCL work with the designers to keep the design under control, especially the finishes.

We had no one to lead the Wailea preconstruction effort as my entire staff was swamped with other projects. So, I would have to serve as preconstruction manager, lead estimator, and chief estimator on this one while in my spare time managing the estimating department.

However, I would get some help from our senior superintendent Mike Finney for construction logistics and scheduling.

The task at hand was monumental; I had never been so buried and overwhelmed with work in all my years. My stress levels were at an all-time high. I was flying by the seat of my pants. The problem was it felt like my pants were around my knees. Even working twelve hours plus a day, seven days a week, I fell further and further behind. I did my best to take Sundays off but often fell short of my best. My only relief was taking weekly two-hour walks along Kailua beach. The warm ocean air and sound of the waves soothed my soul, allowing me to meditate and pray as I walked along the soft sand.

Well, it was that time of year again, and Wayne Melnyk went on his yearly spring family cruise. So, once again, he left me in charge of the office. The previous year was a disaster, with my engagement breaking off and my estimator quitting. But that was last year; this year, I had things more under control, or so I thought.

It was mid-week, and I had just gotten out of a grueling eight-hour meeting with the developer on the Wailea project. My brain felt like mashed potatoes as I retreated to my office. Just as I sat down, Debbie Asato entered my office. "You need to fire your estimating coordinator!" Debbie asserted, pointing and waving her index finger about six inches from my nose. Debbie and my estimating coordinator did not get along; they had been fighting for months now. Wayne and I had many meetings trying to smooth things out between the two ladies but to no avail. Debbie continued to scold me and wave her finger in my face. But with my stress levels high, my patience escaped me like air from a deflating balloon.

I stood up and, in my big bear voice, said, "Debbie, enough. You can go back to your office, or you can leave; I don't care."

Debbie stormed back to her office, grabbed her purse, and left the building.

"Oh darn, there goes Wayne's executive assistant."

It took a few weeks, but eventually, we smoothed things over. Debbie was just looking out for the best interests of PCL, and we've stayed friends to this day. My estimating coordinator eventually left for a better position elsewhere. As for Wayne, well, he took me with him on his family cruise the following year.

Our Wailea client decided to bid out the project for a guaranteed maximum price (GMP). Time is money in the hotel/condo business, and the owner wanted to fast-track the project to get it operational sooner. I warned our client, the drawings were not advanced enough to bid to trades, plus the designers had not been listening to our cost-saving suggestions. As a result, I feared we would get a lot of inflated pricing from the subcontractors.

Unfortunately, my advice fell on deaf ears, and we put the project out on the street for pricing the first week of December 2007. A meeting was scheduled with the owner and developer for the second week of January 2008 to review the numbers.

It took me a few days to assemble all the trade pricing into the estimate. I finished Saturday afternoon, January 5, just in time to head to the big General Contractors Association dinner at the Royal Hawaiian Resort in Waikiki.

As I entered the ballroom, Wayne saw me approaching. From the look on my face and my dead man walking body language, he suspected the news was not good.

"How bad is it?" Wayne asked.

"$420 million," I responded.

Wayne rolled his eyes and took a sip of his drink. "Well, let's enjoy the party, and we'll figure something out on Monday."

Not to downplay the gravity of the situation or embellish the story, I'll just say this. The client's executives and the developer were not pleased with the $420 million price tag. Wayne and I came up with a value engineering list that would get the project down under $380 million, but they wanted none of it. The client was a billionaire from the mainland East Coast and simply did not believe the Hawaii pricing at the time.

A point of contention was the concrete structure. The developers construction manager began to grill me on my structure pricing. "In all my years in Hawaii, I have never seen concrete structure pricing that expensive," he announced, as if he were making some grand declaration.

I agreed the concrete formwork pricing was some of the most expensive I had ever priced, but there were reasons for it. I tried to explain, but the manager didn't even listen, he just kept saying it was too expensive. After two-and-a-half hours of getting grilled by the ownership group, Wayne and I were asked to leave the room for about fifteen minutes. We retreated to Wayne's office with our tails between our legs like two dogs getting scolded for peeing on the carpet.

Wayne called Al Troppmann to fill him in on how the meeting was going.

After the status report, Al said, "Ken, you have been pricing concrete structures for twenty years; I am going to gamble that you know more about concrete and formwork than anyone in that meeting. Of course, you're just being honest, but I think this construction manager is grandstanding in front of his client."

Al continued, "I know I always told you never to give detailed pricing and productivities to clients because it's confidential to PCL. But, this time, I want you to go into full detail; let's see what this guy knows, take him where he doesn't want to go."

Al gave Wayne a few more words of wisdom, and we headed back into the meeting. As I walked down the corridor, I felt like Rocky Balboa heading into round twelve of his heavyweight fight against Apollo Creed. I could hear the Rocky theme song playing in my head.

Entering the meeting room, I went straight to the whiteboard and quickly sketched out the structural slab-to-wall connection.

"OK, how would you terminate the post-tension anchor at the perimeter exposed architectural concrete wall? As you know, the cable has to be tensioned after the wall and slab are poured. But as you can see, the architectural wall face is in front of the tension anchor."

The room was so quiet you could hear a termite sneeze, so I continued.

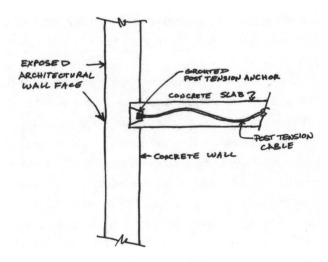

"I'm using a TITAN handset modular formwork shoring system; is there a more economical system you would you suggest? What sort of labor crew mix do you think we should use?"

At this, the construction manager cut me off and spoke. "That's fine, Ken, just double-check your numbers, that's all."

Whoa, I felt like I had just won the heavyweight championship of the world.

The tone of the meeting soon turned for the better. The client wanted to keep moving forward with the project and, thankfully, with PCL as the general contractor.

We agreed to target $345 million as the not to exceed GMP. This time, there was a commitment from the ownership group to work with the designers and PCL to find design solutions and get this project on budget.

In the spring of 2008, after returning from my Caribbean cruise with Wayne and his family, I was fortunate to hire Raymond Woodard, a senior estimator from one of PCL's large mainland competitors. Raymond and his wife moved to Hawaii, and he took on some of our larger projects. The big PCL news in 2008 was the purchase of Nordic Construction. In Hawaii, the new company name was now "Nordic PCL Construction, Inc."

Rob Spangler and his estimating staff were welcome additions to my estimating team. I now managed a group of twelve and received a small promotion from chief estimator level two to chief one.

Through a lot of blood, sweat, and tears, Wayne and I got the Wailea project down to $345 million, and we had a date set to sign the contract. The year 2008 was turning into a record-setting year for PCL in Hawaii. Then all the walls came tumbling down, and the United States economy crashed. The "Great Recession" had begun.

The commercial construction industry was in freefall, the Wailea Beach Resort project got canceled, and many new work opportunities instantly disappeared. During our weekly managers' meeting, we discussed the potential of layoffs. After four years of building a team, to have to lay people off was unsettling.

I still remembered getting laid off by PCL during the 1992 recession. It was life-changing, but at least I was single. My staff were married and had families to support, not to mention we lived on an island.

My stomach was unsettled heading into January 2009. Not from the food poisoning I got from my New Years' Eve potluck party that year, but from the thought of having to lay people off with no place to go. I was praying hard and started to feel the trade winds of change blowing. I loved Hawaii, but as the days progressed, I had this calming feeling it was time to move on.

These were uncertain times. I should have been stressed and worried, but to my surprise, I was not. I'd like to say I was at peace knowing Jesus was with me, but that would be giving myself too much credit. At first, I thought this was just my brain's self-defense mechanism trying to plan an escape route. But as the days passed, I felt more and more that change was coming.

I had accomplished a lot in Hawaii. My career had taken off more than I could have dreamed, but life is not about my accomplishments; it's about my journey to my final destination. I felt I needed to tempt fate; I needed to provide PCL an option. As the saying goes, "It's far better to volunteer than to be drafted."

I talked to Wayne Melnyk. "Look, I'm single, which means I'm more mobile. I love Hawaii, but if I need to go to the mainland for a few years to save from laying off staff, I would be willing to do that. Whatever it takes to get everyone through this recession."

Al Troppmann started considering a couple of options for me. One in Colorado and one in San Diego. But the Colorado project kept getting delayed. So, in April 2009, PCL decided to transfer me to be the chief estimator in PCL's newly formed San Diego district office. The Honolulu PCL staff gave me a big surprise going away party. They totally surprised me, which is very difficult to do, given my analytical brain and all. But Wayne Melnyk and Debbie Asato planned and executed the surprise party with the efficiency of a Navy Seal mission.

My house sold right away and for a reasonable price, which was a surprise, given the recession and all. It was bittersweet as the movers packed up my home on Paaoloulu Way in Kapolei Knolls. So many good memories, plus a few not-so-good ones.

I think the Lord had been preparing my heart for this day. Finally, my broken heart had healed, and I was looking forward to a new adventure. Wayne met me at the hotel in Waikiki for one last dinner. I would be boarding the plane to San Diego the following day. We reminisced about all the fun times, eccentric clients, and crazy situations we had experienced establishing the PCL Honolulu district.

Hawaii deals are made on the golf course, and Wayne and I were always golfing with clients. I'm not much of a golfer, but I can hit the ball a long way. My first problem, I hit pretty much the same distance with every club.

Wayne tells people, "Ken golfs as he estimates; it's all or nothing."

My second problem was my golf clubs. I had these six rusty old clubs that were a bit small for me.

Wayne once told me, "Ken, we are trying to negotiate these deals worth hundreds of millions of dollars, and you keep showing up with these Charlie Brown golf clubs. It's embarrassing. If you don't buy a decent set of clubs, I'm going to buy you a set and deduct it from your Christmas bonus."

So, thanks to Wayne, I have a new set of clubs.

More important than the projects we constructed, or our success was the friendship Wayne and I developed. We learned a lot together, and no one can ever take that away.

After dinner, I walked the streets of Waikiki alone for one last time. Then, bright and early the next morning, the soft Hawaiian music played in the airport as I boarded the plane.

With the trade winds behind me, I was on my way to San Diego.

Lookout, California, here I come.

Chapter 26:

California Dreaming

Brothers and sisters, I do not consider myself yet to have taken hold of it. But one thing I do: Forgetting what is behind and straining toward what is ahead, I press on toward the goal to win the prize for which God has called me heavenward in Christ Jesus. Philippians 3:13-14

Looking back was never part of my life. Up until now, I had never looked back; instead, I was constantly pushing forward. The question I faced now was: forward to what? Was my destiny in San Diego or was it merely another stop on the long road to purpose and meaning?

There were not many homes for sale in Southern California with the housing market crash. Folks were either short selling their house or being foreclosed on by the banks. If they could afford the mortgage, they were trying to ride out the great recession.

I didn't have time to wait on a short sale as PCL was shipping my furniture from Hawaii.

I prayed the same house prayer I had done in Hawaii. Remember? "Not my house but yours, Lord, and I will use it for ministry." My Realtor came across a brand spanking new house in La Costa Ridge, Carlsbad, California, just north of San Diego. Somebody had put the deposit down to build the house then walked away just as it was completed. So, I put in a lowball offer, and to my surprise, the developer accepted.

I now had a brand-new house in La Costa Ridge for a bargain-basement price. OK, Lord, now I just need to figure out how you want me to use it for ministry.

I started attending North Coast Calvary Chapel led by Pastor Mark Foreman. The church had a 30s/40s ministry called 30/40. Yeah, I know, not too overly creative, but that's what it was called. Pastor Adam Stadtmiller led the ministry. I got along with Pastor Adam from the get-go. Maybe it was his lifelong love of football, particularly the San Diego Chargers. Or that he received his BA in religion from Point Loma Nazarene University, which traces its theological roots back to the Methodists and John Wesley.

Pastor Adam asked me to lead and host a 30/40 ministry Bible study group in my house. So, it was pretty straightforward once again how the Lord wanted me to use my home for ministry.

This group was a bit smaller than my Hawaii group but had regulars including Nicole Stewart, Kim Joecken, Bum Cho, Kristen Weaver, Richard Martin, Tony Kovacs, and Maggie Lee. (Not the same Maggie from Hawaii).

Life was pretty uneventful for the remainder of 2009, except for a quick trip back to Hawaii for Brent Martinson and Maggie Li's wedding in October.

Brent & Maggie Martinson, October 9, 2009

I settled in pretty quickly at the PCL office in San Diego. Darin Chestnut had an entire staff set up and had landed a major San Diego Airport Terminal joint venture project. The condominium market had dried up, but PCL had a few university projects in various preconstruction and construction stages. The challenge was securing new work as we navigated through the recession.

Andy Kleimola had transferred from the PCL Orlando office to be the operations manager. I had worked with Andy on that New Orleans Convention Center pursuit a few years back. Andy was very talented, being able to manage construction work plus estimate. I inherited a couple of senior estimators, including Anthony Lee, who could crank out the estimates. Jerry Carlson was a former chief estimator with a small general contractor. Jerry handled all our smaller bids, which we classified as special projects. Then we had a few other estimators we cycled through the department at various times.

The construction industry was at rock bottom. Lots of work had dried up and disappeared. We found ourselves bidding against upward of twelve general contractors on a given project, getting a lot of second and third-place finishes. The low bidders were submitting prices well below our costs. As the months rolled on, the fees and profits went down, and the pressure to get work went up.

Paul Douglas would be taking over from Ross Grieve as PCL's new CEO in 2010. It's hard to believe eighteen years had passed since I first met Paul as he assumed the reins as Ottawa district manager. It would be no easy task for him to navigate PCL through the recession.

Toward the end of 2009, I started using an online dating service called eHarmony. The site matched you based on compatibility after completing this very long questionnaire.

I had tried eHarmony on and off in the past but never had too much luck. The website had four stages of communication, from multiple-choice questions to a list of deal-breakers to short written questions. Then you get to open communication where you see each other's photos, write to each other, exchange phone numbers, etc.

My problem was as soon as matches saw my photo, I would never hear from them again. I had gotten to open communication very few times in the past years, but nothing ever developed.

Once, eHarmony offered a free assessment of my profile. The eHarmony expert told me my written profile and photos looked good.

I mentioned I would get multiple matches a day, but every time I got to the stage where the woman saw my picture, she would disappear, and I wouldn't hear from her again.

The expert told me, "Well, you have a very distinctive look. I would suggest allowing the women to see your photo from day one."

"You think I look distinctive now. You should have seen me when I was born."

Well, I took the expert's advice, allowing the women to see my photo from the get-go. And you know what? It worked! I wasn't wasting my time going through four communication stages anymore as the women would now delete me before stage one.

Oh well, it was the second week of February 2010, and I thought I would give eHarmony another try. By midweek I received a match of a woman who also lived in Carlsbad. She was a nurse whose parents immigrated to the United States from the Philippines. She was born and raised in California, and her name was Tia Fa.

With my photo showing, I did not get deleted by Tia as we progressed through the four communication stages, hitting open communication by Saturday.

I caught the late show at the local movie theater that Saturday evening. Going to bed late that night, I decided not to set my alarm.

I planned to catch the 9:00 a.m. service at North Coast Calvary Chapel only if I woke up in time. I figured I would go to the later service if I slept late.

I woke up at 8:50 a.m. Sunday, February 14, and decided to try and make the 9:00 a.m. service. But, getting to the church auditorium, I found it was completely full. So, I turned to head to the outdoor overflow area when the usher stopped me.

"Sir, we have one available seat."

The chair was about five rows from the front on the left side.

I squeezed by two ladies and sat in the third seat from the aisle, just as the praise and worship song ended.

I noticed the two women I was seated beside looked Filipino. The woman on the aisle wore dark blue jeans, a brown leather jacket, and big, very dark sunglasses. She kept staring toward the ground. It looked like she was in the witness protection program or something.

The lady sitting right beside me sorta looked like Tia Fa's photos, my match from eHarmony. I couldn't tell for sure, though, as she had her hair tied up in a bun, was wearing glasses and an oversized frumpy sweater.

The service ended, and even before the final worship song finished, the two gals shot for the exit like they were making an escape.

As I drove home, I kept thinking, what are the odds I was sitting beside Tia Fa? But if it was her, why didn't she say something? After all, I have a very distinctive look.

Maybe she did recognize me, thus the rush for the exit after church. Eventually, my curiosity got the better of me, and I emailed Tia.

"Yes, that was me," Tia replied.

She told me her real name is Nimfa Santos. She used Tia Fa as her alias on eHarmony, which meant auntie in Filipino. It was the name her young nephews called her.

Nimfa also told me eHarmony had offered her a free week on the site as a special for Valentine's.

"I could not see your photo because I was not a paying customer," she said.

Ahh, I guess that explains why I didn't get deleted.

Nimfa asked if I could meet her for coffee; she had something to discuss with me.

How strange, I thought. What was it that she couldn't just say in an email or phone call? I hope she's not trying to get me into some multi-level marketing scheme. I've tried those in the past only to lose money. I am a terrible salesman.

I met Nimfa for coffee, and after a couple of minutes of small talk, she got right to the point.

"I think you and my housemate would be a good match."

I was not expecting that.

"That wouldn't happen to be the woman in the dark glasses sitting beside you at church?" I questioned.

"Maybe?"

"Is she on eHarmony?"

"Yes, she is."

"If we are compatible, then why didn't eHarmony match us?"

"I don't know, but I do know you two would be a good match."

Nimfa said her friend's alias was "Bound for Glory." She would check with Miss "Bound for Glory" if she were willing to meet me.

Getting home after I met with Nimfa, I found a place on eHarmony where I could see past deleted matches. Sure enough, almost two years ago to the day, while in Hawaii, I was matched with "Bound for Glory," but I had deleted her.

Oops, my bad! But in my own defense, I didn't want a long-distance relationship at the time.

You can probably guess Bound for Glory's response to Nimfa that night. "He deleted me; if we are such a good match, why did he delete me?"

Nimfa had to do some convincing, but eventually, I met Bound for Glory for dinner.

Although she goes by Celine, Bound for Glory's real name is Jocelyn Floresca. "How do you get Celine from Jocelyn?" I asked.

"In my family, we always abbreviate each other's names. So, everyone calls me Celyn, as short for Jocelyn. But it sounds like Celine if you say it with a Filipino accent (Jo-celine). So, I simply go by Celine."

Very interesting, I thought to myself. I learn something new every day. Celine was also a nurse for orthopedic surgeries at Scripps Hospital in La Jolla, not far from PCL's office. Well, I'm pleased to tell you Nimfa was right; Celine and I hit it off and began dating.

Celine grew up in the Philippines until her family moved to the United States when she was fifteen. Her dad, Abraham, was a lawyer in the Philippines, and her mom, Erlinda, worked as a nurse.

Celine has five siblings, including older sisters. Joy married Paul Cabanting, Joan married Joseph Ilagan, and Jo married David Rhode. In addition, she has an older brother Jeff Floresca married to Kristin. Last but not least, Celine's younger sister Karen is married to Gerald Cruz.

Celine also has nine nieces and nephews: Loren, Ben, Abi, Jacob, Hannah, Caleb, Sarah, Nico, and Klay. However, at the time of our meeting, Klay wouldn't be born for a few years yet.

Celine and I at Carlsbad Beach

Early June rolled around, and Celine wanted to go white water rafting on the Kern River in Bakersfield, California. It was a tour she had done in the past. Two rafts were going out on the river that day. The leading guide gave us our safety briefing. He was a tall, burly guy standing well over six foot two with long hair and an impressive beard. He reminded me of Grizzly Adams, that 70s television show about a mountain man with a pet grizzly bear.

The Grizzly Adams guide man explained to us a few essential rules:

- Rule #1: If you end up in the water, keep your legs up and pointing downstream.

- Rule #2: Avoid fallen trees extending into the water. The trees' branches go under the water, creating a strainer of sorts that will trap you underwater, and you will drown.

- Rule #3: To pull a person out of the water and into the raft, grab their life jacket, pushing them down into the water. The life jacket's buoyancy will pop them up out of the water, helping you pull them into the raft.

After putting on our wetsuits, life jackets, and helmets, we all headed down to the river. With the Grizzly Adams man in the lead raft, Celine and I were placed in the second raft with a younger, much smaller guide. We also had two teenage girls in our raft. We would be taking on five "Class 3" to "Class 4" rapids over our five-mile river run that day. The guides pointed out that due to excessive rainfall, the river was swelling. Due to the swelling, all the rapids were closer to a "Class 4." However, the final rapid called Hari-kari would be an angry "Class 5" rapids that day, which is the highest of the levels. As the guide talked, my spider senses began tingling. *I'm not strong in the water; this could be dangerous,* I thought. However, Celine was still up for it, so I had no choice but to man up, despite my hesitation.

We managed to navigate the first four rapids. As our raft continued to float down the river, we started to hear the roar of the final rapids getting louder and louder, reminding me of a childhood trip to Niagara Falls. Finally, coming around a bend in the river, we came face to face with Hari-kari.

"Oh, boy!" I yelled as we hit Hari-kari dead on.

Instantly the raft began to spin. The guide frantically yelled, "Reverse paddle, dig deep, paddle, paddle."

The two girls up front panicked, pulling their oars out of the water, they ducked into the raft as I dug my oar deep, trying desperately to help our guide right the raft. Suddenly, we slammed backward into a large rock without warning, catapulting everyone into the raging river.

My life jacket was about as useless as a foam noodle in a tidal wave as I sunk deep into the river. The torrid undertow sucked me under, spinning me around like a demon-possessed washing machine. The ice-cold water was like sharp knives on my skin.

I frantically flailed around, not knowing which way was up. Then, almost out of breath, my backside suddenly hit the river bottom. I kicked hard, propelling myself upward toward the surface like I had done so many times at Ena and Larry's pool in Spring Arbor, Michigan.

WHACK! My head cracked the underside of the raft, now directly on top of me. Dazed from the sudden blow, I inhaled, instantly filling my lungs with water. Then, everything started to go black as my consciousness departed from me.

I guess this is the end of my life journey, was the last thought entering my mind before I blacked out.

The next thing I remember was coughing and choking water out of my lungs as the river spit me out of the rapids. I was now floating down the center of the river in the swift current.

Where is Celine? I spun around to look for her.

Celine was floating about twenty yards behind me. "Turn around and point your legs downriver. Just try to relax and take deep breaths," Celine yelled, channeling her inner nurse.

Fortunately, she was able to angle herself to shore and safety.

Our raft guide and one of the teenage girls had also gotten to safety. But not me, as the river current was not finished with me yet. Looking downstream, the second teenage girl was desperately clinging onto a tree that had fallen over into the river.

Seeing the young damsel in distress, I channeled my inner Dudley Do-Right. "Here I come to save the day."

I motioned to the girl to move to the end of the tree. "I'll grab you on the way by," I yelled.

I tried to swim a bit to angle myself toward the young lady. But as I have said, I am not skilled in the water. Miscalculating my speed and approach angle, I was now on a collision course with the middle of the fallen tree.

At this point, my only thought was the words of the guides, rule #2: "avoid fallen trees, branches go underwater, they will trap you, you will drown." I turned my left shoulder toward the tree as the full force of my body mass propelled by the raging current slammed into the branches.

That tree trunk snapped like a cheap toothpick. The collision's intensity slingshot the woman toward the shore, where she was able to escape the clutches of the raging river. Half a tree and I were the only things still floating down the river. Then, finally, I spotted Grizzly Adams guide man, with his raft in the shallows near shore. He was yelling and motioning me to angle toward him.

I thumped into the side of the raft. But, before I could catch my breath, Grizzly Adams grabbed my life vest, pushing me down underwater.

My lungs took on a mouthful of river as he tried to pull me up into the raft. However, I was too heavy for him, so he pushed me back under again, trying to use the life jacket bouyancy to hoist me into the raft. As I popped back up out of the river, I swung my leg over the side of the raft. Everyone in the raft grabbed a leg, arm, and hand, rolling me up and into the raft.

Lying flat on my back, I spit out the remaining water in my lungs. I could feel the warm sunshine on my face as I looked up at the clear blue sky. I would live to raft another day.

The guide then said, "Let's all go jump off the thirty-foot rock into the tidal pool; it's lots of fun."

"Nope, I'm good; I can only handle so much fun in one day," I said with my teeth chattering as I tried to fight off hypothermia from my death-defying river run.

Celine and I hit the Sonic Burger drive-in after rafting. Nothing says I survived Hari-kari like a big juicy bacon double cheeseburger, fries, and a shake. Later, we watched the Los Angeles Lakers defeat the Boston Celtics in game seven of the NBA championship.

Celine is a huge basketball fan, and her team is the LA Lakers. It just so happens my sister Debbie is a big Boston Celtics fan.

Next up, Celine said she wanted to run the Carlsbad Half Marathon. Now, I'm a sprinter, not a long-distance runner, but when you're trying to impress a lady and she asks you to train for a half marathon with her, the only answer is, "Sure, let's do it."

Nimfa had run full marathons in the past, so she volunteered to train Celine and me. Our first training session was at 6:00 a.m. sharp on Carlsbad Beach. We would be running three miles on the sand.

As we began to jog, the early morning frigid marine air started to constrict my lungs as I gasped for each breath.

After a while, the arches in my feet began a dull ache as each step became more difficult, followed by a cramp in my side, seemingly screaming at me to give up.

I labored on as my calf muscles began to tighten and constrict. Finally, Nimfa stopped the run, and I dropped to my knees, sucking in the air to catch my breath.

Great, we must be at the halfway point; that wasn't too bad, I thought.

"We've gone one-half mile," Nimfa announced, looking down at the running app on her phone.

"No way, it can't be," I objected. The run app had to be wrong. We must have gone well over a mile, at least.

"Nope, look," replied Nimfa, showing me her phone.

We ended up only going a mile and a half total that day. We would have six short months to build up to the entire 13.1 miles half marathon distance.

During the summer, my neighbor down the street offered me a stay in their large Big Bear Lake cabin up in the mountains. I invited my Michigan cousin Dawn Hawkins, her husband Vern, and daughter Brittany to come along for the weekend.

Dawn and Vern had recently moved to the San Diego area. Vern was a vice president with Comerica Bank, and Dawn was now a semi-retired nurse.

Brittany lived in Carlsbad for a few years now and was training to run a marathon. Brittany was now in her early twenties, and I had not seen her since she was a baby. It's crazy how quickly the years pass by.

I invited Celine and Nimfa to tag along for the weekend adventure. It was an excellent opportunity for Celine to get to know some of my family. In addition, Celine, Dawn, and Nimfa could talk about nursing stuff. It was a fun, relaxing weekend up in the California mountains.

Things were progressing well with Celine, and we talked daily. We spent most of our weekends hanging out, training for our half marathon, and attending church.

I had season tickets for the San Diego Chargers. So, Celine would attend the weekend games with me. Weeknight games went past Celine's bedtime, so Pastor Adam was more than happy to take Celine's ticket for the midweek games.

Tailgating at the San Diego Chargers Game

Adventures in Dating

With my air miles saved up from my Hawaii years, I picked up two first-class round-trip fares to Seattle. We drove up to British Columbia from Seattle, where Celine talked me into zip lining at Whistler Mountain.

Now, I'm not saying I'm afraid of heights. It's just when I'm high on a ledge, it feels like there is a giant vortex trying to suck me over the edge. I had just such a feeling as the guide hooked me to the line. The heavier you are, the faster you go, the guide said as he pushed me off.

I accelerated down that 1,000-foot zipline, high above the mountain gorge, hitting a warp speed in excess of sixty miles per hour. "Ahhhhhhhhhhhhhhhhh!"

The end of the cable was coming fast, and I had no way to slow myself down. Suddenly the cable break kicked in, bringing me to a stop atop a platform high in the trees.

Once all of our group had landed, the guide gave a little nature speech before we hooked up to the next zipline. As he talked, I noticed the ladder from the platform down to the ground, some fifty feet below. *Hey, maybe I can just slip down the ladder and hike back to Whistler Village.* Just as that thought entered my brain, the guide said. "There is one bear per square kilometer in this area of the mountains."

Oh, great, fall a thousand feet off a zipline or get mauled by a bear. I decided ziplining to the village had better survival odds than wrestling a bear. With my luck, there would be a bear waiting for me at the bottom of that ladder.

As Celine and I snacked on sweet potato fries in Whistler Village after our zipline adventure, I thought, *This is a woman I could marry. That's, of course, if I survive the courtship.*

Celine having fun ziplining day   *Me, hoping I survive ziplining day*

We stayed with long-time friends Scott and Lila Yewchuk at their house in the White Rock, British Columbia, area. In addition, we spent a day with old friends Edgar Heyde and Marta from Argentina, who had been married a few years now. It just so happened friends from Hawaii, Brent and Maggie Martinson, were on vacation in the area at the time, so Celine also got to meet them. It was a good time for Celine to ask old friends about me and all my stories.

Late fall 2010, I had decided. I was going to ask Celine to marry me. I ordered the ring but had no idea how to surprise her with it. She would suspect if I planned a fancy dinner or something.

On November 15, PCL was the successful bidder to design and build the California State University San Marcos Student Union Building. When I told Celine about landing the project, she said, "We need to go out to celebrate."

"Let's go out for a fancy pants dinner on Saturday," I replied.

Now I had my opportunity. I booked a reservation at The Marine Room restaurant, right down on the beach in La Jolla, for Saturday, November 20, just after sunset. The plan was to watch the sunset, propose, then have our fancy dinner.

Saturday came, and so did the rain.

"Really, Lord. Did it have to rain today?"

My romantic sunset proposal was ruined. I had to choose to abort or figure out a Plan B. After a short deliberation with me, myself, and I, it was on to "Plan B."

Placing a bunch of boxes in the house foyer, I covered them with a white tablecloth. Then I set the ring on top and spread rose petals everywhere.

After leaving my wallet on the kitchen counter, I drove to pick Celine up for dinner.

As we pulled away from Celine's house, I calmly said, "You know what, I left my wallet at home. We have time, so I'm just going the swing by the house to get it on the way to the restaurant."

"You don't need to do that. I can pay, then you can just pay me back later," Celine insisted.

Oh, no, warning, warning, Plan "B" is in danger of imminent failure; think, Ken, think.

"Well, I don't feel comfortable driving without my driver's license, so I think we need to go get my wallet at the house."

"I can drive," Celine fired back.

"No, you don't like driving the truck, and parking will be tight at the restaurant. So, let's just slip by the house so that I can get my wallet."

"OK," Celine finally said.

Whew, that was a close call, but the plan was back on track. My only problem now was getting Celine into the house foyer. It was still raining, and she was not going to want to get out of the truck.

As we turned down my street, suddenly the rain stopped. Thank you, Jesus! Pulling into the driveway, I asked, "Would you like to come in for a minute while I grab my wallet?"

To my shock and amazement, Celine said, "Yes."

As Celine entered the house, her eyes caught the rose petals on the floor, and then she saw the white sheets and the ring box. Finally, as the reality of the situation caught up with her brain, I walked over and picked up the ring.

I got down onto my one knee.

"Jocelyn Aragon Floresca, will you marry me?"

"Yes," she softly said, nodding her head up and down as the emotion overwhelmed her.

After calling Celine's dad to ask permission to marry his daughter, we headed off to our fancy pants dinner.

I brought my now fiancée Celine home to Sault Ste. Marie to meet my family that Christmas. In the summer, she had met my brother Doug, Grace, and now four-year-old niece Courteney when they visited to go to Disneyland. Celine would experience her first Christmas in the snow. Mom even made Celine her own Christmas stocking, and I was able to get Celine out snowmobiling at Aunt Ruth's property. We also went on a horse-drawn sleigh ride with our family, David and Lori West, and their kids.

My sister Debbie had returned to the Sault area a few years back to be near my parents as they age, working as an intervention foster parent, taking in children from very troubling situations. Debbie lived out in the country, so we did a big winter bonfire at her place.

Christmas Morning 2010, Sault Ste. Marie

Celine was also able to spend time with Aunt Linda and Uncle Butch, and let's not forget my little dog Gabriel who was now thirteen years old. If you are wondering, Gabriel gave Celine two paws up full approval.

I'm pleased to say, Celine survived her Sault Ste. Marie Christmas, a very different cultural experience from what she was used to growing up in the Philippines and California. With Christmas now behind us, Celine, Nimfa, and I completed our first Carlsbad Half Marathon in January 2011. All I will say is whether you run, walk, or crawl, 13.1 miles is a long way to go for a small participation medal, especially since you pay for the award with your entry fee.

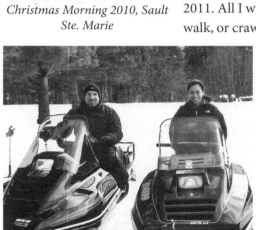

Snowmobiling at Aunt Ruth's

After the big race, we continued with our wedding plans for May 11, 2011. It would be an outdoor wedding at the Grand Palisades Resort overlooking the Carlsbad Flower Fields with the Pacific Ocean in the distance. Pastor Adam Stadtmiller would be doing the ceremony. We enrolled in North Coast Calvary Chapel's marriage preparation course. The classes span three months, covering all aspects of marriage, including conflict resolution, personality differences, finances, dealing with relatives, raising children, etc.

Celine and I, plus Celine and trainer Nimfa, race day

We were also assigned a mentoring couple. The couple would take us through several evaluation tests, determining Celine's and my compatibility. The tests would expose potential areas where we may have conflict in our marriage based on our personalities and communication styles. Our mentor couple was friendly and had been married for many years. The wife said she felt God had given her a calling to help prepare couples for a successful marriage.

"Great!" I said, "I've read many books on marriage and relationships. I have a wealth of head knowledge but minimal practical experience."

Celine and I had been dating for almost a year by this time. We had worked through some conflicts, though we were both a bit older and set in our ways and beliefs.

Celine grew up in the Philippines and California; I grew up in Sault Ste. Marie, Ontario, Canada. Our upbringings couldn't have been more different. So, we had to work through a few things.

Celine had always figured to marry someone Asian. So, I took a DNA test, and although I came back primarily Scottish Highlander, I was also 2% Asian, Pacific Islander. So, how's that for checking the box.

Ultimately, we survived our marriage preparation course. Our mentor couple and the church said they felt we were compatible with no red flags to keep us from getting married. You would think it would be full steam ahead, given the green light from the church, eh. Well, you would be mistaken. Nothing in my life has ever gone smooth or easy, and sure shooting, there was still a month left to derail my up-coming nuptials.

On the day we graduated from our marriage preparation course, Celine and I got in a heated disagreement to the point that my brain left the building. It was a case of analysis paralysis.

We are compatible, but at the same time, very different. *The wedding is only a few weeks away; is this going too fast; am I making a mistake?* My mind froze up like a computer. Do you know when you see that spinning circle on your computer screen? Well, that was my brain at that moment.

Since I was in complete freaking out mode, I don't remember exactly what I said at that point. However, I think I sorta, kinda put the engagement on hold, which sucked for Celine, as the next day was her bachelorette party. That next day I went with my cousin Vern Hawkins and his sons Heath and Jordan to the San Diego Padres game. Vern scored some great seats right next to the third-base line dugout. Vern noticed I was a bit out of sorts and distracted at the game. I gave him a brief synopsis of the events of the past twenty-four hours. Vern told me I should try to talk to Celine later.

I had been texting and leaving Celine messages all day, but she gave me radio silence, only adding to my doubt and paranoia. How can I marry a woman if she won't even talk to me to resolve a conflict? Late Sunday night Celine finally called me back, but she did not want to speak.

"You're not making sense; you need to call the husband from our mentor couple," Celine said.

So, I called the husband of the mentor couple and filled him in on the past two days' events.

"You two are compatible, and you love the Lord. You just need to talk things out." And that's about all he said, which did not help me.

Celine talked to the mentor couple's wife. The wife said to Celine she thought "Ken was supposed to be a relationship expert" and that we should talk to our pastor.

What? These guys are supposed to be our mentor couple, and they don't even want to meet with us? Pastor Adam was away on a mission trip. Besides, for the record, I said I have a lot of book knowledge on relationships but no practical experience.

That mentor wife said she felt it her calling to help couples prepare for marriage. However, I think she needs to find another calling. After another sleepless night, I called Celine first thing in the morning. Celine thought maybe I was going cuckoo, as I was not making much sense, a condition that was very out of character for me.

"You just need to stop thinking. You need to take a few days and pray to the Lord for direction. Then, once you get some direction, let me know," Celine said.

Later that morning, I received a call from Vern, checking to see how I was doing. "Not good," I told him.

"Would you be OK with Dawn talking with Celine?" Vern asked.

"Yes, that would be a good idea," I responded.

My cousin Dawn had gotten to know Celine over the past year, had been married for thirty years to Vern, and also knew me and my family my entire life. Dawn had even been the flower girl at my parents' wedding.

Vern also invited me over for dinner and to attend a men's Bible study that evening. Hopefully, this would help get my spinning mind to settle down.

Dawn filled in Vern and me on her meeting with Celine at dinner. The bottom line, Dawn liked Celine and had assured her I was not a cuckoo. Very conservative Free Methodist values, yes, but no cuckoo.

"Celine loves the Lord and loves you; I don't see any reason why the two of you should not get married," Dawn said.

Vern and I questioned Dawn over a couple of concerns, but Dawn stuck with her assessment of the situation.

The next evening, I did meet Celine for coffee. My brain had calmed down a bit but was now running on sleep deprivation going on three days. So, although a step in the right direction, the meeting didn't go well or poorly. I was still in computer lockdown mode. No matter how hard I tried, I could not get my brain to reboot.

Pastor Adam would be back in two days and would be meeting with me. So, Celine said, "Let's not talk anymore until you get a chance to speak with Pastor Adam."

After another sleepless night of prayer and frustration, I was sitting in my office at work when Jon Runnfeldt knocked on my door. Jon was in his mid-20s and had committed his life to Christ just a couple of years prior. He knew I was struggling and offered to pray for me.

I told Jon how I could not get clear direction from God. I couldn't sense if he was directing me to marry Celine or not marry her. It felt like this big spiritual battle going on in my head for my sanity, and I couldn't tell if it was God or Satan.

Jon said, "You've been a Christian a lot longer than me. But in my limited experience, when it's God working, there's no confusion nor anxiety."

Jon then prayed for me and left the room.

All of a sudden, my anxiety lifted and my brain rebooted. I was thinking clearly again. *Celine and I are compatible; we both love the Lord and love each other; there is no reason we should not get married.*

The next day I met with Pastor Adam. He sat quietly, sipping his coffee as I gave a blow-by-blow description of the past week's events. Then, he smiled and took one more sip of coffee as I finished.

"Well, Ken, I have been pastoring singles for almost twenty years. I find singles will break up relationships over things that married couples deal with daily. You and Celine both love the Lord and love each other. Now, let's have ourselves a wedding."

I met with Celine that evening, clear of mind and heart. I even brought her a gift for the emotional roller coaster I had put her through the past week. It was a pair of earrings to wear with her wedding dress.

We had a lot to do as our wedding was only three weeks away.

Two weeks before the wedding on Good Friday, I went mountain biking to blow off some wedding planning stress.

As I raced around the bend near the end of the trail, I locked up my breaks and came to a skidding halt. There, in the middle of the path staring me down, was the most giant diamondback rattlesnake I had ever seen. This bad boy had to have been six-foot long and over two inches in diameter.

The Bible refers to the serpent as representing evil and specifically Satan. So here I am on Good Friday, two weeks before finally getting married in a stare-down with a giant serpent.

The snake just looked at me, sticking out its forked tongue. I stepped back to a safe distance and tossed a rock at the serpent's head.

The diamondback rattler didn't even flinch as if to say. "Is that all you got?"

He then took one last look at me and slowly slithered away into the underbrush.

That snake encounter was a good reminder. Even if you think your life is going right, there is always evil just around the corner waiting to strike.

He who finds a wife finds what is good and receives
favor from the Lord. Proverbs 18:22

May 6, 2011, the wedding day had finally arrived, and in true McQuarrie fashion, not without a few challenges. Mom needed surgery and had been on a waiting list for over a year, so she could not travel to attend the wedding. It had been forty-three years since she took me in as a baby, and the one year I finally got married, she could not make it. Debbie would stay home with Mom, allowing Dad to come to California for the wedding. The good news was that our videographer was able to livestream the wedding for Mom and Debbie to attend virtually.

Scott Yewchuk was going to be my best man. However, Lila was in the midst of a difficult pregnancy. So, Scott and Lila ended up not being able to attend. Thankfully, Brent Martinson made it from Hawaii and served as my best man. The baby did end up being OK, giving Scott and Lila three children, Zac, Jordin, and Cailin.

Time for birthday cake. L-R Zac, Scott, Cailin, me, Jordin

The song "I Can Only Imagine" by the band Mercy Me began to play. I adjusted the monogrammed cufflinks given to me when I was the ring bearer at Uncle Tom and Aunt Shirley's wedding so many years ago.

Then, my beautiful bride came into view, walking down the aisle toward me. After all these years, it was a surreal experience. As Celine slowly walked toward me, I thought of the words of Pastor Wayne years ago. If you mess up a relationship God favors, he will bring it around for a second chance. I did not realize at the time that those words would be so prophetic in my life.

I was matched with Celine on eHarmony but deleted her. Then, years later, I get matched with Celine's best friend Nimfa on a random free Valentine's week trial. Nimfa cannot see my photos, eliminating the risk of me getting deleted. Remember, God has to work around people's free will.

Valentine's Sunday, the only available seat at church, was beside Nimfa and Celine. Not to mention I almost didn't even go to that service. After getting the church's green light to get married, my brain leaves the building, and I go temporary cuckoo—talk about cold feet.

No worries, though, as it just so happens, my cousin Dawn from Spring Arbor, Michigan, a nurse like Celine, moved to San Diego right about the same time I met Celine. Dawn steps in, providing some wisdom and counseling to get things back on track.

Then, just for good measure, a young Christian provides words and a prayer that help finally reboot my brain.

I wonder what the Lord was thinking about the events leading up to my wedding day?

• • •

It's late November 2003 as the two strangers enter the old, abandoned hospital's back door, carefully stepping down the old rusty stairs to the basement. They continue down a long, dark, empty corridor, with flickering lights providing just enough illumination as they pass by a strange door with the letters M-O-R-G-U-E above it. But the door is swung open, and the room is now empty; everyone is gone. The strangers come to an old workshop with equipment now covered in dusty tarps. Some timeworn tools are just sitting in boxes, left behind by the movers.

At the back of the workshop, the Master builder is welding, making something old into something new again, no doubt. Approaching the Master from behind, one of the strangers calls out, "Lord, we have a problem."

Turning around, the old Master lifts his welding shield, revealing his beard. With a slight grin and eyes radiating with possibilities, he says, "It's Kenny, isn't it?"

"Yes, Lord, we did as you asked, but Kenny insists on going to Hawaii and not San Diego."

"I see; he is stubborn, you know," the Master replies as he turns, rifling through some paper files on the workbench.

Turning back around, the wise old Master grins. "It's only 2003, and he's not due to meet Celine until 2010. So, tell you what, let him go to Hawaii, but just make sure you get him to Carlsbad, California, by 2009 at the latest."

"Yes, Lord, but what if Kenny gets himself married in Hawaii?"

The Master starts to laugh, not a chuckle but a deep belly laugh. "You know Kenny; there is no way he will be able to get himself married without our help."

"You're right," the strangers reply, now both laughing.

"One more thing, let's make sure we get Kenny's cousin Dawn Hawkins and her husband, Vern, down to San Diego for 2010 also."

As the two strangers exit the workshop, one turns back. "Lord, what was up with Kenny going to Orlando for six months? It didn't further his career. Why couldn't he have just stayed in Hawaii all year?"

"Just wait, you'll see. Give it time," the Lord replies.

• • •

"Who gives this woman to be married?" Pastor Adam calls out.

"Her mother and I do," Celine's dad Abe responds.

A short twenty minutes later, Pastor Adam announces, "I now pronounce you husband and wife. You may kiss your bride." Woohoo, we did it, Lord, we are married!

Married, May 6, 2011

Back L-R: Pastor Adam, Nimfa, Celine, Me, Brent
Front L-R: Caleb Ilagan, Sarah Ilagan, Caleb
Cabanting

I hope and pray all the people involved in getting Celine and me to the altar will get a special blessing in Heaven. Especially Nimfa. If she had deleted me and had not seen the potential of Celine and I, this chapter of my life would never have been written.

But it's in the history books now, so on to the next chapter.

Chapter 27:

It Seemed Like a Good Idea

*Therefore we do not lose heart. Though outwardly we are
wasting away, yet inwardly we are being renewed day by day.
For our light and momentary troubles are achieving for us an eternal
glory that far outweighs them all. So we fix our eyes not on what is
seen, but on what is unseen, since what is seen is temporary,
but what is unseen is eternal. 2 Corinthians 4:16-18*

One wedding and a honeymoon in Costa Rica later and Celine and I settled into married life. The rest of the year was relatively ordinary, filled with family occasions and activities with friends. There was no way of knowing or preparing for what lay ahead; it was the proverbial calm before the storm.

When I married Celine, I told her, in many ways, my life had been very ordinary, yet at the same time quite extraordinary. I felt I had been very blessed, and the Lord had been watching over me. Yet somehow it all seemed to come at a price. It's like the storm clouds of life had been chasing me since the day I was born. It was only by the grace of God I was still alive and kicking. The shorter version of that was more about how being married to me means you need to be prepared for a rough ride. The only thing I can guarantee is that no matter how hard life slams us down, I'll be here beside you, keeping my faith in God and soldiering on. Jesus hasn't let me down yet, even if he has made me sweat a few times.

As we began 2012, I wanted the Carlsbad house to feel like our home. "Let's do some renovations and pick new furnishings together, so this house feels like our home as a couple," I told Celine. Even better was how one of Celine's childhood friends from the Philippines, Katrina Nable Villa, is owner of KV Interiors, an interior design company in Los Angeles. We engaged Katrina to add some finishing touches to the house, along with helping to select furnishings.

I enjoyed working with Katrina on the design and construction aspects of the renovation. After all, my whole life had pretty much revolved around design and construction. But eventually, Celine just wanted the project finished and the house put back together. In the end, though, it was mission accomplished. Once finished, the house felt more like our home together than merely the place that Ken bought.

We finished the renovation just in time to fly to Sault Ste. Marie for Mom and Dad's fiftieth wedding anniversary. Celine and I had just celebrated our first year of marriage. By the time we hit fifty years of marriage, I will be ninety-three-years old, Lord willing.

Just us at Mom and Dad's 50th Anniversary, June 23, 2012. L-R
Me, Celine, Grace, Doug, Mom, Dad, Debbie, Courteney

The renovation wasn't the only thing we started in the spring of 2012. Getting married at an older age, Celine and I wanted to create a family right away. We hoped to have a couple of kids the old-fashioned way, then eventually adopt at least one child. I always wanted to adopt at least one, given I was initially an orphan. It was one of my lifelong dreams. Unfortunately, the old-fashioned way was not working. As with all things, time was of the essence, so we visited one of the top fertility specialists in Southern California who recommended in-vitro fertilization. Before we could start the process, Celine would have to undergo two surgical procedures to clear the plumbing, so to speak.

While all this was going on, I made the brilliant decision to make a career change and get my United States citizenship. Just some friendly advice and do listen closely all you guys reading this who are planning to get married or just got married. After only one year of marriage, do not start the in-vitro process, tear the house apart, make a career change, and get new citizenship all at the same time. I was used to my life always going three directions at once, but Celine was not. She just wanted to settle in, slow life down, and start a family. Celine understood the storms of life would be chasing us. She just didn't think I should be doing a rain dance on the front porch.

Technically the great recession ended in 2009, but the road back for the construction industry was a long one. Like many other general contractors, PCL needed to secure new volumes of work. However, the competition was fierce, with many contractors bidding at very low or no fees to keep their companies alive.

PCL needed work, but we were not willing to lose money to get it. San Diego was a challenging market at the time, and we were not having much success. By the spring of 2012, I felt pretty beat down after three years and very little success in landing new work. There were many discussions, rumors, and speculations within PCL as to whether San Diego was a viable market for a whole district office. Should it instead be a satellite office of our Los Angeles district? If San Diego changed to a satellite office, there would be no need for a chief estimator. Adding to all this was Al Troppmann's retiring as president of PCL Construction Services after some forty-five years with the company.

Al hired me in Toronto in 1989, moved me to Seattle in 2000, sent me to Hawaii in 2002, tried to get me to Orlando in 2003, moved me back to Hawaii in 2004 and finally moved me to San Diego in 2009. Not to mention Al farmed me out to several other PCL districts in Canada and the US for short-term assignments over the years. So, it was the end of an era, at least for Al and me. I was not worried about losing my job. The thing was, though, we did not want to move. We intended to say close to Celine's family in California, especially starting our own family. That being said, a move to Los Angeles was out of the question. The lesser air quality of LA affected my asthma, not to mention the insane traffic. It was right about this time of uncertainty I was offered a position as vice president of preconstruction and estimating for a new company called West America.

Darren Mann and Rick Coen were two senior managers in the construction industry that had a falling out with their respective employers. With a mutual vision of how business should be handled, they started their own company called West America.

West America had three sizeable projects lined up and under preconstruction. In addition, it had a financial backer putting ten million of equity into the company. They offered me a profit-sharing incentive that would be rolled over into partial ownership once the company got through the initial start-up years.

After much thought, prayer, and discussion with Celine, I resigned from PCL and accepted West America's offer. It was an excellent opportunity and if I were going to take a chance on something like this, now was the time. I didn't want to get to the end of my career and say what if or I should have. Plus, this would ensure we stayed in San Diego county.

I started my new job at West America in April 2012. Unfortunately, by May, I had determined that of the three projects they had, only one of them, an apartment complex, actually had a reasonable chance of being financed and built. The major problem with that project was the start of construction was at least one year away. It gets even better. You know the sizeable financial backer they had? Well, that guy was about as real as an urban legend; no money ever came in.

Fortunately, Darren Mann had been able to get a two-million-dollar line of credit from an equity partner. Which was all fine and dandy other than the fact we had a staff of around fifteen people without enough work to cover overheads.

Oh boy, Lord, this isn't looking good from where I sit. Oh well, I was here now. I needed to make the best of it—time to get to work.

In anticipation of starting a family, Celine and I decided it was time to set up a family living trust. We wanted to get everything set up before we started having children. The attorney setting up our trust recommended I get my United States citizenship. It would make things easier to administer the trust if something happened to me.

Celine had obtained her American citizenship back in 1992. Since I already had my green card, it would be just a matter of filing the citizenship paperwork and, of course, paying the government fees. Still, I hired an immigration attorney to hasten the process and ensure all the paperwork was in order.

Finally, mid-summer rolled around, and it was time for our first try at in-vitro fertilization. It's quite a process with fertility drugs and hormone shots to stimulate the follicles for multiple egg growth. The more eggs produced, the better the chance of getting a viable embryo. But unfortunately, our biggest challenge was that Celine did not generate many eggs, and we could do nothing about that. After a surgical procedure to retrieve the eggs from the ovaries, the sperm was then introduced to the eggs. Finally, an embryologist monitored the now-fertilized eggs for development into embryos.

Anticipation was high, and Celine and I prayed hard for a successful procedure, as did family and friends. It had been a long six months with Celine having surgeries in March and June to prepare. Celine received a call from the fertility clinic. "Mrs. McQuarrie, you have two viable embryos. The doctor is recommending transferring both embryos."

It was hard to contain our excitement, as we were one step closer to having children and, Lord willing, twins. The doctor carefully inserted our two little, microscopic embryos into Celine's womb at the clinic. Now we would need to wait and see. The following month seemed to go by in slow motion as we marked off the days until Celine's August 22nd pregnancy test. August started with hope and optimism but ended in sadness and despair as the test was negative.

As much as you prepare yourself for bad news, it's still a gut punch when you hear the words, "I'm sorry, your test came back negative."

We would have a month to recover before starting the cycle on our second in-vitro attempt.

October 24, 2012, I took part in my swearing-in ceremony to become an American citizen. My father- and mother-in-law, Abraham and Erlinda Floresca, came down from Los Angeles to attend the ceremony with Celine. It was very reminiscent of when they became citizens so many years ago.

There must have been over twenty countries represented at the ceremony that day. As for me, I now had three citizenships. I'm a citizen of Heaven, Canada, and the good old United States of America.

USA Citizenship Day with Mom and Dad Floresca

Mom finally received the surgery she had been waiting on for over a year and a half back in Canada. Hence, she and Dad were able to visit Southern California that fall. As a result, we were able to celebrate Mom's seventy-sixth birthday, and she finally got to meet all of Celine's family.

We visited Torrey Pines State Natural Reserve on one of our excursions, walking the scenic trails and enjoying the Pacific Ocean's views from the coastal bluffs. Torrey Pines is home to one of the rarest pine trees in the country, the Pinus Torreyana, also referred to as the Torrey Pine.

Mom decided a Torrey pinecone would be a good souvenir, and before Dad or I could object, Mom had plucked one off a low-lying branch. "Hey, Mom, look at that sign!"

The sign said you could be fined or charged for removing the rare pinecone from the park. Mom gasped and quickly dropped the pinecone like a hot potato. We then took a rest break at a nearby bench.

"Is there a curse if you remove a pinecone from the park?" Mom asked.

"No, not here, only in Hawaii."

"Good." Mom said as she got up from the bench. Then, seeing a lone pinecone on the sidewalk, she scooped it up.

"This cone will die on the concrete; I'm just rescuing it," Mom declared as she stuffed the rare pinecone into her purse.

To this day, that endangered Torrey pinecone resides at Primrose Drive in Sault Ste. Marie, all safe and sound right beside the Hawaiian lava rock.

While Mom and Dad were visiting, Celine and I received some discouraging news. We had started our second attempt at in-vitro. But, this time, Celine's body had only produced a couple of eggs, so the chance of getting a viable embryo would be slim at best.

To complicate things, Celine had developed an abscessed tooth. The tooth infection required antibiotics that would further put an embryo at risk if we move forward. As a result, we were forced to abandon this attempt.

Celine took the news hard; she somehow felt it was her fault, which was the furthest thing from the truth. Still, the pressure to have a child weighed heavy on her heart. All we could do at this point was soldier on and have faith that the Lord was with us. We were forced to put the in-vitro on hold for a few months so Celine could deal with her tooth problem.

In early 2013, Celine and I kicked off our third attempt at in-vitro fertilization. Just like attempt number one, we ended up with two viable embryos, even stronger than previously. Trying to keep calm, all we could do was pray as we patiently waited for the March 6th pregnancy test.

On March 7, we planned a trip to Vegas to celebrate Nimfa's birthday. Celine and Nimfa's friend Moriah Testa would be flying down and meeting us in Vegas for the festivities. Before moving to Carlsbad in 2007, both Celine and Nimfa lived in the San Francisco Bay area. They met Moriah, who was just a young child at the time, when they all attended the same church.

Moriah had just graduated from nursing school and worked at a San Francisco Bay Area hospital. Celine and I figured, if we were pregnant, we would celebrate in Vegas. But, if the test was negative, then a fun getaway weekend in Vegas would be just what the doctor ordered to relax and recover.

About two weeks after inserting the embryos, Celine developed a low-grade fever. Hearing this, something deep inside me didn't feel right. However, I buried my emotions deep to be a calming influence on Celine.

The clinic assured us this was not uncommon and told Celine to take some Tylenol to keep the fever down. Still, something didn't feel quite right to me. March 6 rolled around and, once again, a disappointment, as the pregnancy test came back negative. This news was very disheartening and saddened us deeply, as doubt started to chisel away at our faith in starting a family.

Celine, Nimfa, and I headed off to Las Vegas in a rental car Nimfa had picked up. Celine was feeling a bit off, both emotionally and physically. From the earlier failed in-vitro attempts, she knew that her monthly cycle would be hitting with a vengeance. We figured all the hormone shots had something to do with it. As we drove along, Celine began to experience painful cramps and indigestion. I asked her if we needed to head back home, but she wanted to continue. "I'm sure I'll feel better once I get to the hotel," Celine said.

She figured it was just her hiatal hernia acting up, a condition she had suffered from for several years.

We pulled into a fast-food hamburger joint to use the restrooms at about the halfway point. As we approached the entrance, a homeless man was sitting on the ground beside the door. He was quietly leaning against the wall with his arms wrapped around his knees.

I had a very peculiar track record with homeless men, to say the least. So, as I opened the door for Celine, I looked down at the man, expecting him to tell me something about myself in colorful expletives. Or, at the very least, to ask for some money. But nothing of the sort came to pass.

The man looked up at me from under a slightly wrinkled brow, his eyes calm, shimmering with a glint of concern. I nodded, and he gave me a slight smile as he turned and looked away.

I was in and out of the restroom ahead of the ladies. So, I headed to the car to wait for them.

As Celine exited the restaurant, she suddenly hunched over from a cramping pain. Seeing her, the homeless man jumped to his feet. Placing his right hand around her waist, he supported the underside of her left forearm with his left hand. Gently, he helped Celine to the vehicle.

Once Celine was safely seated in the car, the man turned to me. Looking directly into my eyes while pointing his finger to get my attention. "You need to get her to a hospital," the man said.

I thanked the man for his kindness and hopped in the car. With Nimfa now back in the drivers seat we headed on our way.

"You should have bought that guy a hamburger," Celine said as we pulled out onto the street.

"Yeah, you're right. I didn't even think of it."

We never saw that homeless burger joint man again.

Once in Vegas, we picked Moriah up at the airport and headed to the hotel. I suggested checking to see if they had a wheelchair at the hotel.

There is a lot of walking involved in Vegas, and I thought a wheelchair would be a lot easier for Celine, given the cramps she was dealing with.

"A hotel isn't just going to have a wheelchair sitting around," Celine said.

But I figured we were in a prominent Vegas hotel. If I asked for a pink elephant and were willing to pay for it, they would simply ask me, what shade of pink? So, a wheelchair should be easy to get.

Sure enough, within an hour, the hotel delivered a wheelchair to our room.

The four of us had a nice dinner at a famous chef's fancy pants steak restaurant. I'd have to say it was probably the best New York strip steak I had ever eaten. After dinner, Celine was starting to feel lousy. She was in pain and just felt yucky all over. It had been an emotional and tiring twenty-four hours, so Celine and I went back to our room for the evening.

Nimfa said, "Just call if you need the car for any reason," as she and Moriah faded into the crowd of the casino.

Back in the hotel room, Celine could just not get comfortable. We would sit her up, lay her down, turn her right, turn her left, but no position provided relief.

At around 1:30 a.m., I jumped into a taxi heading to a pharmacy to get some medications for Celine's hiatal hernia and cramping. I also grabbed some Diet Coke and M&Ms with peanuts for myself, as it was turning into a long night.

Nothing provided Celine any relief. So finally, at about 3:30 a.m., I called Nimfa and Moriah's room. "Can you bring the car around? I need to get Celine to a hospital."

After driving us to the hospital, I told Nimfa and Moriah to head back to the hotel and get some sleep. Celine and I were going to be a while.

Saying we would be a while at the hospital was an understatement. The hospital staff ran all sorts of tests on Celine. She had to drink these volumes of fluid called contrast for the tests, and when you're already suffering from severe indigestion and cramping, pounding back gallons of contrast ain't no fun. Finally, the doctor approved giving Celine some pain meds. So, at last, some relief as she was feeling no pain with the medication coursing through her veins.

Although she had not slept in over thirty-two hours, she was very talkative, energetic, and happy now; it must have been some good drugs.

It was now after 3:00 p.m. Friday. We had been at the hospital for eleven hours when the doctor came to a diagnosis. The doc said it was an ovarian cyst, and Celine should see her OBGYN when she returned home.

Celine was finally discharged from the hospital emergency room after getting a prescription for some pain meds and a few sleeping pills. Nimfa and Moriah were now at the hospital, so all four of us drove to a pharmacy to pick up Celine's medication. Then, grabbing some takeout dinner, we headed back to the hotel.

There was still time to catch the 7:00 p.m. Beatles tribute Cirque Du Soleil show. Our tickets had been pre-purchased days before. The wheelchair came in handy; I could wheel Celine around to the shows. After the Beatles, we visited the "Real Bodies" Exhibit. It's a world-famous exhibit where real deceased human bodies have been preserved through plastination. They looked like manikins of the anatomy posters you see in your doctor's office.

The display was an explosion of medical and scientific curiosity while, at the same time, it was somewhat creepy.

After the shows, Celine and I retired to our hotel room. With Celine taking a painkiller and her sleeping pill, we both had a good night's sleep. Little did we know this was to be our last good sleep for a long time.

Saturday, March 9, we all hit a fancy hotel brunch buffet. After eating, Celine and I relaxed by the pool all day.

The plan was to drop Moriah back at the airport by 6:00 p.m., then start our four-and-a-half-hour journey back home to Carlsbad. But unfortunately, although enjoying her painkillers, Celine continued to have extreme indigestion. You know the feeling, like when you need to do a big burp but can't.

After dinner at the Boiling Crab, we dropped Moriah off at the airport and started our long trek home. Celine had not been able to eat much, only managing to finish about half of her seafood gumbo with rice. She was now also constipated, probably from the painkillers.

The sun was setting as Celine, Nimfa, and I drove along the lonely desert highway. It wasn't the fun relaxing Vegas weekend we had hoped it would be. But, as the saying goes, "What happens in Vegas stays in Vegas."

Celine felt continually worse as we drove along. Finally, indigestion combined with constipation overtook the pain medication; her stomach began bloating.

We were somewhere in the middle of nowhere, between Vegas and Carlsbad. But, if nowhere was a destination, we indeed had found it. I don't remember who came up with the bright idea, but finally the decision was made to do an enema procedure on Celine to release her bowels.

Now, if this was three guys, there is no way on God's green earth "Let's do an enema" would ever enter the conversation. Instead, we would simply buy the guy some laxatives and a soda. Beyond that, he would be on his own.

But I was with two female nurses, so an enema it would be.

We found an all-night pharmacy and grabbed the supplies. Next, we found and booked a Motel 6 to serve as our procedure room. Alas, after a couple of hours and no results from multiple attempts, we finally abandoned the enema idea.

It was now about midnight, and the gals figured we should just hunker down for the night and hit the road in the morning at first light. However, I felt uneasy hanging around the middle of nowhere, considering Celine's condition.

"We are less than two hours from home. I would feel better making a run for the house. That way, if Celine gets worse, we can just head straight to Scripps Hospital in La Jolla," I said.

The ladies agreed, and we packed up. It was now 12:30 a.m. Sunday, March 10, and we were back on the road. Celine called her friend Lovely, an emergency room nurse, and told her what was happening. Lovely told Celine she should head straight to the hospital. But Celine was exhausted and just wanted to get home.

Arriving at our house just before 2:30 a.m., I got Celine right into bed as she was now feeling nauseated. Nimfa had done all the driving; exhausted herself, she crashed in the spare bedroom.

I placed a pail beside Celine in the bed. It was a good thing as Celine suddenly grabbed the bucket and emptied the contents of her stomach. Initially, I thought this was a good thing, her clearing her stomach, until fifteen minutes later when she threw up again. Even after that, she still didn't want to go to the hospital.

"OK, but if you throw up once more, we are going to the hospital regardless, if only to get you rehydrated," I told Celine, and she fell fast asleep.

At 3:30 a.m., Celine grabbed the pail and filled it for the third time. I dressed her, got her into the truck, and headed to Scripps Memorial Hospital. Nimfa followed us in the rental car.

Once at the hospital, they ran all sorts of tests. I sat there about as useless as a skill saw without a power source.

If you want to build a hospital, I'm your guy, but I'm not medical, so all I could do now was pray and trust the doctors could figure out what was happening with Celine.

Late morning the on-call OBGYN doctor came to talk with Celine. "You have a nasty infection that has shut down your bowels. You are so bloated and swollen it's hard to tell what the source of the infection is. So, I'm going to admit you into the hospital so we can get you on intravenous antibiotics."

The doctor was also surprised the Vegas hospital had released Celine. Her elevated white blood cell count from the Vegas hospital tests showed an infection. We lucked out and Celine got her own private room. They set me up with a cot in the room to stay with her and they gave her some painkillers and sleeping pills to help her sleep through the night.

Moriah adjusted her nursing shifts in San Francisco. She flew down Sunday evening to help Celine and me at the hospital, sleeping on an inflatable mattress on the other side of the room.

I hope and pray you never have to spend the night in a hospital for any reason. But, if you ever do, just know that it's the worst place to try to sleep unless, of course, they give you drugs. I mean, beepers and buzzers are going off all the time. So, if that doesn't keep waking you up, then the yells and moans of patients in other rooms will.

Monday March 11 was a quiet, wait-and-see day. Celine slept on and off, and I grabbed some tools from my truck and fixed things in the hospital room.

I hadn't slept in forty-eight hours and was feeling pretty useless. I guess my nervous energy was channeling my years as hospital Jr. Maintenance Supervisor with Poppa. I fixed a squeaky door hinge, the flush on the toilet, and an old light fixture with this annoying flickering light.

On Tuesday March 12, at mid-morning, Dr. Michael Silverman, a gynecologic oncologist surgeon, visited Celine. Gynecology is a medical practice that deals with women's reproductive systems. Oncology deals with cancer. Either way, the fact that Dr. Silverman was there

Me and Moriah with Celine March 12, 2013

meant things were not good. The antibiotics held the infection at bay, but Celine was not improving. Plus, she had gained over forty pounds from bloating in two days, which would almost be impressive under different circumstances.

The doctor explained that Celine had a terrible infection spread through her abdomen and bowels, shutting everything down. The antibiotics had temporarily slowed the toxicity, but he recommended operating to remove the source of the infection.

"I want to be honest with you. The infection is already widespread, and there is no guarantee that we can get it all. There is also a high probability that Celine will lose her ovaries, uterus, anus, most of the bowels, and possibly some of her stomach. She may end up having to use a colostomy bag," the doctor told us.

The doctor said we could continue with the antibiotics and see if anything changes over the next couple of days. However, there was a risk of the infection overtaking the antibiotics. At that point, it would be too late for surgery or to save Celine.

"I'll leave you two alone to discuss. I wouldn't say it's an emergency. But my recommendation would be to get Celine on the operating table before the sun sets today."

Dr. Silverman then left the room. Fighting back the emotion and tears, I appeared very calm on the outside. "Carpenters don't cry, you know." Still, I was absolutely freaking out on the inside. I'm a contractor, and if you say it needs to be completed by sunset, that constitutes an emergency in my world. After we completed the surgical authorizations, within a short time, Celine's surgery was scheduled for just before sunset that day.

The doctor took me aside. "Mr. McQuarrie, once we finish the initial exploratory portion of the surgery, I will come and talk to you with recommendations. I'm hoping for the best. First, however, you need to prepare yourself. You may have to make decisions that will affect Celine's immediate life and future quality of life."

The gravity of the situation descended on me like a dark cloud. It felt like the total weight of our world had just landed square on my shoulders. I had sleep deprivation and to make matters worse, I was now physically and emotionally exhausted.

I suddenly remembered the words of that homeless guy we encountered on the way to Vegas.

"You need to get her to a hospital," the guy said.

"Lord, was that you trying to send me a message?"

As Celine slipped into her midday nap, I went to the lobby in front of the nurse's station to call my parents. They didn't know yet about Celine.

"Hello," Mom answered.

"Mom?"

"What's wrong?" Mom said as my emotions got the best of me.

Now sniffling with tears streaming down my face like a two-year-old, I barely got the words out. "Celine is really sick, and I can't fix her."

"Oh dear, what happened?"

I tried to tell Mom a short version of the past five days' events, all the while continuing to sniffle, spit and sputter. So much for "Carpenters don't cry."

I continued my story while strangers stared at me as they walked by. I'm sure these folks told their families at the dinner table, "You should have seen this tough-looking bald guy, with a scar on the back of his head, crying like a baby as he talked to his mom on the phone."

After I brought Mom up to speed, she said, "I'm going to hang up now; you need to go be with Celine and pray about it. I will fill your father in, and we will be praying. Keep us posted."

> *I lift up my eyes to the mountains—where does*
> *my help come from? My help comes from the Lord,*
> *the Maker of heaven and earth. Psalms 121:1-2*

I decided to fill Celine's family in by text, as I wasn't in the best condition for repeating the story. Celine's older sister Joan left work early, picked up Mom Floresca in Newhall, and made the 140-mile (225 Kilometer) drive south to San Diego in time for the surgery.

Nimfa came to the hospital for the surgery, then took Mom Floresca back to our house.

Mom Floresca was a retired nurse and wanted to stay a few days to help Celine. Nimfa would shuttle Mom Floresca back and forth from the house as she did not drive. We happened to be in the same hospital where Celine worked as an orthopedic surgery nurse. So, the surgery staff ensured she was getting extra care and attention. Celine's coworker and friend, operating room nurse Joan Taylor, worked a double shift that day to be in the surgery with Celine. Joan's husband, Matt, who is a surgical scrub technician, also stayed late, bringing me status reports from behind the curtain during the surgery.

It appeared to be the Lord was sending Celine and me lots of help and support to get through this nightmare.

The photo I took of Celine in Pre-op, just before I left for the waiting room.

I was with Celine in the pre-op holding room before surgery. It was now time for her to go. I prayed, we said our goodbyes, and I was escorted to the waiting room.

I sat in the waiting room watching the clock tick. Minutes seemed like eternities as I waited for any updates from the doctors. The hospital limited visitors in the surgical waiting area, so Moriah stayed up in the hospital room, praying for Celine as the evening passed by. Meanwhile, Celine's mom, sister Joan, and Nimfa were all very quiet in the waiting room, praying and pondering their thoughts as the evening passed. After hours, Dr. Dale Mitchell emerged from behind a large door. Dr. Mitchell was Celine's regular OBGYN and assisted Dr. Silverman with the surgery.

Dr. Mitchell explained some good news and some bad news. The good news was that they would save Celine's bowels, organs, and uterus. The bad news—the source of infection was the ovaries, most likely from the failed in vitro. One ovary was worse than the other. Just cleaning out the infection may not be good enough, as it could return. The safest course of action was to remove both ovaries and the fallopian tubes, ending Celine's ability to have children and putting her into early menopause.

A conflict of emotions was racing through my very being at that moment. I was ecstatic that Celine had a reasonable prognosis of pulling through. Yet, simultaneously, the decision I was about to make would end her chances of having a child, and time was ticking.

"OK, remove the ovaries," I instructed Dr. Mitchell.

After the ovary removal, doctors scraped and cleaned all infections throughout the abdomen and intestines. Then a lavage wash with a medicated solution was used to clean and disinfect Celine from the inside out. The operation took well over four hours. After the surgery, I was instructed to head back to the hospital room until Celine's anesthetic wore off. Then, the nurse would let me know when it was time to come to the recovery area.

Celine's sister Joan headed back to Newhall. Nimfa drove Mom Floresca back to our house in Carlsbad for the night. Now back in the room, Moriah and I waited. Forty-five minutes passed by, and still no word from the recovery room. I went to the nurse's station, but they told me to wait. Another half-hour passed by; I inquired again but received the same answer. "Go back to the room, Mr. McQuarrie, and we will let you know when your wife is ready."

"I suggest you call the recovery room and let them know I'm on my way. It's been almost an hour and a half. I want to know what's happening with my wife," I said in a friendly but firm enough tone to get my point across. I headed toward the elevator when the corridor doors suddenly swung open. There, on the gurney, was Celine getting wheeled to the room. She was awake but heavily sedated and disoriented.

Celine was initially in the recovery room but started having excessive blood coming out of a drainage tube post-surgery. So, they took her back into surgery and opened her up again to stop the bleeding. I was annoyed that I had not been informed of what was happening. I could have been down there praying for Celine instead of just sitting up in the room thinking everything was OK.

I didn't have time to be angry; my focus was Celine. I was grateful she had survived and appreciated all the attention the doctors and hospital staff had given her.

Celine, being very disorientated, asked me. "Was I in a car accident?"

"No, you are very sick and just had surgery," I replied, holding her hand and wiping her hair away from her eyes.

"Was it my fault?"

"No, it's not your fault; you just sleep now."

"OK," Celine responded as she faded into a deep sleep.

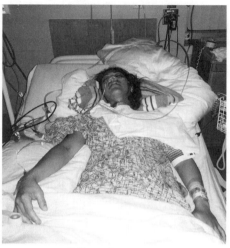

Celine after surgery

She would have night terrors, waking up with hallucinations, and feeling disoriented and confused those first couple nights post-surgery.

Celine was not out of the woods yet; she had a long recovery ahead of her. She could not leave the hospital until her bowels started to work and her white blood cell count dropped, signifying no more infection. At least now, her body had a fighting chance.

She had an impressive, Frankenstein-looking incision. First, they had to open her up from the belly button to well below the beltline. Then, surgical staples were used to close the wound back up.

The doctor told me the staples would leave less of a scar. I'd have to take his word on that because that incision looked scary from where I was standing.

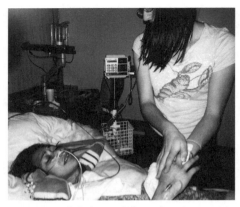

Moriah helping Celine at 2:49 am

On Wednesday, March 13, the hospital inserted a PICC (peripherally inserted central catheter) line called a "pick" line. They put it into Celine's upper arm vein, then thread it through to a large central vein near her heart. This pick line is more durable than a traditional IV and is used to administer fluids, antibiotics, and other medications.

Celine's personal nurse team continued to help. Unfortunately, Moriah had to head back to San Francisco for her shifts but returned a few days later. Nimfa pulled a couple of night shifts while Moriah was away and continued to shuttle Mom Floresca back and forth.

I stayed at Celine's side on my cot, helping with what I could.

By Saturday, March 16, Celine was starting to do better. Her white blood count was beginning to drop, and that forty pounds of fluid she

Back Row: Mom Floresca, Sarah Ilagan, Caleb Ilagan, Dad Floresca, Joan Ilagan, Hannah Ilagan, Joseph Ilagan

had gained was draining. However, I was still very concerned that her bowels were not working. To use the doctor's term, "Her bowels were still very angry."

Some of Celine's family made the drive down to visit on Saturday, and she was allowed to go outside in a wheelchair for some air. Mom Floresca headed back to Newhall with the family. When she initially said she wanted to stay and help, I had some concerns. Mom Floresca was in her mid-70s, quite frail, and had chronic neck and back pain. But you know what, she was a real trooper, didn't complain, and did what she could to help Celine be comfortable.

Other than my fifteen- to thirty-minute power naps, I had now gone seven days without sleep. I tried filling in some short-term disability paperwork for Celine's employer. However, I struggled to get much more than our address and phone numbers correct. Celine insisted I go home for a good night's sleep, and she was right. The minute my head hit my pillow I was comatose for over fifteen hours. Still, I returned to my cot beside Celine the very next day.

Finally, at 8:35 a.m. on Monday, March 18, Celine had a bowel movement. I never thought I would see the day I would be praising Jesus because my wife just took a poop, but that day had arrived! Praise Jesus! Wednesday, March 20, Celine was released from the hospital, and I took her home. It had been a two-week nightmare since we had set out on our fateful trip to Vegas.

Celine would survive the infection, but she had a long physical and emotional recovery ahead of her. She was off work for two months before her doctors approved a modified duty return in late May.

Finally, on June 15, Celine returned to full work responsibilities. Three-and-a-half months had passed since getting sick with the infection.

I returned to work at West America, but the company's financial situation had worsened. The cash flow problems had deteriorated. Overhead costs were eclipsing profits at an accelerated pace. Making matters worse, a developer we worked for held back hundreds of thousands of dollars on extras we had completed. One of the West

America managing partners, Rick Coen, decided to part ways, leaving Darren Mann solely in charge. Before the year was out, several other employees would decide to move on. To help get the company back on track, Darren hired Joe Sayatovich as executive vice president. Joe was in his mid-70s and had lots of business experience.

Joe had owned and managed past drywall and construction companies. As an entrepreneur, he had a rodeo lasso-making business and was part owner of a brewery. Joe even managed a world champion middleweight boxer back in the '80s and '90s. Darren continued to seek financial backers. Several individuals showed interest but never produced the promised funding.

I did get a phone call from Wayne Melnyk and Brad Hendrickson of PCL, seeing if I would like to come back to PCL as chief estimator in Seattle. Wayne had been transferred from Hawaii, assuming the vice president and district manager position in Seattle. Brad, the former chief estimator in PCL's Minneapolis office, was now an operations manager in Seattle. Brad had also been involved with that 2003 New Orleans Convention Center pursuit, and I had helped him out with a New York State courthouse budget back in 2004.

I thanked the guys for the offer, but Celine was in no shape for a stressful move, and I was praying hard that things at West America would work themselves out. So, I declined the offer, at the same time hoping that wasn't Jesus trying to send me a lifeboat off a sinking ship.

Celine and me with newborn nephew Klay Cruz

The year was not all bad news. In September, Celine's youngest sister Karen and her husband, Gerald Cruz, gave birth to Klay Cruz. Celine and I took a trip to the Bay Area to meet our newest nephew, a true blessing amid a rough year for us.

Celine and I met again with the fertility clinic to discuss options. The doctor recommended looking into using an egg donor. Celine's uterus survived the infection and would still be capable of carrying a fetus to term.

The doctor then warned Celine, "As a result of your surgery, you have a lot of adhesions. If you give birth naturally, everything should be fine. However, if complications develop and a C-section is needed, you will be at a high risk of bleeding to death. Regardless, you will need an OBGYN doctor that specializes in high-risk pregnancies."

"I'm not willing to take that chance; it's not worth it. I don't want to lose Celine and be raising a baby without her," I replied, responding to the doctor's prognosis.

"It's not that important to me that my child and I share the same DNA. Let's just adopt. Adoption is safe and guaranteed, and most importantly, there is no chance you will die," I told Celine.

With that, we began the long adoption process, deciding to adopt internationally from Celine's native Philippines. Unfortunately, the entire adoption would take up to five years to complete. As 2014 began, Celine made a career change. Since her surgery, she had struggled with the twelve-hour shifts working on her feet all day.

Making the change from surgical nurse to an employee health nurse at PIH Hospital in Downey, California, would be less stressful and less physical. In addition, she would be commuting by train. However, the blessing was she would only have to work three days a week.

On August 29, 2014, after months of studying and testing, I received my California general contractor's license. Now, I could become the responsible managing officer "RMO" for West America's license and possibly do a bit of house flipping on the side. I even got myself a logo.

Unfortunately, as 2014 came and went, so did West America. Finally, in December, all the walls came tumbling down. There was no longer any money to run the company. Thus, my illustrious career came to a dead stop, forcing me to apply for unemployment. Looking back, leaving PCL for West America and taking the in vitro route for Celine to get pregnant were the two worst decisions of my life to date. I guess life rarely goes as planned, but they seemed like good ideas at the time. Back in Hawaii, I had a successful booming career but no wife. Now I had a wife but no career. OK, Lord, I think I have the priorities in the correct order. Now, a little help on the career front would be much appreciated.

Although I was out of work, I felt surprisingly peaceful. I could relax now that Celine was OK. Besides, I had been working hard for a very long time. So, in a way, it was nice to have a break.

Mom Floresca said, "Leave Ken alone. Let him have some time off."

My mom told me, "Oh well, you always land on your feet; let's just pray about it."

So, when two moms are backing you up, life doesn't get better than that. The thing is, my entire life, many times I've been down but, with Jesus in my corner, I've never been out.

Chapter 28:

Down but Not Out

The Lord makes firm the steps of the one who delights in him;
though he may stumble, he will not fall, for the Lord upholds
him with his hand. Psalm 37:23-24

As 2015 began, I remained calm about the whole no job thing. Celine and I briefly discussed if I should just start up my own business, "McQuarrie Construction Services." I did have a California contractor's license and a logo, after all. With commercial construction, the challenge is always having enough bonding and cash flow. Without a sizeable financial backer, I would end up with the same problems as West America.

A possibility would be to put my old tool belt back on and start small with residential kitchen and bathroom renovations, or try some house flipping. Unfortunately, both of these options take time to develop to the point that they could replace the income I made working for large commercial contractors. Not to mention houses in southern California are insanely expensive.

My best bet was simply looking for an opportunity with an established general contractor. I was facing a big challenge, though. The industry had changed over the past thirty years, especially in the United

States, where companies ask for a university degree as a minimum qualification.

All I had was a community college diploma, thirty years of experience, and a master's degree from the school of hard knocks. The construction industry was experiencing a prolonged, slow recovery from the great recession. As such, there were just not many senior management positions available. I did manage to line up interviews with five large contractors, but no offers. I guess I wasn't very good at interviews. I was starting to get a bit concerned. Maybe Jesus was on vacation or something, but I sure hoped he would help me out sometime soon.

Adrian Ayala, a young estimator I had hired at West America, was also struggling to find a decent job opportunity. He had a construction management degree from Arizona State University. He attended on a football scholarship, playing offensive line for the Sun Devils. Adrian's wife, Jessica, had also been helping us out at West America with marketing.

I had trained Adrian for the past two years and felt he had lots of potential. His experience mainly was from smaller companies, but he wanted to move into the big leagues with a more prominent contractor.

So, I called Darin Chestnut, who had moved back to PCL's Seattle office a few years back and told him about Adrian. PCL hired and moved Adrian and his family to Seattle within a few weeks. He was in the big leagues now. On the other hand, I was still in a league of my own—as in, the league of the unemployed.

Finally, later that month, I had an opportunity through a recruiter. The job was with a developer specializing in wood-framed apartments nationwide. They had recently centralized their estimating in Irving, Texas, near Dallas, and were looking to hire a chief estimator. On Wednesday, April 8, the Texas developer flew Celine and me to Dallas to tour their head office and meet the senior executives. It was a nice four-day, all-expenses-paid trip. I met with the company owners, and Celine and I toured the Dallas/Fort Worth Area.

All the time, I was praying, "Lord is this what you want for us? Are we meant to relocate to Dallas?"

Friday, while still in Dallas, I received a phone call just as Celine and I headed out for dinner. It was Brad Kirsch from Sundt Construction in San Diego. Brad was Sundt's preconstruction vice president, whom I briefly met a few years prior. Sundt was similar to PCL but only about a tenth of the size. It turns out Sundt had just opened an office in Irvine, California, in Orange County. They were looking to hire someone to oversee preconstruction and estimating for that office. Brad said just that week, Greg Mueller, CEO of Tucker Sadler Architects, told him he should speak to Ken McQuarrie about the Orange County position.

I was friends with Greg and his wife Diane, going back ten years, working on multiple projects and pursuits together in Hawaii and Southern California.

The following Wednesday, April 15, now back in San Diego, I interviewed with Sundt regarding the Orange County position. The interview went well, but Brad said they weren't ready to pull the trigger on the position for six months to a year, but he would keep me posted.

That Texas developer made me a decent offer for the chief estimator position near Dallas the next day. So, I set May 11 as my start date, giving us a little over three weeks to get the house up for sale. I liked Texas. The wide-open spaces and the housing costs are less than half that of California. But I really liked that there is no state income tax in Texas. Still, I was a little hesitant that this was the right move for us. At this point, Celine was willing to go wherever needed for my career. I just knew she preferred California in her heart, but I had now gone four months without a paycheck. So, Texas was the best offer out there. Actually, it was the only offer out there.

Celine and I ran around that weekend, starting to plan our big move. She asked me, "You left PCL San Diego partly so we didn't need to leave Southern California. Now we are moving to Texas. Why don't you just ask Deron Brown if there is a PCL opportunity in another state?"

Holy cow, what an epiphany! Why didn't I think of that?

While I was away from PCL, Deron Brown had done very well in Orlando. So well, in fact, he had been promoted a couple of times. As of January 2015, he became president of PCL's United States building operations. That was Al Troppmann's old position. Sunday night, while relaxing in the hot tub, I emailed Deron, filling him in on my little predicament. Deron made a few calls, and a couple of days later, I was contacted by vice president and district manager Aaron Wiehe.

Aaron was a young project engineer in Seattle when I moved from Vancouver in 2000. He was just finishing leading the PCL Hawaii operation a couple of years. His new assignment was to reestablish the San Diego office. PCL San Diego had struggled to secure work over the past few years and was now a fraction of its former size.

Aaron told me he was finalizing his San Diego business plan. He would need to revise the plan and get approval from CEO Paul Douglas to bring me back on board. I expected as much, knowing all senior management positions had to be approved by the CEO.

A couple of weeks passed, and still no word from PCL. In the meantime, Celine and I had no choice but to move forward with our plans for Texas. All the while, we kept praying, "Lord, if it's not your will for us to move to Texas, then show us another path. Oh yeah, and by the way, we would prefer to stay in California, if at all possible."

Just days before loading up for Texas, I received a call from Brad Kirsch at Sundt.

"Ken. There has been a change of plans. We have decided to accelerate our establishment of our Orange County office. So, we want to offer you a position as a preconstruction project manager."

Whoa, talk about a last-minute answer to prayer.

So now, after five months without a paycheck, I had two offers on the table. Still no word from PCL, though. A week after pulling out of the Texas deal and accepting Sundt's position, PCL came through with an offer, ugh!

I called Aaron Wiehe and thanked him for going to bat for me with PCL. Still, I decided to take the Sundt position for a couple of reasons.

First, Sundt was more established in San Diego County and Orange County. Second, I wasn't in Aaron's initial business plan, so my salary's added overhead burden would put pressure on both Aaron and me. Aaron needed to prove that San Diego was a viable office location for PCL.

I had just come through three years of learning the consequences of high overheads with insufficient work volume. Plus, Celine and I were starting the adoption process, and I needed secure work in the same place for the next five years. Aaron understood, wished me well, and said, "Let's keep in touch." Deron Brown also told me to let him know if Sundt didn't work out.

On May 11, 2015, I started my new job with Sundt Construction. They had a contract to build the California Baptist University "Events Center." The new sports facility would allow the university to compete in the NCAA Division 1 for basketball and volleyball.

I would help put together the guaranteed maximum price on the Events Center and then take over for Pam Hermosillo on preconstruction. Pam was a sixteen-year veteran at Sundt and would show me the ropes as she transitioned out of the day-to-day on the project. Tyler Scott would be the senior estimator.

Sundt managed their preconstruction a little differently than I was used to. At PCL, being a chief estimator, I always aided or took the lead in pursuing a project. I would manage the estimators, constructability, costing, and value engineering. However, a project manager would lead the client meetings and the designers. This same project manager would continue on to run the construction.

At Sundt, that front-end pursuit was handled by the area manager. All of the estimators and preconstruction managers reported to the vice president of preconstruction, thus eliminating the chief estimator function as I performed it at PCL. Once a project was secured for preconstruction, it would be handed off to a preconstruction project manager, and an estimator would be assigned. The preconstruction project manager would manage preconstruction, including directing the estimator and negotiating all the trade contracts. When all contracts are awarded at the end of preconstruction, the job would be handed over to the construction project manager to build.

My strength had always been that project pursuit phase. I had built my reputation on the accuracy of my high-level conceptual estimates off mere napkin sketches. Having an estimating background, I liked to be very hands-on with the estimators or anything to do with pricing.

The typical Sundt preconstruction project managers came from a university-educated project management background. On the other hand, I came from an estimating and swinging-a-hammer background.

So, in my new role as a preconstruction project manager with Sundt, I wouldn't be playing to my strengths. On the other hand, I would be getting a chance to negotiate and award all the trade contracts, something I didn't get the opportunity to do in past jobs. The Events Center construction costs started out being significantly over budget. So, my years of experience getting projects back on a budget was about to become my greatest asset as I hit the ground running. Finally, I was back in the game.

Celine had now been working for over a year as an employee health nurse at PIH Hospital in Downey. She gained lots of experience and enjoyed the job, especially the three-day workweek. In addition, the couple days a week she had off provided time to deal with all the stuff we had to do for our adoption.

We were almost a year into our five-year adoption journey. There are a crazy number of hoops to jump through for an adoption. Since we were doing an international adoption, we had even more hurdles to overcome. The process started with filling out endless amounts of paperwork. We had to get multiple references on our ability to raise children.

Celine and I were tasked with writing four-page essays on our upbringing. In these essays, we had to list and describe all immediate family members, their occupations, and their potential involvement with the child. We had to list every address we had lived at since we were eighteen years old. The adoption agency would then run criminal and background checks on us in each listed city.

I had thirteen addresses over the years, having worked in over thirty cities, across two countries, including four provinces and five states. Celine has had eight addresses in California since she was eighteen. All our financial information had to be disclosed. In addition, we had to name guardians for the children, including their financials, in case something happened to us. Our doctors filled in forms and gave us physicals, blood, hepatitis, and tuberculosis testing. Then we had our three hours of testing and evaluation by a psychologist.

Celine and I were fingerprinted multiple times. Then, we had to file petitions to bring the child into the country with the United States Citizenship and Immigration Services (USCIS). Finally, we would be interviewed and approved by a Homeland Security officer to bring the child into the country.

A social worker visited our home to evaluate child safety and prepare a home study report. In addition, there were multiple other social worker visits to interview us, review paperwork, and go over our essays.

One of the most emotionally challenging forms to fill out was the "Type of Child Acceptable to Family." We had to check off what type of child we would accept based on age and physical and emotional conditions in this form.

Since we were adopting a Filipino child, there was no question about race. The challenge was all the special needs conditions. Every time we checked a box, we knew we were eliminating a child.

Our final decision was to accept a child four years old or younger. If there were a sibling group of two, we would be willing to take both children. We were prepared to take kids with allergies, asthma, and physical abnormalities that were correctable with surgery.

We would not accept children with ADHD (attention deficit hyperactivity disorder). The reason was simple: Celine and I would be older parents. I would be fifty years old by the time we received a child placement. We just felt the energy needed to raise hyperactive children might exceed our energy level.

Another requirement to adopt was taking ten hours of online training that focused on challenges and parenting for children from less-than-optimal circumstances. The training covered every behavioral issue you could think of, including some concerning behaviors, to say the least. After the online training, we asked our social worker, "Maybe we should reconsider and only take one child?"

"Don't worry. The training covers all the worst-case scenarios. Many of these things are very rare. The vast majority of adoptions work out just fine," the social worker responded, reassuring us that everything would be OK. Finally, after over a year of paperwork, appointments, interviews, and inquisitions, everything that needed to be filed got filed, and we were approved to adopt.

It was like we were pregnant, only instead of the child coming in nine months, we had three and a half more years to wait.

When all was said and done, between immigrating, getting my United States citizenship, and this adoption, I had been poked by a dozen doctors, accessed by a psychologist, fingerprinted a half dozen times, and filed enough paperwork to fill the Smithsonian. And don't forget the endless interviews and interrogations. I swear the US Government has more information on me than they do on George Washington and Abraham Lincoln combined.

One thing's for sure, Celine and I were getting well trained and prepared to be parents. It was a lot of work, but we considered it a blessing. After all, parents having kids the old-fashioned way don't get trained at all. Plus, don't forget I was once an orphan and foster child myself, spending my early years helping Mom, Dad, and Debbie with many foster children. Dad had been president of the Ontario Children's Aid Society. Debbie had a bachelor's degree in early childhood education and was an intervention foster parent.

Still, Celine and I volunteered to help with the four- and five-year-old Sunday school class at church to prepare for us for young children.

Christmas 2015 Celine and I once again headed to the Great White North to spend Christmas with my parents and family. I realized Celine had not partaken in a boot hockey game yet; I couldn't believe I had overlooked that Canadian rite of passage for her.

We grabbed some old hockey sticks, got Dad, Debbie, Uncle Butch, and Debbie's son Aaron, and headed to the church parking lot. Mom came along for color commentary and a good laugh.

The old guys were against the youngsters, meaning Dad, Uncle Butch, and Debbie against Celine, Aaron, and me.

Aaron was a big kid and played offensive line for his high school football team. He was one of Debbie's foster kids that she adopted.

Game time, it was a couple of degrees below freezing. Even though cold, there was no stretching or warming up or anything like that. This was good old Canadian boot hockey; just drop the ball and game on.

I thought the old guys would be slow, but no chance. They came at us full speed, complete with body checking and slashing. Celine, Aaron, and I got out to a 5-to-3 lead when Uncle Butch picked up a pass from Dad and made a charge for our net.

Suddenly, Uncle Butch's body hit the ground fast and hard. His face slammed the frozen asphalt hard enough to knock a heavyweight boxer out cold.

We helped Uncle Butch to his feet; he was dazed but wanted to continue playing. He had been suffering for years with a brain tumor. The tumor had been progressing and was affecting his equilibrium. But Uncle Butch was a rugged Canadian; there was no way a brain tumor and bad fall would take him out of a hockey game.

Debbie said, "OK, Butch, you're playing goal for Celine and Ken. Aaron, you're with Dad and me now." Celine looked at me like we were all cuckoo as Debbie dropped the ball and pressed toward our goal.

In the end, the game ended in a tie.

After getting home, Celine commented. "I know how you guys are with hockey, but that was intense. And what's up with giving us the injured player? We were winning!"

That would be Uncle Butch's last hockey game. By February 2016, the tumor was winning the battle, and Uncle Butch had to enter hospice. All Celine and I could do now back in California was pray for Uncle Butch.

We decided to move from San Diego County to Orange County to considerably cut down my hour and a half commute to work each day. In addition, Celine landed an employee health nurse position at Hoag Hospital in Orange County about this same time.

It sure seemed like the Lord was aligning the stars for us to start and raise a family in Orange County, California. Since we still had at least three years of waiting on our adoption, Celine and I came up with a brilliant idea. At least brilliant in our minds. The plan was to buy a small townhouse in Orange County and sell our Carlsbad home. First, we would live in the townhouse while looking for an opportunity to build a new home or find an old, dilapidated wreck of a house and rebuild it. Then, after constructing our new home, we would convert the townhouse to a rental property.

I was so excited. It was a dream of Poppa and me to build a house for my family. Unfortunately, Poppa had been gone for many years now, but even still, I could construct it in his honor. As good fortune would have it, we found a brand spanking new two-bedroom townhouse that would work just fine. It was one of the last remaining units in the development and came fully furnished.

March 2016 was a busy month. First, Celine started her new job. Then we moved to our townhouse and put the Carlsbad home on the market, hoping for a quick sale. Have you ever heard the saying, "Hope is not a strategy"? Well, we were more than proving that out. Weeks turned into months, and we didn't get a single offer on the house.

Regardless, Celine and I settled into our new life in Orange County and started attending Saddleback Church, pastored by Rick Warren. We continued to pray for our house to sell before we ran out of money paying two mortgages.

Celine was enjoying her new job. As for me, I liked my work as always but was under more stress than usual, learning the Sundt way of doing things. I have to admit I was surviving but not thriving in my new role. I did enjoy working with the people at Sundt. Robert Stokes was the vice president and area manager for the Orange County office. Then, Ann Poppen took over as vice president of preconstruction from Brad Kirsch. I got along well with both Robert and Ann.

I now had a student housing project at Pepperdine University in Malibu on my plate. Soon we would add a biotech laboratory facility at California State University Los Angeles and The College of Extended Learning building at California State University San Bernardino.

There was a common theme with all the projects: they all had budget challenges. You see, the construction industry started to take off, prices rose, and skilled trade resources were limited on the backside of the recession.

Finally, after three months on the market, we received a single offer on our Carlsbad Home. It was a low-ball offer I wanted to reject.

"What are you doing? It's our only offer after three months on the market; we need to counter," Celine passionately exclaimed.

"Yeah, you're right. Better not blow off our only interested buyer."

After a bit of back and forth on the price, we agreed, and the house was sold.

I had been studying the Orange County housing market for over a year now, and it was not good. Everything was so crazy expensive. Our best bet was to find an old, dilapidated house and completely rebuild it, an exercise that would prove to be much easier said than done.

Celine wanted a one-story home on a cul-de-sac with a park or open space behind it. She wanted the house orientated so natural sunlight would pour through the windows all day. Oh yeah, and we had to get it at a cheap enough price to afford renovations.

On a late July Friday evening, the summer sun was setting on the horizon. I told Celine her wish list for a home was not realistic, at least not in the price range we could afford. Celine's response: "You need to pray about it."

Jeepers, my wife is now sounding like my mom. "OK," I said, "but it's going to take a miracle to find this house." It would be easier to find a purple hippopotamus.

Before lights out that night, I prayed. "Lord, you know it has been my life's dream to build a house for my wife and family. So please help us find the perfect home for us. In Jesus' name, amen." With that, I turned off the bedside lamp and fell asleep.

Saturday morning, the sunlight was peaking around the bedroom window blinds. Celine was already up. I could smell the fresh coffee brewing in our tiny townhouse kitchen as I grabbed the tablet from my bedside table. Opening a real estate app, I searched for a one-story home in Orange County.

To my shock and awe, there staring back at me was a 2,300-square-foot, one-story house on a cul-de-sac, backing onto a park. The family room and kitchen faced southeast, ensuring natural light most of the day. It was an estate sale, only one day on the market.

The house was built in 1977 and was pretty much original, meaning it was a dilapidated wreck. As such, it was at a rock bottom price that would afford us the ability to renovate it completely.

I had just found Celine's purple hippopotamus!

At first, I thought I was dreaming, but after realizing I was, in fact, awake, I went and showed Celine the house. The home was close to Saddleback Church, so we decided to look at it after church on Sunday.

After driving by and viewing the property, I called our Realtor, Candis Kolb, who had just sold our Carlsbad house. "How would you like to do a double closing?" I asked Candis.

Candis checked on the house, but sad news. The owners already had an all-cash offer on the property. Wow, an offer in less than twenty-four hours. I was right; this was a good deal. No matter, we didn't act fast enough. So, Celine and I continued to pray.

About a week later, we got the news. That all-cash house offer fell through. We quickly submitted our proposal and a letter of how we wanted to renovate the house to raise our family. The letter worked, and our offer was accepted.

Unbelievably, we had just bought the purple hippopotamus.

Our Carlsbad house sale closed on August 17, and our new house purchase closed just nine days later, on August 29.

Like a kid in a candy shop, I was so excited to redesign and re-build our new home. So, I grabbed Celine and a tape measure. Within a couple of hours, I had the entire inside of the house measured. I would spend the following week taking the existing floor plan and doing tracing paper overlays of potential layouts. The current home was typical of the '70s, with many small, compartmentalized rooms.

I wanted to create an open concept floorplan with a vaulted ceiling by knocking down interior load-bearing walls and installing a new thirty-foot structural beam. The front entry would be reconfigured, and a back exterior wall pushed out to make room for a dining area. The kitchen would have a large center island.

The existing four bedrooms would be converted into a master suite with two bedrooms. And to complete my design was a new loft space over the double garage.

Existing house floor plan

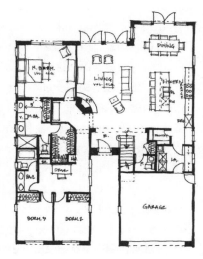

Revised house floor plan

The next step was to get some professional designers on board to finish the design and prepare the building permit submission plans.

Celine and I liked the Southern California Spanish Colonial design. Michael Luna and Associates Architect had experience in this architecture style. We also once again brought on our friend Katrina Nable Villa of KV Interiors for the interior design. I was off and running with design and preconstruction on our future home, which would consume most of my evenings and weekends over the coming months.

My job at Sundt continued to get busier. The Cal Poly Pomona Student housing project was kicking off. This massive project included two eight-story student housing buildings, a dining commons, and relocating a section of Kellogg Road. Sundt would handle the design and construction of the project. Mary Homan would be leading the preconstruction on the Cal Poly project, and Tyler Scott would head the estimating effort. I would be involved in a higher-level oversite as I was busy with our other projects. Soon after Cal Poly housing kicked off, I received a call from my old friend Eric Orquiola. Remember Eric? He was that young chief estimator that I went to help in Orlando way back in 2003. Eric and I had kept in touch over the years. He was now director of preconstruction and estimating at PCL USA head office. Eric's wife, Cathy, was now working for PCL and was being transferred to become the district manager for PCL's California operation.

Eric mentioned developing a business plan to open an Orange County office, asking if I would like to run the preconstruction and estimating. It was an offer I found pretty intriguing.

Celine said, "You should consider going back to PCL. You have a long history with PCL, and It would be less stressful for you."

I wouldn't say I was stressed; it's just I hadn't hit my stride yet with Sundt. The way I see it, construction is quite similar to football. There are policies and procedures which are like a playbook. The thing is, I've always been a very intuitive player relying on prayer and instincts. When I have the ball, my aim is to reach the goal without penalties.

The playbook may say go left, but my instincts tell me to go right. As I break right, the coaches on the sidelines start to worry and may even freak out a little. Over time, though, as my instincts prove correct, the coaches calm down more often than not. They even start counting on me to use my instincts to reach the goal.

I did have a long history at PCL. Over the years, many bosses had developed a trust in my instincts. Sundt was running a different offense than I was used to. I had made some ground on building their faith in me, but I still had a ways to go.

I told Eric with all the projects I had on my plate plus starting my house build, it was not a good time to be making any big moves. But there was also professional integrity. Sundt had entrusted me with over two hundred and fifty million dollars' worth of projects. I needed to see these projects through.

Eric totally understood. "I'll touch base with you as things develop," he told me. So, we left it at that.

On September 27, 2016, at the age of seventy, Uncle Butch lost his battle with a brain tumor and went to be with the Lord. Celine and I booked our flights and headed to Sault Ste. Marie for the funeral. Uncle Butch didn't enter my life until I was twelve years old, but he became the most involved of my uncles. Besides being the "five golden rings" singer at Christmas time, Uncle Butch always joined family events. From boot hockey to family game nights to camping trips.

He would take me to Greyhound hockey games when I was a teenager. He even trained me to make a custom knife from scrap steel, although Mom put an end to my knife making when I cut off the tip of my thumb in a grinding wheel. Luckily Poppa was available to drive Mom and me to the hospital to get the bleeding to stop.

It was also Uncle Butch who gave Poppa and me the plans to build the bed and dresser back in the day.

Uncle Butch stayed with me in Vancouver a couple of times when he flew out to visit his grandson and daughter Sherry (my cousin). Aunt Linda came with him on one such trip but ended up with food poisoning. Not such a memorable trip for Aunt Linda.

*Uncle Butch and
Aunt Linda*

As a self-trained handyman, Uncle Butch was always willing to lend a helping hand or talk sports and politics. His most significant victory in life came not too long after marrying Aunt Linda when he accepted Jesus as his Lord and Savior.

Uncle Butch always told me that was the best decision he ever made and how his life changed for the better after that. As for Celine and me, we didn't know it yet, but we were only a couple of months away from the start of a life-altering event.

Chapter 29:

Living the Dream

Teach me to do your will, for you are my God; may your
good Spirit lead me on level ground. Psalm 143:10

In December 2016, we received a call from our adoption agency. They were sending us the "Special Home Finding List." *Oh, what's that?* I thought. *It sounds somewhat ominous.*

The list was of children in the Philippines passed over for adoption for various reasons. We could choose a child from this list to adopt right away. Or we could wait a couple more years for a placement.

This Special Home Finding List was a gut-wrenching document with pages and pages of children tossed aside. Countless kids with physical abnormalities; many had been abused physically, sexually, and emotionally. Some were abandoned, still others with severe developmental challenges.

As Celine and I reviewed the document, our hearts went out to each and every child. We just wished we could hug each one and make all the pain go away. Unfortunately, what had been done to some of these children was nothing short of evil. Even with my knowledge and experience of orphaned children, it was shocking. It put into perspective how blessed I had been not to have been passed over but adopted into a loving Christian family.

Buried in the middle of the document, Celine spotted a sibling group of three. It said, "The children were voluntarily surrendered by their birth parents due to their incapability to provide for their needs continuously."

The eldest of the three was a ten-year-old boy. The report said he was humble, helpful, quiet, and diligent. Although he could be quite shy, he interacted well with other children and house parents. He related well to his sisters and was described as a loving and caring brother. The boy was also intelligent, helpful in the kitchen, and interested in playing a musical instrument.

The middle child was an eight-year-old girl described as being healthy and active. The report said she loved to sing Christian songs and take part in prayer before meals. She was friendly, sociable, sweet, and affectionate toward her younger sister.

The youngest was a healthy and playful seven-year-old girl who was sensitive to other children's feelings. She loved to be hugged, and could carry on conversations with other children and adults. She was described as being closer to her sister than her brother.

Celine and I were astonished. These kids didn't seem to fit with the other children in this report. Yes, we understood they would have some trauma from being separated from their family. Still, they were described as healthy, sweet, caring, and loving for the most part.

We told our adoption agency we would be interested in learning more about these three kids. In no time, we received a detailed report on them.

The report was extensive and over fifty pages long, including, among other things, a child study report, medical history, psychological evaluations, and a few recent photos.

Their father was sent to jail, but eventually, he was acquitted of the charges and released from prison. During his incarceration, their mother could not support the children. She would leave them alone for long periods.

In late 2011 the three children were placed into the orphanage. Eventually, their mother signed the papers giving voluntary consent to place the children up for adoption.

The children's father was still hoping to get them back. Still, he was not able to financially support them. So finally, he also signed over the children for adoption. The three kids became legally eligible for adoption in spring 2016.

The report made it clear that the kids had been in grave poverty and had suffered from neglect. However, physically they were doing well, and their medical records were reasonably normal for young kids.

The psychological reports provided us with a lot of information.

The boy's report confirmed he was humble, shy, and quiet in his ways. He was free from adjustment problems but lacked some self-confidence. So, he would shut down and retreat into his shell, so to speak, if stressed or upset.

There was evidence of affectional deprivation and a need for acceptance. However, the boy's testing showed he had inner strength and resilience and would benefit from a stable, secure environment.

The middle girl struggled a bit with learning. However, it was felt this could be improved with proper schooling, love, and support.

She was pretty active with a short attention span and average reasoning ability. But she was described as playful and compliant when given a task or asked to do a chore.

The report did mention she tended to be insistent on what she wanted but listened when reprimanded. It also talked about crying and indulging in mild tantrums when angry but clarified she was not a mean child and could be disciplined. So, it sounded like she had a bit of a stubborn streak, but nothing I couldn't relate to.

As for the youngest, she was lively and bubbly with a firecracker personality and quick wit. In addition, her tests showed her to be emotionally stable, a fast learner, and inquisitive. She was also described as having an amiable, friendly nature with no difficulty bonding with her peers.

This little gal seemed like a young mini version of my mom. Looking at her photo and reading about her personality, family and friends would comment, "She could literally be the biological child of you and Celine."

All and all, we didn't see any big red flags in the report.

After praying about it and consulting with my dad and sister from their fostering experience, we decided to request to adopt these three siblings. A response returned saying several families had signified interest in adopting these children. So, as a result, it would take a couple of months before a final decision would be made.

Celine and I were cautiously optimistic about getting the three kids. But unfortunately, it was out of our hands now. All we could do at this point was continue to pray about it.

"Lord, not our will but yours. If we were meant to adopt these kids, we ask your blessing. If not, may the Holy Spirit lead us in the direction we should go."

Oh boy, if we do get these kids, I need to get our house finished and soon. The drawings had been submitted to the building department for permitting, so it was just a waiting game now. I was already entrenched in the house design and wanted to be involved with the construction. My problem, I had a very demanding day job. So, I needed to find a general contractor that I could partner with.

The design was a complicated rebuild, with many unique details to work through. There was a lot of structural work with new concrete foundations and large wood beams. To keep costs under control, I needed a contractor with good carpenters and laborers to execute the job, or as we say in the construction industry, "Self-perform the work."

I would supply various materials and handle certain subcontractors directly from my commercial construction connections.

Our architect recommended two custom house builders. At the same time, I saw Israel Battres, aka "Izzy" of Battres Construction, on one of those house flipping shows. You know, the shows where they renovate a whole kitchen for only $10,000. I checked out Battres's website and they were a family-owned business with some good construction experience for what I wanted.

I met Izzy early one morning at the property. We rolled out the new architectural plans on an old folding table I had set up in the living room. First, Izzy started to flip through the blueprints. Then, with a wrinkled brow and a half-cocked smile, he looked up at me. "This isn't a $10,000 kitchen, you know."

"Yeah, I figured as much."

We walked through the house, and I explained my vision for the home. Izzy and I hit it off from the get-go, and he quickly grasped our dreams for this house. Over the next few weeks, Izzy and I worked on a scope of work, pricing, and detailing what his crews would do and what I would handle on my own.

Oh, yeah, and those two housebuilders our architect recommended? Well, they both bailed on me, saying they were fully booked for at least a year.

Now, please don't tell Izzy he was my only option; we'll keep that our little secret. Truth be told, I felt Battres Construction was the best suited for what I wanted to do. I think Jesus must have scared off the two other contractors, so I couldn't screw it up and not hire Battres.

After many months and resubmissions, the city finally approved our design and issued a building permit. Izzy's team was eager to get started. His brother Rudy Battres would be the project manager, and Rafael Leon, the superintendent.

However, they couldn't get started just yet, as securing the construction financing proved more problematic than anticipated. The problematic part being the bank wouldn't loan us enough money to complete the construction.

Our house construction dreams were at a standstill, short of winning the lottery or getting a mystery inheritance. All Celine and I could do was to pray about it. Not pray to win a lottery, although that would be awesome. Simply pray for the Lord to help us out of our predicament.

That answer to prayer sure didn't take long. Celine's sister Joy worked for a company that provided construction financing. With Joy's reference, I negotiated a deal with their vice president on a construction loan.

Yet, there was one little catch. We were still short on funds to complete the project. So, there was no choice but to sell our townhouse to make up the difference.

Sounds easy, right? But I've never done anything the easy way, so why start now, eh.

We were in the middle of an adoption process. We had already done adoption home studies on two properties with moving to Orange County. Selling the townhouse and moving to a temporary rental would require yet another home study, followed by a fourth study once in our new house.

Celine was starting to get very concerned. When adopting, you are supposed to be stable, meaning staying in one place for five years. Since beginning the adoption process, I was with my third company, Celine, her second.

Now we were staring down the barrel at moving four times in two years. That would almost be impressive under different circumstances.

Maybe this whole house renovation was a bad idea, but I figured I could pull this off with a bit of planning and a lot of prayers. I had been waiting for this opportunity my entire life.

In April 2017, we put the townhouse up for sale while demolition started on the house. The renovation was scheduled for seven months, just in time to cook an American Thanksgiving turkey in our new kitchen.

On Monday, May 15, I called our social worker. "Is there any news on the three kids from the Special Home Finding List? It's been over four months."

"Nothing as of Friday but let me check my email from over the weekend. Hey! I don't believe it! You guys have been selected to adopt the kids!"

The emotion hit me hard, like being blindsided by a linebacker. I fell back into my office chair, speechless. Holy cow, we're going to be parents. Then, about a minute later, the second wave of emotion hit. Holy cow, am I ready to be a dad?

Pulling myself together, I called Celine and gave her the news.

"Celine? Celine? You still there?" The phone was dead silent. I guess that linebacker got to her too. I think it's fair to say, neither of us got much work done that afternoon.

There were still many immigration hoops to jump through, both in the USA and the Philippines. It was expected to take about seven months to get all the clearances to bring the kids to California. For the time being, our lives went into hyperdrive. So much to do, so little time to prepare for these kids.

Ten days after getting the news on the kids, our townhouse not only sold but sold with a rent back clause allowing us to stay in it until December 31. So now we had the funds to finish our house renovation and a place to live. Thank you, Jesus!

The good Lord had to be helping us. I mean, what are the odds of finding the perfect home with complicated financing falling into place? But then, we sold our townhouse right away with a rent-back clause and got approval on the adoption, all in perfect timing. Everything was lining up with the precision of a finely tuned Swiss watch. It was like someone set up the dominos, and all we had to do was push over the first one.

It had been a long journey, but my lifelong dreams of adopting a child and building a house for my wife and kids was becoming a reality. It was like the good Lord had been preparing me for this moment my entire life. This must be my purpose.

"What if we find some hidden problem with the house? You know, like on those renovation shows, they always find something that adds money or blows the schedule," Celine asked.

"We should be fine. We're pretty much tearing this house down and completely rebuilding it. What could we possibly find at this stage?" I responded.

Back at the office, the Cal Poly project, like many others, was having budget and schedule challenges. The job was proving to be a real tiger by the tail. So, I would have to be more hands-on to get it back on track. It was decided Mary Homan would focus on managing the designers. I would roll up my sleeves on the pricing, value engineering, and getting the trades bid and under contract.

To free up some of my time, project director Jeff Truman and estimator Brian Parker would take the lead on the Los Angeles Biotech Laboratory as well as the San Bernardino Extended Learning facility. I would still supply a higher-level oversite of these projects.

With everything I had going on at work, my stress rose as fast as the email count. I was now receiving and responding to over 100 emails per hour. I also attended endless meetings, managed staff, kept the executives happy, and oversaw my own house construction project. Speaking of the house. Can you believe we only got a couple of weeks into construction when I received a call from superintendent Rafael? He had found some structural problems with the size of the roof rafters that needed a redesign and resubmission to the city.

Ugh, the cost impact wasn't half as bad as the four-week schedule delay. But I assured Celine that I was still optimistic that we could make up the schedule delay and get the house completed for Christmas.

Every spare moment I had, and some that I didn't, were now consumed by the house, working with Katrina on the interior design, sourcing the right plumbing fixtures, appliances, tile, and specialty items. In addition to Battres Construction, I used my own contractors for the fire sprinklers, fireplace, exterior landscaping, stair railings, door frames and hardware, carpet, security system, and a few other things.

There were endless details to figure out. Rafael and I were emailing and texting back and forth multiple times a day. I would run to the jobsite most lunch hours. Then, Celine and I would spend our weekends reviewing the progress of construction and shopping for various products we needed to provide. I was in my element, having fun and

Living the dream

loving the process. I was living the dream, and I enjoyed every minute of it.

Now don't get me wrong, Celine was looking forward to the new home, but she just wanted it to get done already. Her focus was on preparing physically and emotionally for our instant family of three kids. We had already sent the children a photo album full of fun family pictures with grandmas and grandpas, aunts and uncles, cousins, and of course, amusing photos of Celine and me.

At 6:00 p.m. Monday, July 17, we would be meeting our children for the first time via Skype.

A nervous excitement descended on us as we connected with Ms. Charlotte, the orphanage director. Ms. Charlotte was slight in stature but big in heart. She would roam into some of the roughest neighborhoods, rescuing young children and bringing them back to her orphanage home.

As Skype started, we saw the children for the first time. The youngest girl's little witty personality jumped through the screen as she instantly connected with Celine and me. She was as described, bubbly, talkative, and very social, asking questions, pointing, and laughing at the various photos we had sent them.

Initially, the middle girl was quieter, watching the computer screen intently with big eyes. She let her younger sister take the lead but soon engaged in the call's excitement. She responded to questions we specifically asked her and asked us a few questions of her own when prompted.

The older boy was quite shy, preferring to sit behind his sisters and quietly watch. His mannerisms were very humble, polite, and gentle. He would look down when asked specific questions, covering his eyes, but with gentle encouragement, would eventually answer. When asked if he had questions for us, he would smile and shake his head, indicating no.

The call was a short forty-five minutes, intensified by the few-second delay in the internet connection, making it difficult not to be talking over each other. The kid's English was better than we expected. However, they were much more comfortable when Celine spoke to them in their own Tagalog dialect.

After the call, Celine and I were emotionally, mentally, and physically exhausted. Trying to keep three young children with English as a second language engaged, excited, and interested for forty-five minutes on the internet with a time delay had its challenges. But the emotion of being called mommy and daddy, and meeting our children for the very first time, was quite overwhelming. That night we prayed to the Lord, thanking him for blessing us with these children and for wisdom and guidance moving forward. We also thanked him for our house under construction, soon home for our family.

We were truly "living the dream." The Lord was setting into motion the desires of our hearts, and we were so thankful.

After talking with Ms. Charlotte and our social worker, we decided it best to start the children off in a small private Christian school as they would be behind in their education versus American children of the same age.

After some searching, we found a small Christian elementary school in Lake Forest called Grace Christian School. Celine and I met with the school principal to discuss a plan for evaluating the children and easing them into American learning. We also prepaid the tuition to ensure there would be available spots for them when the time came.

Grace Community Church owned the school. We felt a smaller, family-oriented church would help our new family. So soon, we switched over from Rick Warren's Saddleback Church and started attending Grace Community. We began attending a home Bible study group led by Alan and Vanessa Russell. Vanessa was Filipino and Alan Scottish. Like Celine and I, except Alan was from Scotland, and I just have Scottish DNA.

Alan and Vanessa had a young boy and adopted a newborn baby boy. We also met Paul and Catherine Nylander in the group, with a young boy and girl of their own. So soon, we would be adding our three children to the mix.

A common practice when adopting children is giving them a new name. It helps signify a new beginning. For example, I was born baby Ian, then Mom and Dad gave me the name Kenneth, moving Ian to my middle name.

We wanted to do something similar for our children. Since they were a bit older, they could make their new names their first or middle name. Ultimately, we would let it be their individual choice to use the name we suggested, pick one of their own, or not to change their name at all.

Celine and I agreed on the following names for the kids. We would name the oldest boy Andrew after my Poppa. Andrew was also Baby Stephan's middle name.

The youngest girl was so much like a little young version of my mom, we would call her Joanna.

I had always liked the name Sofia and thought one day, if I had a little girl, I wanted to name her Sofia. So, Sofia seemed like the perfect name for a special middle girl.

So, it was settled. Our children's new names would be Andrew, Sofia, and little Joanna, at least if they accepted those names. We planned to surprise them with their new names when we flew to the Philippines to get them.

We got the children's sizes from Ms. Charlotte. Celine started to get clothing, toys, books, etc., for the children. Family and friends donated things they knew we would need for three young kids. Moriah, Nimfa, and Celine's sisters even put on a surprise baby shower, or should I say children shower, for us. Well, at least it was a surprise for

Celine, as my job was to get her to the house for the surprise. I even found a neat children's picture Bible with many key Bible stories. I looked forward to reading the children a Bible story each night before bedtime.

Soon it was time for another Skype with the kids. Like the first time, there was still a delay in the sound. But that didn't slow down the video chat. This time around, the kids had many more questions for us.

Little Joanna was even more excited this time than previously, if that was even possible. Sofia was right there beside Joanna smiling and intently taking everything in. She even sang us a praise and worship song; she had a beautiful singing voice.

Andrew, although still shy, asked a few questions and interacted much more than last time.

After talking to all three together, we did some one-on-one time with each child—first little Joanna, then Andrew, followed by Sofia.

When Sofia's turn came, Ms. Charlotte got called out of the room.

"Daddy, what's your favorite color?" Sofia asked.

"It's red," I responded.

"Daddy, zip it," Sofia snapped back, putting her thumb and pointer finger together, moving them from left to right across her face, mimicking closing a zipper.

I was caught off guard as Sofia quickly asked Celine, "Mommy, what's your favorite color?"

"It's orange," Celine started to say. But before she could get the words out, Sofia yelled, "Zip it, Mommy."

Sofia, now getting louder, "DADDY, what's your favorite food?" I tried to get her attention, but Sofia yelled over me, "Zip it, Daddy, zip it."

"MOMMY, ZIP IT. DADDY, ZIP IT." Sofia continued getting louder and louder. "ZIP IT, ZIP IT, ZIP IT." Now virtually out of control, with her face contorted and mere inches from the screen, she just kept screaming, "ZIP IT, ZIP IT, ZIP IT." Then suddenly, just as quickly as she started, she stopped and looked calm, like nothing had happened.

Moments later, Ms. Charlotte came back into the room. The children left, and we had a bit of a chat. She was accommodating in providing us with more information on the children. We discussed their personalities and behaviors, what each struggled with, what they were good at, how their learning and schooling were going. However, we didn't mention the behavior we had just witnessed with Sofia. I wanted to discuss this with Celine before bringing it up with Ms. Charlotte.

Oh, man. Celine and I were more exhausted after this video chat than the previous one, but for a different reason.

Wow! Are we in over our heads? What's up with Sofia?

After my heart rate slowed back down, I said to Celine, "Maybe Sofia was getting frustrated with the delay in the video chat. After all, this was as new to her as it was to us. I'm sure one of her instructors tells the kids to zip it when they're not being quiet in class. She just doesn't know how to interact with a parent."

"Maybe you're right, but you should ask Ms. Charlotte about it," Celine said.

I followed up with an email to Ms. Charlotte explaining what had happened with Sofia. Ms. Charlotte responded, "I am sorry she said that and that I wasn't there! Little monkey! I think it is a bit surreal seeing you on Skype; she wouldn't dare say that to your face. I am now wondering where she heard that saying."

It was reassuring to hear Ms. Charlotte's response that this was an isolated incident. On our next video chat with the kids, Sofia did apologize for acting that way. Still, my gut told me there was a bit more to it. We discussed with my sister Debbie about traveling with us to help when we picked up the children. She has professional experience with child behavioral issues, fostering, and adopting. Debbie was more than willing to come along and looked forward to it.

The house construction wasn't going as quickly as I had hoped. We kept running into challenges to solve and details to figure out.

That December deadline to be out of our townhouse was getting closer and closer. The reality was that we could get word to get the children any day. We kept praying and trusting the Lord had every-thing under control.

Mary Homan and I were making good progress on the Cal Poly housing project at the office. Finally, we now had a path to getting the project's budget back in line without compromising the design quality or cutting the work scope. You gotta love it when a plan comes together.

Cast all your anxiety on him because he cares for you. 1 Peter 5:7

I pushed myself pretty hard between Cal Poly, my other proj-ects, our house, and preparing for the children. There was a full-on Canadian blizzard swirling around my head to the point I struggled falling asleep at night. If I woke up in the middle of the night, my brain would shift into gear, taking off at a hundred miles an hour.

Celine, getting concerned, told me, "You need to slow down; you're under too much stress."

I had been under more pressure than usual working for Sundt over the past year. Remember that trying to learn a new offense stuff? Compound that with the full weight of getting the house finished by the end of December. Then there was the anticipation and planning for becoming a father.

Given all that was going on, it was understandable my blood pres-sure was a bit high at times. But, slow down? How can I slow down? Too many deadlines and so little time.

"I'm not stressed; I'm just busy; I have a lot to get done," I reas-sured Celine.

At least, I didn't think I was stressed until our friendly neigh-borhood building inspector brought our house construction to a standstill.

During any construction project, there are change orders. We had added a number of lights and electrical receptacles. We also changed from one 5-ton air conditioner to two 3-ton units. The inspector wanted us to revise our drawings and resubmit them to the city for approval.

What? I couldn't believe it. That's crazy. Usually, you would just mark the plans with a red pen to show the changes, then go to the city building department and they will sign off on the changes that same day.

It took me two weeks to get the revised plans from the architect combined with four weeks for the city's approval. So, it turned into a six-week delay. Rats, that's it. There is no way the house will be finished on time. So come December 31, we will be with three kids and homeless.

The following week was insanely busy. Then, Friday around 3:30 p.m., I just didn't feel right. I felt lightheaded and a bit nauseous, so I texted Celine and told her I didn't feel well and was heading home early.

"Do you need me to come to get you?" Celine texted back.

"No, I'll stay off the freeway and just take side streets," I replied.

As I was driving, I became dizzy and started to sweat. No problem, I just turned the air conditioner to full blast and managed to make it home. I went straight to the bed and laid down, although the bed felt like it was spinning.

About twenty minutes had gone by when Celine, just getting home from work, burst into the room. Grabbing my arm, she slapped a blood pressure cuff on it.

My blood pressure was almost impressive, clocking in at 218 over 114. Keeping in mind that normal is 120 over 80, Celine almost called 911. However, she kept checking my blood pressure over the next half hour, and it dropped back to a more normal range.

"OK, Monday you're going to see your doctor," Celine stated like she meant business.

I'll let you in on a little secret: when you're married to a Filipina nurse and she talks to you in her "I mean business" nurse's voice, the best thing to do is listen.

Celine was right, and sure enough, the doctor put me on a little pill for high blood pressure, telling me I needed to reduce some stress in my life.

"It's time you call Eric Orquiola about returning to PCL; you could have had a stroke or worse. I don't want to be raising three kids on my own," Celine asserted.

You know what? She was right again. I've always had a high-stress threshold and have been able to push myself hard. Heck, I could sprinkle stress on my corn flakes and down it like a champ. Well, that was OK when I was young and single. However, now I was fifty years old, married, and soon a father of three. My health was starting to catch up with me, and I had a family to think about.

It's hard to imagine going back to work for a company six times the size, with larger projects and shorter deadlines, as a change that would reduce my stress. But it was the system I had been trained in, and I had a long history with PCL. Calling my old friend Eric, I told him I was ready to sit down and seriously discuss a return to PCL.

On October 27, I had coffee with PCL's regional vice president Jack Sample. I knew Jack in passing. He managed the special projects division out of the LA office back when I was chief estimator in San Diego.

Since I had been away from the company, Jack served as vice president and district manager and was recently promoted to regional VP. Thus, Cathy Orquiola would be taking over as district manager.

Jack explained the new plans for the California operation and particularly the Orange County office. My primary focus would be helping grow the OC office. However, the San Diego office also needed some help, particularly with the Seaport Village redevelopment project.

Seaport Village was an ambitious, two-billion-dollar redevelopment of San Diego's downtown waterfront in the early programming and preconstruction phase. Jack and I discussed my employment package and a timeline to start. Once we got the children, I would use twelve weeks of Family and Medical Leave (FMLA). So, the earliest I could begin was probably the beginning of March 2018.

PCL's new CEO, Dave Filipchuk, approved my return to the company. I hadn't met Dave as he came up through the ranks after I had moved to the United States. But, Dave would later tell me, he knew me by reputation. Which I assume is a good thing, although you'd have to ask Dave about that.

So, everything was set for my return to PCL. The timing worked well as I finished preconstruction and contracted the Cal Poly housing project's final trades. All we needed now was permission from the Philippines to fly and pick up the children.

Since the early summer, we had been Skyping monthly with the kids and couldn't wait to bring them home. We would be staying three days at the orphanage with the children to ensure the kids' bond with us. So, it was recommended that we not bring my sister Debbie.

Debbie would have been an enormous help. Not only with her experience in child behavioral issues, but simply by helping us navigate the Philippines, as Celine and I would be outnumbered three kids to two adults.

We were now heading into November, and the house's progression was starting to get very concerning. Celine wanted to get into the house and set it up before the kids arrived. Not to mention we had to be out of the townhouse in less than two months.

We were praying hard, but not hard enough. We had hit a stretch of uncommonly damp and cool days and nights. At least uncommon for Southern California. The challenge was the drywall joint compound was not drying between coats, bringing the construction to a snail's pace as days turned into weeks.

There was no chance the house would be ready by the end of December.

I felt I had let Celine down. I thought I could get this house finished on time, but the complexity of the design, building department delays, and now the weather had finally got the upper hand. Plus, I pushed the detail and quality of construction pretty hard with the trades, which also slowed the project.

I don't think Celine understood why I was such a stickler for detail. She just wanted me to say good enough and call it a day. But Poppa had trained me not to settle for good enough with construction details. Remember Poppa's saying, "If you are going to take the time to do it wrong, why not do it right."

The job was coming along, and all the trades enjoyed how the design and construction were coming together. That's all well and good, but we were about to become homeless. So, Celine and I prayed hard this time for a housing solution.

Vanessa Russell suggested we announce in the church bulletin about our homeless predicament. Sure enough, it worked.

Francis and Laurie Murphy had just renovated their three-bedroom rental property. Fortunately for us, December is not a good time of year to find renters, so they rented the house to us on a month-to-month lease.

Wow, that was an unbelievable answer to prayer, and just in the nick of time. On November 27, 2017, the Philippines gave us approval to come and pick up the children.

December went into hyperdrive. We made final preparations for the children, moved to the rental property, booked all our travel arrangements, and finished my projects at Sundt to go on FMLA. We even decorated for Christmas and had presents waiting under the tree for the kids.

Ms. Charlotte requested we delay our flights a few weeks. The orphanage was on reduced staff over the holidays. She wanted us to get feedback from staff about the children.

Finally, the airport shuttle driver knocked on the door. I helped him load our luggage. Celine and I each had a suitcase as usual. We also had luggage filled with clothing and personal items for our three children this time.

The kids would literally come with only the clothes on their backs and whatever personal items they could stuff into a backpack.

Celine and I were quiet on the hour-and-a-half commute to the airport. Both our minds were spinning.

Did we forget anything? Are we prepared? Will the kids like us?

We were booked on the red-eye flight leaving Los Angeles on Saturday, December 30, 2017, at 10:20 p.m. With a fifteen-hour flight and a sixteen-hour time zone change, it would be 5:35 a.m. on Monday, January 1, 2018, when we landed in Manila.

"Flight attendants, prepare for takeoff," the pilot called out over the intercom.

The jet engines roared as we accelerated down the runway. As the plane gained elevation, it banked slightly, putting us on a collision course with destiny.

Chapter 30:

Mommy, Mommy, Daddy, Daddy

But Jesus called the children to him and said,
"Let the little children come to me, and do not hinder them,
for the kingdom of God belongs to such as these." Luke 18:16

It was just after 6:00 a.m. New Year's Day 2018 as we grabbed our luggage from the carousel in the Manila airport. The adrenalin of excitement overpowered our exhaustion from the jet lag. What a way to kick off the new year, picking up our children and becoming a family.

Exiting through the airport sliding door, the hot, humid air hit us like a warm blanket. This well-dressed gentleman standing in front of the Shangri-La shuttle sign asked us, "You need a ride?"

"Yes, we do. How much to Shangri-La hotel downtown Manila?"

"Eighty US dollars."

"OK, sounds good," I responded.

"Wait a minute. Let me handle this," Celine jumped in.

Celine proceeded to converse with the man in Tagalog. After a couple of minutes, he reduced the fare to $60 US.

"See, he was trying to scam you," Celine pointed out.

Wow, call me naive. I'm sure glad Celine stepped in, or I would have paid $80 plus a tip.

The drive through Manila was, to put it simply, absolutely crazy. So many cars, so little road. Los Angeles traffic is like a drive through the countryside compared to Manila. I have never seen so much traffic congestion and horn honking in my life. Beyond the traffic was the mixture of extreme poverty and wealth, all intertwined like an ancient tapestry.

We later found out that a taxi, Uber, or Lyft ride from the airport was less than $10 US, including tip. I'm not going to say we got scammed by the well-dressed man at the airport. I prefer to say we helped him put food on the table for his family. It's just, that night his family would be eating steak. Welcome to Manila!

After checking in at the hotel, we took full advantage of the New Year's Day buffet. It had been a long trip, and we were tired and hungry. We would be resting for the next three days at the hotel before getting the kids. It would be essential to recharge, get onto the time zone and recover from the long flight. When we picked up the children, I wanted to be at full energy capacity.

Later that afternoon, we met with Ms. Charlotte in the hotel lobby. She was heading out of the country the following day but wanted to meet before leaving. The children had been at the orphanage for five years. So, understandably Ms. Charlotte was disappointed she could not be there when we picked them up. Even so, Ms. Charlotte had some last-minute updates for us on them.

Little Joanna is very social and trusted everyone, she told us, so you have to watch her in public as she will just wander off with strangers. Ms. Charlotte also mentioned Joanna doesn't just cry when hurt or upset; she wails very loudly. So, you will need to hold her to console her until she calms down.

Andrew is well-behaved. However, if he gets emotionally hurt or feels wronged, he retreats into his shell. There is no consoling him until he is ready.

Sofia had finished special classes she was taking to help advance her reading skills, and she did well in the classes.

After hearing about some recent behavioral issues with Joanna, we asked Ms. Charlotte, "What techniques do you use to discipline the children?"

We knew from all our training that children from these backgrounds have trauma. So, discipline can be tricky to navigate, not knowing what deep-seated fears and anxieties may lurk below the surface.

Ms. Charlotte said taking away privileges is the best way. For example, she mentioned a time Joanna acted up and, as a result, was not allowed to go on an outing with the other children.

Another technique that works well, especially with Joanna, is a denial of snacks, Ms. Charlotte explained. For example, if a child is acting up, give the other children a special snack, and the naughty child doesn't get one.

We received many helpful last-minute ideas from our visit with Ms. Charlotte. As a result, we were prepared to pick up the kids more than ever.

Celine decided to get her hair done before getting the kids. The first quoted price for what she wanted seemed like a good deal compared to California rates. However, once in the chair, the hairdresser kept suggesting various upgrades and extras. Assuming the additions were small added costs, Celine agreed.

When she was presented with the final bill, she literally almost fell out of her chair. With tip, the cost was over $300 US. Wow, she could have gotten her hair done in a famous Beverly Hills salon and paid less.

"Well, at least your hair will look good for picking up the kids," I said.

Celine's cousin Ruby and Ruby's daughter Issa, who Celine hadn't seen in years, met us for dinner the following evening. Ruby laughed as Celine told her about the hairdressing adventure.

"They not only ran up the bill on you, but they also charged you the absolute maximum for each little thing," Ruby said.

Wow, we had only been in Manila a couple of days and had been scammed twice already. I was determined not to be taken advantage of the third time. It hit me that I needed to be on high alert. Being in a country for the first time and not speaking the language, I must have my wits about me at all times.

"Since you will only be at the orphanage for a couple of days you won't need all five bags. Let me take a couple of the suitcases home and bring them back when you return to Manila," Ruby suggested.

"Wow, really? Thanks so much. That would really help," Celine responded.

We stuffed what we needed for the next few days into three suitcases. Then, after praying for us and giving us a book on parenting, Ruby and Issa grabbed the spare bags and left.

The big day—Thursday, January 4—had finally arrived. Checking out of the hotel, we loaded our luggage into the back of the small SUV. It would be a long day with an hour-and-a-half drive followed by a two-hour ferry ride. An orphanage representative had been tasked with getting us to the ferry. A missionary from the orphanage would pick us up once we landed on the other side. It was a pleasant sunny day with lower than usual temperatures for the time of year, although there was no denying we were in the tropics with the ever-present humidity.

As we drove through the Philippine countryside from Manila to the Port of Batangas, our guide supplied background on the orphanage and its ministries.

Celine enjoyed asking questions about current places and events of the country she left over thirty years ago. Our guide even knew a bit about our three children's backgrounds.

"Do you know if our kids have been bullied at the orphanage?" Celine asked.

The guide laughed. "Bullied? They're the bullies!"

He told us those kids had been there so long it was like they were the orphanage mafia, especially the girls.

Ahh, man, I was bullied as a child, and now my kids are the bullies. So that's just great, ugh!

The ferry was a small catamaran and sure looked like it was overloaded, by American standards anyway. We ended up inside the front hull of the boat, wedged in like sardines in a tin can with no windows and no air conditioning. Our seats in the front right corner barely afforded us enough room for our legs, and I had to continually lean forward to keep my head from hitting the top of the hull.

I felt like one of those daredevils wedged in a metal barrel to go over Niagara Falls. It was a long bumpy ride; all we could do was hold on and pray there were no deadly waterfalls or something even worse ahead. Well, I'm pleased to report we made it to the island safely, although a bit seasick.

The van pulled off the main road and drove slowly the final thousand feet down a small laneway where the walled and gated orphanage came into view for the first time. I could feel my heartbeat racing as the van came to a stop. So many last-minute feelings descended upon us in a paralyzing swarm of emotions. This is it; the time is now for us to finally become parents.

As we entered the front lobby and headed toward the office, the room suddenly erupted with excitement. "DADDY, DADDY, MOMMY, MOMMY!" little Joanna yelled as she ran down the stairs, followed by Sofia and Andrew.

I dropped down on one knee as Joanna leaped into my open arms, giving me a big hug around the neck as Sofia jumped on my back, hugging me from behind. "Easy on Daddy, girls," Celine called out as she gave Andrew a big hug.

After the pandemonium of our grand reception died down, we were given the key to the small apartment we would be staying in for the next two nights. Joanna grabbed my hand, pulling my arm. "Come on, Daddy, this way."

We walked across a small grassy and muddy courtyard to the other side of the compound. As we entered the tiny ground-level apartment, the three kids charged inside as if being handed the keys to the kingdom.

The apartment was bare-bones, to say the least, with vinyl tile flooring throughout. The small living room had a couple of wooden benches, a small table, and a chair, plus a little TV that only received a couple of fuzzy channels. Two bedrooms were down the narrow corridor with beds made from lumber and plywood, blanketed with a thin two-inch foam pad for a mattress.

The kids' room had a bunk bed on each side. Both bedrooms had ceiling fans and wall-mounted air conditioning units. My inner Canadian was thrilled to see the air conditioning unit as the high heat and humidity wore me down.

A small kitchenette displayed a tiny table and chairs with a refrigerator and microwave. The bathroom had a toilet, sink, and showerhead, all crammed into a three-foot square space, reminding me of a boat or RV bathroom.

The entire apartment was reminiscent of a church campground cottage. It sure wasn't the Shangri-La Hotel, but it would do for a couple of nights until we could get back to Manila.

We expected staff from the orphanage to give us some sort of instructions, a schedule, a tour, or something. But no such directions were provided; we were on our own.

The orphanage held over forty children, ages eight months to twelve years. We sat in on one of the kids' afternoon teachings and craft classes, followed by outdoor playtime and exercises.

As I was standing watching the kids run some races, a diminutive three-year-old boy quietly approached; reaching up, he grabbed my hand. Observing this, little Joanna ran over and pushed the boy out of the way.

"That's my daddy," Joanna said as she scolded the little guy.

"Joanna, that's mean. Yes, I'm your daddy, but we don't turn away other children like that. He was just being friendly." Joanna looked up at me, giggled, and ran back to the games.

All three kids were pretty hyper, all amped up on adrenaline, no doubt, which was understandable at the time. As such, they didn't listen to us at all, coming and going from the apartment as they pleased.

Sofia especially gave a lot of attitude when we tried to talk to her or give directions. We even had to keep the suitcases and room locked as the girls tried to take things.

I wasn't too concerned at the time, as we were in the initial bonding stages. I felt it essential to let the kids come to us as they felt comfortable. Once we left the orphanage, I was convinced they would be less distracted and more apt to listen.

About 6:00 p.m., Celine and I were in the apartment unpacking and getting organized for the next couple of days. We were starving and realized we had not eaten since breakfast. Ms. Charlotte had said the facility would be providing us meals, but nobody had mentioned anything since we had arrived.

Suddenly our kids burst into the apartment. "Mommy, Daddy, let's go; it's time to eat." *Oh, boy, I'm famished,* I thought as the kids led us across the courtyard to the kitchen.

The orphanage children had already eaten. The cooks had left food for our family of five to dine together. When I saw the food, my first thought was, *Oh no, is that it? There's gotta be more food!*

I was staring at only about five cups of rice and maybe four ounces of chopped-up beef steak. Talk about being put on rations.

We portioned out the measly pittance of food and gave thanks. "Lord, thank you for getting us here safely, and bless the food we are about to eat, in Jesus' name, amen." All the while, I was thinking, *Lord, remember the time you multiplied the loaves and fishes to feed a thousand people? Well, we could use that same miracle on the beefsteak right about now.*

As soon as I finished the prayer, the kids dug in, not with their silverware. Instead, they aggressively shoveled the food into their mouths with their hands.

Little Joanna was eating so fast she bit her finger hard. Within seconds rice and beefsteak gravy were dripping down their faces and all over the table and floor.

Celine and I were caught in the middle of the mayhem as the girls started grabbing food off our plates. "Whoa, girls, Mommy and I need some food too," I said as I grabbed Joanna's hand, going for a second helping of my dinner.

After dinner, Sofia jumped up and cleared the table without being asked, helping Celine wash the dishes. I was pretty impressed; she showed signs of being a good little helper.

Leaving the orphanage kitchen, the five of us settled back into the apartment. It had been a very long day for everyone; Celine and I were exhausted from the traveling, emotions, and lack of food. After showering and getting the kids ready for bed, I pulled out the picture Bible to read the kids a bedtime story.

Andrew and Joanna were mesmerized by the picture Bible and excitedly flipped through the pages to pick a story. Sofia stayed back and stayed quiet, just watching. "Daddy, can you read this one?" Joanna asked, picking the story of Joseph and the coat of many colors.

As I began to read, Sofia suddenly started saying, "No, no, no," as she grabbed the Bible and began flipping the pages.

"This one." Sofia pointed, handing me back the book. I started to read once again. "No, no, no," Sofia said louder than before, reaching in and flipping more pages. As I read, Sofia listened for a bit then left the room.

After the story, we said our prayers. These kids must be exhausted, I thought; it's already two hours past their usual bedtime. So, giving Andrew and Joanna a hug, I tucked them into bed. Sofia, though, pulled back; she didn't want a hug.

Returning to our room, I found Celine already half asleep on our double-wide plywood bed. I set the air conditioner on medium and crawled onto my two-inch foam pad.

Fifteen minutes went by when, *Knock, knock, knock.* "Daddy, Sofia keeps kicking me out of bed."

I walked little Joanna back to her room and tucked her in again. "OK, girls, we had a long day, time to go to sleep," I said as I turned off the light and closed the door.

Ten minutes later. *Knock, knock, knock.* "Daddy, Sofia keeps turning the light on and off and won't let me sleep on her side of the room."

"Andrew, can Joanna sleep on your side for tonight?" Andrew jumped to the top bunk, making room for Joanna on the lower.

"OK, kids, have a good sleep," I said as I hit the light and returned to the room where Celine was now sound asleep.

Five minutes later. *Knock, knock, knock.*

Oh boy, welcome to fatherhood!

Finally, around 2:00 a.m. the girls settled down. I was so exhausted and hungry I couldn't see straight. I doubled up my foam pad as my shoulder sank into the plywood bed frame below.

At least I had an air conditioner; thank you, Lord, for small mercies. With the nice cool air flowing over me, I fell into a deep sleep.

Suddenly I awoke, startled by a kerplunk sound as the air conditioner fan ground to a halt. I couldn't believe it; the power had gone out.

Looking over, I saw Celine was in a deep sleep. My phone clock displayed 2:32 a.m. The apartment was pitch black. Using the light of my phone to guide me, I went to check on the kids. Good, they were all sound asleep.

Making my way to the front of the apartment, I opened the door. The hot, humid night rushed in like I had opened a fiery furnace.

I stepped out into the heavy darkness, clouds blocking the stars. There were no emergency lights, streetlights, or anything. It was nothing but blackness. I could hear the faint sound of a dog barking in the distance, like an old friend calling out from across the abyss.

"Lord, are you out there? Are you keeping a watch over us?"

I went back to bed, and just as I laid down, the power kicked back on, and the fresh cool air from the air conditioner started to flow once again. Ahh, peace at last.

I must have fallen asleep for a good fifteen minutes when Celine popped up. "Did you hear that? Someone's coughing."

Before waiting for my response, Celine was out the door and down the hall to the kids' room.

Little Joanna had developed a cough. "I hope she's not coming down with a cold," Celine said as she gave Joanna some cough medicine and brought her into our room.

After about a half hour, Joanna fell asleep on the bed with Celine and me. I checked my phone. *OK, it's 3:30 a.m.; maybe I can get some sleep now.*

3:45 a.m. *Knock, knock, knock.* It was Andrew and Sofia. "We can't sleep," they said.

"Come on in," I told them, motioning them into the room.

Within minutes all five of us were curled up on the plywood bed asleep from exhaustion.

Morning came fast. 4:50 a.m., to be exact. The kids were up, excited and raring to go. Joanna's cough had cleared up so I made some coffee, and Celine got the kids glasses of milk.

Then, finding some SkyFlakes, aka Filipino soda crackers, in the cupboards, we sat down for a game of UNO.

I'm not much of a card player, but Andrew and Sofia were regular card sharks. Unfortunately, poor Joanna and I were left holding most of the cards, meaning we lost badly. However, Joanna took it in stride, and her infectious giggle made the game all the more entertaining.

Breakfast was much like dinner the previous evening. There was about enough porridge to half fill a bowl for each of us. Less, of course, considering the amount the kids spilled down their fronts. At least we got them to partially use a spoon this time. We were making progress!

After breakfast, I went back to the apartment with the kids while Celine hung around to chat with the caregivers in Tagalog.

Andrew found a basketball game to watch on the TV while Sofia sat on the floor with some pencil crayons and paper. Joanna sat with me, reading a book and asking questions.

After a while, Joanna calmly walked over and picked up one of Sofia's pencil crayons. Sofia leaped onto Joanna's back and violently pulled the pencil crayon from her hand, causing a deep scratch.

Joanna began to cry and wail uncontrollably. I picked her up and sat back on the bench, embracing and trying to console her. Sofia went to the TV, trying to change the channel.

Andrew repeatedly asked Sofia to stop, gently pushing her back. Then, without warning, Sofia started screaming and ferociously hitting and kicking Andrew.

Holding Joanna in my right arm, I reached out with my left, grabbing Sofia around the waist, pulling her toward me, just in time for Andrew's punch to miss its mark.

Andrew, now shaking, stood at guard with fists clenched, ready to defend himself should I let go of Sofia. Once Sofia stopped kicking, I let her go, and she retreated to the bedroom, slamming the door behind her. After calming down Joanna and Andrew, I went to talk to Sofia, but she stayed under the bed covers, not saying a word.

"OK, when you're ready to talk, I'll be in the front room with your brother and sister," I told Sofia as I left her alone.

One hour had passed by when Sofia ran through the room. "Sorry," she yelled as the front screen door slammed behind her.

Later that morning, Celine and I met with the children's teacher. She was a volunteer missionary who knew the kids well. It was so gracious of her to take the time to write down some notes to help us with each child.

From the teacher's notes:

Andrew is good in biology, science, and sports but still needs some work on writing and speaking English.

Andrew has genuine faith in God and loves Christmas and worship songs. He has a very tender heart and processes his thoughts internally. You need to give him time and space alone to process his thoughts. Change is hard for him. He can shut down when he is upset and become uncommunicative for hours before he is ready to interact again.

Andrew only does what is needed, although he is capable of much more. Unfortunately, he rushes through his work and makes needless mistakes.

Sofia is making significant improvements in her overall learning and schoolwork. Once she realizes she is capable of doing something, she accelerates at it.

Sofia lacks initiative and needs a lot of prodding and encouragement. She's untidy, disorganized, and does not sit still. She has low self-esteem, so she has adopted a sassy, "I'll tease you just to annoy you" attitude.

You need to help Sofia not tease others as she can do this relentlessly. She also takes things that are not hers. Make sure the rules are clear and follow through with consequences. Sofia will not respect you unless you stick to your guns.

Little Joanna is a natural academic who loves reading and has a real thirst for knowledge. She's a quick learner, and if she wanted and worked hard, she could be a doctor someday. Her attitude can prevent her from learning and achieving her potential. However, she is a social butterfly who needs a secure source of love and affirmation. Joanna needs firm boundaries. If you want to love this child, you have to lovingly and firmly let her know that you are in charge. Help her make friends and encourage her when she is kind to younger kids, as she can be mean at times. Joanna has a very tender heart, and once you have earned her trust and affirmed boundaries, she can be delightful.

The teacher gave us four pages of notes on each child, outlining strengths, weaknesses and social development, and made recommendations for the next steps in nurturing, guiding, and teaching these young souls.

We briefly discussed the girls' hyperactivity and struggle to sit still. Once we get back to the USA, the teacher suggested we have the girls professionally evaluated for attention deficit hyperactivity disorder, "ADHD."

Oh, great. ADHD was one of the things that we specifically said we would not accept on the "Type of Child Acceptable to Family" form. Oh well, I guess that ship has sailed.

Celine and I were so appreciative of the teacher's time with us. The information she supplied would be beneficial moving forward.

So many behavioral things mentioned were not uncommon for many children, even those with natural birth parents. But there was also some obvious stuff that we needed to navigate with caution, understanding, love, and grace.

"That was great information," I said to Celine as we walked back to the apartment. "What did you find out from the Filipina caregivers?"

"Well, Andrew is really liked. They all had nice things to say about Andrew.

"Joanna is, you know, Joanna, they would say as they rolled their eyes.

"Joanna's social and fun but can be mean and disrespectful at times. However, she can't lie; ask her a question, and she will answer truthfully.

"Sofia lies and steals. You have to keep an eye on her in a store; they think she's a kleptomaniac and can be a bully."

These kids were in extreme survival mode, especially the girls. So, the sooner we could get them out of that environment, the better. The orphanage was not a bad place. It's just that they had been there far too long. I had to go to the orphanage office and get on the internet to take care of some adoption paperwork and download childhood photos of the children. Celine hung back at the apartment with the kids. The internet connection was intermittent and slow. It was taking forever. As I sat there staring at the little circle go around and around on the computer screen, little Joanna burst through the office door.

"My name's Joanna," she proudly proclaimed. "I'm Sofia," her sister called out, running in right behind Joanna.

"Oh, so Mommy told you your new names?" I said as Joanna jumped up on my lap.

I told the girls how special those names were to me, and that's why Mommy and I picked them just for you.

Andrew liked his new name also. All three of them wanted these to be their new American names. So, from that point on, the three kids were officially Andrew, Sofia, and Joanna.

We even made a little game about it. If you referred to one of the kids by their wrong name, everyone else could give you a light flick on the forearm. The girls especially had fun with this, as Celine and I constantly called them by their wrong names.

The name changes were a real turning point with the kids. They were now listening to us more, and we were starting to become a real family.

Lunchtime rolled around. Celine, Andrew, and Joanna were already over at the dining room as Sofia and I headed over from the apartment. Sofia, about twenty feet ahead of me, suddenly pulled down her pants and, bending over, gave me a moon (exposed her bare bottom).

"Sofia, pull your pants up. Don't do that; it's disrespectful," I called out. Then, quickly pulling up her pants, she grinned and ran into the building.

After lunch, Celine decided to go into the little town to look for a food store. We were famished and wanted to get something to keep in the apartment. Andrew went with Celine, and I stayed back with the girls.

Celine and Andrew went to town on a motorized tricycle taxi. They had been gone quite a while, but just as I was starting to get concerned, they arrived back.

"It's a good thing you didn't go with us. It was insanely crowded and dirty," Celine told me as she and Andrew carried a few bags from their haul into the apartment. "We couldn't even find any real food, only snack food."

"Snack food sounds good to me. I think I've lost about five pounds in a day and a half," I said as I stuffed a candy bar into my mouth.

That evening the orphanage was putting on a going-away party for the kids. So, we all cleaned up for the photo op. Celine's sister Jo had gotten us all matching red shirts with our names on the back and "Team McQuarrie" on the front.

In addition, at the request of little Joanna, we had brought little party gift bags for all the orphanage children. The five of us had a fun time spending part of the afternoon filling the gift bags.

After the party, back at the apartment, we gave the kids their backpacks to pack their belongings. They were thrilled with their new packs. Andrew's had a Spiderman theme, and the girl's packs were from the Disney movie *Frozen*. Sofia had an Elsa pack, and Joanna had Anna.

The kids didn't have much, just a few small personal items and some favorite clothes.

Andrew showed me some peso coins he had been saving and asked if he could buy something in Manila. "Of course, you can," I responded. Then, reaching into my suitcase, I pulled out a leftover gift bag from the party.

"Here you go," I said, handing him the little empty cloth bag. "This will be perfect for storing your coins."

It was close to midnight by the time we were all packed up and read the kids their Bible story. Even Sofia must have been tired as she was not as disruptive that night, although she still refused a good night hug.

It had been a full day, but now with the air conditioner humming, Celine and I fell into a deep sleep.

Knock, knock, knock. "Mommy, Daddy, we can't sleep." I looked up, and all three kids were standing in the doorway. I looked at my phone as the digital display showed 3:40 a.m. *Well, at least that's three more hours of sleep than I got last night,* I thought to myself.

"Come on, kids. Why don't you sleep in here tonight? Tomorrow is a big day."

I can't even begin to comprehend the excitement and emotion the kids were feeling that night. They had spent more than half their young lives in the orphanage. Yet, everything they knew was about to change.

Saturday, January 6, 5:00 a.m. came early, and there was no more sleep to be had. The kids were excited and energized, anxious to leave the orphanage behind.

Our ride was scheduled to pick us up a 9:30 a.m. to catch the 10:30 a.m. ferry to the mainland. We splurged on the Fast Cat Ferry this time, as it was bigger, faster, and most importantly, air conditioned.

While checking his backpack, Andrew became very distraught. Some of his peso coins were missing. He frantically searched everywhere but could not find them. I had a suspicion of what may have happened to the coins but, without any proof, I kept my thoughts to myself.

"Well, maybe they'll show up. Here, you can have these coins," I said, handing Andrew some spare change I had in my briefcase.

A day later, some mysterious coins showed up in a pocket of Celine's purse. "How did these coins get here?" Celine asked.

"Hmm, I think we have a very sneaky coin thief, but I don't think your purse was the smartest hiding place for the plunder," I laughed.

The kids were all cleaned up, packed, and ready to go with an hour to spare. We told them it was all right to say last goodbyes to their friends, but their backpacks needed to stay in the apartment.

As Celine and I finished packing in the bedroom, Sofia walked in.

"Daddy, Joanna's outside with her backpack."

"Joanna, come over here," I called out as I walked out into the courtyard. Joanna finished hugging a little boy and skipped over to where I was standing with the backpack over her shoulders.

"What did I tell you about keeping the backpacks in the apartment?" I asked Joanna. Looking up at me, she giggled and walked back inside.

Celine, taking me aside, said, "Sofia and Andrew are expecting you to discipline Joanna. We can't just let her ignore us."

"Yeah, I agree."

"Let's try that discipline technique Ms. Charlotte talked about, withholding snacks," Celine suggested.

"That's a good idea."

We had seen that the kids were aggressive and possessive about food in general, so we did not want to intensify that. Instead, we decided to give Andrew and Sofia each two Starburst candies. Since Joanna did not listen to Daddy, she received only one Starburst candy. We figured this was a way to ease into disciplining the children.

The technique worked. At least, I think it worked, sort of. Little Joanna apologized for not listening, then asked if she could give her candy to the little boy.

"Yes, of course. That's very nice of you to do that, Joanna," I affirmed.

Our ride was a bit late, but we made it to the ferry terminal on time, putting our luggage through an X-ray machine. Then, an official-looking man grabbed the bags and put them in a roped-off area.

"Come on, let's go," Celine called out as she and the girls headed down the crowded pier.

"What about our bags?" I yelled back.

"Don't worry, they will load them onto the boat. Now come on!" Celine insisted, motioning Andrew and me to follow.

The long pier was jam-packed with a sea of Filipinos pushing upstream toward the ferry. I forced my way forward, making way for Andrew trailing behind me.

As I got closer to the boat, I noticed passengers handing their belongings to men loading them onto the ferry. Suddenly I had a real bad feeling about our luggage.

"Celine! Celine! You and the girls, get on the boat; Andrew and I need to go back to get our luggage," I yelled out.

My racing heart dropped about twenty beats at the relief of seeing our bags still sitting now just outside the roped-off area.

I approached the man standing over our stuff. "That's our luggage," I said with a firm and authoritative voice as I handed the guy a $10 US bill.

Catching the man a bit by surprise, he turned and looked up at me with a stern stare. Then, realizing I was about three inches taller and, without doubt, had a sixty-pound weight advantage, he quietly took the ten-dollar bill.

Andrew and I grabbed the luggage and made a mad dash for the ferry, but we got separated. Just as Andrew reached the boat and started across the narrow gangplank, a man on the dock stopped me. "Larger bags loaded back there, back there, you go back there," the man said as he kept pointing.

Andrew had made it onto the boat deck, and there was no way he would be able to reverse course on the narrow gangplank as the crowds made a last rush to get on the vessel.

"Andrew, go inside the boat and find Mom and your sisters," I yelled as I forced my way down the pier to the rear of the ferry.

As the boat horn sounded, I tossed our suitcases from the dock over the side of the ship. A guy that looked like Filipino Gilligan caught the bags and moved them to a storage area as I leaped onto the ferry.

Well, that seemed to be more complicated than it needed to be, I thought. Regardless we were all on the boat as it pulled away from the pier.

I found Celine, Andrew, and the girls in the center of the air-conditioned cabin. I would have the next hour and a half to catch my breath.

Now, I wish I could say, "With our newly formed family, we sailed west into the sunset and lived happily ever after." But it was only 10:30 a.m., the boat was heading north, and we were oblivious to the brewing storm heading our way.

Chapter 31:

The Thriller in Manila

We do not want you to be uninformed, brothers and sisters, about the troubles we experienced in the province of Asia. We were under great pressure, far beyond our ability to endure, so that we despaired of life itself. Indeed, we felt we had received the sentence of death. But this happened that we might not rely on ourselves but on God, who raises the dead. 2 Corinthians 1:8-9

We arrived at the mainland dock where our driver from a couple of days ago was waiting for us.

Before loading into the SUV, I gave all the kids some money to buy their own snacks at the gift shop. They each bought their favorites and stuffed their backpacks.

We wanted the children to feel secure that there would always be food. So, there was no need to sneak or compete over food. Having their snacks in their backpacks would help provide them some of that security.

As we made our long drive to Manila, we stopped at a Jollibee for lunch. Jollibee is a famous Filipino fast-food restaurant known for its fried chicken and is popular with kids. While at lunch, our driver noticed little Joanna had lice in her hair. He was right, and upon further investigation, we discovered all three kids had lice.

"We are going to have to quarantine when we get to the hotel," Celine told me.

Wow, this was the trip that just keeps giving.

A good meal in the books meant it was time to get back on the road, and about an hour later, we arrived at Discovery Suites in downtown Manila, the hotel where we would be staying for the next few days.

I had a pocket full of pesos, so I gave each child a couple for being good on the long trip. "Here you go, guys. You did really good on our long journey today."

Celine had to take little Joanna to the restroom. So, Andrew, Sofia, and I went to the hotel lounge to take advantage of the free juice and snacks. As I was getting the kids some juice, I caught Sofia handing Andrew her pesos out of the corner of my eye.

"Daddy, I lost my pesos," Sofia told me as I approached the sofa where they were sitting.

Yes, Sofia was lying and trying to scam me. But, at that moment, I had a decision to make. Would it be punishment or a life lesson?

This little girl had some issues that we would have to work on over the long haul, and we were not going to solve her emotional challenges in one day.

Andrew looked up in fear, now realizing he was a naive participant in his sister's scam.

"Hmm, well, that is a problem," I said as I reached into the side pocket of my briefcase.

"Here you go. In the McQuarrie household, you never need to worry about losing your pesos," I said as I handed Andrew and Sofia each a few coins.

As we entered our high-rise hotel suite, my eyes were drawn to the view of the downtown Manila skyline that seemed to go on forever. From my vantage point, I counted eight new high-rise towers under construction. In addition, there was a new high-rise going up right beside our hotel. It couldn't have been much more than fifty feet away.

I could throw a football to the construction workers on the upper decks if I opened a window.

I was taken aback by the number of California OSHA safety violations I saw on the construction site, like no perimeter guardrails and too many trip hazards to count. In addition, the construction workers were not wearing any hard hats, vests, gloves, or safety glasses. Oh well, I wasn't there to critique the local construction industry. Instead, we needed to get the kids settled in.

Have you heard the term "the kids are bouncing off the walls?" Well, I can now say I have seen it firsthand. These kids were used to running wild within a walled compound. They tore through this two-bedroom hotel condo like three little Tasmanian Devils.

Andrew was excited, but the two girls were borderline uncontrollable. Little Joanna kept picking up phones and would just randomly push buttons. Sofia was running around jumping and climbing on everything. I even walked into the room to catch her climbing a glass shelving unit to get at the TV remote control.

The girls were constantly fighting with each other. Andrew tried to ignore his sisters as much as possible, but it was like we had three completely unrelated children. You would think with all these three kids had been through, they would be a close-knit group. But I can assure you that was not the case.

Eventually, we were able to get the kids calmed down to a dull roar. Then, while Celine washed everyone's hair with lice shampoo, I did my best to childproof the hotel room.

Collecting all the phones, I hid them in a closet, along with all the breakable room decorations. Then I sealed clothes from the orphanage in plastic bags for quarantine and wiped down the backpacks and their contents.

The room service menu was surprisingly cheap when converting the pesos to US dollars. So, I was able to order a bunch of food for dinner. After having a late dinner, we were all ready for bed. Lord knows there was not much sleep to be had these past couple of days. *These kids must be prepared to crash, I thought. I know I sure am.*

As usual, I read the kids a Bible story. However, Sofia was even more disruptive during the story than the past couple of nights. She didn't listen to the story at all, going in and out of the room as I read. Eventually, all three were in bed. We had Sofia and Joanna in one queen-sized bed and Andrew in the other. I turned off the light and closed the door.

It only took five minutes before Joanna was at our bedroom door. "Daddy, Sofia keeps kicking me." *Jeepers, don't these kids ever sleep?*

Taking Joanna back to the room, I put her in the bed with her brother, who was already half asleep.

"I'm not tired at all," Sofia proclaimed.

"That's OK, just try to be quiet so your brother and sister can sleep," I said as I turned off the light and closed the door.

I didn't even get to the bed before the blaring of a loud radio filled the hotel suite. Sofia had the music on full blast. The radio incident kicked off an hour of back and forth trying to get the girls to settle down. Little Joanna was exhausted and wanted to sleep, but Sofia kept being disruptive, making noise, turning on lights, and fighting with her younger sister.

Finally, I said. "If you don't settle down in the next five minutes, I'm going to have to take your pesos until you decide to behave."

Of course, there was no settling down. So, I took Joanna's pesos out of her backpack. However, Sofia's coins seemed to be missing.

"She has them under her pillow," Andrew told me.

"Thanks, Andrew. OK, girls, I'm going to hold on to your pesos until the morning. Now, go to sleep."

About fifteen minutes went by when there was a knock on our bedroom door. "Sofia is opening and closing our door," Joanna said.

As I walked out into the living area, I was shocked to see Sofia slumped over on the floor in a trance-like state, opening and closing the door while making very unsettling chanting and moaning sounds. Celine told me to go and get some sleep, and she would work with Sofia. As Celine tried to talk to Sofia in Tagalog, she began to slither across the floor like a snake, slumping under the kitchen chairs.

At one point, Sofia went over and opened the hotel room door, stepping outside into the hallway. "Where are you going, Sofia? Do you want to leave? Do you want to go back to the orphanage? Is that what you want?" Celine asked.

"Your daddy is a very kind and patient man, and he and I want you to come to California with us. We're going to be a family with you, Andrew, and Joanna," Celine continued, but Sofia remained silent in her trance.

It took about thirty minutes, but eventually Sofia snapped out of it and even apologized for being so disruptive. Finally, she went to bed and fell asleep. The poor little gal, she must have been exhausted.

The Sunday morning sun peeked through the window. As my eyes opened, the bedside clock showed 6:00 a.m. It was strangely quiet. *I better check on the kids,* I thought as I rolled over only to see all three kids standing at the bedroom door in their pajamas.

"Come on in, guys," I said as all three excitedly jumped on the bed. It was a new day, and our first full day as a family on our own.

The mornings were already becoming a fun tradition of joking around with the kids. We'd laugh about the events of the previous day and talk about all the fun and exciting things ahead of us.

Each morning the kids would count down the number of sleeps before we flew to California.

After getting freshened up, we headed down to the hotel's complimentary breakfast buffet. As our eyes peered into the restaurant for the first time, all five of us came to an abrupt stop, like we were a choreographed dance troupe.

Oh boy, I thought, *this is going to be very interesting.*

I think Celine and the kids were thinking the exact same thing I was. The restaurant was jam-packed with well-dressed folks enjoying a quiet Sunday brunch.

We had been working with the kids on their table etiquette, but I wasn't sure we were ready for prime time just yet.

"Good morning, sir. We have a private room set up with a projector playing cartoons. Would you like to eat in there so the kids can watch?" the hostess asked.

"YES! Yes, that would be great, thank you," I replied with a sigh of relief.

We had a really good time at breakfast. Were the kids messy? Well, yes. But judging from the smaller-than-average amount of food spilled on the table and floor, we were making significant progress.

I was pleased and proud of how well-behaved and helpful the children were, especially Sofia, as she helped Celine and me get food and bring it back to the table.

After breakfast, we headed to the pool. It just seems to be a universal and timeless fact that kids love a swimming pool.

Our kids were no exception; the only challenge was they couldn't swim. However, swimming offered an excellent opportunity for bonding and building trust as I taught the kids.

Now, I've already established that I'm not particularly good in the water. I'm much better at sinking than I am at swimming. But, given that the hotel pool was only three-and-a-half feet deep, I figured I could manage.

After some initial apprehension and getting used to their inflatable water wings, the girls took to the water like a couple of little mermaids. Their squeals of glee and laughter filled the pool deck with fun and excitement, while Andrew preferred the warmer, calmer waters of the hot tub.

After building up their confidence, the girls decided they wanted a swimming race, with me walking beside them, of course.

"Ready, on your mark, get set, GO!"

The girls were off frantically kicking and splashing as they slowly moved across the top of the water. Joanna got out ahead when suddenly Sofia grabbed Joanna by the hair, pulling her under the water as she swam over the top of her.

I quickly plucked little Joanna out of the water. The squeals of glee were now loud, uncontrollable wailing and crying. "It's OK; it's OK, I've got you," I said as Joanna held me tightly around the neck.

"Your sister didn't mean to pull you underwater. It was an accident. She was just trying to get ahead of you," I reassured Joanna. Honestly, it felt more like I was trying to convince myself than Joanna.

All and all, it was a good morning at the pool. The children had fun, and we were starting to feel like a real family. In fact, the kids did so well that morning that we told them that we would take them out for Jollibee and ice cream for dinner.

Back in the hotel room, the kids were so hyper, it was difficult to have even two minutes of peace. Andrew wasn't too bad, but the girls constantly needed something. They were either getting into something, fighting, or complaining about something.

I did something I said I would never do to control the pandemonium. I turned on the television and let them play with the computer tablet. It's incredible; you turn that TV on, and kids will sit still and quiet for hours. After that, I never criticized parents who use electronics for babysitting their kids ever again.

With the children now calmed down, Celine and I had a chance to think, organize, and plan. I was even able to check up on the house construction back home, something I had neglected since picking up the kids.

"Daddy, my nuts are missing. I can't find them; they are gone," little Joanna told me in a panic, showing me her open backpack.

Joanna had bought herself a bunch of little flavored nut packets as part of her backpack snacks.

"There are still a few packets left. Are you sure you didn't eat some already?"

"No, I didn't eat them," Joanna replied, now in tears and flipping over the sofa cushions, frantically looking for her nuts.

I kneeled down, looking at Joanna face to face. "Well, maybe they'll show up. But I tell you what. Next time we go to a store, I'll buy you some more nuts." Joanna seemed OK with my response but asked me to hold on to her backpack and keep it safe.

Hmm, I wondered if Andrew's coin thief and Joanna's nut thief were one and the same. But, without any proof, I kept my thoughts to myself.

We went for an afternoon swim before taking the kids to the mall and dinner. A maintenance man walked across the pool deck and went through a locked gate onto the roof. Little Joanna, curious about what he was doing, followed.

"Joanna, come back over here. That's dangerous," I called out.

Ignoring my warning, she started to climb the gate. "Joanna, no, that's dangerous. You can fall off the roof!" I asserted, now running over to grab her. But she still kept climbing, pretending not to hear me.

Reaching her in the nick of time, I grabbed her around the waist. "Let go of the gate, let go, let go. Joanna, it's dangerous; you need to let go." As I pulled her back, she continued holding on to the gate bars but finally let go as I pulled her away to safety.

Walking over to a deck chair, I sat down, placing Joanna on my lap. "You need to listen to me. That was very dangerous. You could get hurt. Now I want you to sit here with me for five minutes."

Joanna kept squirming as I held her, then she started to pinch the skin on my arms. "Joanna, you need to stop that. If you're not going to listen, you won't be able to go for Jollibee and ice cream with your brother and sister."

"Just let go of her and see what she does," Celine suggested.

As I let go, Joanna slid off my knee and stomped her heel into the top of my foot three times, then sat on the floor beside me with her arms crossed in defiance.

Soon it was time to head back to the room. Celine helped Andrew and Sofia rinse off at the pool-side shower.

"OK, go see Mommy and get rinsed off," I told Joanna, still sitting at my feet.

Little Joanna got up and stomped toward Celine. Then, stripping off her water wings, she threw them as far into the pool as she could.

"OK, Joanna's not going for Jollibee and ice cream tonight," I called out.

Sofia went and got a long rescue pole from the lifeguard and fished Joanna's water wings out of the pool. That evening Celine took Andrew and Sofia to the shopping mall, and I stayed back with little Joanna to eat leftovers from lunch.

She loves to read, so I read her some books and helped her read English. After that, I taught her how to use the tablet. She was a quick learner and found a video to make a hollow 2-liter chocolate coke bottle filled with M&M's.

"Daddy, Daddy, can we do this when we get to California?" Joanna asked as she showed me the chocolate Coke bottle video.

"Yes, of course, we can. That looks like fun."

After all was said and done, it was some memorable father-daughter bonding time.

After about an hour, Celine, Andrew, and Sofia returned with Jollibee takeout.

"Sofia didn't think it was fair that you don't get ice cream and Jollibee because Joanna was bad. So, we got you some Jollibee and came back to eat as a family," Celine told me.

"Thank you, Sofia, that was very nice of you," I said as we all sat down for dinner.

We had started a tradition at dinner of saying two good things that happened during the day and one bad thing. The idea was to spark discussion and let the kids know it's OK when bad things happen, and we can talk about it.

"OK, what are two good things today?" Celine asked.

Sofia right away said, "We went to the pool twice today."

Andrew followed, "We went to the mall."

"What's one bad thing today?" I asked.

"ME!" Joanna blurted out, throwing her hands up in the air with a big smile and giggle.

We all couldn't help but laugh. "Yes, you had quite the day."

The Canadian side of the family is going to love this girl's sense of humor, I thought to myself. *Especially Mom.*

Joanna did not want to eat the leftovers from lunch, making her the only child I've ever met that doesn't like leftover pizza. I grabbed some SkyFlake soda crackers and gave them to her.

"Here you go. If you're not going to eat the leftovers, you can have these crackers. Nobody goes hungry in the McQuarrie household."

That night after the Bible story, the kids settled down and went to bed right away. Sofia didn't stay in the room for the Bible story but did go right to sleep. All and all, it had been a good day, our first full day as a family on our own.

Monday 6:00 a.m. seemed to come fast after our first whole night's sleep since picking up the kids. Once again, all three came running in, jumping on the bed.

"OUCH!" I yelled as the pain shot through my groin.

"SORRY. Sorry, it was an accident. I was just biting the covers. I didn't mean to bite you," Sofia claimed.

Well, one thing for sure, I was now fully awake.

Monday was another full day of swimming, watching videos, and just hanging out as a family. The kids were far more work than we could have possibly imagined, but Celine and I were hitting our stride and enjoying being first-time parents.

Andrew was coming out of his shell more and more every day. He was a good kid, well-behaved, and he always listened. He had been a big help, especially for Celine, going to the store multiple times.

Initially, Andrew was more comfortable talking to Celine in Tagalog but was now opening up to me and speaking more English. In addition, he enjoyed searching for information about Jesus on the internet. "Daddy, Daddy, look at this," he would call out when finding a story about Jesus.

Little Joanna was becoming my right-hand gal. If I were doing something, she would be right there at my side, joking and giggling, asking lots of questions. Without a doubt, she had my sense of humor.

Sofia seemed to be starting to settle in. She preferred to spend time with Celine, helping organize things for the day. Sofia was a good little worker. If something needed doing and she knew how, you could consider it done. Her eagerness to help reminded me of myself helping Poppa back when I was her age.

That afternoon Celine's cousin Ruby and her daughter Issa returned to bring us the suitcases they had been holding.

As we were visiting, Celine mentioned going to the mall with Andrew and Sofia and looking for new shoes for the kids. They had found shoes for Andrew but could not find Sofia's size. They had also picked up a couple of sizes to try for Joanna. One pair fit her, and one did not.

Ruby volunteered, "Let me return the pair of shoes that didn't fit Joanna and look again for shoes for Sofia."

There were a few other items that Celine had previously picked up but didn't fit that also needed to be returned. So, Ruby and Issa grabbed the bags and headed to the mall.

Sofia was helping Celine in the bedroom, organizing and sorting stuff from the suitcases. They were having a good mother-daughter time chatting and arranging. Then, after a while, Sofia came out to watch some TV.

I went into the bedroom to see how Celine was doing, and she had a puzzled face and wrinkled brow. "What's up?" I asked.

"Sofia and I were sitting on the bed talking and organizing things. Then without warning, she took her foot, rubbed it into my crotch, and grinned."

"Yikes, that's not good."

"She mooned you, then bit your crotch, and now this. Do you think she's been abused?"

"Anything's possible, we don't know the whole story on these kids. So, it's something we should keep an eye on. But it could simply be a nine-year-old girl starting to figure things out."

Ruby and Issa returned from the mall. They did find a cute pair of shoes for Sofia, but unfortunately, they were a bit large.

"Oh, well, we can always return them," I said.

As Ruby and Issa were leaving, we found out they didn't have a car. So, it took over an hour each way commuting on public transit and uber to visit us.

"Wow, we didn't know. You should have told us. You have to let us pay you back for that," Celine insisted.

"No, we're fine, just glad we could help." So responded Ruby as she and Issa left.

It had been another good day. The next day at 10:30 a.m., we would meet with the Philippine Authority for a final interview and pick up the kids' passports.

"You can wear your old running shoes for the interview in the morning. Then we will take you shopping for new shoes after," Celine told Sofia.

"Two more sleeps, two more sleeps," Andrew said as he crawled into bed. Yes, two more nights of sleep, and we'd be getting on a plane to California.

"Daddy, can you hold onto my backpack and coins tonight?" Sofia asked as she gave me a big hug for the first time.

"Of course," I said as I tucked her into bed. Little Joanna was already fast asleep. Tomorrow was going to be a big day.

It was Tuesday, January 9, and the big day had arrived. Today we would get the final OK to bring the kids back to California. We were all excited and raring to go. After hitting the breakfast buffet, we headed back to the room to all get cleaned up for our big interview.

The kids were all excited as they put on their brand-new outfits. "Mommy, can I wear my slippers instead of my old running shoes?" Sofia asked.

In the Philippines, sandals are referred to as slippers.

"Of course, you can," responded Celine.

"Can I wear my socks with my slippers?"

"Yes, but the socks may make your slippers tight. But you can try it and see what you like best."

Sofia went into the bedroom to get her socks. Andrew and Joanna were watching TV.

"OK, guys, it's nine o'clock. It's time to head down to the lobby and call for a ride."

We all started to head out the door. All of us, except for Sofia, that is. Sofia was standing in the bedroom doorway.

"Sofia, let's go. We're going to be late," I said as I waited for her. But she just looked at me for a moment, then retreated into the bedroom and locked the door.

"Sofia, what's wrong?" I asked, standing outside the door. But nothing but silence came back.

Celine tried talking to Sofia, but she was not responding. I called hotel services to come and unlock the door. A half hour had now gone by, and Sofia would not talk or come out of the room.

"Let's try just stepping out into the hallway and see if she follows," Celine suggested.

That worked, sort of. Finally, after about two minutes, Sofia poked her head out the hallway door.

"Come on, Sofia, we're all waiting for you," I said with a big smile, motioning her to come along. But at that, she retreated back into the hotel room.

"Well, I guess we're going to be late," I said as I opened the door and Celine, Andrew, Joanna, and I stepped back into the hotel suite vestibule.

Sofia was just standing there motionless. Suddenly, she turned to make a beeline for the bedroom. Celine quickly stepped in front of her, grabbing her arm. "Wait a minute, Sofia."

Sofia squirmed to get around Celine as Celine tried to block her path and calm her down by speaking in Tagalog.

"I'M GOING TO KILL YOU, YOU MOMMY YOU," shrieked Sofia as she lunged toward Celine.

Backing up to get out of the way, Celine slammed into the hotel room vestibule wall as Sofia unleashed a barrage of kicking, scratching, and hitting, all the while wailing at the top of her lungs.

Regaining her composure, Celine slapped at Sofia's legs, hoping to ward off the sudden unexpected attack.

Confusion blanketed the faces of Andrew and Joanna. They stood by, wanting to help but not knowing what to do.

Jumping to Celine's defense, I approached Sofia from behind, putting my arms around her waist, trying with all my strength to pull her off Celine. But Sofia just yelled louder and louder as she kicked more and more violently.

"YOU MOTHER F%#@ERS, I'M GOING TO KILL YOU," Sofia continued to scream.

Celine got hold of Sofia's legs, trying to keep a firm grasp while attempting to soothe her in Tagalog.

Celine wanted to calm her while I was trying to hold her back. Instead, it seemed to only infuriate her more. Sofia started violently scratching at Celine's arms, pinching them with such force that she was pulling off chunks of skin.

As Celine's arms became covered in blood, I realized I needed to get her out of harm's way. Reaching around, I grabbed Sofia by the ankles, allowing Celine to pull herself away from the onslaught of injury.

"Mommy, Mommy, we are going to be late, we are going to be very, very late," little Joanna loudly called out as she became more and more concerned.

With me now holding her by the ankles, Sofia leaned over, and I felt a sharp, tingling pain shoot up my arm as her teeth clamped down just above my wrist. She then attempted to pinch off chunks of my skin as she had done to Celine just moments ago, but my leathery hide was strong enough to hold off the assault.

Sofia screamed hysterically, "I AM SATAN'S, YOU MOTHER F%#@ERS, I'M GOING TO KILL YOU. I'M GOING TO KILL YOU JUST LIKE THEY DID ON TV."

Celine started to pray for Sofia, now moaning, muttering, and shaking her head violently. At this, I released my grip on Sofia's legs and gently placed my hand on the top of her head as I began to pray.

Sofia's ear-piercing screams became even louder, if that was even possible. Then, after about a minute of prayer, Sofia suddenly went silent. Finally, realizing no one was holding her, she jumped up and ran into the bedroom, locking the door.

Not a minute later, the bedroom door swung open; Sofia threw the Bibles of all three children plus the dress she had been wearing out of the room.

The Scriptures hit the ground with a resounding thud, followed by the door slamming as Sofia retreated into the bedroom.

"What do we do now?" Celine asked.

"I don't know; this is too much. I'm done."

As the four of us sat there stunned at what we had just experienced, my mind was spinning. So, that was a good question. What do we do now?

"I guess I need to call the Philippine Authority. I don't think we are going to be able to make our interview," I said.

We called the Authority and talked with the social worker. After we explained what happened, the social worker asked to speak to the children. Andrew was now distraught and did not want to talk. On the other hand, Joanna was more than happy for the chance to talk on the phone.

Joanna gave the social worker a detailed blow-by-blow description of what she had just witnessed.

The social worker then said, "We are here until four p.m., so if you can get Sofia to calm down, you can come later. In the meantime, write down everything that happened and email it to us."

After our phone call, I contacted hotel services again to unlock the kids' bedroom door. "Can you completely disable the lock this time?" I asked.

"Sofia said, 'I'm going to kill you just like they did on TV.' That's scary," Celine said.

Celine was so right. That statement sent a chill through me as well. Just a few months prior, we had watched a TV mini-series about a pair of brothers who had murdered their parents. At the time, Celine said,

"What if our children try to kill us?" My response was, "I don't think we have anything to worry about."

So yes, Sofia's words were downright eerie, I thought as I hid all the sharp knives in the kitchen.

I started to think; maybe I missed something about Sofia. So, I went back and read line by line the Special Home Finding List information, the Child Study Report, and other notes we had on Sofia.

I read the lines, and I read between the lines. But I could not find anything that would indicate the type of extreme behavior we had witnessed over the past few days.

Yes, the reports on Sofia said she was slow in school with a short attention span and average reasoning ability and had mild temper tantrums. But that describes many young kids, and it sure doesn't mean they are violent.

The reports said Sofia loves to sing Christian songs, participates in prayer, is friendly, sociable, sweet, and affectionate toward her younger sister. It specifically said she can be disciplined and is not a mean girl.

The reports contradicted what the caregivers and teacher told us at the orphanage—namely, that Sofia lies, steals, teases, and can be mean to the younger children.

Celine and I had now witnessed Sofia lying, stealing, being mean to her younger sister, and being violent toward both her brother and sister. That behavior was bad enough, but the violence toward Celine was a deal-breaker for me.

I wouldn't have been thrilled if Sofia had attacked me, but I would have just dealt with it. The fact that she attacked Celine, her new mother, like that—well, that is just not OK on so many levels.

We were still in the honeymoon stage with these kids. If that's how Sofia treated her mother now, what would she be like in six months or a year?

Sofia appeared to be an extremely troubled little girl, and at nine years old, I can't believe this behavior just started in the past couple of days. It also shed new light on the "zip it" incident we had witnessed during the Skype meetings months ago.

I felt like we were being scammed as if somebody had purposely withheld from us critical information about Sofia.

It was like there was two Sofias, one a sweet, helpful little girl and the other a troubled young soul.

I talked to Celine about my concerns. "We don't know what's going on with her. What if she acts up on the plane or at United States Customs? I'm very concerned about your safety as well as Andrew and little Joanna," I told Celine.

After much discussion, we decided we could not adopt Sofia at this time, as we did not know what was going on with her. We would still be prepared to take Andrew and little Joanna, but Sofia had too many unknowns. I was not willing to put Celine at risk and was now starting to think about the safety of our young nieces and nephews back home as well.

I sat down and wrote the Authority the email they requested.

After six days with the children, we have not been able to handle Sofia. I wrote that she lies and steals and was unwilling to take correction for disobedience. I explained how Sofia could be a sweet girl and how she wanted to bring ice cream home for me. But at the same time she had been exhibiting escalating violence toward Celine, Joanna, and Andrew. I told about Sofia attacking Joanna and Andrew in the orphanage apartment. I mentioned how Andrew and little Joanna responded well and were bonding with us, how denial of snacks was Joanna's best form of discipline. Then I discussed that first night in Manila when Sofia acted up. First, I took the pesos away, which was followed by the moaning and chanting behavior she exhibited.

Of course, I reiterated the events of that morning and the violent attack against Celine. I pointed out that we had not been made aware of this violent behavior from our information during the adoption process.

So, with heavy hearts, we have decided not to adopt Sofia.

After over four-and-a-half hours, Sofia came out of the bedroom now wearing a T-shirt and shorts, said she was sorry, and asked if she could play with the tablet. So, Sofia sat beside me as I helped her surf the internet.

Another half hour passed by, then once again we were on our way to meet with the Philippine Authority.

As we waited in the hotel lobby for our ride, Sofia would not stand with the family. Instead, she kept running around, even going behind the reception desk. She would not listen to the hotel staff or me telling her not to go behind the desk.

Finally, the car arrived, and we all piled in.

Once at the Authority, we met with two social workers. They told us they would not separate the children, and we needed to take all three or none of them.

"We will give you a couple of minutes to decide, but it sounds like you have already made up your minds," one social worker said.

I was a bit taken back that the two workers were not offering any suggestions or insight into the behavior we had witnessed. I felt we were being forced into deciding without all the facts. It's like we only had two choices: take the red pill or take the blue pill.

"We don't know what's happening with Sofia; she needs professional help. What's going to happen to the kids?" I asked.

"There will be an investigation, and Sofia will be evaluated. If considered not adoptable, all three children will be placed into foster care," the social worker told us.

My heart sank; the thought of the kids going into foster care crushed my soul, but I had no choice.

"OK, well, we are not prepared to take all three children at this time," I confirmed.

"Give us a couple of minutes to tell the children, and then you can say goodbye. But don't tell the kids why you are leaving them," the social worker said, which I thought was very strange.

The entire meeting lasted less than ten minutes.

A short time later, little Joanna walked into the room and over to me.

"Daddy, are we going now?"

Looking over toward the social worker, I whispered, "Did you tell them?"

The social worker nodded to indicate yes.

Fighting back the tears, I had to tell Joanna we would not be taking her with us. She listened but didn't seem to comprehend what was happening. In the lobby, Andrew was crying uncontrollably. I prayed with him and tried to comfort him as best I could.

"You're a good boy; this isn't your fault. The Lord will watch over you. I know he will."

But no amount of comforting would soothe the hurt and pain Andrew was feeling.

Celine went outside and sat down with the two girls. Celine held out her arms to Sofia, showing the bloody scars from the earlier attack.

"This is not OK. Because of this, we cannot take you," Celine told Sofia.

At this, little Joanna started to wail. Then, with tears streaming down her face, she turned to Celine.

"I will miss you, Mommy; I will miss you very much."

Sofia stared emotionless at Celine then said, "Can I have my tsit-sirya?" A Filipino term referring to the snacks she had in her backpack.

After ten minutes of trying to console Andrew, I felt lightheaded and dizzy. I walked over to a bench and sat down for a few seconds to catch my breath. Little Joanna was now sitting on a bench on the other side of the lobby.

Just as I was about to go over to Joanna, Celine called from outside, "Come on, our ride is here."

Who called for a ride? I'm not ready to go. I need to finish saying goodbye to the kids, I thought, as I walked outside and got into the vehicle.

It was time to go.

Sofia frantically ran into the street after us as the car pulled away. It took three adults to hold her back as she screamed and cried desperately.

It felt like my heart had been ripped from my chest. *How can this be happening, Lord? What possible good can come from this?*

Neither Celine nor I said a word during the short ride to the hotel; our hearts and minds were still with the kids and the pain they must be in. In just six days, we went from the most exciting trip of our life to an incomprehensible nightmare.

There was an eerie silence as we entered the hotel room. With the sun's setting, empty darkness began to fill the suite. It just felt wrong; this was not how things were supposed to end.

A part of us died that day in Manila, and we would never be the same again.

Celine almost died from in-vitro fertilization, and now she was viciously attacked by a nine-year-old girl we are trying to help. Why was this happening?

We packed up the kid's stuff as a social worker would be dropping by soon to pick up their belongings. We stuffed their backpacks with snacks and as many new clothes as would fit. What didn't fit into packs we put in bags.

It was hard to focus on the task at hand. *This can't be happening. I must be dreaming; wake up, Ken, wake up.* But there was no waking up; the nightmare was real. After giving the kids' belongings to the social worker, Celine and I ordered dinner and went to bed early.

We talked a little about what had just happened, but we were exhausted mentally and physically. Celine fell asleep right away, but I couldn't sleep. The construction site across the street was very noisy. *They must be working a three to eleven shift*, I thought. *So, I'll just read until eleven p.m.*

Eleven p.m. came and went, but the construction noise increased. This construction is insane. It can't be legal to be that noisy into the night in a downtown hotel district. Soon it was midnight, then 1:00 a.m., but the construction noise raged on.

I tried earplugs, pillows, and blankets over my head. Unfortunately, nothing helped as the construction sounds tormented me, becoming louder and louder.

My brain was now numb from exhaustion; *I need sleep, please let me sleep*, I prayed. But there was no relief. Instead, the echoes of tower cranes dropping loads were relentless. High-pitched squeals of power tools, loud voices yelling in languages I couldn't understand.

It was now 3:00 a.m. I looked over at Celine, and she was sound asleep. How can she sleep through all the racket outside? Am I going crazy? Am I the only one with noises in my head?

I walked out into the dark hotel living room and stood still, looking out the floor-to-ceiling windows. From construction across the street, shadows streamed through the glass, circling on the walls behind me like a tribal war dance.

The construction tower rose high into the night sky, standing over me like a maniacal beast. The very symbol of my life's work was now my torment in my darkest hour. Fiery sparks and smoke spewed from the tower's core, occasionally illuminating the shadowy figures scurrying around the concrete deck.

My soul was aching. My heart felt like it was in a vice. *My Lord, my God, where are you? Why have you forsaken me?*

I just stood there staring deep into the belly of the beast. "You've been chasing me my whole life but LEAVE MY WIFE ALONE."

Chapter 32:

The Road Back

The righteous cry out, and the Lord hears them; he delivers them from all their troubles. The Lord is close to the brokenhearted and saves those who are crushed in spirit. The righteous person may have many troubles, but the Lord delivers him from them all; he protects all his bones, not one of them will be broken. Psalm 34:17-20

Wednesday, January 10, the light started to slowly peek over the horizon as the new day sun began to extinguish the darkness of the night. Although not refreshed, Celine awoke from her deep slumber as wounds from the previous day's events remained heavy on her heart. The silence in the hotel room was deafening. This morning there would be no kids laughing, joking, and jumping on the bed. Of course, this morning was quiet and empty, other than the construction noise.

Today would be a day of rest as we prepared to fly back to California. Celine's cousin Ruby booked us a hotel closer to the airport and arranged ground transportation.

We spent the morning packing. I put the hotel room back together, all the phones, knives, and decorations reset to their original location. As I exited the room, I took one last look. The place looked like the past few days had never happened. All that was left were the memories of what could have been.

As we drove, my mind kept playing over and over the events of these last days. I couldn't make sense of what had just happened. What was I missing? Is this my fault? Is this how our seven-year-long journey to have children ends?

Lord Jesus, where are you? Why didn't you help us?

So much prayer went into this adoption. Now the children are traumatized, and Celine is devastated. I am in complete and utter shock. What will become of Andrew, Sofia, and little Joanna? I felt like I had just let so many people down; my head was spinning. I thought I was ready. I really thought I could help these kids.

As the car pulled into the hotel porte-cochere, my eyes gazed skyward, catching first sight of the letters "MARRIOTT." It was like seeing an old friend that had come to take me in.

Marriott was the company that launched my career to new heights with all those Hawaiian construction projects so many years ago.

It was like the Lord was sending me a message, "Remember, I am always with you; tonight, I will bring you rest." And that night, I had my first decent night's sleep in a week.

Morning came quickly, and we headed down to the hotel lobby. "I'd like to check out," I said as I tossed the room key onto the front counter.

"I can help you with that, Mr. McQuarrie. I hope you enjoyed your stay in Manila."

"Our stay was a memorable one, that's for sure."

• • •

As the plane gained elevation, Manila faded into the distance. The aircraft banked slightly, turning toward the United States. I would have the next fifteen hours to process what just happened as Celine and I made the long journey back to California.

Nimfa had taken time off work to pick us up at the Los Angeles airport. Since initially setting Celine and me up on a date back in 2010, she was now married and living in Seal Beach, California, with her husband, Nick Taylor. So, Nimfa dropped us off at our rental home and headed back to work.

The door hinge moaned as if just waking up from a long slumber as we pulled our luggage into the dimly lit house. A Christmas tree stood on guard, watching over Christmas presents, waiting for children who were no longer coming.

Fresh Filipino food sat waiting on the counter, left by friends to welcome the kids to their new home, another stark reminder of what could have been.

Celine and I slept for almost twenty hours straight that first day back. The events in the Philippines continued to weigh heavy on our hearts as we tried to restart our lives. But we didn't even know where to begin.

I had enough banked vacation to last me until the middle of February. So, I decided to use the time to focus on getting our house construction finished.

I set my start day with PCL Construction to February 12. Celine returned to work on January 22, a little over a week after returning from the Philippines.

As Celine started working again, I pressed hard to finish the house. We had now been under construction for nine months with no end in sight. I just had to get it completed quickly to move in and begin rebuilding our lives.

"Why are you so detailed and picky with the house? Just get it finished!" Celine would reiterate every evening as I gave her updates on the daily progress. Naturally, I was excited about seeing all the final touches of the design come together. However, as the days progressed, Celine became more agitated and anxious about just getting the house done.

I totally understood Celine's frustration. And, given what we had just been through, I thought she was holding it together rather well. You see, we just needed to get some normalcy into our lives. I needed to get this house done so Celine could unpack both physically and emotionally.

On January 29, our adoption agency contacted me. Unfortunately, the Philippine Authority was dropping us as potential adoptive parents.

"After thorough review and deliberation, the Board resolved to drop the McQuarrie couple from the Roster of Approved Applicants. The Board is concerned regarding the manner in which the couple responded to the needs of the children. Lack of pre-adoption training and preparation as prospective adoptive parents for a sibling group was raised as a concern."

Holy cow, talk about getting blindsided by a linebacker. I had to read it about ten times just for it to sink in. Lack of pre-adoption training and preparation. What do you call the past five years of training and preparation, psychological exams, references, and evaluations, not to mention my entire life and family background?

We had even planned to bring my sister Debbie to the Philippines. We figured her bachelor's degree in early childhood education and the fact she was an intervention foster parent might come in handy. But it was recommended Debbie not come due to the importance of initial bonding between the kids, Celine, and me.

We had also heard from our social worker in California that after we drove away that night leaving the kids, Sofia had another episode. The Filipino social workers could not handle Sofia, so they used little Joanna to talk to her sister and calm her down.

Professional social workers had to rely on a seven-year-old little girl to handle Sofia, and it's Celine and I that lack training? Seriously?

The thing that upset me the most was that blaming us for what happened would not help Sofia in the least. She showed violence toward her sister and brother on the first day we were at the orphanage. In my opinion, she was a very troubled little girl who needed some professional help.

I also noticed that the letter from the Philippines was dated January 18, only one week after we left the kids. The day we left the children, we provided a written statement of events via email. However, even with that, in our final meeting, Celine and I were allowed to reconsider and take the children with us if we wanted.

So, one week after we leave the Philippines, we are considered unfit to adopt. That makes absolutely no sense.

If they had concerns about any of our statements, they could have asked for further explanation and clarification. In addition, we would have been more than happy to provide added detail and information on the six days we were with the children, especially if the information would aid in evaluating and helping Sofia.

Our adoption agency was as surprised as I was. Our social worker suggested we appeal the decision.

"We will request for you to be reconsidered for a single child under the age of two as initially planned. We can also let the Philippines know you are willing to take additional training," the social worker suggested.

"That sounds good. This adoption has been costly, and our funds are getting tight. Do you think any of the fees and expenses we have paid so far may be credited toward a future adoption?" I asked.

"Possibly, but let's work on the appeal first, then we can look into that afterward. We don't want to give the wrong impression by talking finances while appealing."

"Fair enough. The money's not a big deal. It was just a question."

I talked to my sister Debbie about what had just happened. She wasn't surprised.

"You and Celine didn't do anything wrong. But, unfortunately, it's not uncommon when something goes wrong with an adoption or fostering, they blame the parents. Unfortunately, the authorities involved rarely admit any wrongdoing or mistake on their part. So, just prepare yourself. Anything you say or try to explain will probably be taken out of context and used against you. I hope I'm wrong, but I've seen it too many times."

"That's very interesting," I said to Debbie.

The day after the attack by Sofia, we received an email from the kids' teacher. She was concerned that notes she had provided on the kids might have contributed to our decision not to adopt.

The teacher wrote: "The notes were part of a much longer conversation with many more details. Any such notes could be taken out of context, and I could be blamed for your decision not to move forward with the adoption by the powers that be."

Of course, I reassured the teacher the decision not to adopt was based on other circumstances and not her notes. But I found the "notes could be taken out of context" comment quite interesting, as that seemed to be what was happening to us.

That evening Celine was not happy as I filled her in on the events of my day.

"Why are you moving forward on another adoption? We haven't even processed what happened in the Philippines. Why didn't you discuss this with me first? Why isn't the house finished? Stop being so OCD. You're too picky; just let Battres Construction get it done," Celine told me.

Hmm, I tried to explain to Celine that I wasn't starting a new adoption but just reacting to a letter from the Philippines. As far as the house goes, I wasn't OCD; I just wanted things done right.

It's common to start a list of fixes called a punch list that needs attention as the construction completes. I will admit my punch list was somewhat more exhaustive than usual, but I was convinced Celine would love the results.

The more I tried to explain myself, the more agitated Celine became. I understood she was working through all the stages of mourning and grief. But, for the rest of that week, it was like someone had covered the floor with eggshells, and I kept stepping on them.

Saturday, February 3, was a cooler and overcast day. Celine and I did a long morning walk, followed by breakfast and some running around. In the afternoon I was doing some work on the computer and Celine was watching some TV.

"Why did the Lord let us go through this? What good can come from it?" Celine asked.

"I don't know, hard to say. We just need to move forward."

"But what about the kids? Are you OK that the kids are traumatized? How can you just move forward?"

"I'm not OK with it. But I'm at peace with it."

"That doesn't even make sense; how can you be at peace? What's the Lord telling you?"

Celine was now getting quite upset. "Was it because Sofia wasn't bonding with you like the other two, so you just walked away from her. Is that what you do? You just push people away."

"No, of course not; that has nothing to do with it," I responded.

"I'm not blaming you for what happened, but if you are at peace with it, what's the Lord telling you? Why are you at peace? Tell me, what's the reason we are going through this?"

Celine said she wasn't blaming me for what happened, but it sure felt like I was taking the blame. Trying to de-escalate the situation, I calmly responded, "Well, the Lord doesn't speak to me like that. I just have faith that somehow this is all for a purpose, and the Lord will work it for good. But it may take years or a lifetime before it all makes sense."

Well, my attempts at de-escalating the situation were not working. The more I opened my mouth, the more upset Celine became. She was hurting, something was broken, and I couldn't fix it. Jeepers, I didn't even know what it was.

Suddenly this random thought flooded into my brain, and I blurted out, "Would you be willing for us to go see a counselor to help us process all this?"

Did I just say that? I thought as Celine said, "OK, yes, let's do that."

I spent the next week networking and finding a good Christian family counselor with experience in adoptions. I ended up with multiple recommendations for Mark Chevalier, who just happened to have availability to meet with us on Wednesday, February 14. Yes, that just randomly happened to be Valentine's Day. But I guess it was available as not many couples go to counseling on Valentine's Day. In the meantime, we continued to pray for Andrew, Sofia, and little Joanna. It pained us to think of what they must be going through emotionally.

We had some connections in the Philippines and were able to get some updates on the children. They were doing a little better toward the end of January, and Sofia was getting some professional help. All we could do was continue to pray and trust that the Lord had a plan that was bigger than any of us.

After not getting a response from the Philippines on our appeal, our social worker suggested sending a request to refund some of our processing fees. At the same time, I decided to look into some of our legal rights with this whole international adoption process. I think I was working through my own stages of grief, and I was in my "ticked off" stage at this point.

I researched a couple of law firms specializing in international law and even found a Los Angeles firm that specifically dealt with the Philippines.

Also, both the United States and the Philippines are members of The Hague Convention, an international agreement to safeguard intercountry adoptions. I could always file a complaint to The Hague Convention through the U.S. Department of State.

One could say I was preparing for a fight.

On Monday, February 12, 2018, as I started my new job returning to PCL, I couldn't help but reflect back on the summer of 2003. I had taken a detour from Hawaii to Orlando, Florida, only to move back to Hawaii six months later. It seemed so random at the time that I even questioned God.

During my time in Orlando working for Deron Brown, I developed a good friendship with Eric Orquiola and met his wife, Cathy. Fast forward fifteen years, Deron is now the president of PCL's US operations and Cathy Orquiola, the California district manager. They open a new office in Orange County, California, just a few miles from where I'm building my dream home.

Here I am in the most stressful time of my life, given a new start with an old familiar company, working for people I've known for fifteen years, in a newly opened office, just a few miles from my house. The trip to Orlando didn't make sense to me in 2003, and California wasn't even on my radar. The fact that the events and relationships of that time would come back to help me fifteen years later with the precise timing of a space shuttle launch is unmistakable.

That cannot be a random coincidence. Only the good Lord could have orchestrated such a plan.

The same week I started my job, Celine and I met with counselor Mark Chevalier. We opened up by telling Mark a bit about ourselves, how we met, and our seven-year journey to start a family. We then got into the events of our Philippines trip.

The emotions were still raw, and Celine struggled to tell her story. I spotted a tissue box on Mark's shelf and handed it to Celine. As for me, I held my emotions down. It was sort of awkward opening up to this complete stranger.

After patiently listening to our stories, Mark took a deep breath and began to speak slowly.

"I'm not saying you made a right or wrong decision not to take the kids, but it sounds like Sofia has reactive attachment disorder (RAD). From my experience working with families who adopt children with RAD, I can tell you; usually, one parent has to quit their job to focus on the child. A lot of money gets spent on psychologists and counseling, and the strain on the family sometimes leads the parents to divorce."

Reactive attachment disorder was quite the revelation. I knew about potential attachment issues with adopted children, but this was the first time I heard the term "reactive attachment disorder."

Apparently, RAD is not a very common disorder but can be pretty intense. As babies, we need affection, lots of comforting, and love to feel secure.

When we don't have a loving parent or caregiver or are neglected and abused, it can really mess us up emotionally. So, when this happens, we may not develop the ability to have healthy attachments with others, especially parents or caregivers. As a result, we may also struggle with proper social interactions.

Now I'm no expert, but it seems many, if not most, of us had some struggles as babies. Our parents weren't perfect and probably struggled with their own issues when we came onto the scene. You and I may have our quirks, but that's not reactive attachment disorder.

Most neglected or abused children do not develop RAD automatically from what I've read. But a child with RAD may have behaviors that include looking for affection from complete strangers or trouble accepting comfort when distressed, even from familiar adults. More extreme symptoms include withdrawal from interaction with people, violence toward caregivers, siblings, animals, and even themselves. This reactive attachment disorder would explain some of the behavior we witnessed in the Philippines.

After explaining reactive attachment disorder, Mark addressed Celine and me. "The events in the Philippines didn't cause a rift in your marriage; it exposed one," Mark started.

"Ken, you have a strong mind, and you have trained your mind to make wise decisions based on logic and facts. This has served you well most of your life; I'm sure you make the right decisions most of the time. However, when the challenges in the Philippines presented themselves, you made decisive and probably good decisions, but you left Celine behind."

"But the decisions I was making were to keep Celine safe, and we did discuss whether or not to adopt Sofia. I didn't just make that decision on my own," I responded to Mark.

"You're correct you did consult with Celine. But you didn't attune with her."

"Attune? What do you mean attune?"

"Celine was in a very emotional place, and you didn't take the time to understand what she was feeling. Because of this, she couldn't feel that bond or connection with you. Instead, she felt lonely, isolated, and left behind."

Talk about hitting the nail on the head. Mark was bang on; I'm not good at the emotional, touchy-feely stuff. If you need help with a plumbing leak in the middle of the night, I'm your guy, just call, and I'll be right over. But if you call feeling depressed and need a hug, I'm more apt to tell you to drink a warm glass of milk. Then, I will bring you some cookies the next day to make you feel better.

I've always lived my life like playing a game of football. If there is an obstacle in the way, I'll run right through it or around it. If I get knocked down, I simply get up and run it again. I've trained myself not to let emotions get in the way. As Mark explained reactive attachment disorder, it made me reflect on my start to life. I don't think I was neglected those first three months as an orphan in the hospital. However, I'm sure I didn't get the attention and nurturing a newborn would typically receive from a mother.

Remember, Joanna McQuarrie's journal said I was the best baby. I would just eat and sleep. I didn't cry because I had already learned it didn't get me anywhere. Now that being said, from three months old on, I did get plenty of nurturing. So, I have emotions, and I care very deeply for others. My challenge is I hold my feelings deep, and only occasionally do they bubble to the surface. My stoic nature can cause me to seem aloof or disconnected at times. I show my love through acts of service, not through emotional attuning.

My problem wasn't loving and caring for people. My problem was connecting on that deeper emotional level, allowing a person to feel cared for and loved. It's probably why I didn't get married until forty-three years old. The rift that got exposed between Celine and me was because that emotional connection was weak. We had a decent marriage, but our bond wasn't strong enough to withstand the storm due to the lack of attuning when the crisis hit.

I thought the counseling session would deal with the failed adoption. Instead, it was about me learning to attune. Mark said, "I can help you guys, but it's going to take a while."

"Ah, how long is a while?"

"We would need to meet once a week for six to eight months."

Say what, six to eight months! My initial thought was that's insane. *I mean, I got it, attuning, can't I just read a book or something?*

Celine was OK with the six to eight months, and when Mark agreed to cut his regular fee in half to help us, well then, I figured God had something to do with this so I'd better pay attention.

Mark gave us some homework to help me with attuning. The main exercise for the week was when Celine told me something about her day. I need to ask her, "How did that make you feel?"

It seems easy, right? Well, not so fast. I am hard-wired to be an overcomer and fixer. Present me with a problem and my brain goes into hyperdrive, trying to figure out the next best course of action. If Celine were to say, "That door squeak is annoying," she'd barely get the words out of her mouth and I'd be reaching for the WD-40. Fix the squeak, no more annoyed wife, and life is good, right?

Well, not so fast; that's fixing, not attuning. To attune, I need to respond, "Oh, and how does that make you feel?"

I still couldn't quite figure out when I was supposed to fix the door, though.

The following week Mark asked me, "How did you do with your assignment from last week?"

"I think I did OK," I responded.

"How do you think he did, Celine? Mark asked.

"Hmm, not so well," Celine responded.

Darn it, you see, Celine still felt I was more focused on solving the problem than really understanding or feeling her emotions. Simply asking how she felt is not the same as feeling or understanding her frustration or pain level.

Mark explained, "When Celine tells you what she's feeling, you need to hold on to that, ask probing questions to understand and feel what she's feeling. For example, is she sad like a death in the family, or is the sadness more like she forgot to record her favorite show? Avoid questions trying to figure out or solve the problem. Do you understand?"

"Uh, sort of, I think I so," I responded. But who was I kidding? How could I understand her feelings unless I found out what caused the feelings in the first place? It seemed like backward logic to me.

Mark then had Celine and I sit directly across from each other. Celine was to talk about something that upset her that week. My job was to hold on to her emotion and ask probing but not solution-based questions.

I'm not lying; this was extremely difficult. First, I'd asked one or two good questions, and then without even thinking, I would ask something that would start steering the conversation to a fact-finding mission or solution. Every time I did this, Mark would jump in and stop me, and we'd have to start over.

This counseling process was awkward on many levels. Having another person two feet from you while you're having a touchy, feely conversation with your wife was bad enough. But being constantly interrupted, like getting the buzzer on a game show, was quite distracting. The whole process felt more like atonement than attunement, but still, I soldiered on.

We continued our weekly sessions and assignments with Mark. Meanwhile, I continued to press hard on getting the house finished. Finally, all the hard work paid off when on March 16, 2018, we received the final signoff on the occupancy permit from the city. It was a historic day for me, fulfilling a childhood dream.

Kitchen Before

Kitchen After

Family Room Before

Family Room After

With all the excitement of our new home, I had almost forgotten about our appeal with the Philippines. Driving home one evening, I called our adoption agency for an update.

Our social worker said our appeal had been rejected, and the letter from the Philippines was not very nice.

"That's sort of expected. Email it to me so we can figure out our next move," I told her.

As I came to a stoplight, I opened up the email from the Philippines.

"We acknowledge receipt of your email dated January 30, 2018, regarding Mr. and Mrs. McQuarrie's desire to continue to be considered to adopt a single child.

By email dated February 8, 2018, Mr. and Mrs. McQuarrie requested a refund for the processing fees, pre-travel fees, and the child-caring agency donation they had endorsed for the adoption of the siblings.

Andrew, Sofia, and Joanna are attending sessions with a therapist since being left behind by the McQuarrie's last January 9, 2018. The caregivers reported that the siblings were distraught and had none of their usual passion for their daily routines.

Interview of the children and Mr. and Mrs. McQuarrie's report of the incident showed Mr. and Mrs. McQuarrie lack the empathy and understanding of the children's psychological needs:

1. Denial of snacks.

2. On their first night in Manila, they were given each a peso coin but were taken back for misbehavior.

3. Aggressive behavior ensued over Sofia's wanting to wear socks with slippers.

4. According to Sofia, Mrs. McQuarrie hit her in her leg.

5. The children overheard the couple saying, "We can change our minds about these kids."

Literature states that disturbing behaviors are often triggered by a child's deep, primal fear. The manner by which Mr.

and Mrs. McQuarrie dealt with the alleged 'misbehavior' was a threat to the children's safety and security. It is disheartening to know that the couple is more concerned about a refund rather than requesting information on the status of the children."

Wow! Our social worker was right. It was not a very nice letter. But it was just as Debbie had warned. They took our statements assuming the most extreme worst case possible and used it against us.

- The interview with us referred to in the letter lasted all of ten minutes, and at the time, we were in complete shock. They could have asked us to stay a couple more days, meet with a psychologist, try to figure things out. But, instead, they just said take all three kids or leave them.

- We only used denial of snacks when we gave little Joanna one Starburst candy instead of two. The children had their backpacks full of their favorite snacks at all times. In my letter to the Philippines, I said denial of snacks works best with Joanna, simply reiterating what Ms. Charlotte had told us. Maybe I should have said treats instead of snacks.

- On the first night in Manila, I did take the coins back from Sofia and Joanna and returned them the following day. Joanna wasn't very interested in the coins, but Sofia did react to this. So, I admit the coin thing was probably a mistake on my part. However, Sofia asked me to hold onto her backpack, including her coins, to keep them safe in subsequent days.

- The coins were the only time we tried any discipline with Sofia. Andrew was never disciplined and was a wonderful boy the whole time. With Joanna, we tested the Starburst thing. Then, of course, there was the night she had to stay in the hotel with me instead of going to the mall. However, it turned into a memorable father-daughter bonding time.

- Sofia decided to wear socks with her slippers. We were OK with that. We felt bad we could not find new shoes in her size, but it was not for lack of trying. Sofia was even with Celine on one of the trips to the mall looking for new shoes. We had told her we would keep looking. We don't know what triggered her to lock herself in the bedroom and subsequently attack us. We had a fun morning together as a family. Sofia had been watching TV with her brother and sister before the incident.

- During the attack, Celine did slap Sofia's leg. It was because Sofia was kicking Celine at the time. I was there, and it was not a very hard slap.

- I'm not sure what the kids overheard about changing our minds about taking them. We never had any discussions or thoughts, for that matter, about returning the kids before Sofia attacked Celine. I had even sent an email to my family the night before the attack giving them an update. We were looking forward to getting the kids back to California. The kids may have overheard something after the attack, as we decided not to take Sofia at that time but always said we would take Andrew and Joanna.

- We only questioned refunding fees after the Philippines banned us from adopting. However, international adoption is costly, and it was a simple question if some of our expenses could be credited to use in a future adoption.

- We had not requested follow-up information on the children from the Philippine Authority. Instead, we were getting updates from connections we had made during our trip there. We were very concerned about the children and their well-being.

We treated the children with the utmost love, gentleness, kindness, and grace. In my opinion, at no time were the children in any danger, either physically or emotionally.

As the stoplight turned green and I began to accelerate, I had an overwhelming feeling of peace. The words Jesus spoke in Luke 23:34 flooded into my mind. "Father, forgive them, for they do not know what they are doing."

The Philippines Authority was correct in the fact we were not the best parents for these three kids. If Sofia, Andrew, and Joanna have any sort of reactive attachment disorder, it will take specially gifted parents to work through that. My mother had a special gift for little children, helping many kids in her lifetime, not the least of which was me.

My sister Debbie worked with troubled children and, before that, developmentally challenged adults. So, I deeply understood about gifted parents having special skills or experience in raising troubled children. Here I am in counseling, learning how to attune with my wife emotionally so I probably wouldn't have been the best person for working with kids suffering from attachment disorders. If we had brought the kids home, I would have done what I always do. First, pray to the Lord for help, then lean in and meet the challenge head-on.

If Celine and I had known Sofia's behavioral tendencies ahead of time—that is, the stuff we learned from the orphanage caregivers— well, maybe we never would have gone down the path with these three. But that's neither here nor there.

The Philippine Authority's perception of what happened those six days with Andrew, Sofia, and Joanna may not be accurate. But they were just looking out for the children's best interest. I'm sure they are understaffed for the sheer number of children they deal with daily.

Any legal action or complaint filing would not help Andrew, Sofia, and Joanna. Ms. Charlotte offered to return the mandatory donation we gave the orphanage. By then we knew that wasn't the right thing to do. We told her to keep it; the orphanage was doing a wonderful ministry, helping hundreds of children. The best course of action moving forward for Celine and I was continually praying for Andrew, Sofia, and Joanna that the Lord would bring them special gifted parents. The perfect parents for them.

We had faith that the Lord was working in the lives of these children and would somehow bring victory over this most unfortunate experience for all.

During our next counseling session, the focus was on the letter from the Philippines, forgiving and moving forward. It was a good session.

One new thing that came up during our discussion was Celine's feelings of not being needed. Or, more specifically, feeling not needed by me. This time, I sensed what she felt. Our dreams of having a child had once again ended in devastating results. For me, I was simply searching for a life purpose. For Celine, it was more than that. She was from a big family. She had a natural desire to be a nurturing mother, to be needed by a child. Unfortunately, this desire had once again been shattered, snatched away from her at the last minute. She felt like she was being punished like she had somehow failed.

My natural independence only intensified Celine's feelings. I had always been an individual-type guy. When I was a toddler, mom could place me in my sandbox with my Tonka trucks, and I'd play alone for hours. I had my own apartment in college. Once I moved West, I was entirely on my own for years. I didn't get married until forty-three years old. Mom taught me to cook and be street smart and Poppa to fix things. Dad taught me to focus on the essential aspects of my faith and be gracious and kind to others.

I was just so used to doing things independently, without relying on anyone else but Jesus and me. Ecclesiastes 4:12 talks about the strength of a cord of three strands. The three strands were supposed to be Jesus, Celine, and me in our marriage. Wanting to not burden Celine with worrying about me in our day-to-day lives, I denied her to be an equal strand, an equal partner. As a result, I wasn't fully letting her strengths reinforce my weaknesses. Thus, she wasn't feeling needed. I thought that was one of our best counseling sessions to date. Plus, I was starting to attune with Celine's feelings, and as Jesus is my witness, I determined to now rely more on Celine.

That following Saturday, we moved the last of our stuff from the rental house and storage into our new home. It was Easter weekend, and we were excited to have our first sleep in the new place. On Sunday, we attended Easter service and headed to Celine's sister Karen's place in San Elijo. Karen and Gerald were hosting a family Easter get-together. Celine's brother Jeff and wife Kristin were visiting from Illinois, and it just also happened to be Jeff's birthday.

Celine's sister Jo organized some team relay games in the afternoon. Unfortunately, our team was slightly behind after the three-legged race and running with an egg on a spoon. So, it was up to me to close the gap in the run with a balloon between your legs.

I was pitted against my niece Sarah, now nine years old. She had been only two years old when she served as a flower girl at our wedding. But she was nine now, and there was no way I was going to let her beat me. Sarah got a quick lead, but I remembered my old broad jumping skills in elementary school. Bringing my feet together, I recoiled and made a giant leap forward.

It worked; I was catching up. Then, using my momentum from the first jump, I made a second leap, this time even farther, although coming down slightly off-balance. Finally, with no time to readjust, I launched into my third leap. I now felt like I was flying as my body soared completely horizontal four feet off the ground.

Suddenly everything went into slow motion. *Uh oh, this isn't good* was the last thought running through my brain as Newton's law of gravity snatched me from midair.

My body plummeted to the ground hard, like I had been dropped from an airplane, my right arm pinned beneath me. The sharp pain shooting through my arm was dulled only by my head slamming the ground, rendering me half unconscious.

Dazed and confused, I tried to roll over.

"Call 911!" my sister-in-law Kristin yelled.

Oh darn, am I dead? Am I having an out-of-body experience? I then started feeling dizzy and nauseous. *OK, I must not be dead yet.*

Celine helped me get up onto a chair, but the whole yard seemed to be spinning. I felt cold as beads of sweat poured down my bald head, glistening in the afternoon sun.

"How many fingers am I holding up?" Celine asked.

"Umm, three."

"What year were you born?"

"1967."

"On a level of one to ten, what's your pain level?"

"Uh, about 6 or 7."

After fifteen minutes, the yard stopped spinning, I stopped sweating, and nausea subsided. I felt better, but I can't say the same for my arm. It had swollen to nearly double its normal size. I was pulled out of the game and taken to the locker room. Or, in this case, the family room sofa.

My sister-in-law Jo, a nurse, tightly wrapped my arm in ice. Then, it was suggested that maybe I should go to the hospital. But, nah, this wasn't my first rodeo. I wanted to just sleep on it, then see how it felt in the morning. Celine decided the party was over for me, and we headed home. But, not before getting a to-go piece of Jeff's birthday cake from my sister-in-law Karen.

Every little bump was causing sharp pains in my arm on the drive home, so we decided to pull into a hospital emergency room—if

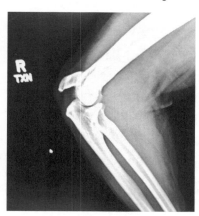

Yep, it's broken

for nothing else, just to get some painkillers.

"Yep, it's definitely broken," the doctor said as he showed us the X-ray.

No, way! The X-ray looked like something from a Bugs Bunny cartoon.

"Well, my friend, you're going to need a steel plate and some screws to put you back together. So, for tonight, I'll put it in a hard splint and give you a prescription for painkillers. An elbow break is excruciatingly painful. You're going to need more than Tylenol. But at least you have your own personal nurse to look after you," the doctor commented.

"But he said his pain was only a seven, doc," Celine questioned.

"Yeah, but I have a high pain tolerance," I interjected.

But the doctor just smiled. "You mentioned he was dizzy, sweating, and nauseous. Once the symptoms tell you the patient is in shock, you discount anything they say from that point on."

Just like that, Celine got an answer to her prayers of feeling needed as I was broken and would need lots of help.

"Lord, I appreciate the quick response to Celine's prayers, but next time could you please come up with a better game plan?"

After fifty years of walking away unscathed from tree falls, contact sports, car accidents, crazy close calls, and bizarre circumstances, I was finally a broken man. Now it would take all the good doctors and surgeons to put Humpty Dumpty back together again.

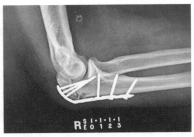

My elbow all screwed up, as in fixed

The broken elbow finally slowed me down. Over the next couple of months, Celine and I kept to ourselves as we settled into our new home. The past seven years of marriage had been insane, and it was time to settle down and focus on building that strong strand of three, Jesus, Celine, and me.

In the coming months, I had to rely on Celine to do even the simplest tasks. With my broken elbow, simply getting dressed and taking a shower was a challenge. We had lots of time now to practice attuning. As my arm began healing, so did the rift in our marriage. We were getting stronger by the day.

As June rolled around, our counselor Mark wanted us each to tell a little about our childhood.

"Sometimes how were raised gives insight to why we react specific ways to life's challenges," Mark said.

Celine went first, talking about how she was the second youngest of six siblings. Her parents both worked, so the kids were with caregivers most of the time.

"Education was important, and mistakes or failing were frowned upon. My dad was very strict, and it made me feel afraid to fail," Celine shared.

As Celine continued, her eyes became moist; a tear broke free, rolling down her right cheek.

"I feel like a failure not being able to have children," she said as her shoulders began to slump forward from the weight of the emotion.

I handed her the box of tissue as Mark began to speak.

"Our experiences as children shape the way we react to life as adults. It's not necessarily good or bad but is part of who we are. Celine, as a child, your parents weren't around; your reactions and emotions had to be more significant or dramatic to get attention, being one of six kids.

"Ken, from what you've shared, you had a lot of support growing up. Your mother, father, grandfather were all there, allowing you a safe place to fail. As a result, your reactions to things are less because you didn't need significant reactions to get attention. If you failed, it was OK; you could simply try again.

"So, you can see how your upbringing affects how you process or react. Celine, is there something about Ken you don't quite understand?" asked Mark.

"Yes, the house. Why was he so OCD about the house construction?"

"Ken, tell me about the house."

"Well, I've mentioned about my grandfather, Poppa. At first, he didn't want anything to do with me, but then we bonded over construction from the time I was a little guy."

As I began my story, those deep-down emotions started to bubble up; I took a short deep breath to push the feeling back down, but to no avail. It stuck in my throat like I swallowed a golf ball. My eyes became puffy; I sniffled, tears flooding down my face. Celine handed me the box of tissues as I continued.

"Poppa would refer to me as 'The Boy,' like I was the only one, like I was special. We always talked about building a house together when I was old enough, but that day never came. He always told me, 'If you're going to take the time to do it wrong, then why not do it right.' But he would always have patience with me, as he showed me the right way. I just wanted to do it right with this house in honor of Poppa. I just wanted to make Poppa proud of me."

Celine grabs the tissue box back from me, now choking back her own emotions, tears spilling down her cheeks; she wipes her nose.

"What are you feeling?" Mark asked Celine.

Now sniffling and wiping tears from her eyes, Celine's voice trembled as she tried to respond.

"I didn't know; I didn't know. I mean, I knew about Ken's relationship with his grandfather. But I didn't know about the house and what it meant to him. I was so focused on having children that I missed it. I missed being a part of that with him. I said I didn't blame him for what happened in the Philippines, but I realize now I did blame him, and it wasn't his fault. It wasn't anybody's fault."

Looking up at Mark, it looked like even his eyes were starting to get a bit puffy.

After giving Celine and me a minute to regain our composure, Mark said, "Your lives together began when you started dating. But, before that, both of you had lived separate lives for many years. So, for this week's homework assignment, I want you to write each other a story from your life. The life you had before you met. Your memories from when you were growing up."

"Me, write a story? I barely passed English class in school. I'm no writer," I responded.

Mark smiled. "I'm not saying write a novel. It's more like a letter, just write down some memories of your life you can share. Just like our session today, this will help you to understand each other better."

"OK, I'll give it a try," I said.

That night, the session with Mark was a real breakthrough, at least a breakthrough for me. Celine and I learned a lot about each other that day. I felt I was starting to feel the attuning for the first time.

That night Celine fell asleep as soon as her head hit the pillow, exhausted from the emotional roller coaster a few hours before. So, I pulled out a journal and pen and began to write.

I wrote about the circumstances of my birth, foster care at three months old, arriving at the McQuarrie's, and brain surgery. I scribbled notes down for about an hour then fell asleep.

In the morning, I handed Celine my journal. As she began to read, her brow wrinkled, followed by her face contorting as if in pain. Finally, after a couple of long minutes, she looked up.

"Is it that bad?" I asked.

"No, it's not that it's bad. It's … you should write this."

"I just did."

"No, I mean you should write your story, your whole story."

"You mean like a book? I can't write a book. I barely passed English class; my spelling and grammar are terrible. I think when they operated on my head, they must have cut a wire or something leading to that part of my brain."

"No, you can't spell, and yes, your grammar is terrible, but you tell stories all the time, and people like your stories. People remember your stories."

Celine was right about one thing, the fact that I tell a lot of stories. When I was young, Mom would tell me stories repeatedly of how I came to be a McQuarrie. I loved Bible stories about Moses, Joseph, and King David as a little guy. I guess not being good at English, I often used stories of my life to explain myself or try to relate to others.

"Stories are one thing, but to write a book, you have to have a point or a purpose, not just a bunch of stories," I said to Celine.

"Well, you should pray about it," Celine responded.

The following week Mark Chevalier said, "I don't think you two need to meet with me anymore. If you want to do a follow-up session in a year or so, that's fine, but I think you two are going to be just fine."

Wow, Mark initially said it would take six to eight months to fix our marriage. But here we are, good to go after only four months. Woohoo! Thank you, Jesus!

The attuning thing was quite the eye-opener for me. I had come a long way in the past four months but knew this was something I would need to work on for the rest of my life. As the weeks turned into months, I kept praying about writing my stories.

"Lord, is this something I should be doing?"

Yes, I had some stories, but my life seemed pretty ordinary. However, some extraordinary things did happen to me. I guess I would say my life has been extraordinarily ordinary.

Joseph was sold as a slave in the Bible but became the second most powerful man in Egypt, saving millions from starvation. Moses went to a foster family at three months old, just like me. But later, he leads millions of Hebrews to the promised land, where they form the nation of Israel.

In the 1700s, John Wesley started the Methodists and traveled hundreds of thousands of miles preaching the gospel. And in more recent times, Billy Graham evangelized the world, leading millions of people to accept Jesus Christ as their Lord and Savior.

As for me, I've done nothing but live my life chasing some sort of meaning and purpose. Nothing worth writing home to Mom about, that's for sure. Still, I continued to pray, and as I did, memories came flooding back like a returning ocean tide. Details of my long-forgotten life were now fresh in my mind like they happened yesterday. I remembered the good and bad, happy and painful memories from scars healed long ago.

I began making notes as the memories started to form the chapters of my life. I began to see a pattern as biblical truths started to reveal themselves. The events in the Philippines had shaken my core beliefs. The months following our return from Manila were actually strengthening my faith. I thought God had abandoned Celine and me, but that was furthest from the truth.

Through my memories, I could now see clearly that God has always been with me, continually working in my life. In every chapter of my life, no matter how the odds were stacked against me, in life and death situations, when things were totally out of my control, some-how, someway, the Lord always showed up.

Of course, I'm not talking miraculous miracles, although I would argue there have been a few. God seemed to make use of a sudden change in circumstance, a gifted physician, or a perfect stranger to help in the nick of time. Thus, whether random or not, the events of my life were used to propel me toward some purpose. As the months passed by, it started to become more clear. Finally, it became unmis-takable that my stories were not about me. My stories were about God. More specifically, about Jesus, how he has always been present and active in my life, that he loves me and has a plan and purpose for me. I may not have figured out my purpose yet, but I had figured out this book was about Jesus.

February 2019 rolled around. It had now been one year since "The Thriller in Manila." Celine and I headed off to Sault Ste. Marie to visit my parents. I wanted Celine to experience winter like I did growing up. Oh boy, would I get my wish.

A polar vortex had descended upon the middle of North America. If you were to throw a hockey stick at the center of the vortex, you'd pretty much hit Sault Ste. Marie dead on. We arrived in 20-below tem-peratures, with winds driving the cold down to almost 40-below at times.

Celine even got to experience shoveling snow in the middle of a snowstorm when the winds picked up for a couple of days. Oh yeah, and we also got her out to a Soo Greyhounds hockey game. Unfortunately, the Hounds lost to the Sudbury Wolves that night.

While visiting, sitting in front of a warm fireplace drinking coffee and eating goodies, I interviewed Mom and Dad. I walked through recollections of my early childhood and asked questions about baby Stephen and their knowledge of where I came from. Mom and Dad were able to add a few details and perspective, but most importantly, they verified that the stories from my recollections were true.

It was a good visit with Mom and Dad, walking down memory lane in the place where it all began for me so many years ago.

An old, abandoned wing of the Plumber Memorial Hospital is still standing. I could still remember the smell of grease and sawdust of the basement workshop where I spent afternoons with Poppa. But, of course, I also remember the emergency room that I visited so often, struggling to breathe.

Long demolished was Sir James Dunn High School where I played my first football game, although my elementary school, Ben R. McMullin, was still there on Purgatory—I mean Paradise—Avenue. You remember that old dirt path through the bush where I almost met my demise at the hands of the first-grade bullies? Well, it's now a paved walkway through a subdivision.

"Canadians are so hardy; how do you survive weather like this?" Celine asked as we started our trek back to California.

"Well, it toughens you up for life, that's for sure."

We arrived back in California late Sunday night. Monday evening, Celine went to bed early, suffering from jet lag and the three-hour time difference.

I turned on the computer and pulled up a blank document.

OK, Lord. If I'm going to do this, then I'm gonna need your help. Don't let me screw this up.

After all, this book is not about me. It's about you!

And away we go ... When I came into this world, there were no baby showers, no celebrations, no father handing out big cigars, or first photo being passed around the office. Grandma, grandpa, aunts, and uncles would not be visiting, pinching my chubby cheeks and saying how cute I was. You see, I was an orphan, unwanted, cold, hungry, and alone ... or was I?

Chapter 33:

So What?

I will not leave you as orphans; I will come to you. Before long, the world will not see me anymore, but you will see me. Because I live, you also will live. On that day, you will realize that I am in my Father, and you are in me, and I am in you. John 14:18-20

While living in Hawaii, I was invited to a restaurant to celebrate a friend's birthday. Unfortunately, traffic was terrible that day, and I was running late. To make matters worse, it took me almost a half hour to find parking.

"Sorry for being so late. It took me forever to find a parking spot," I said as I sat down at the table.

A friend quickly responded, "I found one fast. I just prayed, 'Lord, help me find parking,' and a spot opened up right away."

"Me too," another friend added.

As I ordered my meal, another latecomer showed up. "Trouble finding parking?" I asked.

"No, as I entered the parking lot, I just prayed, and a spot opened up."

OK, I felt I had a strong faith, but seriously, children in the world are dying of cancer, and the Lord helps you get a parking spot! That almost made me feel angry.

About a month later, I was rushing to meet Brent at the Dole Cannery movie theaters for a 10:30 pm late show. Unfortunately, traffic was all backed up, and by the time I entered the parking garage, it was already 10:25 pm.

"OK, Lord, are you going to help me get parking? I'm going to be late," I said out loud, almost sarcastically.

As I pulled up the parking garage ramp, a car pulled out from the first parking space in front of the elevator to the theater lobby. Pulling into the spot, I jumped out of my car and made a few short steps to the elevator. Someone had already pushed the elevator call button, so I was able to step in without even breaking stride. I was in my seat just as the movie previews began at 10:30 p.m. sharp.

Although I appreciated getting to my movie on time, I can't say it answered my question. If the Lord is willing to help me get a parking spot, why won't he heal my asthma? Why does he let children die or be abused and neglected?

I had spent my life searching for a purpose or reason for me even to be alive. But now, this minor parking incident shifted my focus, changed my thought process. I was still searching for my purpose, but now it was like, "What's God's purpose for this world, and how do I fit into that purpose?"

Over the years, I have been asked to pray for someone with a terminal illness many times. Unfortunately, however, 100 percent of the time, that person died. There are all sorts of conclusions you could come to about that, not the least being: don't ask me to pray for you if you are sick.

There are all sorts of illnesses in this world, combined with natural disasters, violence, war, slavery, human trafficking, assault, murder, rape, and the list goes on. So many people fall victim to terrible evil through no fault of their own.

Now, I wish I had an answer to why God has allowed so much terrible stuff in this world for so long, but I don't. Smarter people than me have tried to figure it out for centuries. Looking back throughout history, it's clear to me we live in a fallen world. God created us with free will, and humanity has used that free will to perpetuate violence and evil since the beginning of time.

> *As it is written: There is no one righteous, not even one ... For all have sinned and fall short of the glory of God. Romans 3:10, 23*

It's like my parable of the pollywog; human beings have collectively allowed evil into our jars, and the daily consequences play out in the news. Then if that's not enough, the world moans with natural disasters, pestilence, and disease as if the very earth is sick.

> *"I have told you these things, so that in me you may have peace. In this world you will have trouble. But take heart! I have overcome the world." John 16:33*

Jesus spoke the words of John 16:33 to his disciples mere hours before being taken from them and crucified. He had just been sharing about what would be happening in the coming hours and the months to follow, how he would be leaving them for a while but that they would see him again. Jesus also mentioned the Spirit of Truth (the Holy Spirit).

Jesus talked figuratively, so his disciples didn't quite understand. I can imagine myself sitting there with the apostles. I'd be like, "Say what? What are you talking about, Jesus?"

They didn't understand, but that day Jesus revealed his purpose, the reason why he came from God the Father and entered the world. He came to die as a living sacrifice to pay for our sins, so that through his resurrection, he would defeat sin once and for all.

> *For God so loved the world that he gave his one and only son, that whoever believes in him shall not perish but have eternal life. John 3:16*

God created the world; can he fix it? But, of course, he could just hit control-alt-delete and reboot the whole universe. And the day is coming when he will do just that, but not today.

Jesus told his followers, "In this world you will have trouble." So, we know Jesus didn't come to take all our troubles away. So, the problems of this world will continue, for the time being, anyway.

God didn't cause sin to come into the world, but he did allow it. God created us in his image to have free will, a sense of fairness, and justice. He made us for a relationship with himself, but it's our choice.

The thing about free will is that you need a choice. Humanity had a choice and chose sin. So now there is a new choice between this fallen world with sin or the redemptive saving grace of Jesus Christ, who paid the price for our sins.

For God did not send his Son into the world to condemn the world,
but to save the world through him. John 3:17

A long, long time ago, King Nebuchadnezzar of Babylon (modern-day Iraq) conquered Israel and carried many people into exile from Jerusalem to Babylon. The prophet Jeremiah wrote a letter to the exiles. In this letter, Jeremiah told them they would be in exile for seventy years, after which God would fulfill his promise to bring them back. Then he told them:

"For I know the plans I have for you," declares the Lord,
"plans to prosper you and not to harm you, plans to give
you hope and a future." Jeremiah 29:11

I don't know about you, but if someone told me, "Hey Kenneth, you're going to be held captive for seventy years, but don't you worry. After it's over, I have plans for you to prosper, to give you hope and a future."

Well, I'd kind of give him my squinty eyes look and say, "Seriously, that's supposed to cheer me up?"

However, God didn't just say, "See ya in seventy years." Instead, he told them to settle down, have sons and daughters, increase in number, and pray to the Lord for peace and prosperity in their city of exile. Then, after seventy years, he would return them to Israel, the promised land.

> *"I will make you into a great nation, and I will bless you;*
> *I will make your name great, and you will be a blessing. I will bless*
> *those who bless you, and whoever curses you I will curse; and all*
> *peoples on earth will be blessed through you." Genesis 12:2-3*

You see, God's intent was always to bless the world through the nation of Israel, to reestablish his relationship with humanity that had been severed by sin. Thus, long before Babylon, God promised Abraham that his descendants would become a great nation, that through his descendants, all the people on the earth would be blessed.

Later on, through Moses, God made a covenant with Israel starting with the Ten Commandments. However, Israel had fallen away from God over the centuries, breaking the covenant he had made with them. God sent them many warnings to smarten up, but they just kept doing their own thing. Over time, they chose to turn their backs on God.

So, to set things back on track, God allowed the exile to Babylon. It might have seemed like God was abandoning his chosen people, but that was not the case. Instead, he used what seemed like a lousy circumstance to refocus the Israelites, strengthen them, and refine them. Finally, after seventy years as promised, God did return the people to Israel, giving the nation a renewed faith, future, and hope.

> *For this reason Christ is the mediator of a new covenant, that those*
> *who are called may receive the promised eternal inheritance—now*
> *that he has died as a ransom to set them free from the sins committed*
> *under the first covenant. Hebrews 9:15*

God's first covenant with Israel was based on the Ten Commandments, laws, rules, and regulations. So, you see, sin was still in the world, and the first covenant was to help people understand what sin was. These commandments also proved that there was no way a person could live without breaking at least one of these laws. It showed that all have sinned and come short of the glory of God.

The good news is God always knew sin would keep us from him, and there is no way we can live a sinless life. That's why Jesus came into this world to show us the way, to reestablish our connection with God. Jesus lived as a sinless example, a living sacrifice paying the price for our sins.

When Jesus defeated sin through his death and resurrection, he established a new covenant for all humanity past, present, and future. This new covenant is no longer just for Israel and no longer based on laws and regulations.

Through Jesus, God's promise to Abraham, blessing all the people on the earth through him, was fulfilled.

Not only did God fulfill his promises, but now the words from God spoken by Jeremiah, "'For I know the plans I have for you,' declares the Lord, 'plans to prosper you and not to harm you, plans to give you hope and a future,'" ring true for those who accept the new covenant through Jesus Christ.

Then I saw "a new heaven and a new earth," for the first heaven and the first earth had passed away, and there was no longer any sea. I saw the Holy City, the new Jerusalem, coming down out of heaven from God, prepared as a bride beautifully dressed for her husband. And I heard a loud voice from the throne saying, "Look! God's dwelling place is now among the people, and he will dwell with them. They will be his people, and God himself will be with them and be their God. 'He will wipe every tear from their eyes. There will be no more death' or mourning or crying or pain, for the old order of things has passed away." Revelation 21:1-4

It's great news that through Jesus Christ, God gives us a new future and a hope of an eternity with him. But what happens in the meantime? We still have to live in this messed up world with many daily troubles.

Jesus made it very clear that you will have problems in this world, to say the least.

And we know that in all things God works for the good of those who love him, who have been called according to his purpose. Romans 8:28

The Bible tells us in all things, God works for the good of those who love him. The question is, what is the good he is referring to? Is it a good job, living in Hawaii or Southern California? What about getting to build your dream house? Is it having children and a dog?

Proverbs 18:22 says he who finds a wife finds what is good, so is that what the Bible is referring to?

Do I consider all these things blessings? Of course, I do. But the problem is just because I may have some of these things and someone else does not, it doesn't mean I'm more blessed than they are.

These are all good things, but they are temporary in the context of eternity, plus they don't always bring happiness. And we have all heard the saying, "Be careful what you wish for."

The "good" is not what we consider good, but what God considers good.

The good God is referring to in Romans 8:28 is Jesus Christ. And he is working in all things to conform us into the image of Jesus.

Just like God used Israel's exile to Babylon to refine them, he uses the circumstances of this world to refine us into the image of Christ.

I have yet to meet a perfect human being in my fifty years. Whether we admit it or not, we all struggle with our character flaws; I know I do. Maybe you struggle with anger or lack of patience. How about anxiety and fear? Pride and insecurity seem to go together like peanut butter and jelly.

You may be able to hide your flaws from the world, but you know what they are, and guess what? So does God.

We have all heard the old saying, "What doesn't kill you makes you stronger." Well, this is true as long as you are not left scarred, bitter, and emotionally damaged.

My broken elbow is stronger with the titanium plates and screws, but I can't say it's better. God uses the circumstances of life not only to make you stronger but to make you better.

God is working in our lives to help develop the attributes of Jesus Christ in us.

Galatians 5:22-23 says, *"But the fruit of the Spirit is love, joy, peace, forbearance [patience], kindness, goodness, faithfulness, gentleness, and self-control. Against such things there is no law."*

If I struggle with anxiety and stress, the Lord will continue to allow me to get into stressful situations to help strengthen me in this area. It won't be until I learn to rely on the Lord and stop stressing that the stressful situations will disappear. The Lord will also use increasingly stressful circumstances to help build up my ability to handle more stress.

For over thirty years, I have made my career in a very high-stress, deadline-driven industry; the pressures and expectations on me now are ten times that of when I started my career. But over the years, the Lord helped me get through increasingly stressful times, building up my stress tolerance. Because of this, I can handle exponentially more stress now than when I was in my 20s.

I did end up on blood pressure pills, so maybe this is not the best example, but the need for medication was more my own doing. Plus, remember I'm still a work in progress.

I have come up against many challenges, heartache, pain, and flat-out bad luck in my life. I could probably go through each story or chapter in my life and point out how God used the situation to work on a specific fruit of the Spirit in me. But this book is getting long, and Celine tells me I need to wrap it up. So, I'll just point out the big elephant in the room.

My biggest challenge in life has always been emotional attuning with people. I hold my emotions very deep, most likely contributed to or caused by the circumstances when I came into this world.

My first doctor, Dr. Cole, told Mom that she had seen many babies come into the world with challenges, and they either give up and die or fight to survive. Dr. Cole said I was a fighter.

I can feel love and make emotional attachments, but the person won't feel loved if I don't attune with them. Instead, they may feel lonely, isolated, and left behind as I go off to slay my next dragon.

Looking back on my life, the Lord gave me plenty of chances to develop my attuning. I've lived in so many places and met so many people—made some good friendships and met some folks I'd like to forget. But I was so focused on chasing my purpose that I kept failing the opportunities to develop deeper relationships with the people right in front of me.

But God isn't finished with me yet. The Philippines adoption was the noblest challenge in my life that turned into my worst nightmare, but God used it for ultimate victory.

"Why did the Lord let us go through this? What good can come from it?" Celine asked on that cloudy Saturday back in February 2018.

I don't think we will ever fully know the ramifications on the lives of the folks involved in our "Thriller in Manila." I don't believe God caused those events to happen, but he used them to help expose and heal a rift in Celine's and my marriage. In doing so, I had a breakthrough in learning to attune, or more simply love, as Jesus loves.

> *"Love is patient, love is kind. It does not envy, it does not boast, it is not proud. It does not dishonor others, it is not self-seeking, it is not easily angered, it keeps no record of wrongs. Love does not delight in evil but rejoices with the truth. It always protects, always trusts, always hopes, always perseveres ... And now these three remain: faith, hope and love. But the greatest of these is love." 1 Corinthians 13:4-7, 13*

But what about Andrew, Sofia, and little Joanna? Well, Celine and I continue to pray for them. However, we did receive a newsletter from the orphanage announcing that they were adopted. We don't know what their names are now but they have found their forever family, praise Jesus! I just know the Lord is working in their lives and the lives of their new parents.

I know that God is working in all things for good in my life, and through Jesus Christ, I have a hope and future. But that gets me back to the one thing that has eluded me my whole life.

What is my purpose?

Well, it turns out my purpose has been right in front of me my whole life. My purpose is actually the same as your purpose. That purpose is just to live our lives to glorify God.

A simple way to do that is to tell your story, and through it give all glory to God. I'm not saying write a book; that would be crazy; who would do a thing like that? But what I am saying is when difficulties in life strike you down, lean into Jesus for help because whether you believe it or not, he's already there helping. Then when you have victory in the situation, be sure to tell someone how the Lord strengthened you in your time of trouble.

You may be surprised how the most minor victories may become the most enormous encouragement in another person's life.

Shortly before Jesus's crucifixion, a woman poured some expensive perfume on him. When she did this, she was rebuked by the people in the room. Talk about a stressful situation. But Jesus said she did a beautiful thing. The perfume was symbolic of preparing his body for burial.

Jesus also said. *"Truly I tell you, wherever the gospel is preached throughout the world, what she has done will also be told, in memory of her"* Mark 14:9.

This woman was just living her life and glorified Jesus through a small act. Moreover, this woman's story is in the Bible, which has sold an estimated five billion copies over the centuries. Talk about hitting it out of the park with her story glorifying God.

If you don't think your story matters, I have news for you; it does matter because you matter. You are not an accident.

For you created my inmost being; you knit me together in my mother's womb. I praise you because I am fearfully and wonderfully made; your works are wonderful, I know that full well. My frame was not hidden from you when I was made in the secret place, when I was woven together in the depths of the earth. Your eyes saw my unformed body; all the days ordained for me were written in your book before one of them came to be. How precious to me are your thoughts, God! How vast is the sum of them! Were I to count them, they would out- number the grains of sand—when I awake, I am still with you.
Psalm 139:13-18

I resulted from an unplanned, unwanted pregnancy, but scrip- tures tell me I wasn't a mistake. So, I know from personal experience that you are not a mistake either. God planned you; he loves you and, through Jesus, has promised you hope and a future.

Now, I may not always be the sharpest tool in the shed, but there is one thing I know for sure.

"Jesus loves you, this I know. For my Bible tells me so. All of us to him belong, we are weak, but he is strong. Yes, Jesus loves you. Yes, Jesus loves you. Yes, Jesus loves you. My Bible tells me so."

In this world, terrible evil things will continue to happen. Life isn't always fair, and happiness is not a guarantee. However many days we have in our lives, it's all but a moment in time. Baby Stephen only lived ten days, struggling to survive. However, through his tragic death, I was given a gift to live the life I've had.

Baby Stephen went straight to heaven, while I have had to toil through the trials of life. But by putting faith in Jesus as my Lord and Savior, and because of his grace and promise, I will meet Stephen in person for the first time one day.

You know, maybe you have never accepted Jesus as your Lord and Savior. Or maybe you did years ago, but over time, life has gotten in the way, and he's no longer Lord of your life. Well, if that's you, then I have some awesome news: as long as you are still breathing, it's never too late to reach out to Jesus.

But what does it say? "The word is near you; it is in your mouth and in your heart," that is, the message concerning faith that we proclaim: If you declare with your mouth, "Jesus is Lord," and believe in your heart that God raised him from the dead, you will be saved. For it is with your heart that you believe and are justified, and it is with your mouth that you profess your faith and are saved. Romans 10:8-10

*For it is by grace you have been saved, through faith—
and this is not from yourselves, it is the gift of God—
not by works, so that no one can boast. Ephesians 2:8-9*

You can't earn your way into heaven by doing good things or following laws and regulations. There are no cosmic scales of justice at the end of life that weigh your good deeds against your bad to determine whether you make it into the promised land. Remember the first law-based covenant God made with Israel through Moses? Well, it proved that we couldn't earn our way into heaven by keeping the law.

Clearly no one who relies on the law is justified before God, because "the righteous will live by faith." Galatians 3:11

God's plan all along was for Jesus to be our Savior, to be the perfect sacrifice, to pay the price for humanity's sins past, present, and future.

Scripture foresaw that God would justify the Gentiles by faith, and announced the gospel in advance to Abraham: "All nations will be blessed through you." So those who rely on faith are blessed along with Abraham, the man of faith. Galatians 3:8-9

The simple fact is that all you have to do for salvation is to put your faith in Jesus Christ and accept him as your Lord and Savior. There are no special prayers, rituals, or handshakes required; just believe in your heart and confess with your mouth that Jesus is Lord, and you will be saved.

If you're anything like me, to commit in my heart and mind, sometimes it helps me write it down or say it aloud. If you are ready to make that commitment to Jesus, you can write or speak something like this:

"Dear Jesus, I know that I'm a sinner, and no matter how hard I try, I cannot be good enough; I am tired of doing it on my own. Lord, I believe you died for my sins and rose from the dead. I am asking you to forgive me of my sins and enter into my heart. I humbly invite you to be my Lord and Savior from this moment forward. In Jesus' name. Amen."

Then, just for good measure, you can pray this when you go to bed tonight.

"Now I lay me down to sleep. I pray the Lord my soul to keep. If I should die before I wake, I pray the Lord my soul to take. In Jesus' name. Amen."

Now, if you just said that prayer in your heart and currently are not attending a church, here's what I want you to do. Put this book down and go to the internet. Search for a respectable local Christian church.

When you find one you like, check out the "What We Believe" section of their website.

Remember you're looking for:

- The Trinity: God the Father, God the Son (Jesus), and God the Holy Spirit. He's one God existing in three forms.

- That all humanity has sinned and come short of the glory of God.

- Jesus Christ is our Lord and Savior who died as a sacrifice for our sins and rose from the dead. It's through faith in him that we are saved. We cannot earn our salvation through good deeds, rules, and regulations.

- The Holy Bible is the only authoritative scripture.
- We live for the glory of God alone.

Once you find a church you like, there's one last thing to do. I want you to contact the church pastor and tell 'em "The Orphan Carpenter" sent you.

May the Lord bless you, may his face truly shine upon you. In Jesus' name. Amen.

Kenneth Ian McQuarrie
The Orphan Carpenter

"However, I consider my life worth nothing to me; my only aim is to finish the race and complete the task the Lord Jesus has given me – the task of testifying to the good news of God's grace." Acts 20:24

Tribute to Mom

Joanna Ellen McQuarrie (Mom)
Born November 18, 1936
Went home to Jesus July 19, 2020

During the writing of this book, Mom passed away due to complications from Alzheimer's. In the final chapter of her life, this terrible disease took her memories and pieces of who God made her to be.

Mom's answer to all life's challenges was always, "We'll have to pray about that." And pray we did, but the progression of the disease was relentless. Still, during her moments of clarity and peace, she turned her prayers toward the Lord, that he would have mercy and take her home.

On July 19, 2020, to even the doctor's amazement, her prayers were answered when the Lord took her home early, stopping the progression of the disease mid-course.

"In this world you will have trouble. But take heart! I have overcome the world," Jesus said.

Mom knew all too well about the trouble in this world, enduring the death of her newborn son, followed by the loss of her mother to cancer only a few years later. Yet, her faith in the promises of Jesus only grew stronger.

Mom had natural gifting for nurturing children, especially younger ones, evident in the many babies she helped as a foster mom and a lifetime of being a babysitter, caregiver, and Nanna to many other children. I was blessed to be the baby she kept, raising me as her own. I had nowhere to go, and she took me in, medical challenges and all.

You've just read the many stories of how Mom loved and supported me from that very first day back in December 1967. Since leaving Sault Ste. Marie, Ontario, I have lived in numerous cities throughout Canada and the USA, including seven years in Hawaii. Along the way, I have shared my stories of Mom and her faith. How she and Jesus have continued to look out for me and mold me into who I am today.

Mom was born and raised on Saint Joseph's Island, a small island with a population of around 1,000 people at the time. She lived most of her adult life on Primrose Drive in Sault Ste. Marie. Her lifetime took place in a 100 km radius in Northern Ontario.

But, in December 1967, Jesus came calling. Joanna McQuarrie picked up the phone and answered the call.

Hundreds, maybe even thousands of people have heard the stories over the years. The stories of love, faith, and dedication Joanna had for one little baby boy that no one else wanted.

*"The Lord took my baby and has sent me
this one because he needs my help."*

And help she did.

Over the years, many people have asked me, "Don't you wonder who your real mother is and where she is now?"

My real Mother is Joanna Ellen McQuarrie, and now she is with Jesus.

"For I know the plans I have for you," declares the Lord, "plans to prosper you and not to harm you, plans to give you hope and a future."
Jeremiah 29:11

Acknowledgments

First off, I want to thank Jesus Christ for all you have done and continue to do in my life. I wouldn't have made it this far in life if it weren't for you.

Next is Ron and Joanna McQuarrie, or as I know you, Mom and Dad. You took a chance on me many years ago, and your love and support have never wavered. It is just as big sister Debbie says, "You don't set the bar as gracious, loving parents; you are the bar."

Then, Poppa, you weren't so sure about taking me in, still dealing with your emotions of baby Stephen passing. But your doubts only lasted about a minute. After that, you became my defender and mentor, my biggest supporter. It was taking me under your wing, sparking my interest, teaching me carpentry and construction skills that would one day launch me on a wonderful adventure to far-off exotic places.

Let us not forget Nanna. Sadly, you were only around for my first five years. But you were the matriarch of the family and a big part in my becoming a McQuarrie. I'm your grandson, and that's all there is to it.

From my first day in the McQuarrie household, Debbie, you were my big sister. You have always watched over and protected me. You literally saved my life from drowning at the hands of bullies. If you had not been there that cold November day in 1972, well, this would have been a very short book.

My younger brother, Dougie, or I guess I should call you Doug now since you're all grown up. I hope I'm your favorite brother since I'm the only one you've got. You have always trusted and believed in me. As kids or since we grew up, you never doubted me with any of my hair-brained schemes. Now you may have scratched your head a few times and thought, What the heck? But doubt me, you did not.

To my wife, Celine, you are the love of my life and my greatest blessing from God on this side of heaven. I told you being married to me meant you needed to be prepared for a rough ride because the storm clouds of life had been chasing me since the day I was born. But you committed to being my wife through the good and bad. The Lord has brought us through some pretty big storms in the past ten years, but you have stood by me every step of the way. This book would never have become a reality without your encouragement to write it and patience for me to finish it.

Celine, I look forward to what the Lord has planned for the next chapter of our lives together. Thank you for all you do for me. I love you.

Family Tree

On May 2, 1969, just a few months before my second birthday, I was no longer an orphan. I now had my forever family. Unfortunately, I could not fit a story about everyone into this book. My entire life, aunts and uncles have supported and accepted me as one of the family. Here is my forever family.

The McQuarries:
Neil and Minerva McQuarrie – Grandpa and Grandma
1. Marjorie (McQuarrie) Lion - Aunt Marj (Chapter 11)
   - Norm Lion – Uncle Norm (Chapter 11)
2. Kenneth McQuarrie – Uncle Ken (Chapter 11)
   - Hazel McQuarrie – Aunt Hazel (Chapter 11)
3. Ruth (McQuarrie) Marshal – Aunt Ruth (Chapter 6, 26)
   - Charlie Marshal – Uncle Charlie (Chapter 6)
4. Ron McQuarrie – Dad
5. Shirley (McQuarrie) Scott – Aunt Shirley (Chapter 11, 26)
   - Tom Scott – Uncle Tom (Chapter 11, 26)

The 10 Tribes of Hawdon:
Willy and Nellie Hawdon (Great Grandpa and Grandma) (Ch. 4)
1. Margaret Emily (Hawdon) Bjornaa – Nanna
   - Andrew Bjornaa – Poppa
     o Joanna – Mom
     o Linda – Aunt Linda (Uncle Butch) (Chapters 4, 5, 6, 12, 13, 26, 28)
     o Marilyn – Aunt Marilyn (Chapters 4, 7)
2. Anne Mable (Hawdon) Young – Aunt Anne

- William Young – Uncle Bill
3. Horace Reginald Hawdon – Uncle Reg (Chapters 10, 14, 20)
    - Bessie Hawdon – Aunt Bessie (Chapters 10, 14, 20)
4. Ellen Rosaline (Hawdon) Gilbertson – Aunt Rose (Chapter 10)
    - Bernt Gilbertson – Uncle Bernt (Chapter 10)
5. Dorothy Violet (Hawdon) Campbell – Aunt Dot (Chapter 8, 14)
    - Frank Campbell – Uncle Frank (Chapter 8)
6. Reuben Crozier Carlyle Hawdon – Uncle Carl
    - Olive Hawdon – Aunt Olive
7. Marion Alice (Hawdon) Hyndman – Aunt Marion (Chapter 14)
    - John Hyndman – Uncle John (Chapter 14)
8. Maureen Gwyneth (Hawdon) McIntyre – Aunt Maureen
    - Cecil McIntyre – Uncle Scotty
9. Charles Edward Hawdon – Uncle Ed (Chapter 14)
    - Merle Hawdon – Aunt Merle (Chapter 14)
10. Julia Pearl (Hawdon) McFadden – Aunt Julie (Chapter 11)
    - James McFadden – Uncle Jim (Chapter 11)

Thanks to all for your love and support over the many years